the life

MATTHEW FLINDERS

BY

ERNEST SCOTT

With Introduction by Professor Stuart Macintyre

Angus&Robertson
An imprint of HarperCollins*Publishers*

Cover photographs
Flinders' map of Terra Australis, reproduced with permission from the Tooley Collection, National Library of Australia.
Matthew Flinders R.N. 1814, stipple engraving, Rex Nan Kivell Collection NK1379, National Library of Australia U6553.
Stewartia serrata, Ferdinand Bauer, c. 1804, gouache, National Library of Australia R4747.
Sextant, Image Library, State Library of New South Wales, ML: R148.
Page from Flinders' journal of the *Investigator*, vol 1, 3 September 1801, p. 88 (ML Flinders Project digital ref: A055)

Angus&Robertson
An imprint of HarperCollins*Publishers,* Australia

First published by Angus & Robertson Ltd., Sydney, in 1914
This reissued edition published in 2001 by
HarperCollins*Publishers* Pty Limited
ABN 36 009 913 517
A member of the HarperCollins*Publishers* (Australia) Pty Limited Group
http://www.harpercollins.com.au

A percentage of the royalties from the sale of this edition are donated by HarperCollins to the Matthew Flinders Collection at the State Library of New South Wales.

HarperCollins*Publishers*
25 Ryde Road, Pymble, Sydney, NSW 2073, Australia
31 View Road, Glenfield, Auckland 10, New Zealand
77–85 Fulham Palace Road, London W6 8JB, United Kingdom
Hazelton Lanes, 55 Avenue Road, Suite 2900, Toronto, Ontario M5R 3L2
and 1995 Markham Road, Scarborough, Ontario M1B 5M8, Canada
10 East 53rd Street, New York NY 10022, USA

National Library of Australia Cataloguing-in-Publication data:

Scott, Ernest, 1868–1939.
The life of Matthew Flinders.
Bibliography.
Includes index.
ISBN 0 207 19717 2.
1. Flinders, Matthew, 1774–1814. 2. Explorers – Great Britain – Biography. 3. Australia – Discovery and exploration. I. Title.
910.92

Cover and internal design by Matt Lobina, HarperCollins Design Studio
Typeset in 11/13.5pt Stempel Garamond by HarperCollins*Publishers*
Printed and bound in Australia by Griffin Press on 79gsm Bulky Paperback

4 3 2 1
04 03 02 01

CONTENTS

INTRODUCTION vii
EDITOR'S NOTE xiii
PREFACE TO ORIGINAL EDITION xv
CHRONOLOGY xviii

I BIRTH AND ORIGINS 1
Place of Flinders among Australian navigators — Birth — Flemish origins — Pedigree — Connection with the Tennysons — Possible relationship with Bass — Flinders' father — Donington

II AT SCHOOL AND AT SEA 9
Education — *Robinson Crusoe* — Aspirations for a naval career — His father's wish — John Flinders' advice — Study of navigation — Introduction to Pasley — Lieutenant's servant — Midshipman on the *Bellerophon* — Bligh and the *Bounty* mutiny

III A VOYAGE UNDER BLIGH 21
The second breadfruit expedition — Flinders in the *Providence* — Notes from Santa Cruz — At the Cape — Tahiti — In Torres Strait — Encounter with Papuans — Return to England

IV THE BATTLE OFF BREST 30
The naval war with France — The battle of 1 June 1794 — Flinders as gunner — Pasley wounded — Flinders' journal of the engagement — Effect of Pasley's wound on the career of Flinders

V AUSTRALIAN GEOGRAPHY BEFORE FLINDERS 47
The predecessors of Flinders — How Australia grew on the map — Mediaeval controversies on antipodes — Period of vague speculation — Sixteenth-century maps — The Dutch voyagers — The *Batavia* on the Abrolhos Reef — The *Duyfhen* in the Gulf — Torres — The three periods of Australian maritime discovery — Geographers and their views of Australia — The theory of the dividing strait — Cook and Furneaux — The untraced southern coast

VI THE *RELIANCE* AND THE *TOM THUMB* 56
Governor Hunter — Captain Waterhouse — Flinders' passion for exploring new countries — Joins the *Reliance* — Hunter on the strategic importance of the Cape —Sailing of *Reliance* and *Supply* for New South Wales — Flinders' observations — Arrival at Port Jackson — George Bass — The *Tom Thumb* — Exploration of George's River — A perilous cruise — Meeting with Aboriginals — The midshipman as valet — Port Hacking — Patching up the *Reliance* — Voyage to South Africa

VII THE DISCOVERY OF BASS STRAIT 70
Bass in the Blue Mountains — Supposed strait isolating Van Diemen's Land — Bass's whaleboat voyage — Wilson's Promontory — Escaped convicts — Discovery of Westernport — Return to Port Jackson

VIII THE VOYAGE OF THE *FRANCIS* 88
The wreck of the *Sydney Cove* — Discovery of Kent's Islands — Biological notes — Seals — Sooty petrels — The wombat — Point Hicks

IX CIRCUMNAVIGATION OF TASMANIA 95
Flinders in command of the *Norfolk* — Bass's association with him — Twofold Bay — Discovery of Port Dalrymple — Bass Strait demonstrated — Black swans — Albatross Island — Tasmanian Aboriginals

X THE FATE OF GEORGE BASS 104
Bass's marriage — Part owner of the *Venus* — Voyages after pork — A fishing concession — South American enterprise — Unsaleable gods — A 'diplomatic-looking certificate' — Bass's last voyage — Probable fate in Peru — His missing letters

XI ON THE QUEENSLAND COAST 112
Flinders and the Isaac Nichols case — Exploration on the Queensland coast — Moreton Bay

XII THE *INVESTIGATOR* 117
Return to England in the *Reliance* — Sir Joseph Banks — Marriage of Flinders — Ann Chappell and Chappell Island — The Franklins — Publication of *Observations on the Coasts of Van Diemen's Land, on Bass Strait and its Islands* — Anxiety about French expedition — The *Investigator* commissioned — Equipment of ship — The staff and crew — East India Company's interest — Instructions for the voyage — The case of Mrs Flinders — Sailing orders delayed — the incident at the Roar — Life on board — Crossing the Line — Australia reached

XIII THE FRENCH EXPEDITION 142
Origin of Baudin's expedition — His instructions — Baudin's dilatoriness — In Tasmanian waters — Waterhouse Island

XIV SOUTH COAST DISCOVERY 147
The south coast of Australia — Method of research — Aboriginals at King George's Sound — Discovery of Spencer's Gulf — Loss of Thistle and a boat's crew — Memory Cove — Port Lincoln — Kangaroo Island — St Vincent's Gulf — Pelicans — Speculations on the fate of La Pérouse

XV FLINDERS AND BAUDIN IN ENCOUNTER BAY 160
The sighting of *Le Géographe* — Flinders visits Baudin — Their conversations — Flinders invites Baudin to visit Port Jackson

XVI FLINDERS IN PORT PHILLIP 167
Grant's discoveries — Murray discovers Port Phillip — King Island — Flinders enters Port Phillip — Ascends Arthur's Seat — The *Investigator* aground — Cruise in a boat — Ascends Station Peak — Flinders' impression of the port — Arrival in Port Jackson — Healthiness of his crew

XVII THE FRENCH AT PORT JACKSON: PÉRON THE SPY 176
Arrival of *Le Géographe* at Port Jackson — State of the crew — Hospitality of Governor King — Rumours as to French designs — Baudin's gratitude — Péron's report on Port Jackson — His espionage — Freycinet's plan of invasion — Scientific work of the expedition

XVIII AUSTRALIA CIRCUMNAVIGATED 190
Overhaul of the ship — The *Lady Nelson* — Flinders sails north — Discovery of Port Curtis and Port Bowen — Through the Barrier Reef — Torres Strait — Remarks on Coral Reefs — The Gulf of Carpentaria — Rotten condition of the ship — Melville Bay discovered — Sails for Timor — Australia circumnavigated — The *Investigator* condemned — Illness of Flinders — News of father's death — Letter to stepmother — Letters to Mrs Flinders — Letter to Bass — The end of the *Investigator*

XIX THE CALAMITY OF WRECK REEF 205
New plans — Flinders sails in the *Porpoise* — Remarks on Sydney — Wrecked — Conduct of the *Bridgewater* — Plans for relief — Stores available — Voyage in the *Hope* to Sydney — Franklin's description of the wreck

XX TO ILE-DE-FRANCE IN THE *CUMBERLAND* 215
King receives new of the wreck — The *Cumberland* — Wreck Reef reached — Voyage to Timor — Determination to sail to Ile-de-France — Flinders' reasons — Arrival at Baye du Cap — Arrival at Port Louis

XXI GENERAL DECAEN 222
Decaen's early career — His baptism of fire — War in the Vendée — The Army of the Rhine — Moreau — Battle of Hohenlinden — Moreau and Napoleon — The peace of Amiens — Decaen's arrival at Pondicherry — His reception — Leaves for Ile-de-France — His character and abilities

XXII THE CAPTIVITY 231
Flinders' reception by Decaen — His anger — Imprisoned at the Café Marengo — His papers and books — His examination — Refusal of invitation to dinner — Decaen's anger — His determination to detain Flinders — King's despatches — Decaen's statement of motives — Flinders asks to be sent to France

XXIII THE CAPTIVITY PROLONGED 249
Decaen's despatch — A delayed replay — Flinders' occupations — His health — The sword incident — Anniversary of the imprisonment — Aken's liberation — The faithful Elder

XXIV THE CAPTIVITY MODIFIED 257
Thomas Pitot — Removal to Wilhelm's Plains — The parole — Madame D'Arifat's house — Hospitalities — Flinders studies French and Malay — Further exploration schemes — The residence of La Pérouse — Work upon the charts — King's protest and Decaen's anger — Elder's departure

XXV THE ORDER OF RELEASE 264
Influences to secure release — The order of release — Receipt of the despatch — Decaen's reply — Flinders a dangerous man — Reason for Decaen's refusal — State of Ile-de-France — Project for escape — Flinders' reasons for declining

XXVI THE RELEASE 273
Blockade of Ile-de-France — Decaen at the end of his tether — Release of Flinders — Return to England — The plagiarism charge — Flinders' papers — Work of Péron and Freycinet

XXVII LAST YEARS AND DEATH OF FLINDERS 282
Flinders in London — Prolonged and severe work — His illness — Death of Flinders — His last words — Treatment of his widow by the Admiralty

XXVIII CHARACTERISTICS 290
Personality — Portraits — Flinders' commanding look — Geniality — Conversational powers — Gentleness — Kindness to wounded French officer — Advice to young officers — An eager student — The husband

XXIX THE NAVIGATOR 299
Technical writings — The marine barometer — Variations in the compass — Praise of other navigators — Love for his work

XXX THE NAMING OF AUSTRALIA 304
The name Australia given to the continent by Flinders — The 'Austrialia del Espiritu Santo' of Quiros — De Brosses and 'Australasia' — Dalrymple and 'Australia' — Flinders' use of the word in 1804 — His use of it in a French essay in 1810 — Persistent employment of the word in letters — Proposes the word 'Australia' to Banks — His fight for his word — 'Terra Australia' — The footnote of 1814

APPENDIX A — BAUDIN'S ACCOUNT OF ENCOUNTER BAY 311
APPENDIX B — PÉRON'S REPORT ON PORT JACKSON 315
APPENDIX C — NAMES GIVEN BY FLINDERS TO IMPORTANT AUSTRALIAN COASTAL FEATURES 338
MAPS FROM ORIGINAL EDITION 345
BIBLIOGRAPHY 357
INDEX 361
PICTURE CREDITS 372

INTRODUCTION

The story of Matthew Flinders has an enduring appeal to Australian readers. Born in the Lincolnshire village of Donington in 1774, he was lured from the family trade of medicine to the romance of naval exploration by reading *Robinson Crusoe*. He learned the skills of navigation and cartography as a midshipman on a voyage to Tahiti under the command of William Bligh. Having returned to England, he saw action in 1794 in one of the first great naval battles in the war against France. Next year Flinders sailed to the new settlement of Sydney with his friend George Bass, and undertook hazardous trips in small boats to explore the waterways to the south and the north. In 1798 they confirmed the existence of Bass Strait and circumnavigated Van Diemen's Land.

These exploits brought Flinders the patronage of Sir Joseph Banks, and a commission from the Admiralty to make a full coastal exploration of Australia. He returned to southern waters on the *Investigator* in 1801, leaving behind his new wife. For the next two years he performed his task with extraordinary application in a defective ship, conscious all the time of a rival French expedition. The first person to circumnavigate Australia, he set off with his charts on the return voyage to England and was shipwrecked. An epic passage of 1,200 kilometres in an open boat brought him back to Sydney, and he set off again in a leaky schooner. Limping into port at Mauritius at the end of 1803, he was arrested by its French governor and remained in captivity until 1810. He finally returned to his homeland in failing health and lived just long enough to write the monumental account of his great voyage. The book was published the day before he died.

The life of Flinders has both a personal fascination and a monumental significance. The poignancy of the long separation from his wife, Ann Chappell, provided the title for Ernestine Hill's popular biography, *My Love Must Wait*. His affection for his most constant companion on the travels, a cat—'my faithful, intelligent Trim'—found expression in *A Biographical Tribute to the Memory of Trim*, which he wrote during the captivity on Mauritius. His skill as a seaman and his lasting significance as a mapmaker and namer of Australia have been celebrated in numerous books of maritime history. When this account by Ernest Scott of the life of Flinders appeared in 1914, it was the first comprehensive biography. If Flinders put Australia on the map as a complete island-continent, then Scott gave precise outline and substance to a figure of legendary significance.

The name of Matthew Flinders is to be found around the coast of Australia. There is a Flinders Bay on the south-west corner of the continent, a Flinders River that flows into the Gulf of Carpentaria in the far north-east. Flinders Island lies in Bass Strait, a group of smaller islands make up the Flinders group off Cape York Peninsula. A mountain in Queensland, a full range in South Australia, a peninsula in the Northern Territory, a township and a federal electorate in Victoria, a suburb of Brisbane and a University in Adelaide were all named after him. A species of tree, *Flindersia*, extends from Queensland into New South Wales.

Flinders himself was responsible for the name of this country. The Dutch named the western part they had found early in the seventeenth century New Holland. Cook called the eastern part he discovered in the late eighteenth century New South Wales. Flinders, who was the first to sail around the whole at the opening of the nineteenth century, decided that it needed a new name and revived an earlier one. As Ernest Scott relates, he announced his choice to his brother in a letter written in 1804: 'I call the whole island Australia or Terra Australis.'

Terra Australis, a Latin phrase meaning the Southern Land, had previously been used to refer to the land that was supposed to lie in the southern hemisphere. Flinders, having established its precise location, gave it the less cumbersome form. His superiors preferred the older designation, so Flinders had to use that one for the book he wrote of his epic *Voyage to Terra Australis*; but in a footnote he explained his personal preference: 'Had I permitted myself any innovation upon the original term, it would have been to convert it into Australia; as being more agreeable to the ear, and an assimilation to the names of the other great portions of the earth.' The passage caught the eye of Governor Macquarie, who adopted Flinders' suggestion and the name Australia soon entered general usage.

Flinders was not well rewarded for his services. The Royal Navy promoted him upon his return to England but a request to backdate the promotion was refused, as was an application to receive full pay while writing the *Voyage*. His widow was denied a pension such as had been granted to the widow of Captain Cook. But in 1853 the newly self-governing colonies of New South Wales and Victoria both voted a pension of £100 a year each to Mrs Flinders; she had died in the previous year so the pension went to her daughter. The daughter inherited the sea trunk of Flinders' papers, and in 1875 her son, Flinders Petrie, sent transcripts and a few original documents to J. J. Shillinglaw, a Victorian public servant who planned to write a biography. Soon afterwards Petrie presented the narrative of an early voyage of Flinders to that indefatigable collector Sir Redmond Barry, who was president of the trustees of the Victorian Public Library, and subsequently he had Shillinglaw transfer the material in his custody to the library.

These were the records that Ernest Scott found when he began to research the history of Australian maritime exploration in the early years of the twentieth century. He was then in middle age and working as a Hansard reporter of the Commonwealth Parliament that sat in Melbourne. Scott had come to Melbourne in 1893 as Ernest Besant-Scott, with a new wife who was the daughter of Annie Besant, the famous English theosophist. Scott edited the journal of the Australian theosophists whose aim was to foster 'a Universal Brotherhood of Humanity without distinction of race, sex, caste or colour'. But his marriage soon broke down and he turned for companionship to male friends with similar literary and intellectual interests. It was to a men's dining club in 1907 that he first outlined the result of his investigation into French naval exploration.

The French expedition of Nicolas Baudin was sent six months ahead of that of Flinders. Previous historians had seen it as part of the competition for supremacy between the two great powers. They argued that under the guise of a scientific venture to map the coast, conduct astronomical experiments and collect specimens, the expedition was intended to collect military information that would enable France to challenge British control of Australia. Scott used French records to show that there was no such ulterior motive. He acquitted the French of deceit only to convict them of incompetence. Baudin's expedition was dilatory and careless, his men were stricken with scurvy and racked by jealousy. He arrived in Australian waters first but turned left up the Western Australian coast and made a clockwise circumnavigation, whereas Flinders proceeded on an anti-clockwise circuit along the uncharted portion of the south coast. When the two parties met off the south coast of Australia, the Englishman was generous with his sound knowledge, the Frenchman ungracious with his own slipshod navigation.

Scott published his findings in 1910 in a book, *Terre Napoléon*, and followed it with another two years later on a doomed earlier French explorer of the South Seas. By this time he was working on the biography of Matthew Flinders, stimulated by the approaching centenary of Flinders' death. The book was in manuscript by the middle of 1913, when he applied successfully for the chair of history at the University of Melbourne. Its preface is dated June 1914, just a few weeks before the outbreak of the Great War that Australia immediately entered in support of Britain. The title, *The Life of Captain Matthew Flinders, R.N.*, lays stress on the importance of the Royal Navy and control of the oceans that separated the two countries. Scott's exploration histories are coloured by the mounting rivalry of the European powers and their competition for control of overseas territories—the French, the Dutch and the Germans all had colonies in the islands that fringed northern Australia. They are also providential histories that celebrate Australia's good fortune to have been settled by 'a race that knew how to woo her with affection and to conquer her with their science and their will'.

Scott's Flinders embodies all these qualities. He is a man of controlled passion whose circumnavigation is an act of sexual conquest. He risks the safety of his ship to hug the flanks of a landmass 'virgin to geographical science' so that no inlet or river mouth should escape attention. It is 'hard, persistent, straining work' calling for great powers of endurance. His paternity is registered by the names he bestows on the country—a list of them at the end of the original edition takes up nine pages—so that Scott dubs him the Great Denominator. Above all, he named Australia and Scott's account of this achievement met a growing desire among his contemporaries to create historical foundations for the new Commonwealth. In 1911 the Victorian Government declared 19 April—the day Cook first sighted Australia—Discovery Day. On Discovery Day of 1912 Scott attended a ceremony in the You Yang range of mountains overlooking Port Phillip to unveil a plaque on Station Peak, which Flinders had climbed in 1802 during his great voyage. Alfred Deakin pronounced Flinders 'one of the greatest of Australians', announced that a new naval base at Westernport would be named after him and thanked 'that brilliant writer, Mr Ernest Scott' for revealing his full greatness.

The present-day reader of Scott's biography is struck by its unashamedly heroic tone. He has few of the sensitivities that inhibit those who now write Australian history. Distinctive characteristics are attributed to different European races as if they were self-evident. The encounters with the 'Aboriginal natives', as he calls them, are presented as overtures of friendship in a doomed effort to soften the dispossession that must follow for the country to fulfil its destiny. The metaphors of sexual conquest are employed without concern for their implications. We are struck by the reverence of the author and the exuberance of his prose.

These aspects of the book were less remarkable to those who first read it. They were struck, as Scott meant them to be, by his close attention to the documentary record. As a self-conscious practitioner of the new school of scientific history, he insisted always on going back to the original sources and testing every claim by careful assessment of the evidence. He followed the dictum of Lord Ranke, the founder of that school, that 'the truth was more interesting and beautiful than the romance'. By establishing the truth about Flinders, he was enhancing his status and the country's historical foundations. Strict fidelity made for an authoritative form of monumental history.

Scott wrote his book with all the records that were available to him: the published writings of Flinders and his contemporaries; the transcripts of Flinders' papers made for Shillinglaw and deposited in the Melbourne Public Library; further transcripts of French original material and British records in the Public Record Office; other manuscripts held by the Mitchell Library in Sydney. New monuments to Flinders were raised afterwards in Melbourne and Sydney to secure the papers still held by his grandson. The Mitchell Librarian visited Flinders Petrie in London and inspected these papers in the same year that Scott's book appeared. Petrie agreed that the papers as well as personal relics belonged in Australia and offered them in 1918 to the first state to erect a statue of Flinders costing at least £2,000. The government of New South Wales commissioned a British sculptor. Meanwhile the Victorians had commenced an appeal for a statue of Flinders in 1911. The collection of funds was slow and the Victorian government did not know of Petrie's negotiations with New South Wales until it was too late. The statue in Macquarie Street, Sydney, outside the Mitchell Library, was unveiled in 1925, just two weeks before the Governor-General unveiled Web Gilbert's grander one on the corner of the street named after Flinders in Melbourne. By then the papers were in the Mitchell Library.

There are additional original sources that Scott did not use: other family papers now in the National Maritime Museum in London, charts and papers of Flinders held by the Hydrographic Department of the British Ministry of Defence, and writings in the Royal Greenwich Observatory. Flinders knew full well the value of his charts and journals. He tackled the hazardous voyage back to England in an unfit vessel in order that they could be published before those of his French rival. A fine penman, he was a faithful correspondent to his family and an assiduous one to his patrons. Other legendary navigators such as Cook and Bligh left few intimate records of their voyages. Flinders created a wealth of information.

Naval historians have reworked Flinders since Scott. The most distinguished of them is Geoffrey Ingleton, an officer in the Hydrographic Service of the Royal Australian Navy, and his 1986 study, *Matthew Flinders: Navigator and Chartmaker*, has authoritative status. Ingleton's Flinders is something less than Scott's Great Denominator. He charted the unknown section of the southern coast but failed his instructions to make an accurate survey of the Torres Strait and north-west coast. His running surveys were reasonably accurate but given the limitations of time and resources they could be no more than preliminary, and claims for their lasting value—repeated by Scott—could not be sustained.

Ingleton draws attention to Flinders' misfortunes (he first grounded the *Investigator* while still on the English coast), his errors of judgment (such as the attempt to take his wife with him), his oversights (he failed to spot the outlet of the Murray as well as other rivers in northern Australia). His biggest blunder, says Ingleton, was the decision to proceed with the return voyage to England on a vessel quite unfitted for the voyage. The subsequent detention on Mauritius was due entirely to his arrogant and irrational behaviour. He could not know that war had resumed between Britain and France while he was away, but he should have known that the passport given to him by Baudin applied to the vessel he had abandoned in Australia, and it was folly to antagonise the French governor. Ingleton also disagrees with Scott's assessment that the captivity broke Flinders' health; rather, he diagnoses the illness that killed him by the age of 40 as gonorrhoea, contracted at Tahiti while a midshipman with Bligh.

Yet Scott gives Flinders to us during the years in Mauritius pondering the lessons he had learned: 'I shall learn patience in this island, which will perhaps counteract the insolence acquired by having had unlimited command over my fellow men.' Flinders was a short, spare, intense man. He sought authority and exercised it with single-minded determination in pursuit of his goals. He took risks and accepted the consequences. Fortune smiled on him until he had completed his major goal, and he survived the subsequent disappointments to lodge his claim to fame. This fetching account of an epic life story helped to secure it.

Professor Stuart Macintyre,
Ernest Scott Professor of History;
Dean, Faculty of Arts, The University of Melbourne, 2001

EDITOR'S NOTE

In preparing this reissued edition of Ernest Scott's biography of Matthew Flinders I have endeavoured to make the text as accessible as possible to the contemporary reader with a bare minimum of departures from the original. The concept of posthumous editing is fraught with intellectual and ethical problems, and with that foremost in my mind I decided upon an approach of minimal editorial intervention: changes in the text have been made only when I felt they were absolutely essential for clarity and intelligibility, or where there were orthographic errors.

Changes have been made to the manner in which quotations are set and the positioning of quotation marks. An attempt has been made to impose a degree of consistency with respect to hyphenation, spelling, capitalisation, punctuation, footnoting and the use of numbers and dates—which was not apparent in the original edition. More importantly, I have endeavoured to provide definitions of archaic expressions and nautical terms, to unravel idiosyncratic syntax and to explain some of Scott's literary and historical allusions with which the modern general reader may well be unfamiliar. These definitions and explanations appear within square brackets immediately after the matters in question.

Curiously, neither the author nor the original publisher thought it necessary or even desirable to provide translations of Latin and French quotations; presumably, it was thought axiomatic in 1914 that readers would find such assistance patronising. Today, it can no longer be assumed that either the common reader, or, for that matter, the academic historian, is likely to have a sound working knowledge of these two languages. Accordingly, I have also provided translations of such passages or phrases in square brackets in the text. Where fashions in the writing of proper nouns have changed, I have adopted the more modern form: Scott's original Lapérouse and Dentrecasteaux appear in the text in the more familiar form of La Pérouse and D'Entrecasteaux.

No attempt has been made to rein in Scott's discursive style, to restrain his whimsy or even to tone down his occasionally florid turn of phrase except where intelligibility was at stake. However, on a few occasions arcane literary quotations, whose only reason for inclusion appears to have been to enhance the author's reputation for erudition, have been dispensed with.

Moreover, it goes without saying that Scott was a man of his times, and his prejudices are no longer, by and large, ours; while we may recoil from the use of the term 'savages' to describe any number of indigenous Pacific peoples, while we may be amused by his quaint, old-fashioned gallantry with respect to women, and while his empire loyalty and pride in his 'race' will be hardly comprehensible to many twenty-first-century readers, no attempt has been made to sanitise his opinions or to moderate or modernise his sentiments.

It is my hope that this light but explanatory editorial approach to this excellent, well-researched and entertaining biography will contribute to the enjoyment and enlightenment of contemporary readers and will assist them in some small measure to make their own judgments and come to their own conclusions about the achievements and character of one of the most significant explorers of the past 200 years.

Neil Thomas, Leichhardt, Sydney, 2001

PREFACE TO ORIGINAL EDITION

The subject of this book died 100 years ago. Within his 40 years of life, he discovered a very large area of what is now an important region of the earth; he participated in stirring events which are memorable in modern history; he applied a vigorous and original mind to the advancement of knowledge, with useful results; and he was the victim of circumstances which, however stated, were peculiarly unfortunate, and must evoke the sympathy of everyone who takes the trouble to understand them. His career was crowded with adventures: war, perilous voyages, explorations of unknown coasts, encounters with savages, shipwreck and imprisonment. These are the elements which go to make up his story. He was, withal [as well], a downright Englishman of exceptionally high character, proud of his service and unsparing of himself in the pursuit of his duty.

Yet up to this time [1914] his biography has not been written. There are, it is true, outlines of his career in various works of reference, notably that contributed by Sir J. K. Laughton to the *Dictionary of National Biography*. But there is no book to which a reader can turn for a fairly full account of his achievements, and an estimate of his personality. Of all discoverers of leading rank Matthew Flinders is the only one about whom there is no ample and convenient record.

This book endeavours to fill the gap.

The material upon which it is founded is set forth in the footnotes and the bibliography. Here the author takes pleasure in acknowledging the assistance he has received from several quarters. A previous book brought him the acquaintance of the grand-nephew of that Comte de Fleurieu who largely inspired three famous French voyages to Australia—those of La Pérouse, D'Entrecasteaux and Baudin—all of which have an important bearing upon the subject. The Comte A. de Fleurieu had long been engaged in collecting material relative to the work and influence of his distinguished grand-uncle, and in the most generous manner he handed over to the author his very large collection of manuscripts and note-books to be read, noted, and used at discretion. Even when a historian does not actually quote or directly use matter bearing upon his subject, it is of immense advantage to have access to documents which throw light upon it, and which enable an in-and-out knowledge of a period and persons to be obtained. This book owes much of whatever value it may possess to Monsieur de Fleurieu's assistance in this respect, and the author thanks him most warmly.

The Flinders papers, of which free use has been made, were presented to the Melbourne Public Library by Professor W. M. Flinders Petrie. They are described in the bibliography. The transcripts of family and personal documents were especially valuable. Although they were not supplied for this book, Professor Flinders Petrie gave them [to the library] in order that they might be of use to some biographer of his grandfather, and the author begs to thank him, and also Mr E. La Touche Armstrong, the chief librarian, in whose custody they are, and who has given frequent access to them.

The rich stores of manuscripts in the Mitchell Library, Sydney, have been thoroughly examined, with the assistance of Mr W. H. Ifould, principal librarian, Mr Hugh Wright, and the staff of that institution. Help from this quarter was accorded with such grace that one came to think giving trouble was almost like conferring a favour.

All copies of documents from Paris and Caen cited in this book have been made by Madame Robert Hélouis. The author was able to indicate the whereabouts of the principal papers, but Madame Hélouis, developing an interest in the subject as she pursued her task, was enabled, owing to her extensive knowledge of the resources of the French archives, to find and transcribe many new and valuable papers. The author also wishes to thank Captain Francis Bayldon, of Sydney, who has kindly given help on several technical points; Miss Alma Hansen, University of Melbourne, who was generous enough to make a study of the Dutch *Generale Beschrijvinge van Indien*—no light task—to verify a point of some importance for the purpose of the chapter on 'The Naming of Australia'; and Mr E. A. Petherick, whose manuscript bibliography, containing an immense quantity of material, the fruit of a long life's labour, has always been cheerfully made available.

Professor Flinders Petrie has been kind enough to read and make some useful suggestions upon the personal and family passages of the book, which has consequently benefited greatly.

The whole work has been read through by Mr A. W. Jose, author of *The History of Australasia*, whose criticism on a multitude of points, some minute, but all important, has been of the utmost value. The help given by Mr Jose has been more than friendly; it has been informed by a keen enthusiasm for the subject, and great knowledge of the original authorities. The author's obligations to him are gratefully acknowledged.

It is hoped that these pages will enable the reader to know Matthew Flinders the man, as well as the navigator; for the study of the manuscript and printed material about him has convinced the author that he was not only remarkable for what he did and endured, but for his own sake as an Englishman of the very best type.

Ernest Scott, Melbourne, June 1914

CHRONOLOGY

1774 (16 March)	Born at Donington.
1789 (23 October)	Enters the Royal Navy.
1790 (31 July)	Midshipman on the *Bellerophon*.
1791–93	Voyage in the *Providence*.
1793 (September)	Rejoins the *Bellerophon*.
1794 (June)	Participates in the battle off Brest.
1795 (February)	Sails for Australia in the *Reliance*. Meets George Bass.
1796 (March)	Cruise of the *Tom Thumb*.
1797 (December)	Bass's whaleboat voyage.
1798 (January)	Discovery of Westernport.
1798 (January)	Flinders' voyage in the *Francis*.
1798 (31 January)	Flinders obtains lieutenant's commission.
1798 (October)	Voyage of the *Norfolk*.
1798 (November)	Discovery of Port Dalrymple.
1798 (December)	Bass Strait demonstrated.
1799	Return to Port Jackson.
1799 (July)	Exploration on Queensland coast.
1800 (March)	Return to England in the *Reliance*.
1800 (October)	Arrival in England.
	Plan of Australian Exploration.
1800 (December)	The *Investigator* commissioned.
1801 (17 January)	Publication of *Observations*.
1801 (16 February)	Obtains commander's rank.
1801 (April)	Marriage of Flinders.
1801 (18 July)	Sailing of the *Investigator*.
1801 (December)	Australia reached.
1802 (February)	Discovery of Spencer's Gulf.
1802 (March)	Discovery of Kangaroo Island and St Vincent's Gulf.
1802 (April)	Meeting of Flinders and Baudin in Encounter Bay.
1802 (May)	Flinders in Port Phillip.
1802 (July)	Voyage to Northern Australia.
1802 (August)	Discovery of Port Curtis and Port Bowen.
1802 (November)	In the Gulf of Carpentaria.

1803 (April)	Return voyage; Australia circumnavigated.
1803 (June)	Sydney reached; the *Investigator* condemned.
1803 (10 July)	Sails in the *Porpoise*.
1803 (17 August)	Wrecked on the Barrier Reef. Voyage in the *Hope* to Sydney.
1803 (8 September)	Arrival in Port Jackson.
1803 (21 September)	Sails in the *Cumberland*.
1803 (November)	Timor reached.
1803 (17 December)	Arrival at Ile-de-France; made a prisoner.
1804 (April)	Removal to the Garden Prison (Maison Despeaux).
1805	Removal to Wilhelm's Plains.
1806 (21 March)	French Government orders release of Flinders. (Rec'd 20 July 1807)
1810 (13 June)	Release of Flinders.
1810 (24 October)	Return to England.
1814 (19 July)	Death of Flinders.

I

BIRTH AND ORIGINS

MATTHEW FLINDERS was the third of the triad [trio] of great English sailors by whom the principal part of Australia was revealed. A poet of our own time, in a line of singular felicity, has described it as the 'last sea-thing dredged by sailor Time from Space';[1] and the piecemeal, partly mysterious, largely accidental dragging from the depths of the unknown of a land so immense and bountiful makes a romantic chapter in geographical history. All the great seafaring peoples contributed something towards the result. The Dutch especially evinced their enterprise in the pursuit of precise information about the southern Terra Incognita [Unknown Land], and the nineteenth century was well within its second quarter before the name New Holland, which for over a hundred years had borne testimony to their adventurous pioneering, gave place in general and geographical literature to the more convenient and euphonious designation suggested by Flinders himself, Australia.[2]

But, important as was the work of the Dutch, and though the contributions made by French navigators (possibly also by Spanish) are of much consequence, it remains true that the broad outlines of the continent were laid down by Dampier, Cook and Flinders. These are the principal names in the story. A map of Australia which left out the parts discovered by other sailors would be seriously defective in particular features; but a map which left out the parts discovered by these three Englishmen would gape out of all resemblance [bear little resemblance] to the reality.

---

1 Bernard O'Dowd, *Dawnward* (1903).

2 Not universally, however, even in official documents. In the Report of the Committee of the Privy Council, dated 1 May 1849. 'New Holland' is used to designate the continent, but 'Australia' is employed as including both the continent and Tasmania. See Grey's *Colonial Policy* I, pp. 424 and 439.

Dampier died about the year 1712; nobody knows precisely when. Matthew Flinders came into the world in time to hear, as he may well have done as a boy, of the murder of his illustrious predecessor in 1779. The news of Cook's fate did not reach England till 1781. The lad was then seven years of age, having been born on 16 March 1774.

His father, also named Matthew, was a surgeon practising his profession at Donington, Lincolnshire, where the boy was born. The Flinders family had been settled in the same town for several generations. Three in succession had been surgeons. The patronymic indicates a Flemish origin, and the work on English surnames[3] that bids the reader looking for information under 'Flinders' to 'see Flanders', sends him on a reasonable quest, if to no great resulting advantage.

The English middle-eastern counties received frequent large migrations of Flemings during several centuries. Sometimes calamities due to the harshness of nature, sometimes persecutions and wars, sometimes adverse economic conditions, impelled companies of people from the Low Countries to cross the North Sea and try to make homes for themselves in a land which, despite intervals of distraction, offered greater security and a better reward than did the place whence they came. England derived much advantage from the infusion of this industrious, solid and dependable Flemish stock; though the temporary difficulty of absorption gave rise to local protests on more than one occasion.

As early as 1108, a great part of Flanders 'being drowned by an exudation or breaking in of the sea, a great number of Flemings came into the country, beseeching the King to have some void place assigned them, wherein they might inhabit'.[4] Again in the reign of Edward I we find Flemish merchants carrying on a very large and important trade in Boston, and representatives of houses from Ypres and Ostend acquired property in the town.[5] In the middle of the sixteenth century, when Flanders was boiling on the fire of the Reformation, Lincolnshire and Norfolk provided an asylum for crowds of harassed refugees. In 1569 two persons were deputed to ride from Boston to Norwich to ascertain what means that city adopted to find employment for them; and in the same year Mr William Derby was directed to move Mr Secretary Cecil, Queen Elizabeth's great minister, to 'know his pleasure whether certain

---

[3] Barker, *Family Surnames* (1903), p. 143.

[4] Holinshed's *Chronicle* (edition of 1807), II, p. 58.

[5] Pishey Thompson, *Collections for a Topographical and Historical Account of Boston and the Hundred of Skirbeck* (1820), p. 31.

strangers may be allowed to dwell within the borough without damage of the Queen's laws'.[6]

During one of these peaceful and useful Flemish invasions the ancestors of Matthew Flinders entered Lincolnshire. In the later years of his life he devoted some attention to the history of his family, and found record of a Flinders as early as the tenth century. He believed, also, that his people had some connection with two men named Flinders or Flanders, who fled from Holland during the religious persecutions, and settled, in Queen Elizabeth's reign, in Nottinghamshire as silk stocking weavers. It would be very interesting if it were clear that there was a link between the family and the origins of the great Nottingham hosiery trade.

Matthew Flinders himself wrote the note: 'Ruddington near Nottingham (it is four miles south of the town) is the place whence the Flinders came'; and he ascertained that an ancestor was Robert Flinders, a Nottingham stocking weaver.

A family tradition relates that the Lincolnshire Flinders were amongst the people taken over to England by Sir Cornelius Vermuyden, a Dutch engineer of celebrity in his day, who undertook in 1621 to drain 360,000 acres of fen in Norfolk, Lincolnshire and Cambridgeshire. He was financed by English and Dutch capitalists, and took his reward in large grants of land which he made fit for habitation and cultivation. Vermuyden and his Flemings were not allowed to accomplish their work of reclamation without incurring the enmity of the natives. In a petition to the King in 1637 he stated that he had spent £150,000, but that £60,000 of damage had been done 'by reason of the opposition of the commoners', who cut the banks of his channels in the night and during floods. The peasantry, indeed, resisted the improvements that have proved so beneficent to that part of England, because the draining and cultivation of so many square miles of swamp would deprive them of fishing and fowling privileges enjoyed from time immemorial. Hardly any reform or improvement can be effected without some disruption of existing interests; and a people deeply sunk in poverty and toil could hardly be expected to contemplate with philosophical calm projects which, however advantageous to fortunate individuals and to posterity, were calculated to diminish their own means of living and their pleasant diversions. The dislike of the 'commoners' to the work of the 'participants' led to frequent riots, and many of Vermuyden's Flemings were maltreated. He endeavoured to

[6] Boston Corporation mss., quoted in Thompson, *History and Antiquities of Boston* (1856).

allay discontent by employing local labour at high wages; and was courageous enough to pursue his task despite loss of money, wanton destruction, and many other discouragements.[7] Ebullitions [outbursts] of discontent on the part of fractious Fenlanders did not cease till the beginning of the eighteenth century.

A very simple calculation shows that the great-grandfather of the first Matthew Flinders would probably have been contemporary with Sir Cornelius Vermuyden's reclamation works. He may have been one of the 'participants' who benefited from them. The fact is significant as bearing upon this conjecture, that no person named Flinders made a will in Lincolnshire before 1600.[8]

It is, too, an interesting circumstance that there was a Flinders among the early settlers in New England, Richard Flinders of Salem, born 1637.[9] He may have been of the same family as the navigator, for the Lincolnshire element among the fathers of New England was pronounced.

The name Flinders survived at Donington certainly for 30 years after the death of the sailor who gave lustre to it; for in a directory published in 1842 occur the names of 'Flinders, Mrs. Eliz., Market Place', and 'Flinders, Mrs. Mary, Church Street'.[10]

The Flinders papers, mentioned in the preface, contain material which enables the family and connections of the navigator to be traced with certainty for seven generations. The genealogy is shown by Table 1.

There is also an interesting connection between Flinders and the Tennysons, through the Franklin family. Lord Tennyson, when Governor of South Australia, in the course of his official duties, in March 1902, unveiled a memorial to his kinsman on Mount Lofty, and in April of the same year a second one in Encounter Bay. Table 2 illustrates the relationship between him who wrote of 'the long wash of Australasian seas' and him who knew them as discoverer.

The Flinders papers also contain a note suggesting a distant connection between Matthew Flinders and the man who above all others was his choice friend, George Bass, the companion of his earliest explorations. Positive proof is lacking, but Flinders' daughter, Mrs Petrie, wrote 'we have reason to think that Bass was a connection of the family', and the point is too interesting to be left unstated. Table 3, overleaf, shows the possible kinship.

---

[7] See *Calendar of State Papers*, Domestic Series, for 1619–23–25–38–39, *et seq*.; and White's *Lincolnshire*, p. 542.

[8] See C. W. Foster, *Calendar of Lincoln Wills*, 1320–1600 (1902).

[9] Savage, *Genealogical Dictionary of the First Settlers of New England* (Boston, USA, 1860).

[10] William White, *History, Gazetteer and Directory of the City and Diocese of Lincoln* (1842), p. 193.

TABLE 1

John Flinders, b. 1682, d. 1741, settled at Donington as a farmer, m. 1702, Mary Obray or Aubrey

John Flinders, surgeon at Spalding, born 1737, still living in 1810

John Flinders, Lieutenant in Royal Navy, b. 1766, d. 1793

Matthew Flinders, surgeon at Donington, b. 1750, d. 1802, m. 1773, Susannah Ward, 1752–1783

Matthew Flinders the Navigator, b. 16 March 1774, d. 19 July 1814, m. 1801, Ann Chappell, b. 1770, d. 1852

Samuel Ward Flinders, b. 1782, d. 1842, Lieut. in Royal Navy, married and left several children

Ann Flinders, b. 1812, d. 1892, m. 1851, William Petrie, b. 1821, d. 1908

Professor W. M. Flinders Petrie, eminent scholar and Egyptian archaeologist, b. 1853, m. 1897, Hilda Urlin

John Flinders Petrie
Ann Flinders Petrie

TABLE 2

Matthew Flinders (father of Matthew Flinders the navigator) married as his second wife Elizabeth Weekes, whose sister, Hannah Weekes, married Willingham Franklin of Spilsby

Sir John Franklin, b. 1786, midshipman of the *Investigator*, Arctic explorer, Lieut.-Governor of Van Diemen's Land (Tasmania) 1837–44, d. 1847

Sarah Franklin, married 1812 Henry Sellwood, solicitor, of Horncastle

Louisa Sellwood married Charles Tennyson-Turner, poet, brother of Alfred Tennyson

Emily Sarah Sellwood, b. 1813, d. 1896, m. in 1850 Alfred Tennyson, Poet Laureate, b. 1809, d. 1892

Hallam, Lord Tennyson, b. 1852; Governor of South Australia 1899–1902; Governor-General of Australia, 1902–04

TABLE 3

John Flinders of Donington, b. 1682, d. 1741
(great-grandfather of the navigator)

|

Mary Flinders, third and youngest daughter, b. 1734,
married as her third husband—Bass

|

George Bass, who had three daughters, and is believed to have been an uncle or cousin of George Bass, Matthew Flinders' companion in exploration.

It is clear from the particulars stated above that the tree of which Matthew Flinders was the fruit had its roots deep down in the soil of the little Lincolnshire market town where he was born; and Matthew himself would have continued the family tradition, inheriting the practice built up by his father and grandfather (as it was hoped he would do), had there not been within him an irresistible longing for the sea, and a bent of scientific curiosity directed to maritime exploration, which led him on a path of discovery to achievements that won him honourable rank in the noble roll of British naval pioneers.

His father earned an excellent reputation, both professional and personal. The career of a country practitioner rarely affords an opportunity for distinction. It was even less so then than today, when at all events careful records of interesting cases are printed in a score or more of professional publications. But once [only on one occasion do] we find the elder Matthew Flinders in print. The *Memoirs* of the Medical Society of London[11] contain a paper read before that body on 30 October 1797: 'Case of a child born with variolar pustules, by Matthew Flinders, surgeon, Donington, Lincolnshire'. The essay occupies three pages, and is a clear, succinct record of symptoms, treatment and results, for medical readers. The child died; whereupon the surgeon expresses his regret, not on account of infant or parents, but, with true scientific zest, because it deprived him of the opportunity of watching the development of an uncommon case.

Donington is a small town in the heart of the fen country, lying ten miles south-west of Boston, and about the same distance, as the crow flies, from the black, muddy, western fringe of the Wash. It is a very old town. Formerly it was an important Lincolnshire centre, enjoying its weekly Saturday market, and its four annual fairs for the sale of

[11] Vol. IV, p. 330 (1779).

horses, cattle, flax and hemp. During Flinders' youth and early manhood the district grew large quantities of hemp, principally for the Royal Navy. In the days of its prosperity Donington drew to itself the business of [the surrounding] agricultural neighbourhood. But the drainage of the fens and the making of good roads over what had once been an area of amphibious uncertainty, neither wholly land nor wholly water, had the effect of largely diverting business to Boston. Trade that came to Donington when it stood over its own tract of fen, like the elderly and respectable capital of some small island, now went to the thriving and historic port on the Witham. Donington stopped growing, stagnated, declined. On the map of Lincolnshire included in Camden's *Britannia* (1637) it is marked 'Dunington', in letters as large as those given to Boston, Spalding and Lincoln. On modern maps the name is printed in small letters; on some in the smallest, or not at all. That fact is fairly indicative of its change of fortunes. Figures tell the tale with precision. In 1801 it contained 1,321 inhabitants; in 1821, 1,638; in 1841 it reached its maximum, 2,026; by 1891 it had gone down to 1,547; in 1901 to 1,484; at the census of 1911 it had struggled up to 1,564.[12]

The fame conferred by a distinguished son is hardly a recompense for faded prosperity, but certain it is that Donington commands a wider interest as the birthplace of Flinders than it ever did in any other respect during its long, uneventful history. The parish church, a fine Gothic building with a lofty, graceful spire, contains a monument to the memory of the navigator, with an inscription in praise of his character and life, and recording that he 'twice circumnavigated the globe'. Many men have encircled the earth, but few have been so distinguished as discoverers of important portions of it. Apart from this monument, the church contains marble ovals to the memory of Matthew Flinders' father, grandfather, and great-grandfather. They were provided from a sum of £100 left by the navigator, in his will, for the purpose.

It is interesting to notice that three of the early Australian explorers came from Lincolnshire, and were all born at places visible in clear weather from the tower of St Botolph's Church at Boston. While Flinders sprang from Donington, George Bass, who co-operated with him in his first discoveries, was born at Aswarby, near Sleaford, and Sir John Franklin, who sailed with him in the *Investigator*, and was subsequently to become an Australian Governor and to achieve a

[12] Allen, *History of Lincolnshire* (1833), I, 342; *Victoria History of Lincolnshire*, II, p. 359; Census Returns for 1911.

pathetic immortality in another field of exploration, entered the world at Spilsby. Sir Joseph Banks, the botanist of Cook's first voyage, Flinders' steadfast friend, and the earliest potent advocate of Australian colonisation, though not actually born in Lincolnshire, was the son of a squire who at the time of his birth owned Revesby Abbey, which is within a short ride of each of the places just named.

II

AT SCHOOL AND AT SEA

YOUNG Flinders received his preparatory education at the Donington free school. This was an institution founded and endowed in 1718 by Thomas Cowley, who bequeathed property producing nowadays [1914] about £1,200 a year for the maintenance of a school and almshouses. It was to be open to the children of all the residents of Donington parish free of expense, and in addition there was a fund for paying premiums on the apprenticeship of boys.

At the age of twelve the lad was sent to the Horbling Grammar School, not many miles from his own home. It was under the direction of the Rev. John Shinglar. Here he remained three years. He was introduced to the Latin and Greek classics, and received the grounding of that mathematical knowledge which subsequently enabled him to master the science of navigation without a tutor. If to Mr Shinglar's instruction was likewise due his ability to write good, sound, clear English, we who read his letters and published writings have cause to speak his schoolmaster's name with respect.

During his school days another book besides those prescribed in the curriculum came into his hands. He read *Robinson Crusoe.* It was to Defoe's undying tale of the stranded mariner that he attributed the awakening in his own mind of a passionate desire to sail in uncharted seas. This anecdote happens to be better authenticated than are many of those quoted to illustrate the youth of men of mark. Towards the end of Flinders' life the editor of the *Naval Chronicle* sent to him a series of questions, intending to found upon the answers a biographical sketch. One question was: 'Juvenile or miscellaneous anecdotes illustrative of individual character?' The reply was: 'Induced to go to sea against the wishes of friends from reading *Robinson Crusoe.*'

The case, interesting as it is, has an exact parallel in the life of a famous French traveller, René Caillé, who in 1828, after years of extraordinary effort and endurance, crossed Senegal, penetrated Central Africa, and was the first European to visit Timbuctoo. He also had read Defoe's masterpiece as a lad, and attributed to it the awakening in his breast of a yearning for adventure and discovery. 'The reading of *Robinson Crusoe,*' says a French historian, 'made upon him a profound impression.' 'I burned to have adventures of my own,' he wrote later; 'I felt as I read that there was born within my heart the ambition to distinguish myself by some important discovery.'[1]

Here were astonishing results to follow from the vivid fiction of a gouty pamphleteer who wrote to catch the market and was hoisted into immortal fame by the effort: that his book should, like a spark falling on straw, fire the brains of a French shoemaker's apprentice and a Lincolnshire schoolboy, impelling each to a career crowded with adventure, and crowned with memorable achievements. There could hardly be better examples of the vitalising efficacy of fine literature.

A love of *Robinson Crusoe* remained with Flinders to the end. Only a fortnight before his death he wrote a note subscribing for a copy of a new edition of the book, with notes, then announced for publication. It must have been one of the last letters from his hand. Though out of its chronological order, it may be appropriately quoted here to connect it with the other references to the book which so profoundly influenced his life: 'Captain Flinders presents his compliments to the Hydrographer of the *Naval Chronicle*, and will thank him to insert his name in the list of subscribers in his new edition of *Robinson Crusoe*; he wishes also that the volume on delivery should have a neat, common binding, and be lettered.—London Street, July 5, 1814.'

It seems clear that Flinders had promised himself the pleasure of re-reading in maturity the tale that had so delighted his youth. Had he lived to do so, he might well have underlined, as applicable to himself, a pair of those sententious observations with which Defoe essayed to give a sober purpose to his narrative. The first is his counsel of 'invincible patience under the worst of misery, indefatigable application, and undaunted resolution under the greatest and most discouraging circumstances'. The second is his wise remark that 'the height of human wisdom is to bring our tempers down to our circumstances, and to make a great calm within under the weight of the greatest storm without'. They were words which Flinders during strenuous years had good cause to translate into conduct.

The edition of the book to which he thus subscribed was undertaken largely on account of his acknowledgment of its effect upon his life.

---

[1] Gaffarel, *La Politique coloniale en France* (1908), p. 34.

The author of the *Naval Chronicle* sketch of his career[2] wrote in a footnote: 'The biographer, also happening to understand that to the same cause the Navy is indebted for another of its ornaments, Admiral Sir Sydney Smythe, was in a great measure thereby led to give another studious reading to that charming story, and thence to adopt a plan for its republication, now almost at maturity'; and he commended the new issue especially 'to all those engaged in the tuition of youth'.

One other anecdote of Flinders' boyhood has been preserved as a family tradition. It is that, while still a child, he was one day lost for some hours. He was ultimately found in the middle of one of the sea marshes, his pockets stuffed with pebbles, tracing the runlets of water, so that by following them up he might find out whence they came. Many boys might have done the same; but this particular boy, in that act of enquiry concerning geographical phenomena on a small scale, showed himself father to the man.

'Against the wish of friends,' Flinders wrote, was his selection of a naval career. His father steadily but kindly opposed his desire, hoping that his son would adopt the medical profession. But young Matthew was not easily thwarted. The call of the sea was strong within him, and persistency was always a fibrous element in his character.

The surgeon's house at Donington stood in the market square. It remained in existence till 1908, when it was demolished to give place to what is described as 'a hideous new villa'. It was a plain, square, one-storey building with a small, low surgery built on to one side of it. Behind the door of the surgery hung a slate, upon which the elder Flinders was accustomed to write memoranda concerning appointments and cases. The lad, wishing to let his father know how keen was his desire to enter the navy, and dreading a conversation on the subject—with probable reproaches, admonitions, warnings, and a general outburst of parental displeasure—made use of the surgeon's slate. He wrote upon it what he wanted his father to know, hung it on the nail, and left it there to tell its quiet story.

He got his way in the end, but not without discouragement from other quarters also. He had an uncle in the navy, John Flinders, to whom he wrote asking for counsel. John's experience had not made him enamoured of his profession, and his reply was chilling. He pointed out that there was little chance of success without powerful interest [without patronage]. Promotion was slow and favouritism was rampant. He himself had served eleven years, and had not yet

[2] Vol. XXXII (1814).

attained the rank of lieutenant, nor were his hopes of rising better than slender.

From the strictly professional point of view it was not unreasonable advice for the uncle to give. A student of the naval history of the period finds much to justify a discouraging attitude. Even the dazzling career of Nelson might have been frustrated by a long protracted minority had he not had a powerful hand to help him up the lower rungs of the ladder—the 'interest' of Captain Suckling, his uncle, who in 1775 became Comptroller of the Navy, 'a civil position, but one that carried with it power and consequently influence'. Nelson became lieutenant after seven years' service, in 1777; but he owed his promotion to Suckling, who 'was able to exert his influence on behalf of his relative by promptly securing for him not only his promotion to lieutenant, which many waited for long, but with it his commission, dated April 10, to the *Lowestofte*, a frigate of 32 guns'.[3]

That even conduct of singular merit, performed in the crisis of action, was not sufficient to secure advancement, is illustrated by a striking fact in the life of Sir John Hindmarsh, the first Governor of South Australia (1836). At the battle of the Nile, Hindmarsh, a midshipman of fourteen, was left in charge of the *Bellerophon*, all the other officers being killed or wounded. (It was upon this same vessel, as we shall see later, that Flinders had a taste of sea fighting.) When the French line-of-battle ship *L'Orient* took fire she endangered the *Bellerophon.* The boy, with wonderful presence of mind, called up some hands, cut the cables, and was running the ship out of danger under a sprit sail, when Captain Darby came on deck from having his wounds dressed. Nelson, hearing of the incident, thanked young Hindmarsh before the ship's company, and afterwards gave him his commission in front of all hands, relating the story to them. 'The sequel,' writes Admiral Sir T. S. Pasley, who relates the facts in his journal, 'does not sound so well. Lord Nelson died in 1805, and Hindmarsh is a commander still, in 1830, not having been made one till June, 1814.' A man with such a record certainly had to wait long before the sun of official favour shone upon him; and his later success was won, not in the navy, but as a colonial governor.

There was, then, much to make John Flinders believe that influence was a surer way to advancement than assiduous application or natural capacity. His own naval career did not turn out happily. A very few years afterwards he received his long-delayed promotion, served as

[3] Mahan, *Life of Nelson* (edit. of 1899), pp. 13–14.

lieutenant in the *Cygnet*, on the West Indies station, under Admiral Affleck, and died of yellow fever on board his ship in 1793.

John Flinders' letter, however, concluded with a piece of practical advice, in case his nephew should be undeterred by his opinion. He recommended the study of three works as a preparation for entering the navy: Euclid, John Robertson's *Elements of Navigation* (first edition published in 1754) and Hamilton Moore's book on navigation. Matthew disregarded the warning and took the practical advice. The books were procured, and the young student plunged into their problems eagerly. The year devoted to their study in that quiet little fen town made him master of rather more than the elements of a science which enabled him to become one of the foremost discoverers and cartographers of a continent. He probably also practised map-making with assiduity, for his charts are not only excellent as charts, but also singularly beautiful examples of scientific drawing.

After a year of book-work Flinders felt capable of acquitting himself creditably at sea, if he could secure an opportunity. In those days entrance to the Royal Navy was generally secured by the nomination of a senior officer. There was no indispensable examination; no naval college course was necessary. The captain of a ship could take a youth on board to oblige his relatives, 'or in return for the cancelling of a tradesman's bill'.[4] It so happened that a cousin of Flinders occupied the position of governess in the family of Captain Pasley (afterwards Admiral Sir Thomas Pasley) who at that time commanded HMS *Scipio*. One of her pupils, Maria Pasley, developed into a young lady of decidedly vigorous character, as the following incident sufficiently shows. While her father was commander-in-chief at Plymouth, she was one day out in the Channel, beyond the Eddystone, in the Admiral's cutter. As the country was at war, she was courting danger; and in fact, the cutter was sighted by a French cruiser, which gave chase. But Miss Pasley declined to run away. She 'popped at the Frenchman with the cutter's two brass guns'. It was like blowing peas at an elephant; and she would undoubtedly have been captured, had not an English frigate seen the danger and put out to the rescue.

Flinders' cousin had interested herself in his studies and ambitions, and gave him some encouragement. She also spoke about him to Captain Pasley, who seems to have listened sympathetically. It interested him to hear of this boy studying navigation without a tutor up among the fens. 'Send for him', said Pasley, 'I should like to see what stuff he is made of, and whether he is worth making into a sailor.'

---

[4] Masefield's *Sea Life in Nelson's Time* (1905) gives a good account of the practice.

Young Matthew, then in his fifteenth year, was accordingly invited to visit the Pasleys. In the later part of his life he used to relate with merriment, how he went, was asked to dine, and then pressed to stay till next day under the captain's roof. He had brought no night attire with him, not having expected to sleep at the house. When he was shown into his bedroom, his needs had apparently been anticipated; for there, folded up neatly upon the pillow, was a sleeping garment ready for use. He appreciated the consideration; but having attired himself for bed, he found himself enveloped in a frothy abundance of frills and fal-lals [finery], lace at the wrists, lace round the neck, with flutters of ribbon here and there. When, at the breakfast table in the morning, he related how he had been rigged [attired], there was a shriek of laughter from the young ladies; the simple explanation being that one of them had vacated her room to accommodate the visitor, and had forgotten to remove her nightdress.

The visit had more important consequences. Captain Pasley very soon saw that he had an exceptional lad before him, and at once put him on the *Alert.* He was entered as 'lieutenant's servant' on 23 October 1789. He remained there for rather more than seven months, learning the practical part of a sailor's business. On 17 May, 1790, he was able to present himself to Captain Pasley on the *Scipio* at Chatham, as an aspirant of more than ordinary efficiency; and remained under his command until the next year, following him as a midshipman when he left the *Scipio* for the *Bellerophon* in July 1790.

This famous ship, which carried 74 guns, and was launched in 1786, is chiefly known to history as the vessel upon which Napoleon surrendered to Captain Maitland on 15 July 1815, after the Waterloo *débacle.* She took a prominent part in Nelson's great battles at the Nile and Trafalgar. But her end was pitifully ignoble. After a glorious and proud career, she was converted into a convict hulk and renamed the *Captivity.*

During this preliminary period Flinders learnt the way about a ship and acquired instruction in the mechanism of seamanship, but there was as yet no opportunity to obtain deep-water experience. He was transferred to the *Dictator* for a brief period, but as he neither mentions the captain nor alludes to any other circumstance connected therewith, it was probably a mere temporary turnover or guardship rating not to lose any time of service [an assigned position which would enable Flinders to maintain continuity of service].[5]

[5] *Naval Chronicle* (1814).

His first chance of learning something about the width of the world and the wonder of its remote places came in 1791, when he went to sea under the command of a very remarkable man. William Bligh had sailed with James Cook on his third and fatal voyage of discovery, 1776–80. He was 23 years of age when he was selected by that sagacious leader as one of those young officers who 'under my direction could be usefully employed in constructing charts, in taking views of the coasts and headlands near which we should pass, and in drawing plans of the bays and harbours in which we should anchor' for Cook recognised that constant attention to these duties was 'wholly requisite if we would render our discoveries profitable to future navigators'.[6]

Bligh's name appears frequently in Cook's journal, and is also mentioned in King's excellent narrative of the conclusion of the voyage after Cook's murder. He was master of the *Resolution*, and was on several occasions entrusted with tasks of some consequence: as for instance on first reaching Hawaii, when Cook sent him ashore to look for fresh water, and again at Kealakeakura Bay (16 January 1779) when he reported that he had found good anchorage and fresh water 'in a situation admirable to come at'. It was a fatal discovery, for on the white sands of that bay, a month later (14 February), the great British seaman fell, speared by the savages.

On each of Cook's voyages a call had been made at Tahiti in the Society group. Bligh no doubt heard much about the charms of the place before he first saw it himself. He was destined to have his own name associated with it in a highly romantic and adventurous manner. The idyllic beauty of the life of the Tahitians, their amiable and seductive characteristics, the warm suavity [pleasantness] of the climate, the profusion of food and drink to be enjoyed on the island with the smallest conceivable amount of exertion, made the place stand out in all the narratives of Cook's expeditions like a green-and-golden gem set in a turquoise sea, a lotos-land 'in which it seemed always afternoon', a paradise where love and plenty reigned and care and toil were not. George Forster, the German naturalist who accompanied Cook on his second voyage, wrote of the men as 'models of masculine beauty', whose perfect proportions would have satisfied the eye of Phidias or Praxiteles; of the women as beings whose 'unaffected smiles and a wish to please ensure them mutual esteem and love' and of the life they led as being diversified between bathing in cool streams, reposing under tufted trees, feeding on luscious fruits, telling tales, and playing the flute. In fact,

[6] Cook's *Voyages* (edition of 1821), V, p. 92.

Forster declared, they 'resembled the happy, indolent people whom Ulysses found in Phæacia, and could apply the poet's lines to themselves with peculiar propriety:

To dress, to dance, to sing our sole delight,
The feast or bath by day, and love by night.'

In Tahiti grew an abundance of breadfruit. It was in connection with this nutritious food, one of nature's richest gifts to the Pacific, that Bligh undertook a mission which involved him in a mutiny, launched him upon one of the most dangerous and difficult voyages in the annals of British seamanship, and provided a theme for a long poem by one of the greatest of English authors. Byron it was who, writing as though the trees sprouted quartern loaves ready baked, said of it ('The Island', II, 11):

The bread-tree, which without the ploughshare yields
The unreaped harvest of unfurrowed fields,
And bakes its unadulterated loaves
Without a furnace in unpurchased groves,
And flings off famine from its fertile breast,
A priceless market for the gathering guest.

Breadfruit had been tasted and described by Dampier in the seventeenth century. His description of it has all the terse directness peculiar to the writing of the inquisitive buccaneer, with a touch of quaintness that makes the passage desirable to quote:[7]

The breadfruit, as we call it, grows on a large tree as big and as tall as our largest apple trees. It hath a spreading head full of branches and dark leaves. The fruit grows on the boughs like apples; it is as big as a penny loaf when wheat is at five shillings the bushel. The natives of this island (Suam) use it for bread. They gather it when full-grown; then they bake it in an oven, which scorcheth the rind and makes it black; but they scrape off the outside black crust and there remains a tender thin crust and the inside is soft, tender and white, like the crumb of a penny loaf. There is neither seed nor stone in the inside, but all is of a pure substance like bread; it must be eaten new, for if it is kept above twenty-four hours it becomes dry and eats harsh and chokey; but 'tis very pleasant before it is too stale.

[7] Dampier's *Voyages* (edition of 1729), I, p. 294.

By Dampier, who in the course of his astonishing career had consumed many strange things—who found shark's flesh 'good entertainment', and roast opossum 'sweet wholesome meat'—toleration in the matter of things edible was carried to the point of latitudinarianism. We never find Dampier squeamish about anything which anybody else could eat with relish. To him, naturally, the first taste of breadfruit was pleasing. But Cook was more critical. 'The natives seldom make a meal without it', he said, 'though to us the taste was as disagreeable as that of a pickled olive generally is the first time it is eaten.' That opinion, perhaps, accords with the common experience of neophytes in tropical gastronomy. But new sensations in the matter of food are not always to be depended on. Sir Joseph Banks disliked bananas when he first tasted them.

The immense popularity of Cook's voyages spread afar the fame of breadfruit as an article of food. Certain West Indian planters were of [the] opinion that it would be advantageous to establish the trees on their islands and to encourage the consumption of the fruit by their slaves. Not only was it considered that the use of breadfruit would cheapen the cost of the slaves' living, but—a consideration that weighed both with the planters and the British Government in view of existing relations with the United States—it was also believed that it would 'lessen the dependence of the sugar islands on North America for food and necessaries'.[8]

The planters petitioned the Government to fit out an expedition to transplant trees from the Pacific to the Atlantic. Sir Joseph Banks strongly supported them, and Lord Hood, then First Lord of the Admiralty, was sympathetic. In August 1787, Lieutenant Bligh was appointed to the command of the *Bounty*, was directed to sail to the Society Islands, to take on board 'as many trees and plants as may be thought necessary', and to transplant them to British possessions in the West Indies.

The vessel sailed, with two skilled gardeners on board to superintend the selection and treatment of the plants. Tahiti was duly reached, and the business of the expedition was taken in hand. One thousand and fifteen fine trees were chosen and carefully stowed. But the comfortable indolence, the luxuriant abundance, the genial climate, the happy hospitality of the handsome islanders, and their easy freedom from compunction in reference to restraints imposed by law and custom in Europe, had a demoralising effect upon the crew of the *Bounty.* A stay of 23 weeks at the island sufficed to subvert discipline and to persuade

[8] Bryan Edwards, *History of the British West Indies* (1819), I, p. xl.

some of Bligh's sailors that life in Tahiti was far preferable to service in the King's navy under the rule of a severe and exacting commander.

When the *Bounty* left Tahiti on 14 April 1787, reluctance plucked at the heart of many of the crew. The morning light lay tenderly upon the plumes of the palms, and a light wind filled the sails of the ship as she glided out of harbour. As the lazy lapping wash of the waters against the low outer fringe of coral was lost to the ear, the *Bounty* breasted the deep ocean; and as the distinguishable features of green tree, white sand, brown earth, and grey rock faded out of vision—wrapped in a haze of blue, till at last the only pronounced characteristic of the island standing up against the sky and sea was the cap of Point Venus at the northern extremity—the departure must have seemed to some like that of Tannhäuser from the enchanted mountain, except that the legendary hero was glad to make his return to the normal world, whereas all of Bligh's company were not. For them, westward, whither they were bound,

> *There gaped the gate*
> *Whereby lost souls back to the cold earth went.*

The discipline of ship's life, and the stormings and objurgations [vehement reproaches] of the commanding officer, chafed like an iron collar. At length a storm burst.

On 28 April the *Bounty* was sailing towards Tofoa, another of the Society Islands. Just before sunrise on the following morning Bligh was aroused from sleep, seized and bound in his cabin by a band of mutineers, led out by the master's mate, Fletcher Christian, and, with eighteen companions, dropped into a launch and bidden to depart. The followers of Christian were three midshipmen and 25 petty officers and sailors. They turned the head of the *Bounty* back towards their island paradise; and as they sailed away, the mariners in the tossing little boat heard them calling 'Hurrah for Tahiti!'

The frail craft in which the nineteen loyalists were compelled to attempt to traverse thousands of miles of ocean, where the navigation is perhaps the most intricate in the world, was but 23 feet long by 6 feet 9 inches broad and 2 feet 9 inches deep. Their provisions consisted of 150 pounds of bread, sixteen pieces of pork, each about two pounds in weight, six quarts of rum, six bottles of wine, and 28 gallons of water. With this scanty stock of nourishment, in so small a boat, Bligh and his companions covered 3,618 miles, crossing the western Pacific, sailing through Torres Strait, and ultimately reaching Timor.

That Bligh was somewhat deficient in tact and sympathy in handling men, cross-grained, harsh, and obstinate, is probably true. His language was often lurid, he lavished foul epithets upon his crew, and he was not reluctant to follow terms of abuse by vigorous chastisement. He called Christian a 'damned hound', some of the men 'scoundrels, thieves and rascals', and he met a respectful remonstrance with the retort: 'You damned infernal scoundrels, I'll make you eat grass or anything you can catch before I have done with you.' Naval officers of the period were not addicted to addressing their men in the manner of a lady with a pet canary. Had Bligh's language been the head and front [worst aspect] of his offending, he would hardly have shocked an eighteenth-century fo'c'sle. But his disposition does not seem to have bound men to him. He generated dislike. Nevertheless it is credible that the explanation which he gave goes far to explain the mutiny. He held that the real cause was a species of sensuous intoxication which had corrupted his crew. Bligh wrote:

> *The women of Tahiti are handsome, mild and cheerful in their manners and conversation, possessed of great sensibility, and have sufficient delicacy to make them admired and loved. The chiefs were so much attached to our people that they rather encouraged their stay among them than otherwise, and even made them promises of large possessions. Under these and other attendant circumstances equally desirable, it is perhaps not so much to be wondered at, though scarcely possible to have been foreseen, that a set of sailors, many of them void of connections, should be led away; especially when in addition to such powerful inducements they imagined it in their power to fix themselves in the midst of plenty on one of the finest islands in the world, where they need not labour, and where the allurements of dissipation are beyond anything that can be conceived … Had their mutiny been occasioned by any grievance, either real or imaginary, I must have discovered symptoms of their discontent, which would have put me on my guard; but the case was far otherwise. Christian in particular I was on the most friendly terms with; that very day he was engaged to have dined with me; and the preceding night he excused himself from supping with me on pretence of being unwell, for which I felt concerned, having no suspicions of his integrity and honour.*

Support is given to Bligh's explanation by a statement alleged to have been made by Fletcher Christian a few years later, the genuineness of which, however, is open to serious question. If it could be accepted,

Christian acquitted his commander of having contributed to the mutiny by harsh conduct. He ascribed the occurrence 'to the strong predilection we had contracted for living in Tahiti, where, exclusive of the happy disposition of the inhabitants, the mildness of the climate, and the fertility of the soil, we had formed certain tender connections which banished the remembrance of old England from our breasts'. The weight of evidence justifies the belief that Bligh, though a sailor of unequivocal skill and dauntless courage, was an unlikeable man, and that aversion to service under him was a factor contributing to the mutiny, which cannot be explained away.

Bligh is the connecting link between Cook and Flinders. Bligh learnt under Cook to experience the thrilling pleasure of discovery and to pursue opportunities in that direction in a scientific spirit. Flinders learnt the same lesson under Bligh, and bettered the instruction. Cook is the first great scientific navigator whose name is associated with the construction of the map of Australia; so much can be said without disparagement of the adventurous Dutchmen who pieced together the outline of the western and northern coasts. Flinders was the second; and Bligh, pupil of the one and teacher of the other, deserves a better fate than to be remembered chiefly as a sinister figure in two historic mutinies, that of the *Bounty*, and that which ended his governorship of New South Wales in 1808. Much worse men have done much worse things than he, have less that is brave, honourable, enterprising and original to their credit, and yet are remembered without ignominy. It is said by Hooker: 'as oftentimes the vices of wicked men do cause other their commendable virtues to be abhorred, so the honour of great men's virtues is easily a cloak to their errors'. Bligh fell short of being a great man, but neither was he a bad man; and the merit of his achievements, both as a navigator and amid the shock of battle (especially at Copenhagen in 1801, under Nelson), must not be overlooked, even though stern history will not permit his errors to be cloaked.

Notwithstanding the failure of the *Bounty* expedition, Sir Joseph Banks pressed upon the [British] Government the desirableness of transplanting breadfruit trees to the West Indies. He also proved a staunch friend to Bligh. The result was that the Admiralty resolved to equip a second enterprise for the same purpose, and to entrust the command of it to the same officer.

We may now follow the fortunes of Matthew Flinders under the tutelage of this energetic captain.

III

A VOYAGE UNDER BLIGH

BLIGH'S second expedition was authorised by the Admiralty in March 1791, and the commander was consulted as to 'what sort of vessel may be best adapted to the object in view'. The *Providence*, a 28-gun ship, was chosen, with the brig *Assistant* as a tender. The latter was placed in charge of Lieutenant Nathaniel Portlock. Flinders, eager for sea experience, joined the *Providence* as a midshipman on 8 May, and thus had the advantage of being under the immediate direction of her captain.

He took this step with Pasley's concurrence, if not actually upon his advice. The captain wrote him an encouraging letter asking him to send from time to time observations on places visited during the voyage; and his *protégé* complied with the injunction. It is to this fact that we owe some entertaining passages from young Flinders' pen concerning the voyage. The letters despatched to Pasley are lost; but Flinders, with the love of neatness which was ever characteristic of him, sent only fair copies, and some of his original drafts remain in manuscript. Pasley's letter was as follows:[1]

> *Bellerophon,*
> *Spithead,*
> *June 3rd, 1791*
>
> *Dear Flinders,*
>
> *I am favoured with your letter on your return from visiting your friends at the country, and I am pleased to hear that you are so well satisfied with your situation on board the Providence. I have little doubt of your gaining the good opinion of Capt. Bligh, if you are equally attentive to your duty there as you*

[1] Flinders' Papers.

were in the Bellerophon. *All that I have to request in return for the good offices I have done you is that you never fail writing me by all possible opportunities during your voyage; and that in your letters you will be very particular and circumstantial in regard to every thing and place you may chance to see or visit, with your own observations thereon. Do this, my young friend, and you may rest assured that my good offices will not be wanting some future day for your advancement. All on board are well. Present my kind remembrances to Captain and Mrs. Bligh, and believe me, yours very sincerely,*

THOMAS PASLEY.

The *Providence* and *Assistant* left England on 2 August. From Santa Cruz in Teneriffe Flinders sent his first letter to Captain Pasley. It is worth while to quote a few passages:[2]

Not a large town; streets wide, ill-paved and irregular. The houses of the principal inhabitants large; have little furniture, but are airy and pleasant, suitable to the climate. Most of them have balconies, where the owners sit and enjoy the air. Those of the lower classes ill-built, dirty, and almost without furniture. In the square where the market is held, near the pier, is a tolerably elegant marble obelisk in honour of Our Lady of Candelaria, the tutelar goddess of the place. The Spaniards erected this statue, calling it Our Lady, keeping up some semblance of the ancient worship that they might better keep the Tenerifeans in subjection. At the top of the obelisk is placed the statue, and at its base are four well executed figures, representing the ancient kings or princes of Teneriffe, each of which has the shin-bone of a man's leg in his hand. This image is held in great honour by the lower classes of people, who tell many absurd stories of its first appearance in the island, the many miracles she has wrought, etc.

We visited a nunnery of the order of St. Dominic. In the chapel was a fine statue of the Virgin Mary, with four wax candles burning before her. Peeping through the bars, we perceived several fine young women at prayers. A middle-aged woman opened the door halfway, but would by no means suffer us to enter this sanctified spot. None of the nuns would be

[2] Flinders' Papers.

prevailed upon to come near us. However, they did not seem at all displeased at our visit, but presented us with a sweet candy they call Dulce, and some artificial flowers, in return for which Mr. Smith[3] *gave them a dollar. In general these people appear to be a merry, good-natured people, and are courteous to and appear happy to see strangers. We found this always the case, although they said we were no Christians; but they generally took care to make us pay well for what we had. They live principally upon fruits and roots, are fond of singing and dancing, and upon the whole they live as lazily, as contentedly, and in as much poverty as any French peasant would wish to do.*

The Cape of Good Hope was reached in October, and Flinders told Captain Pasley what he thought of the Dutch colonists:

The Dutch, from having great quantities of animal food, are rather corpulent. Nevertheless they keep up their national characteristic for carefulness. Neither are they very polite. A stranger will be treated with a great deal of ceremony, but when you come to the solid part of a compliment their generosity is at a stand. Of all the people I ever saw these are the most ceremonious. Every man is a soldier and wears his square-rigged hat, sword, epaulets, and military uniform. They never pass each other without a formal bow, which even descends to the lowest ranks, and it is even seen in the slaves.

On 10 April 1792, Bligh's ships anchored at Tahiti, where they remained till 19 July. There was no disturbance this time, and the relations between Bligh and his crew were not embarrassed by the indulgent kindness of the islanders. Their hospitality was not deficient, but a wary vigilance was exercised.

At Tahiti Bligh found the major part of the crew of a whaler, the *Matilda*, which had been wrecked about six days' sail from the island. Some of the men accepted passages on the *Providence* and the *Assistant*; some preferred to remain with the natives; one or two had already departed in one of the lost ship's boats to make their way to Sydney.[4] Two male Tahitians were persuaded to accompany the expedition, with a view to their exhibition before the Royal Society, in England, when at length, laden with 600 breadfruit trees, it sailed for the West Indies.

---

[3] The botanist.

[4] This incident is reported in the *Star*, a London newspaper, 2 March 1793.

The route followed from the Friendly Islands to the Caribbean Sea was not *via* Cape Horn (since that cold and stormy passage would have destroyed every plant), but back across the Pacific, through Torres Strait to Timor, thence across the Indian Ocean and round the Cape of Good Hope. St Helena was reached on 17 December, and Bligh brought his ships safely to Kingston, St Vincent's, on 13 January 1793. Three hundred breadfruit trees were landed at that island, and a like number taken to Jamaica. The plants were in excellent condition, some of them eleven feet high, with leaves 36 inches long. The gardener in charge reported to Sir Joseph Banks that the success of the transplantations 'exceeded the most sanguine expectation'. The sugar planters were delighted, and voted Bligh £500 for his services.[5] To accentuate the contrast between the successful second expedition and the lamentable voyage of the *Bounty*, it is notable that only one case of sickness occurred on the way, and that from Kingston it was reported that 'the healthy appearance of every person belonging to the expedition is remarkable'.[6]

But though nothing in the nature of a mutiny marred the voyage, Flinders' journal shows that Bligh's harshness occasioned discontent. There was a shortness [shortage] of water on the run from the Pacific to the West Indies, and as the breadfruit plants had to be watered, and their safe carriage was the main object of the voyage, the men had to suffer. Flinders and others used to lick the drops that fell from the cans to appease their thirst, and it was considered a great favour to get a sip. The crew thought they were unfairly treated, and somebody mischievously watered some plants with sea-water. When Bligh discovered the offence, he flew into a rage and 'longed to flog the whole company'. But the offender could not be discovered, and the irate captain had to let his passion fret itself out.

Bligh published no narrative of this expedition; but Flinders was already accustoming himself to keep careful notes of his observations. Twenty years later, when preparing the historical introduction to his *Voyage to Terra Australis*, he wrote out from his journal (and with Bligh's sanction published) an account of the passage of the *Providence* and *Assistant* through Torres Strait, as a contribution to the history of navigation and discovery in that portion of Australasia. From the Pacific to the Indian Ocean the passage was accomplished in nineteen days. 'Perhaps,' commented Flinders, 'no space of 3½ degrees in length

[5] Southey, *History of the West Indies* (1827), III, p. 61.

[6] *Annual Register*, 1793.

presents more dangers than Torres Strait, but with caution and perseverance the captains, Bligh and Portlock, proved them to be surmountable, and within a reasonable time.' Bligh's Entrance and Portlock Reef, marked on modern charts, are reminders of a feat of navigation which even nowadays, with the dangers accurately described, and the well-equipped Torres Strait pilot service to aid them, mariners recognise as pregnant with serious risks. On this occasion it was also attended with incidents which make it worth while to utilise Flinders' notes, since they are of some biographical importance.

The highlands of the south-eastern extremity of Papua (New Guinea) were passed on 30 August, and at dusk on the following day breakers 'thundering on the reef' were sighted ahead. On 1 September the vessels edged round the north end of Portlock Reef. Thence the monotonous record of soundings, shoals, reefs seen and charted, passages tried and abandoned, in the prolonged attempt to negotiate a clear course through the baffling coral barrier, is relieved by the story of one or two sharp brushes with armed Papuans in their long, deftly handled canoes. On 5 September, while boats were out investigating a supposed passage near Darnley Island, several large canoes shot into view. One of these, in which were fifteen 'Indians', black and quite naked, approached the English cutter, and made signs which were interpreted to be amicable. The officer in charge, however, suspecting treacherous intentions, did not think it prudent to go near enough to accept a green coconut held up to him, and kept his men rowing for the ship. Thereupon a native sitting on the shed erected in the centre of the canoe, called a direction to the Papuans below him, who commenced to string their bows. The officer ordered his men to fire in self-defence, and six muskets were discharged.

> *The Indians fell flat into the bottom of the canoe, all except the man on the shed. The seventh musket was fired at him, and he fell also. During this time the canoe dropped astern; and, the three others having joined her, they all gave chase to the cutter, trying to cut her off from the ship; in which they would probably have succeeded, had not the pinnace arrived at that juncture to her assistance. The Indians then hoisted their sails and steered for Darnley Island.*

Flinders had watched the encounter from the deck of the *Providence*, and his seaman's word of admiration for the skill of the savages in the management of their canoes, is notable. 'No boats could have been manoeuvred better in working to windward, than were these canoes of the naked savages. Had the four been able to reach the cutter, it is difficult to say whether the superiority of our arms would have been equal to the great difference of numbers, considering the ferocity of these people and the skill with which they seemed to manage their weapons.'

Five days later, between Dungeness and Warrior Islands, there was a livelier encounter. A squadron of canoes attacked both ships in a daring and vigorous fashion. The *Assistant* was pressed with especial severity, so that Portlock had to signal for help. A volley of musketry had little effect upon the Papuans; and when one wing of the attacking squadron, numbering eight canoes, headed for the *Providence*, and a musket was fired at the foremost, the natives responded with 'a great shout and paddled forward in a body'. Bligh had one of the great guns of the ship loaded with round and grape shot, and fired fair into the first of the long Papuan war canoes, which were full of savage assailants. The round shot raked the whole length of the craft, and struck the high stern. Men from other canoes, with splendid bravery, leaped into the water, and swam to the assistance of their comrades, 'plunging constantly to avoid the musket balls which showered thickly about them'. So hard was the attack pressed, that three of the *Assistant*'s crew were wounded, one afterwards dying; and 'the depth to which the arrows penetrated into the decks and sides of the brig was reported to be truly astonishing'. But bows and arrows, on this as on many another occasion, were no match for gunnery; so that, after a hot peppering, the Papuans gave up the fight, paddling back to a safe distance as fast as they could, without exposing themselves to fire. They rallied beyond reach of musket balls, as though for a second onslaught, but a shot fired over their heads from the *Providence* served to convince them of the hopelessness of their endeavour, and they abandoned it.

An incident not without heroic pathos is recorded by Flinders. One native was left sitting alone in the canoe which the gun-shot of the *Providence* had raked and splintered. The men in the canoes which had made good their flight observed their solitary companion, and some of them returned to him; whereafter 'with glasses, signals were perceived to be made by the Indians to their friends on Dungeness Island, expressive, as was thought, of grief and consternation'. Whether the lone warrior was too severely wounded to be moved, or whether he was some Papuan Casabianca clinging to his shattered craft 'whence all but he had fled' or been killed, or hurled into the sea, we are not told. [Casabianca was a Corsican naval officer's son who died in heroic circumstances with his father at the battle of Aboukir in 1798. He is the 'boy on the burning deck' in Felicia Heman's eponymous poem.] But that canoe had been foremost in attack, perhaps the flagship of the squadron; and the memory of that solitary warrior still sitting upon the floating wreck while his defeated companions returned to him, and then left him, to explain his case with gestures of grief to those on the island, clings to the memory of the reader, as it did to that of the young observer and historian of the encounter.

No more natives were seen during the passage through Torres Strait, nor were there other incidents to enliven the narrative, unless we include the formal 'taking possession of all the islands seen in the Strait for His Britannic Majesty George III, with the ceremonies used on such occasions' (16 September). The name bestowed upon the whole group of islands was Clarence's Archipelago.

Flinders described the natives whom he saw carefully and accurately; and his account of their boats, weapons, and mode of warfare is concise and good. Some friendly Darnley Islanders were described as stoutly made, with bushy hair; the cartilage between the nostrils cut away; the lobes of the ears split, and stretched 'to a good length'.

> *They had no kind of clothing, but wore necklaces of cowrie shells fastened to a braid of fibres; and some of their companions had pearl-oyster shells hung round their necks. In speaking to each other, their words seemed to be distinctly pronounced. Their arms were bows, arrows, and clubs, which they bartered for every kind of iron work with eagerness, but appeared to set little value on anything else. The bows are made of split bamboo, and so strong that no man in the ship could bend one of them. The string is a broad slip of cane fixed to one end of the bow; and fitted with a noose to go over the other end when strung. The arrow is a cane of about four feet long, into which a pointed piece of the hard, heavy, casuarina wood is firmly and neatly fitted; and some of them were barbed. Their clubs are made of casuarina, and are powerful weapons. The hand part is indented, and has a small knob, by which the firmness of the grasp is much assisted; and the heavy end is usually carved with some device. One had the form of a parrot's head, with a ruff round the neck, and was not ill done.*
>
> *Their canoes are about fifty feet in length, and appear to have been hollowed out of a single tree; and the pieces which form the gunwales are planks sewed on with fibres of the coconut and secured with pegs. These vessels are low forward, but rise abaft; and, being narrow, are fitted with an outrigger*

> *on each side to keep them steady. A raft, of greater breadth than the canoe, extends over about half the length, and upon this is fixed a shed or hut, thatched with palm leaves. These people, in short, appeared to be dexterous sailors and formidable warriors, and to be as much at ease in the water as in their canoes.*

On 19 September the two ships, with caution and perseverance, had threaded their dangerous way through the intricate maze of reefs and shoals of Torres Strait, and found open sea to the westward. In latitude 10° 8½' 'no land was in sight, nor did anything more obstruct Captain Bligh and his associates in their route to the island Timor'.

It is easy to imagine the delight with which these experiences thrilled the young midshipman on the *Providence.* His eighteenth birthday was spent in the Pacific, in the early autumn of a hemisphere where the sea was not yet cloven by innumerable keels, and where beauty, enchantment and mystery lay upon life and nature like a spell. A few years previously he had been a schoolboy in the flattest, most monotonous of English shires. Broad fields, dykes and fen had composed the landscape most familiar to his eye. In these surroundings he had dreamt, as a boy will, of palm-fanned islands in distant climes, of adventures with savage peoples, of strange seas where great fishes are, and where romance touches all that is with its purple light. Far horizons steeped in marvels had bounded the vision of his imagining eye. His passion was to see and do in realms at the back of the sunrise. He wanted to sail and explore in parts represented by blank spaces on the map.

These dreams of the boy, basking with *Robinson Crusoe* under remote skies, were suddenly translated into a reality as dazzling-bright and wonderful as anything pictured in pages often and fondly conned [studied]. This was his first voyage, and he was serving under a commander who had lived the romance that other men wrote and read about, who was himself a living part of an adventure whose story will be told and retold to the centuries, and who had served under as great and noble a captain as ever trod an English deck.

The very nature of the voyage was bound to stimulate that 'passion for exploring new countries', to use Flinders' own phrase, the hope for which was a strong factor in prompting him to choose the sea as a career. It was a voyage whose primary object involved a stay in two of the loveliest regions on the earth, the paradise of the Pacific and the gem-like Antilles. The pride and pleasure of participation in discovery were his forthwith. A new passage through an intricate and dangerous strait was found and charted; a whole archipelago was delineated, named, and taken possession of for the British nation. The world's knowledge was increased. There was something put down on the map which was not there before. The contact with the islanders in the strait gave a brisk element of adventure to the expedition; and certainly Papuan warriors are foes as wild and weird as any adventurer can desire to meet. The rescuing of wrecked mariners at Tahiti added a spice of adventure of another sort. From beginning to end, indeed, this voyage must have been as full of charm as of utility.

The effect it had upon the future life of Matthew Flinders was very striking. The whole of the salient features of his later career follow from it. He made the most of his opportunities. Captain Bligh found him a clever assistant in the preparation of charts and in making astronomical observations. Indeed, says an expert writer, although Flinders was as yet 'but a juvenile navigator, the latter branch of scientific service and the care of the timekeepers were principally entrusted to him'.[7] These facts indicate that he was applying himself seriously to the scientific side of his profession, and that he had won the confidence of a captain who was certainly no overindulgent critic of subordinates.

The *Providence* and the *Assistant* returned to England in the latter part of 1793. Before Flinders once more sighted the Australian coastline he was to experience the sensations of battle, and to take a small part in the first of the series of naval engagements connected with the Revolutionary and Napoleonic era.

[7] *Naval Chronicle*, Vol. XXXII, p. 180.

IV

THE BATTLE OFF BREST

WHEN Bligh's expedition returned, Europe was staggering under the shock of the French Revolution. The head of Louis XVI was severed in January; the knife of Charlotte Corday was plunged into the heart of Marat in July; Marie Antoinette, the grey discrowned Queen of 38 years, mounted the scaffold in October. The guillotine was very busy, and France was frantic amid internal disruption and the menace of a ring of foes.

The English governing classes had been clamouring for war. It seemed to many political observers that it was positively needful to launch the country into an international struggle to divert attention from demands for domestic reform. 'Democratic ambition was awakened; the desire of power, under the name of reform, was rapidly gaining ground among the middling ranks; the only mode of checking the evil was by engaging in a foreign contest, by drawing off the ardent spirits into active service and, in lieu of the modern desire for innovation, rousing the ancient gallantry of the British people.'[1] French military operations in the Netherlands, running counter to traditional British policy, were provocative, and the feeling aroused by the execution of Louis immediately led Pitt's ministry to order the French Ambassador, Chauvelin, to leave London within eight days. He left at once. On 1 February, acting on Chauvelin's report of the disposition and preparations of Great Britain, France formally declared war.

Flinders was with Bligh, peacefully landing breadfruit trees in the West Indies, when this momentous opening of a 22-year conflict occurred. When the expedition reached England, every port and dockyard on the south coast was humming with preparations for a great naval struggle. The Channel Fleet, under Lord Howe's command, was

---

[1] Alison, *History of Europe* (1839), II, p. 128.

cruising in search of the enemy's ships of war. Flinders' patron, Pasley, who had hoisted his broad pennant as commodore on the *Bellerophon*, was actively engaged in this service. In October 1793, he was detached by Howe to look for five French vessels that had some time before chased the British frigate *Circe* into Falmouth. Howe himself, with a fleet of 22 sail, put to sea later in the same month. On 18 November his squadron sighted six French ships of the line and some frigates, and gave chase. But they were seen late in the day, and soon darkness prevented an engagement. On the following morning the enemy was again sighted by the chasing squadron under Pasley; but the *Latona* signalled that the French were in superior strength, and the British detachment retired.[2] Howe's cruise was barren of results, and the British fleet returned to Torbay. Naval operations were suspended for several months.

Flinders naturally took advantage of the earliest opportunity to report himself to the friend who had first helped him into the King's navy. Pasley, who was promoted on 12 April 1794, to the rank of Rear-Admiral of the White, again welcomed him on board the *Bellerophon* and, hearing from Captain Bligh excellent accounts of his diligence and usefulness, appointed him one of his aides-de-camp. It was in this capacity that he took part in the great battle off Brest on 1 June 1794, signalised [made notable] in British naval history as 'the glorious First of June'.

Lord Howe, with the Channel Fleet (34 ships of the line and fifteen frigates) put to sea on 2 May with two purposes: first, to convoy to a safe distance from the probable field of hostilities a squadron of 148 British merchantmen bound for various ports; second, to intercept and destroy a French fleet which was known to be convoying a large company of provision-ships from America. War, bad harvests, the disorganisation of industry, and revolutionary upheavals, had produced an acute scarcity of food in France, and the arrival of these vessels was awaited with intense anxiety. To prevent their arrival, or to destroy the French squadron, would be to strike a serious blow at the enemy. Howe had under him a fleet eager for fight; against him, a foe keenly aware how vitally necessary to their country was the arrival of the food-ships.

The French fleet (26 ships of the line) under the command of Villaret-Joyeuse, put to sea from Brest on 16 May. Some foggy days intervened. On the 28th Howe sighted them. The French admiral formed his ships in a close line. Howe's plan was first to get his fleet to windward of the enemy, then to sail down, pierce his line, and engage his vessels to leeward.

The *Bellerophon* was in action shortly after coming within striking

---

[2] James, *Naval History* (1837), I, p. 60.

distance, on 28 May. Pasley, at six o'clock in the evening, attacked the French rear, his immediate antagonist being the *Révolutionnaire*, [which was armed with] 110 guns. A hot duel, maintained with splendid intrepidity by the British rear-admiral, continued for over an hour and a quarter, for the other ships of the British fleet were unable to get up to support the fast-sailing *Bellerophon.* She was severely handled by her large antagonist, and was hampered in her ability to manoeuvre by a shot which injured her mainmast. Pasley therefore, on a signal from the admiral, bore up. The *Révolutionnaire* was now attacked from a distance by the *Russell*, the *Marlborough* and the *Thunderer*, and endeavoured to make off, but was blocked by the *Leviathan.* The *Audacious* took up the work which the *Bellerophon* had commenced, and, laying herself on the lee quarter of the *Révolutionnaire*, poured a rain of shot into her. The fight was continued in a rough sea far into the twilight of that early summer evening; until, about ten o'clock, the *Révolutionnaire* was a mere floating hulk. Her flag had either been lowered or shot down, but she was not captured, and was towed into Rochefort on the following day. The *Audacious* was so badly knocked about that she was of no use for later engagements, and was sent home.

This was Matthew Flinders' first taste of war.

Howe's plan for the big battle that was imminent involved much manoeuvring, and, as Nelson wrote in his celebrated 'plan of attack' before Trafalgar, 'a day is soon lost in that business'. The British manoeuvred to get the weather gauge [to get to windward of the enemy]; Villaret-Joyeuse to keep it. On 29 May Howe in the *Queen Charlotte* pierced the French line with two other ships, the *Bellerophon* and the *Leviathan*, and there was some fighting. The *Bellerophon* got to windward of the enemy by passing in front of the French *Terrible*, of 110 guns, and put in some excellent gunnery practice. She sailed so close to the French ship to starboard as almost to touch her, and brought down the enemy's topmast and lower yards with a broadside, whilst at the same time she raked the *Terrible* with her larboard [port] guns.[3]

Both 30 and 31 May were foggy days, and neither fleet could see the other. On 1 June there was a blue sky, a brilliant sun, a lively sea, and a wind that favoured the plans of the British admiral. The signal for close action was flown from the masthead of the *Queen Charlotte.* Howe ordered his ships to sail on an oblique course down upon the French line,

---

[3] There is an interesting engraving of the *Bellerophon* passing through the French line and firing both her broadsides in the *Naval Chronicle*, Vol. I, and a plan of the manoeuvre, showing the course of the *Bellerophon*, in James's *Naval History.*

the two fleets having during the night lain in parallel lines stretching east and west. The intention was to break the French line near the centre, each British captain sailing round the stern of his antagonist, and fighting her to leeward, thus concentrating the attack on the enemy's rear, cutting it off from the van [the leading section of the fleet], and preventing flight.

The *Bellerophon* was the second ship in the British line, next after the *Caesar.* Flinders was upon the quarterdeck as she steered through her selected gap, which was on the weather quarter of the *Eole*; and an anecdote of his behaviour on that memorable occasion fortunately survives. The guns on the quarterdeck were loaded and primed ready for use, but Pasley did not intend to fire them until he had laid himself on the lee of his chosen adversary, and could pour a broadside into her with crushing effect. There was a moment when the gunners were aloft trimming sails. As the *Bellerophon* was passing close under the stern of the French three-decker—within musket-shot, James says[4]—Flinders seized a lighted match and rapidly fired as many of the quarterdeck guns as would plump shot fairly into her.[5] Pasley saw him and, shaking him by the collar, said, sternly: 'How dare you do that, youngster, without my orders?' Flinders replied that he 'thought it a fine chance to have a shot at 'em'. So it was, though not in conformity with orders; and probably Pasley, as good a fighter as there was in the fleet, liked his young aide-de-camp rather the more for his impetuous action.

The guns of the *Bellerophon* were opened upon the *Eole* at 8.45, and battered her severely. The British vessel was subjected in turn, however, not only to the fire of her chosen victim, but also to that of the *Trajan.* At ten minutes to eleven o'clock a shot from the *Eole* took off Pasley's leg, and he was carried down to the cockpit, whereupon the command devolved upon Captain William Hope. It must have been a distressing moment for Flinders, despite the intense excitement of action, when his friend and commander fell; it was indeed, as will be seen, a crucial moment in his career. A doggerel bard of the time enshrined the event in a verse as badly in need of surgical aid as were the heroes whom it celebrates:

Bravo, Bowyer, Pasley, Captain Hutt,
Each lost a leg, being sorely hurt;
Their lives they valued but as dirt,
When that their country called them![6]

---

[4] *Naval History*, I, p. 154.

[5] *Naval Chronicle*, XXXII, p. 180.

[6] *Naval Songs and Ballads*—Publications of the Navy Record Society, Vol. XXXIIL, p. 270.

The fight was continued with unflagging vigour, in the absence of the gallant rear-admiral, who, as another lyrist of the event informs us, smiled and said:

Fight on my lads and try
To make these rebel Frenchmen know
That British courage still will flow
To make them strike or die.

At a quarter before noon the *Eole* had received such a hammering that she endeavoured to wear round [to come around on the other tack] under shelter of her leader; but in doing so she lost mainmast and foretopmast. The *Bellerophon*, too, had by this time been sufficiently hard hit to cause Hope to signal to the *Latona* for assistance. Her foretopmast and maintopmast had gone, and her mainmast was so badly damaged as to be dangerous. Her rigging was cut to pieces, all her boats were smashed, and she was practically as crippled as was her brave commander, upon whom the surgeons had been operating down below, amid the blood of the cockpit and the thunder and smoke of the cannon.

The battle ended about one o'clock. The French fleet was badly beaten, and Villaret-Joyeuse at the end of the day drew back to Brest only a battered, splintered and ragged remnant of the fine squadron which he had commanded. Still, the French provision-ships slipped by and arrived safely in port. The squadron had been sent out to enable them to get in, and in they were, though it had cost a fleet to get them in. Nelson used the phrase 'a Lord Howe victory' disparagingly. Nothing short of a complete smashing of the enemy and the utter frustration of his purposes would ever satisfy that ardent soul.

For the sake of clearness, the general scheme of the battle has been described, together with the part played in it by the *Bellerophon*; but we fortunately have a detailed account of it by Flinders himself. Young as he was, only a few weeks over twenty years of age, he was evidently cool, and his journal is crowded with carefully observed facts, noted amidst the heat and confusion of conflict; and it is doubtful whether there is in existence a better story of this important fleet action. The manuscript of his journal occupies 40 foolscap pages. It is much damaged by sea-water, the paper in some parts having been rendered quite pulpy. But the sheets relating to 1 June are entirely legible. As the reader will see, there is here no rhetoric, no excited use of vivid adjectives to give colour to the story. It is a calmly observed piece of history. Read attentively, it enables one to live through the stirring events with which it deals in a singularly thrilling style. We feel the crash and thunder and hustle of battle far more keenly from the detailed accumulation of occurrences here presented than any scene-painting prose could make us do. The journal begins on 7 September 1793, when Flinders joined the *Bellerophon*, and continues till 10 August 1794, when he quitted her. In the early part it deals principally with cruising up and down the Channel looking for the enemy's ships. Occasionally there was a skirmish. We may select a few instances from this period, before coming to what immediately preceded the great day:

> *Wednesday, 11th (September, 1793) a.m. Hoisted a broad pennant by order of Lord Howe, Capt. Pasley being appointed a commodore of the fleet. Weighed and anchored in our station in Torbay.*
>
> *Monday, November 18th.*[7] *Saw nine or ten sail, seemingly large ships, standing towards us. The admiral made the* Russell *and* Defence *signals to chase, also the* Audacious; *and soon after ours. By this time the strange ships had brought to, hull down, to windward, seemingly in some confusion. The* Ganges' *signal was also made to chase. At 9 the admiral made the sign for the strange fleet being an enemy, and for our sternmost ships to make more sail. At 10 the signal to engage as the other ships came up was made. The enemy had now hauled their wind, and standing from us with as much sail as they could carry. Split one jib; got another bent as fast as possible. We were now the headmost line of battle ship and gaining fast upon the enemy; but the main part of our fleet seemed rather to drop from them. St. Agnes N. 34° E. 89 miles. Ship all clear for action since 9 o'clock.*
>
> *Tuesday, November 19th, 1793. Judge six of the enemy's ships to be of the line, two frigates and two brigs ... On the wind shifting at 4 in a squall, tacked, as did the* Latona, *which brought her near the rear of the enemy's ships, at which she fired several shot; she tacked again at 5, and fired, which the sternmost of their ships returned. At dark the enemy passed to windward of us, about 5 or 6 miles ... 12, set top-gallant-sails, but obliged to take them in again for fear of carrying away the masts. Sundry attempts were made during the night to set, but as often obliged to take them in. At 12 lost sight of all our ships except one frigate. The weather very hazy, with squalls at times,*

[7] See note 11, p. 41.

and at 2 a heavy shower of rain, which lasted a considerable time. When it cleared a little, saw two or three of the enemy's ships ahead of the others on the lee bow. Very thick and hazy, with much rain. Made the signal that the enemy had bore away. Saw the Latona *and* Phoenix, *who seemed suspicious of each other, but on discovering they were friends both bore away after one of the enemy's ships ... About 9, the* Phoenix *and* Latona *being the only friends in sight, the latter made the signal for the enemy being superior to the ships chasing. Soon after we made the signal to call the frigates in... In the firing the preceding evening the* Latona *received a shot between wind and water in the breadroom, and another in the galley; but happily no one was hurt and but little injury received.*

An amusing example of an attempt to 'dodge', under false colours, is related on the following day. The trick did not succeed.

Wednesday, November 27th, 1793, a.m. Hazy weather. Squadron in company. Saw a strange ship to the southward, who hoisted an Union Jack at the main topmast head and a red flag at the fore. The Phoenix *being ahead made the private signal, but the stranger not answering she made the signal for an enemy. We immediately made the general signal to chase. At 10 the* Phoenix *and* Latona *fired a few shots at her, upon which she hoisted French colours, discharged her guns, and struck. She proved to be* La Blonde *of 28 guns and 190 men. The squadron brought to. The French captain came on board and surrendered his sword to the commodore. Separated the prisoners amongst the squadron. An officer of the* Phoenix *sent to take charge of the prize and a party of men from each ship.*

Tuesday, December 1st, 1793. Brought to. The Phoenix *sent into Falmouth, Mr. Waterhouse, Lieutenant, sent in her to take charge of the* Blonde *prize.*

The French fleet, as related above, put out of Brest on 16 May 1794. Flinders tells us how they were sighted, and what happened during the days preceding the great battle:

Friday, May 23rd. The Southampton *brought a strange brig into the fleet and destroyed her ... a.m. A fine little ship, called the* Albion, *of Bermuda, set on fire by the* Glory. *The* Aquilon *brought a strange ship into the fleet. A galliot, with Dutch colours inverted, passed through the fleet, having been set on fire by the* Niger ... *A French man-of-war, captured and brought into the fleet by the frigates, was set on fire.*

Saturday, May 24. The ship brought into the fleet by the Aquilon *left us and stood to the eastward. She was bound to Hull, and was part of a Dutch convoy, most of which had been taken and destroyed by the French fleet on Wednesday last.*

Sunday, May 25th. At daybreak saw four sail to windward; our squadron sent in chase. Fired a shot and brought to a French brig, man-of-war. Made signal that the prize was not secure, and chased a large ship further to windward, apparently of the line, and with another ship in tow. Tacked as soon as she was on our beam. She had cast off her prize as soon as we fired at the brig. In passing, fired at and brought to a French corvette; but left her for the fleet to pick up. Passed to leeward of the ship the chase had in tow. She appeared to be a large merchantman and had up American colours. The frigates in chase picked her up soon after. At 10 the chase was nearly hull down, and gained upon us. Stood back to the fleet, being recalled by signal. Saw one of the prizes in flames, and found the three had been destroyed at noon; 162 leagues W. by S. of Ushant.

In the ensuing pages we are brought into the thick of the battle.

Wednesday, May 28th. Saw two strange sail, one of which the Phoenix *spoke, and soon after made signal for a strange fleet S.S.W. About 8, we counted 33 sail, 24 or 25 of which appeared to be of the line, and all standing down towards us. At 8.30 our signal was made to reconnoitre the enemy—as we were now certain they were. A frigate of their's was likewise looking at us. At noon the enemy's fleet S.W. to W.S.W., on the larboard tack under an easy sail in line ahead, and distant 3 or 4 leagues. Our fleet 3 or 4 leagues to leeward in the order of sailing or under a press of sail. Ushant N. 82° E. 143 leagues.*

Thursday, May 29th, 1794. Fresh gales with rain at times, and a swell from the westward. Repeated the general signals for chase, battle, etc. Kd.[8] *ship occasionally, working to*

[8] 'Kd. Ship' is an expression which puzzled Professor Flinders Petrie, who appended a note to the Flinders papers, suggesting that it could hardly mean kedged. Captain Bayldon supplies an exceedingly interesting explanation:

windward under a press of sail, our squadron and the frigates in company, and our fleet a few miles to leeward. About 3 the Russell, *being a mile or two to windward of us, began to fire on the enemy's rear, as they were hauling on the larboard tack, and continued to stand on with the* Thunderer *and frigates, to get into their wake. We tacked a little before the rear ship was on our beam, which enabled us to bring them to action a considerable time before the other ships could come up to our assistance. Our first fire was directed on a large frigate which brought up the enemy's rear, but she soon made sail and went to windward of the next ship (a three-decker)*[9] *on whom we immediately pointed our guns. In a few minutes she returned it with great spirit, our distance from her being something more than a mile. My Lord Howe, seeing us engaged with a three-decked ship, and the next ahead of him frequently giving us a few guns, made the* Russell *and* Marlborough*'s signals to come to our assistance, they being on the weather quarter. About dusk more of the fleet had got up with us, the signal having been made to chase without regard to order. The* Leviathan *and* Audacious, *particularly, passed to*

---

[8] ***Cont'd.***

'Without the least doubt "Kd. Ship" means "tacked ship". "Kd." is either a private abbreviation of Flinders' for "tacked" or else he intended to have written "Tkd". There is no nautical term beginning with K which would make the least sense under the circumstances. "Kedged" is utterly inadmissable; both fleets were under way in pretty heavy weather. "Working to windward" practically means "tacking ship". So why did Flinders mention an obvious fact, "tacked ship"? Because the weather was bad, strong breezes, heavy swell, and therefore it was very hazardous to tack ship (on account of throwing the sails aback) and also many ships could not be forced into tacking with a heavy head swell. Consequently it is usual to wear ship under these conditions (turn her round before the wind). So he then mentions "under a press of sail", to force her up into the wind (also making it a risky manoeuvre, for they could easily lose their masts—foremast especially). Hence he was proud of the manoeuvre, so mentions, "tacked ship occasionally, under a press of sail". On the 29th May at 8 a.m., the French van wore in succession. (Fresh wind, heavy head sea). Soon after noon (Flinders' old nautical time gives May 30th) Lord Howe signalled the British fleet to tack in succession. The leading ship, the *Caesar*, instead of obeying, made the signal of inability and wore round. The next ship, the *Queen*, also wore. So (at 1.30 p.m.) Lord Howe set the example in the *Queen Charlotte* and tacked. Pasley's *Bellerophon* followed him, and tacked also; the *Leviathan* tacked and followed her. These three ships were the only ones to tack. All the remainder wore, and so did the French. Either their captains would not take the risk, or else could not force their ships through the heavy head sea. So I expect Flinders and the "Bully ruffians" felt elated at their performance and he intended to record "Tkd. Ship".'

[9] The *Révolutionnaire.*

windward of us, and came to close engagement; the first keeping as close to him to leeward as she could fetch, and the latter fetching to windward of him, laid herself athwart his stern and gave a severe raking. The headmost of the French fleet were apparently hove to, but made no effort to relieve their comrade. At this time our maincap was seen to be so badly sprung as to oblige us to take in the main topsail; the larboard topsail sheet block was likewise shot away. Got down the topgallant yard and mast, and, the ship being scarcely under command, we made the signal for inability. Soon after the Admiral called us by signal into his wake. The enemy's rear ship about 9 had his mizzenmast gone and he bore down towards us, the Russell *and* Thunderer *striking close to his weather quarter and lee bow, keeping up a severe fire, but he scarcely returned a shot. Having got clear of them he continued coming down on us, apparently with the intention of striking to our flag, but firing a shot now and then. He was intercepted by one of our ships, who running to leeward of him soon silenced his guns, and, we concluded, had obliged him to strike. The enemy's fleet were now collected about 3 miles to windward, carrying lights, as did ours. We were in no regular order, it having been broken up by the chase. A.M., employed securing the maincap, etc. All hands kept at quarters. Fresh breezes and hazy weather. At daybreak the enemy's line was formed about 2 miles distant, and our commander in chief made the signal to form the line of battle, and take stations as most convenient. We bore down and took ours astern of the* Queen Charlotte, *the* Marlborough *and* Royal Sovereign *following. About 8 our fleet tacked in succession, with a view to cut off the enemy's rear; the* Caesar *leading and my Lord Howe the 10th ship. As soon as our van were sufficiently near to bring them to action, the enemy's whole fleet wore in succession, and ran to leeward of their line in order to support their rear, and edged down van to van. At 10 the firing commenced between the headmost ships of both lines, but at too great a distance to do much execution, and the Admiral made the signal to tack in succession in order to bring the enemy to close action, but not being taken notice of, about noon it was repeated with a gun. The* Leviathan, *being next ahead of the Admiral, fired some guns, but the* Queen Charlotte *and those astern did not attempt it. Hazy weather at noon with a considerable swell from the westward. Latitude observed to be 47° 35' N. NOTE—We found this morning at daybreak that the* Audacious *was missing, and we concluded was the ship who had secured the prize, neither being in sight.*[10]

Friday, May 30th. Fresh breezes and hazy weather. The signal for the van to tack was again repeated, when the Caesar *made the signal of inability; but at last they got round, and the Admiral made signal to cut through the enemy's line; but finding our leading ships were passing to leeward, we tacked a considerable time before the ships came in succession, and luffed up as close to them as possible. The enemy were now well within point-blank shot, which began to fall very thick about us, and several had passed through our sails before we tacked. Immediately we came into the* Queen Charlotte's *wake we tacked, lay up well for the enemy's rear, and began a severe fire, giving it to each ship as we passed. My Lord Howe in the* Charlotte *kept his luff, and cut through their line between the 4th and 5th ship in the rear. We followed, and passed between the 2nd and 3rd. The rest of the fleet passed to leeward. Their third ship gave us a severe broadside on the bow as we approached to pass under her stern, and which we took care to return by two on her quarter and stern. Before we had cleared her, her fore and maintop masts fell over the side, and she was silenced for a while, but it was only till we had passed her. Their rear ship received several broadsides even from our three-deckers, but kept her colours up. The* Orion *then ran down to her, but getting upon her beam and too far to leeward was obliged to leave her, and she got to her own fleet, whom we were now to windward of. Lord Howe made the signal to tack, and for a general chase, but few of the van ships were able to follow him. For ourselves, we lay to, to reeve new braces and repair the rigging, which was entirely cut to pieces forward. The foresail was rendered useless, and was cut away, and being only able to set a close-reefed main topsail for fear of the cap giving way, we were not able to follow his lordship. The French perceiving how few followed them, rallied, tacked, and supported their disabled ships, and even made a feint to cut off*

[10] Of course this surmise was incorrect. The *Audacious* had not secured the *Révolutionnaire* which was towed into Rochefort by the *Audacieux* (curious similarity in names). The *Audacious* badly crippled made her way to Plymouth alone.— [Captain Bayldon's note].

the Queen, *who was rendered a wreck. The Admiral, seeing their intention, bore down with several of the heavy ships who had not been engaged, and forced them to leeward of our disabled ships. At 5.30 having got a new foresail bent, and the rigging in a little order, we bore down and joined the Admiral; who soon after formed the line in two divisions, and stood to the westward under an easy sail abreast of the enemy, who were to leeward in a line ahead; the disabled ships in both fleets repairing their damages, several of theirs being without topmasts and topsail yards. At sunset saw two ships pass to windward, conjectured to be the* Audacious *and prize. Employed splicing and knotting the rigging, and repairing sails, not one of which but had several shot through them. The truck of the foretopgallant mast was likewise shot away. A.M., thick foggy weather. Saw the enemy at times N.N.W. 4 or 5 miles. At noon very foggy. Latitude 47° 39' N. by dull observation.*

Saturday, May 31st, 1794. Lost sight of the enemy and only four of our own ships in sight. People employed repairing sail, rigging, etc., with all expedition. At noon thick and foggy. No enemy in sight; 30 sail of our own ships.

Sunday, June 1st, 1794.[11] *Moderate breezes and foggy weather. Before two it began to clear up. Saw the enemy to leeward, 8 or 9 miles distant, and made the signal for that purpose. Soon after the whole fleet bore down towards them by signal. The enemy were edging away from the wind, and several of their ships were changing stations in the line; some of them without topmasts and topsail yards. About 7, the van of our fleet being within three miles of the enemy's centre, the heavy ships in the rear a considerable way astern, the Admiral made the signal to haul to the wind together on the larboard tack, judging we should not be able to bring on a general action to-night. At sunset the enemy were in a line ahead from N.W. by W. to N.E. by E. about four miles distant, and apparently steering about two points from the wind. At 11 the* Phaeton *passed along the line, and informed the different ships that Lord Howe intended carrying single reefed T.S.F. sail, jib and M.T.M.S. sail.*[12]

[11] Nautical reckoning in Flinders' day was twelve hours ahead; *i.e.*, his 1 June began at noon on 31 May. Occurrences following 'a.m.', happened on 1 June by the Almanac.

[12] Letters probably denote single reefed Top Sails, Fore sail, jib and Main Topmast and Main Stay sails.

After speaking us he kept on our lee bow; each ship carrying a light by signal. A.M., fresh breezes and cloudy. At daybreak the enemy not in sight, our rear ships a long way astern, their signal made to make more sail; when the line became tolerably connected, the whole fleet bore away and steered N.W. by signal. A little before six saw the enemy in the N. by E. about 3 leagues. Made the signal to the Admiral for that purpose, who by signal ordered the fleet to alter the course to starboard together, bearing down towards them. About 8, being nearly within shot of the enemy's van, hove to for the rear of the fleet to come up. Lord Howe made the signal 34, which we understood was to pass through the enemy's line, but it did not seem to be understood by the rest of the fleet. At 8.10 the signal was made to bear up and each engage his opponent. We accordingly ran down within musket shot of our opponent, and hove to, having received several broadsides from their van ships in so doing. We now began a severe fire upon our opponent, the second ship in the enemy's van, which she returned with great briskness. The van ship likewise fired many shot at us, his opponent the Caesar keeping to windward, not more than two points before our beam in general, and of course nearly out of point-blank shot. About 8.30 Admiral Graves made his and the Russell's signal to engage their opponent; we likewise made Captain Molloy's (the Caesar) signal twice to bear down and come to close action. About 9 the action became general throughout the two fleets, but the Tremendous kept out of the line, but on being ordered in by signal from the Admiral, she bore down after some time. A little before 11 our brave Admiral (Pasley) lost his leg by an 18-pound shot, which came through the barricading of the quarter-deck. It was now the heat of the action. The Caesar was not yet come close to his opponent, who in consequence of that fired all his after guns at us. Our own ship kept up a severe fire, and by keeping well astern to let the Caesar take her station, their third van ship shot up on our quarter, and for some time fired all his fore guns upon us. Our shot was directed on three different ships as the guns could be got to bear. In ten or fifteen minutes we saw the foremast of the third ship go by the board, and the second ship's main-top-sail-yard down upon the cap. Otherwise the two headmost had not received much apparent injury, at least in the rigging. At 11¼, however, they both bore away and quitted the line, their

Admiral being obliged to do the same some time before by the Queen Charlotte. *On seeing the two van ships hauling upon the other tack, we conjectured they meant to give us their starboard guns. The* Caesar's *signal was immediately made by us to chase the flying ships. On his bearing down they were put into confusion, and their ship falling down upon them they received several broadsides from the* Leviathan *and us, before they could get clear; which when they effected they kept away a little, then hauled their wind in the starboard tack, and stood away from the opposing fleets. And now, being in no condition to follow, we ceased firing; the main and foretopmast being gone, every main shroud but one on the larboard side cut through, and many on the other, besides having the main and foremasts with all the rigging and sails in general much injured. We made the* Latona's *signal to come to our assistance, and got entirely out of action. When the smoke cleared away, saw eleven ships without a mast standing, two of whom proved to be the* Marlborough *and* Defence. *The rest were enemy's, who, notwithstanding their situation kept their colours up, and fired at any of our ships that came near them. The* Leviathan's *opponent particularly (the same ship whose foremast we shot away) lying perfectly dismasted, the* Leviathan *ran down to him to take possession; but on her firing a gun to make him haul down his colours, he returned a broadside, and a severe action again commenced between them for nearly half an hour, and we could see shot falling on the water on the opposite side of the Frenchman, which appeared to have gone through both his sides, the ships being at half a cable's length from each other. The* Leviathan *falling to leeward could not take the advantage of him her sails gave her, and, seeing his obstinacy, left him, but not before his fire was nearly silenced. About 11.30 the firing was pretty well ceased on all sides, the* Queen *having only a foremast standing was fallen to leeward between the two fleets. She stood on the larboard tack to fetch our fleet, keeping to the wind in an astonishing manner, which we afterwards learnt was effected by getting up boat's sails abaft. In this situation every ship she passed gave her a broadside or more, which she returned with great spirit, keeping up an almost incessant blaze. After she had stood on past the fleets, she wore round and stood back, pursuing the same conduct as before, but the French, having collected their best-conditioned ships in a body, and being joined by two or three other disabled ships, were making off, having apparently given up all ideas of saving the rest. On this our fleet stood down a little, and the* Queen *joined. We were now employed knotting, splicing, repairing, etc., the rigging, cutting away the wrecks of the fore and main topmasts, and securing the lower masts. Fortunately no accident happened with the powder, or with guns bursting. We had but three men killed outright (a fourth died of his wounds very soon after) and about 30 men wounded, amongst whom five lost their limbs, and the other leg of one man was so much shattered as to be taken off some time after. Our brave Admiral was unfortunately in this list, as before observed. Captain Smith of the Marines and Mr. Chapman, boatswain, were amongst the wounded on the second day. Most of our spars were destroyed, and the boats severely injured. About noon we had still fine weather and the enemy standing away from us, except one ship, which did not seem injured, and paraded to windward, as if with the intention of giving some of us disabled ships a brush. However, we were well prepared for him, having got tolerably clear of the wreck, and he stood back again and out of sight, having spoken one of their wrecks. Lord Howe made the signal to form the line as most convenient, but it was a long time before that movement could be effected.*

Flinders wrote in his journal an estimate of the French sailors who were put on board his ship as prisoners. It is of some historical value:

Their seamen, if we may judge from our own prisoners, are in a very bad state both with respect to discipline and knowledge of their profession; both which were evidently shown by the condition we saw them in on the 31st, many of them being without topmasts and topsail yards, and nearly in as bad a state as on the 29th after the action. 'Tis true they were rather better when we saw them in the morning of June 1st. Out of our 198 prisoners there certainly cannot be above 15 or 20 seamen, and all together were the dirtiest, laziest set of beings conceivable. How an idea of liberty, and more so that of fighting for it, should enter into their heads, I know not; but by their own confession it is not their wish and pleasure, but that of those who sent them; and so little is it their own that in the Brunswick *(who was engaged yardarm and yardarm with the* Vengeur*) they could see the French officers cutting down the*

> *men for deserting their quarters. Indeed, in the instances of the* Russell *and* Thunderer *when close to the* Révolutionnaire, *and ours when cutting through the line, the French do not like to come too close. A mile off they will fight desperately.*

Pasley's loss of a leg had a decisive effect upon the career of Matthew Flinders. So fine a sailor and so tough a fighting man would unquestionably, if not partially incapacitated, have had conferred upon him during the following years of war commands that would have led to his playing a very prominent part in fleet operations. As it was, he did not go to sea again, though he was promoted through various ranks to that of Admiral of the Blue (1801). He became commander-in-chief at the Nore in 1798, and at Plymouth in 1799. Had he received other sea commands, his vigorous, alert young aide-de-camp might have continued to serve with him, and would thus have just missed the opportunities that came to him in his next sphere of employment. What young officer would not have eagerly followed a gallant and warm-hearted admiral who had first placed him upon a British quarterdeck and had made him an aide-de-camp? As it was, the chance that came to Flinders about two months after the battle off Brest was one that ministered to his decided preference for service in seas where there was exploratory work to do.

Pasley's influence upon the life of Flinders was so important, that a characterisation of him by one who has perused his letters and journals must be quoted.[13] 'It is impossible,' writes Miss L. M. Sabine Pasley, 'not to be impressed from these journals with a strong feeling of respect for the writer, so simple-minded, so kind-hearted, such a brave old sailor of his time—rough, no doubt, in manners and language, but with an earnest and genuine piety that shows itself from time to time in little ejaculations and prayers, contrasting, it must be owned, rather strongly with the terms in which the "rascally Yankies" are alluded to in the same pages.' What Howe thought of him is recorded in a letter which he sent to the rear-admiral a fortnight after the battle, regretting that 'the services of a friend he so highly esteemed and so gallant an officer, capable of such spirited exertions, should be restrained by any disaster from the continued exertion of them'. There is also on record a letter to Pasley

[13] *Memoir of Admiral Sir T. S. Pasley*, by Louisa M. Sabine Pasley. Sir T. S. Pasley was the grandson of Flinders' admiral. It unfortunately happens that the journals of 'old Sir Thomas' which are extant do not cover the period when Flinders acted as his aide-de-camp. Miss Sabine Pasley was kind enough to have a search made among his papers for any trace of Flinders' relations with him, but without success.

from the Prime Minister, a model of grace and delicate feeling, in which Pitt signified that the King had conferred on him a baronetcy 'as a mark of the sense which His Majesty entertains of the distinguished share which you bore in the late successful and glorious operations of His Majesty's fleet', and assured him 'of the sincere satisfaction which I personally feel in executing this commission'.

On the south-western coast of Australia, eight years later, Flinders remembered his first commander when naming the natural features of the country. Cape Pasley, at the western tip of the arc of the great Australian Bight, celebrates 'the late Admiral Sir Thomas Pasley, under whom I had the honour of entering the naval service'.[14] On some current maps of Australia the cape is spelt 'Paisley', an error which obscures the interesting biographical fact with which the name is connected.

It is notewothy that though the career of Flinders as a naval officer covers the stormiest period in British naval history, the whole of his personal experience of battle was confined to those five days, 28 May to 1 June 1794. The whole significance of his life lies in the work of discovery that he accomplished, and in the contributions he made to geography and navigation. Yet he was destined to feel the effect of the enmity of the French in a peculiarly distressing form. His useful life was cut short largely by misfortunes that came upon him as a consequence of war, and work which he would have done to the enhancement of his reputation and the advancement of civilisation was thwarted by it.

[14] Flinders, *Voyage to Terra Australis*, I, p. 87.

V

AUSTRALIAN GEOGRAPHY BEFORE FLINDERS

IN order that the importance of the work done by Flinders may be adequately appreciated, it is necessary to understand the state of information concerning Australian geography before the time of his discoveries. Not only did he complete the main outlines of the map of the continent, but he filled in many details in parts that had been traversed by his predecessors. This is a convenient point whereat to interrupt the narrative of his life with a brief sketch of what those predecessors had done, and of the curiously haphazard mode in which a partial knowledge of this fifth division of the globe had been pieced together.

There never was, until Flinders applied himself to the task, any deliberately planned, systematic, persistent exploration of any portion of the Australian coast. The continent grew on the map of the world gradually, slowly, almost accidentally. It emerged out of the unknown, like some vast mythical monster heaving its large shoulders dank and dripping from the unfathomed sea, and metamorphosed by a kiss from the lips of knowledge into a being fair to look upon and rich in kindly favours. It took two centuries and a half for civilised mankind to know Australia, even in form, from the time when it was clearly understood that there was such a country, until at length it was mapped, measured and circumnavigated. Before this process began, there was a dialectical stage, when it was hotly contested whether there could possibly be upon the globe lands antipodean to Europe; and both earlier and later there were conjectural stages when makers of maps, having no certain data, but feeling sure that the blank southern hemisphere ought to be filled up somehow, exercised a vagrant fancy and satisfied a long-felt want by decorating their drawings with representations of a Terra Incognita having not even a casual resemblance to the reality.

The process presents few points of resemblance to that by which the discovery of America was accomplished. Almost as soon as Europe came into touch with the western hemisphere, discovery was pursued with unflagging energy, until its whole extent and contour were substantially known. Within 50 years after Columbus led the way across the Atlantic (1492), North and South America were laid down with something approaching precision; and Gerard Mercator's map of 1541 presented the greater part of the continent with the name fairly inscribed upon it. There were, it is true, some errors and some gaps, especially on the west coast, which left work for navigators to do. But the essential point is that in less than half a century Europe had practically comprehended America as an addition to the known world. There was but a brief twilight interval between nescience [ignorance] and knowledge. How different was the case with Australia! Three hundred years after the date of Columbus's first voyage, the mere outline of this continent had not been wholly mapped.

During the Middle Ages, when ingenious men exercised infinite subtlety in speculation, and wrote large Latin folios to prove each other wrong in matters about which neither party knew anything at all, there was much dissertation about the possibility of [the] antipodes. Bishops and saints waxed eloquent upon the theme. The difficulty of conceiving of lands where people walked about with their heads hanging downwards, and their feet exactly opposite to those of Europeans, was too much for some of the scribes engaged in the debate. The Greek, Cosmas Indicopleustes, denounced the 'old wives' fable of Antipodes', and asked how rain could be said to 'fall', as in the Scriptures, in regions where it would have to 'come up'.[1] Some would have it that a belief in the antipodes was heretical. But Isidore of Seville, in his *Liber de Natura Rerum* [Book Concerning the Nature of Things], Basil of Caesarea, Ambrose of Milan, and Vergil Bishop of Salzburg, an Irish saint, declined to regard the question as a closed one. 'Nam partes eius (*i.e.* of the earth) quatuor sunt,' argued Isidore. [There are four parts of the earth.] Curiously enough, the copy of the works of the Saint of Seville used by the author (published at Rome in 1803), was salvaged from a ship which was wrecked on the Australian coast many years ago. It is stained with sea-water, and emits the musty smell which tells of immersion. An inscription inside the cover relates the circumstance of the wreck. Who possessed the book one does not know; some travelling scholar may have perused it during the long voyage from Europe; and one fancies him, as the ship bumped upon the rocks, exclaiming 'Yes, Isidore was right, there *are* antipodes!'

[1] *The Christian Topography of Cosmas*, translated by J. W. McCrindle, p. 17 (Hakluyt Society).

From about the fourth quarter of the sixteenth century until the date of Abel Tasman's voyages, 1642–44, there was a period of vague speculation about a supposed great southern continent. The maps of the time indicate the total lack of accurate information at the disposal of their compilers. There was no general agreement as to what this region was like in its outlines, proportions, or situation. Some cartographers, such as Peter Plancius (1594) and Hondius (1595), trailed a wavy line across the foot of their representations of the globe, inscribed Terra Australis upon it, and by a fine stroke of invention gave an admirable aspect of finish and symmetry to the form of the world. The London map of 1578, issued with George Best's *Discourse of the Late Voyages of Discoverie*, barricaded the south pole with a Terra Australis not unlike the design of a switch-back railway. Molyneux's remarkable map, *circa* 1590, dropped the vast imaginary continent, and displayed a small tongue of land in about the region where the real Australia is; suggesting that some voyager had been blown out of his course, had come upon a part of the western division of the continent, and had jotted down a memorandum of its appearance upon his chart. It looks like a sincere attempt to tell a bit of the truth. But speaking generally, the Terra Australis of the old cartographers was a gigantic antipodean imposture, a mere piece of map-makers' furniture, put in to fill up the gaping space at the south end of the globe.

A few minutes devoted to the study of a map of the Indian Ocean, including the Cape of Good Hope and the west coast of Australia—especially one indicating the course of currents—will show how natural it was that Portuguese and Dutch ships engaged in the spice trade should occasionally have found themselves in proximity to the real Terra Australis. It will also explain more clearly than a page of type could do, why the western and north-western coasts were known so early, whilst the eastern and southern shores remained undelineated until James Cook and Matthew Flinders sailed along them.

A change of the route pursued by the Dutch on their voyages to the East Indies had already conduced [led] to an acquaintance with the Australian coast. Originally, after rounding the Cape, their ships had sailed north-east to Madagascar, and had thence struck across the Indian Ocean to Java, or to Ceylon. As long as this course was followed, there was little prospect of sighting the great continent which lay about 3,000 miles east of their habitual track. But this route, though from the map it appeared to be the most direct, was the longest in duration that they could take. It brought them into the region of light winds and tedious tropical calms; so that very often a vessel would lie for weeks 'as idle as a painted ship upon a painted ocean', and would occupy over a year upon the outward voyage. In 1611, however, one of their commanders discovered that if, after leaving the Cape, a ship ran not north-east, but due east for about 3,000 miles, she would be assisted by the winds, not baffled by calms. Henrick Brouwer, who made the experiment, arrived in Java seven months after leaving Holland, whereas some ships had been known to be as long as eighteen months at sea. The directors of the Dutch East India Company, recognising the importance of the discovery, ordered their commanders to follow the easterly route from the Cape in future, and offered prizes to those who completed the voyage in less than nine months. The result was that the Dutch skippers became exceedingly anxious to make the very utmost of the favourable winds, which carried them eastward in the direction of the western coasts of Australia.

Thus it happened that in 1616 the *Eendragt* stumbled on Australia opposite Shark's Bay. Her captain, Dirk Hartog, landed on the long island which lies as a natural breakwater between the bay and the ocean, and erected a metal plate to record his visit; and Dirk Hartog Island is the name it bears to this day. The plate remained till 1697, when another Dutchman, Vlaming, substituted a new one for it; and Vlaming's plate, in turn, remained till 1817, when the French navigator, Freycinet, took it and sent it to Paris.

After Hartog reported his discovery, the Dutch directors ordered their ships' captains to run east from the Cape till they sighted the land. This would enable them to verify their whereabouts; for in those days the means of reckoning postions at sea were so imperfect that navigators groped about the oceans of the globe almost as if they were sailing in darkness. But here was a means of verifying a ship's position after her long run across from the Cape, and if she found Dirk Hartog Island, she could safely thence make her way north to Java.

But ships did not always sight the Australian coast at the same point. Hence it came about that in 1619 J. de Edel 'accidentally fell in with' the coast at the back of the Abrolhos. Pieter Nuyts, in 1627, 'accidentally discovered' a long reach of the south coast. Similarly, in 1628, the *Vianen* was 'accidentally', as the narrative says, driven on to the north-west coast, and her commander, De Wit, gave his name to about 200 miles of it. In 1629 the Dutch ship *Batavia* was separated in a storm from a merchant fleet of eleven sail, and ran upon the Abrolhos Reef. The captain, Francis Pelsart, who was lying sick in his cabin at the time of the misadventure, 'called up the master and charged him with the loss of the ship, who excused himself by saying he had taken all the care he could;

and that having discerned the froth at a distance he asked the steersman what he thought of it, who told him that the sea appeared white by its reflecting the rays of the moon. The captain then asked him what was to be done, and in what part of the world he thought they were. The master replied that God only knew that; and that the ship was on a bank hitherto undiscovered.' The story of Pelsart's adventure was recorded, and the part of the coast which he saw was embodied on a globe published in 1700.

To the accidental discoveries must be added those made by the Dutch prompted by curiosity as to the possibility of drawing profit from the lands to the south of their great East India possessions. Thus the Dutch yacht *Duyfhen,* sent in 1605 to examine the Papuan islands, sailed along the southern side of Torres Strait, found Cape York, and believed it to be part of New Guinea. The great discovery voyages of Tasman, 1643 and 1644, were planned in pursuit of the same policy. He was directed to find out what the southern portion of the world was like, 'whether it be land or sea, or icebergs, whatever God has ordained to be there'.

In 1606 the Spaniard Torres also probably saw Cape York, and sailed through the strait which bears his name. He had accompanied Quiros across the Pacific, but had separated from his commander at the New Hebrides, and continued his voyage westward, whilst Quiros sailed to South America.

It is needless for present purposes to catalogue the various voyages made by the Dutch, or to examine claims which have been preferred on account of other discoveries. It may, however, be observed that there are three well-defined periods of Australian maritime discovery, and that they relate to three separate zones of operation.

First, there was the period with which the Dutch were chiefly concerned. The west and north-west coasts received the greater part of their attention, though the voyage of Tasman to the island now bearing his name was a variation from their habitual sphere. The visits of the Englishman Dampier to Western Australia are comprehended within this period.

The second period belongs to the eighteenth century, and its hero was James Cook. He sailed up the whole of the east coast in 1770, from Point Hicks, near the Victorian border, to Cape York at the northern tip of the continent, and accomplished a larger harvest of discovery than has ever fallen to the fortune of any other navigator in a single voyage. To this period also belongs Captain George Vancouver, who in 1791, on his way to north-western America from the Cape of Good Hope, came upon the south-western corner of Australia and discovered King George's Sound.

In the following year the French admiral, D'Entrecasteaux, despatched in search of the missing expedition of La Pérouse, also made the south-west corner of the continent, and followed the coast of the Great Australian Bight for some hundreds of miles. His researches in southern Tasmania were likewise of much importance.

The third period is principally that of Flinders, commencing shortly before the dawn of the nineteenth century, and practically completing the maritime exploration of the continent.

A map contained in John Pinkerton's *Modern Geography* shows at a glance the state of knowledge about Australia at the date of publication, 1802. Flinders had by that time completed his explorations, but his work was not yet published. The map delineates the contour of the continent on the east, west, and north sides, with as much accuracy as was possible, and, though it is defective in details, presents generally a fair idea of the country's shape. But the line along the south coast represents a total lack of information as to the outline of the land. Pinkerton, indeed, though he was a leading English authority on geography when his book was published, had not embodied in his map some results that were then available.

The testimony of the map may be augmented by a reference to what geographical writers understood about Australia before the time of Flinders.

Though Cook had discovered the east coast, and named it New South Wales, it was not definitely known whether this extensive stretch of country was separate from the western 'New Holland' which the Dutch had named, or whether the two were the extremities of one vast tract of land. Geographical opinion rather inclined to the view that ultimately a strait would be found dividing the region into islands. This idea is mentioned by Pinkerton. Under the heading 'New Holland' he wrote:[2] 'Some suppose that this extensive region, when more thoroughly investigated, will be found to consist of two or three vast islands intersected by narrow seas, an idea which probably arises from the discovery that New Zealand consists of two islands, and that other straits have been found to divide lands in this quarter formerly supposed to be continuous.' The discovery that Bass Strait divided Australia from Tasmania was probably in Pinkerton's mind; he mentions it in his text (quoting Flinders), though his map does not indicate the strait's existence. He also mentions 'a vast bay with an isle', possibly Kangaroo Island.

---

[2] *Modern Geography*, II, p. 588.

Perhaps it was not unnatural that competent opinion should have favoured the idea that there were several large islands, rather than one immense continent stretching into 30 degrees of latitude and 45 of longitude. The human mind is not generally disposed to grasp very big things all at once. Indeed, in the light of fuller knowledge, one is disposed to admire the caution of these geographers, whose beliefs were carefully reasoned but erroneous, in face of, for instance, such a wild ebullition [outburst] of venturesome theory as that attributed to an aforetime [former] Göttingen professor,[3] who considered that not only was Australia one country, but that it made its appearance upon this planet in a peculiarly sudden fashion. His opinion was that 'the vast continent of Australia was originally a comet, which happening to fall within the limits of the earth's attraction, alighted at length upon its surface'. 'Alighted at length' is a mild term, suggestive of a nervous lady emerging from a tram-car in a crowded street. 'Splashed' would probably convey a more vigorous impression.

The belief that a strait would be found completely dividing New Holland was a general one, as is shown by several contemporary writings. Thus James Grant in his *Narrative of a Voyage of Discovery* (1803), expressing his regret that his orders did not permit him to take his ship, the *Lady Nelson*, northward from Port Jackson in 1801, speculated that 'we might also betimes have ascertained if the Gulf of Carpentaria had any inlet to Bass Straits, and if it be discovered secure more quickly to Great Britain the right of lands which some of our enterprising neighbours might probably dispute with us. And this I trust will not be thought chimerical [fanciful] when it was not known whether other Straits did not exist as well as that dividing New Holland from Van Diemen's Land.' Again, the Institute of France in preparing instructions for the voyage of exploration commanded by Nicolas Baudin (1800) directed a search to be made for a strait which it was supposed divided Australia 'into two great and nearly equal islands'.

Another interesting geographical problem to be determined, was whether a great river system drained any part of the Australian continent. In the existing state of knowledge the country presented an aspect in regard to fluvial features [relating to rivers] wholly different from any other portion of the world. No river of considerable importance had been found. Students of geography could hardly conceive that there should be so large an area of land lacking outlets to

---

[3] Professor Blumenbach according to Lang, *Historical Account of New South Wales* (1837), II, p. 142.

the sea; and as none had been found in the parts investigated so far, it was believed that the exploration of the south coast would reveal large streams flowing from the interior. Some had speculated that within the country there was a great inland sea, and if so there would probably be rivers flowing from it to the ocean.

A third main subject for elucidation when Flinders entered upon this work, was whether the country known as Van Diemen's Land was part of the continent, or was divided from it by a strait not yet discovered. Captain Cook entertained the opinion that a strait existed. On his voyage in the *Endeavour* in 1770, he was 'doubtful whether they are one land or no'. But when near the north-eastern corner of Van Diemen's Land, he had been twenty months at sea, and his supplies had become depleted. He did not deem it advisable to sail west and settle the question forthwith, but, running up the eastern coast of New Holland, achieved discoveries certainly great enough for one voyage. He retained the point in his mind, however, and would have determined it on his second voyage in 1772–74 had he not paid heed to information given by Tobias Furneaux. The *Adventure*, commanded by Furneaux, had been separated from the *Resolution* on the voyage to New Zealand, and had cruised for some days in the neighbourhood of the eastern entrance to Bass Strait. But Furneaux convinced himself that no strait existed, and reported to that effect when he rejoined Cook in Queen Charlotte's Sound. Cook was not quite convinced by the statement of his officer; but contrary winds made a return to the latitude of the supposed strait difficult, and Cook though 'half inclined to go over to Van Diemen's Land and settle the question of its being part of New Holland' decided to proceed westward. As will be seen hereafter, Flinders helped to show that the passage existed.

There were also many smaller points requiring investigation. Cook in running along the east coast had passed several portions in the night, or at such a distance in the daytime as to render his representation of the coastline doubtful. Some groups of islands also required to be accurately charted. Indeed, it may be said that there was no portion of the world where, at this period, there was so much and such valuable work to be done by a competent and keen marine explorer, as in Australia.

A passage in a manuscript by Flinders may be quoted to supplement what has been written above, as it indicates the kind of speculations that were current in the conversation of students of geography.[4]

---

[4] Called an 'Abridged Narrative'—Flinders' Papers.

The interior of this new region, in extent nearly equal to all Europe, strongly excited the curiosity of geographers and naturalists; and the more so as, ten years after the establishment of a British Colony at Port Jackson on the east coast, and the repeated effort of some enterprising individuals, no part of it beyond 30 leagues from the coast had been seen by an European. Various conjectures were entertained upon the probable consistence of this extensive space. Was it a vast desert? Was it occupied by an immense lake—a second Caspian Sea, or by a Mediterranean to which existed a navigable entrance in some part of the coasts hitherto unexplored? or was not this new continent rather divided into two or more islands by straits communicating from the unknown parts of the south to the imperfectly examined north-west coast or to the Gulf of Carpentaria, or to both? Such were the questions that excited the interest and divided the opinion of geographers.

Apart from particular directions in which enquiry needed to be pursued, it was felt in England that the only nation which had founded a settlement on the Australian continent was under an obligation to complete the exploration of the country. The French had already sent out two scientific expeditions with instructions to examine the unknown southern coasts; and if shipwreck had not destroyed the first, and want of fresh water diverted the second, the credit of finishing the outline of the map of Australia would have been earned for France. Flinders wrote:

Many circumstances, indeed, united to render the south coast of Terra Australis one of the most interesting parts of the globe to which discovery could be directed at the beginning of the nineteenth century. Its investigation had formed a part of the instructions to the unfortunate French navigator, Lapérouse, and afterwards of those to his countryman Dentrecasteaux; and it was not without some reason attributed to England as a reproach that an imaginary line of more than two hundred and fifty leagues' extent in the vicinity of one of her colonies should have been so long suffered to remain traced upon the charts under the title of Unknown Coast. This comported ill with her reputation as the first of maritime powers.

We shall see how predominant was the share of Flinders in the settlement of these problems, the filling up of these gaps.

VI

THE RELIANCE AND THE TOM THUMB

APART from Admiral Pasley, two officers who participated in Lord Howe's victory on 'the glorious First of June', had an important influence upon the later career of Flinders. The first of these, Captain John Hunter, had served on the flagship *Queen Charlotte.* The second, Henry Waterhouse, had been fifth lieutenant on the *Bellerophon.* Flinders was under the orders of both of them on his next voyage.

Hunter had accompanied the first Governor of New South Wales on the *Sirius*, when a British colony was founded there in 1788, and was commissioned by the Crown to assume the duties of Lieutenant-Governor in case of Phillip's death. When the office fell vacant in 1793, Hunter applied for appointment. He secured the cordial support of Howe, and Sir Roger Curtis of the *Queen Charlotte* exerted his influence by recommending him as one whose selection 'would be a blessing to the colony' on account of his incorruptible integrity, unceasing zeal, thorough knowledge of the country, and steady judgment. He was appointed Governor in February 1794, and in March of the same year HMS *Reliance*, with the tender *Supply*, were commissioned to convey him to Sydney.

Henry Waterhouse was chosen to command the *Reliance*, under Hunter, at that officer's request. He expressed to the Secretary of State a wish that the appointment might be conferred upon an officer to whom it might be a step in advancement, rather than upon one who had already attained the rank of commander; and he recommended Waterhouse as one who, though a young man and not an old officer, was 'the only remaining lieutenant of the *Sirius*, formerly under my command; and having had the principal part of his nautical education from me, I can with confidence say that he is well qualified for the charge'.

It is probable that Flinders heard of the expedition from his *Bellerophon* shipmate, Waterhouse, who by the end of July was under orders to sail as second captain of the *Reliance*. Certainly the opportunity of making another voyage to Australian waters, wherein, as he knew, so much work lay awaiting an officer keen for discovery, coincided with his own inclinations. He wrote that he was led by his passion for exploring new countries to embrace the opportunity of going out upon a station which of all others presented the most ample field for his favourite pursuit.

The sailing was delayed for six months, and in the interval young Flinders was able to visit his home in Lincolnshire. Whatever opposition there may have been to his choice of the sea as a profession before 1790, we may be certain that the Donington surgeon was not a little proud of his eldest son when he returned after a wonderful voyage to the isles of the Pacific and the Caribbean Sea, and after participation in the recent great naval fight which had thrilled the heart of England with exultation and pride. The boy who had left his father's house four years before as an anxious aspirant for the King's uniform now returned a bronzed seaman on the verge of manhood. His intelligence and zeal as a junior officer had won him the esteem and confidence of distinguished commanders. He had looked upon the strangeness and beauty of the world in its most remote and least known quarters, had witnessed fights with savages, threaded unmapped straits, and had, to crown his youthful achievements, striven amidst the wrack and thunder of grim-visaged war. We may picture his welcome: the strong grasp of his father's hand, the crowding enthusiasm of his brother and sisters fondly glorying in their hero's prowess. The warnings of uncle John were all forgotten now. When the midshipman's younger brother, Samuel Ward Flinders, desired to go to sea with him, he was not restrained, and, in fact, accompanied him as a volunteer on the *Reliance* when at length she sailed.

Hunter took not merely an official but a deep and discerning interest in the colonisation of Australia. He foresaw its immense possibilities, encouraged its exploration, promoted the breeding of stock and the cultivation of crops, and had a wise concern for such strategic advantages as would tend to secure it for British occupation. He perceived the great importance of the Cape of Good Hope from the point of view of Australian security; and a letter which he wrote to an official of the Admiralty while awaiting sailing orders for the *Reliance* (25 January 1795), is perhaps the first instance of official recognition of Australia's vital interest in the ownership of that post. There was cause for concern. The raw and ill-disciplined levies of the French, having at the outbreak of the Revolutionary wars most unexpectedly turned back the invading armies of Austria and Prussia, and having, after campaigns full of dramatic changes, shaken off the peril of the crushing of the fatherland by a huge European combination, were now waging an offensive war in Holland. Pichegru, the French commander, though not a soldier by training, secured astonishing successes, and, in the thick of a winter of exceptional severity, led his ragged and ill-fed army on to victory after victory, until the greater part of Holland lay conquered within his grip. In January he entered Amsterdam. There was a strong element of Republican feeling among the Dutch, and an alliance with France was demanded.

When this condition of things was reported in England, Hunter was alarmed for the safety of the colony which he was about to govern. The Cape of Good Hope was a Dutch possession. Holland was now under the domination of France. Might not events bring about the establishment of French power at the Cape? 'I cannot help feeling much concerned at the rapid progress of the French in Holland,' he wrote,

> *and I own shall not be surprised if in consequence of their success in that country they make a sudden dash at the Cape of Good Hope, if we do not anticipate them in such an attempt. They are so very active a people that it will be done before we know anything of it, and I think it a post of too much importance to be neglected by them. I hope earnestly, therefore, that it will be prevented by our sending a squadron and some troops as early as possible. If the Republicans once get a footing there, we shall probably find it difficult to dislodge them. Such a circumstance would be a sad stroke for our young colony.*

The course which Hunter then advised was that which the British Government followed, though more because the Cape was the 'halfway house' to India, than for the protection of Australian interests. An expedition was despatched later in the year to protect the Cape against French occupation, and in September the colony, by order of the Stadtholder of Holland, accepted British protection.

The *Reliance* and the *Supply* left Plymouth on 15 February 1795, amongst a very large company of merchantmen and ships of the navy convoyed by the Channel Fleet under Lord Howe, which guarded them till they were beyond the range of possible French attacks and then sailed back to port.

From Teneriffe, which Hunter reached on 6 March, he wrote a despatch to the Government stating his intention to sail, not to the Cape of Good Hope, but to Rio de Janeiro in Brazil, and thence to New South Wales. His avoidance of the more direct route was due to the causes explained above. 'In the present uncertain state of things between the French and Dutch,' he had written before sailing, 'it will be dangerous for me to attempt touching at the Cape on my way out'; and writing from Rio de Janeiro in May he explained that he did not 'conceive it safe from the uncertain state of the Dutch settlements in India to take the Cape of Good Hope in my way to Port Jackson, lest the French, following up their late successes in Holland, should have been active enough to make an early attack on that very important post'. In a despatch to the Duke of Portland he commented strongly on the same circumstance, expressing the opinion that 'if the French should be able to possess themselves of that settlement it will be rather unfortunate for our distant colony'.

Hunter had to complain of discourteous treatment received from the Portuguese Viceroy, who kept him waiting six days before according an interview, and then fixed an appointment for seven o'clock in the evening, when it was quite dark. 'As His Excellency was acquainted with the position I held, I confess I expected a different reception,' wrote Hunter; and he was so much vexed that he did not again set foot ashore while his ships lay in port. The incident, though not important in itself, serves, in conjunction with Hunter's avoidance of the Cape, to illustrate the rather limp condition of British prestige abroad at about the time when her authority was being established in Australia. With her army defeated in the Low Countries, her ships deeming it prudent to keep clear of the Cape that formed the key to her eastern and southern possessions, and her King's representative subjected to a studied slight from a Portuguese official in Brazil, she hardly appeared, just then, to be the nation that would soon shatter the naval power of France, demolish the greatest soldier of modern times, and, before her sword was sheathed, float her victorious flag in every continent, in every sea, and over people of every race and colour.

On this voyage, as on all occasions, Flinders kept a careful record of his own observations. Sixteen years later, a dispute arose, interesting to navigators, as to the precise location of Cape Frio in Brazil. An American had pointed out an error in European charts. It was a matter of some importance, because ships bound for Rio de Janeiro necessarily rounded Cape Frio, and the error was sufficiently serious to cause no small risk if vessels trusted to the received reckoning. The *Naval Chronicle* devoted some attention to the point; and to it Flinders sent a communication stating that on consulting his nautical records he found that on 2 May 1795, he made an observation, reduced from the preceding noon, calculating the position of the Cape to be latitude 22° 53' south, longitude 41° 43' west. His memorandum was printed over a facsimile of his signature as that of 'a distinguished navigator', and was hailed as 'a valuable contribution towards clearing up the difficulty concerning the geographical position of that important headland'.[1] For us the incident serves as an indication of Flinders' diligence and carefulness in the study of navigation. He was but a midshipman at the time, and it will be noticed that it was a personal observation which he was able to quote, not one taken as part of his duty as an officer.

The *Reliance* arrived at Port Jackson on 7 September, and in the following month Flinders, with a companion of whom it is time to speak, commenced the series of explorations which made his fame.

This companion was George Bass, a Lincolnshire man like Flinders himself, born at Aswarby near Sleaford. He was a farmer's son, but his father died when he was quite a child, and his mother moved to Boston. She managed out of her widow's resources to give her son an excellent education, and designed that he should enter the medical profession. In due course he was apprenticed to a Boston surgeon, Mr Francis—a common mode of securing training in medicine at that period. He 'walked' [did the rounds of] the Boston hospital for a finishing course of instruction, and won his surgeon's diploma with marked credit.

Bass had from his early years shown a desire to go to sea. His mother was able to buy for him a share in a merchant ship; but this was wrecked, whereupon, not cured of his love of the ocean, he entered the navy as a surgeon. It was in that capacity that he sailed in the *Reliance.* He was then, in 1795, 32 years of age.

All the records of Bass, both the personal observations of those who came in contact with him, and the tale of his own deeds, leave the impression that he was a very remarkable man. He was six feet in height, dark-complexioned, handsome in countenance, keen in expression, vigorous, strong, and enterprising. His father-in-law spoke of his 'very penetrating countenance'. Flinders called him 'the penetrating Bass'. Governor Hunter, in official despatches, said he was 'a young man of a well-informed mind and an active disposition', and one who was 'of much ability in various ways out of the line of his profession'. He was gifted with a mind capable of intense application to any task that he took in hand. Upon his firm courage, resourcefulness and strength of purpose, difficulties and dangers acted merely as the whetstone to the finely tempered blade. He undertook hazardous enterprises from the sheer love of doing hard things which were worth doing. 'He was one,'

[1] *Naval Chronicle*, Vol. XXVI.

wrote Flinders, 'whose ardour for discovery was not to be repressed by any obstacle nor deterred by danger.' He seemed to care nothing for rewards, and was not hungry for honours. The pleasure of doing was to him its own recompense. That 'penetrating countenance' indexed [served to indicate] a brain as direct as a drill, and as inflexible. A loyal and affectionate comrade, preferring to enter upon a task with his chosen mate, he nevertheless could not wait inactive if official duties prevented co-operation, but would set out alone on any piece of work on which he had set his heart. The portrait of Bass which we possess conveys an impression of alert and vigorous intelligence, of genial temper and hearty relish. It is the picture of a man who was abundantly alive in every nerve.

Flinders and Bass, being both Lincolnshire men, born within a few miles of each other, naturally became very friendly on the long voyage to Australia. It was said of two other friends, who achieved great distinction in the sphere of art, that when they first met in early manhood they 'ran together like two drops of mercury', so completely coincident were their inclinations. So it was in this instance. Two men more predisposed to formulate plans for exploration could not have been thrown together. A passion for maritime discovery was common to both of them. Flinders, from his study of charts and books of voyages, had a sound knowledge of the field of work that lay open, and Bass's keen mind eagerly grasped the plans explained to him. It would not have taken the surgeon and the midshipman long to find that their ambitions were completely in tune on this inviting subject. 'With this friend,' Flinders wrote, 'a determination was found of completing the examination of the east coast of New South Wales by all such opportunities as the duty of the ship and procurable means could admit. Projects of this nature, when originating in the minds of young men, are usually termed romantic; and so far from any good being anticipated, even prudence and friendship join in discouraging, if not in opposing them. Thus it was in the present case.' The significance of that passage is that the two friends made for themselves the opportunities by which they won fame and rendered service. They did not wait on Fortune; they forced her hand. They showed by what they did on their own initiative, with very limited resources, that they were the right men to be entrusted with work of larger scope.

Nevertheless it is unwarrantable to assume that Governor Hunter discountenanced their earliest efforts. It was presumably on the passage quoted above that the author of a chapter in the most elaborate modern naval history founded the assertion that 'the plans of the young discoverers were discouraged by the authorities. They, however, had resolution and perseverance. All official help and countenance were withheld.'[2] But Flinders does not say that 'the authorities' discouraged the effort. 'Prudence and friendship' did. They were not yet tried men in such hazardous enterprises; the settlement possessed scarcely any resources for exploratory work, and the dangers were unknown. Official countenance implies official responsibility, and there was not yet sufficient reason for setting the Governor's seal on the adventurous experiments of two young and untried though estimable men. When they had shown their quality, Hunter gave them every assistance and encouragement in his power, and proved himself a good friend to them. In the circumstances, 'prudence and friendship' are hardly to be blamed for a counsel of caution. The remark of Flinders is not to be interpreted to mean that the Governor put hindrances in their way. They were under his orders, and his positive discountenance would have been effectual to block their efforts. They could not even have obtained leave of absence without his approval. But John Hunter was not the man to prevent them from putting their powers to the test.

No sooner had the two friends reached Sydney than they began to look about them for means to undertake the exploratory work upon which their minds were bent. Bass had brought out with him from England, a small boat, only eight feet long, with a five-foot beam, named by him the *Tom Thumb* on account of her size.[3] In this diminutive craft the two friends made preparations for setting out along the coast. Taking with them only one boy, named Martin, with provisions and ammunition for a very short trip, they sailed the *Tom Thumb* out of Port Jackson and made southward to Botany Bay, which they entered. They pushed up George's River, which had been only partly explored, and pursued their investigation of its winding course for twenty miles beyond the former limit of survey. Upon their return they presented to Hunter a report concerning the quality of the land seen on the borders of the river, together with a sketch map. The Governor was induced from what they told him to examine the country himself; and the result was that he founded the settlement of Bankstown, which still remains, and boasts the distinction of being one of the pioneer towns of Australia.

---

[2] Sir Clements Markham in *The Royal Navy, a History*, IV, p. 565.

[3] Flinders' Papers; 'Brief Memoir' mss. p. 5. Some have supposed the measurements given in Flinders' published work to have been a misprint, the size of the boat being so absurdly small. But Flinders' *Journal* is quite clear on the point: 'We turned our eyes towards a little boat of about 8 feet keel and 5 feet beam which had been brought out by Mr. Bass and others in the *Reliance*, and from its size had obtained the name of *Tom Thumb*.'

The adventurers were delayed from the further pursuit of their ambition by ship's duties. The *Reliance* was ordered to convey to Norfolk Island an officer of the New South Wales Corps required for duty there, as well as the Judge Advocate. She sailed in January 1796. After her return in March, Bass and Flinders, being free again, lost no time in fitting out for a second cruise. Their object this time was to search for a large river, said to fall into the sea to the south of Botany Bay, which was not marked on Cook's chart. As before, the crew consisted only of themselves and the boy.

It has always been believed that the boat in which this second cruise was made, was the same *Tom Thumb* as that which carried the two young explorers to George's River; indeed, Flinders himself, in his *Voyage to Terra Australis*, Vol. I, p. xcvii, says that 'Mr. Bass and myself went again in *Tom Thumb*'. But in his unpublished journal there is a passage that suggests a doubt as to whether, when he wrote his book, over a decade later, he had not forgotten that a second boat was obtained for the second adventure. He may not have considered the circumstance important enough to mention. At all events in the journal, he writes 'As *Tom Thumb* had performed so well before, the same boat's crew had little hesitation in embarking in another boat of nearly the same size, which had been since built at Port Jackson.' There was, it is evident, a second boat, no larger than the first, or that fact would have been mentioned, and she was also known as the *Tom Thumb*. She was *Tom Thumb* the Second. Only by that assumption can we reconcile the *Voyage* statement with the journal, which, having been written up at the time, is an authoritative source of information.

They left Sydney on 25 March, intending to stand off to sea till evening, when it was expected that the breeze would bring them to the coast. But they drifted on a strong current six or seven miles southward, and being unable to land, passed the night in the boat. Next day, being in want of water, but unable to bring the *Tom Thumb* to a safe landing place, Bass swam ashore. While the filled cask was being got off a wave carried the boat shoreward and beached her, leaving the three on the beach with their clothes drenched, their provisions partly spoiled, and their arms and ammunition thoroughly wet. The emptying and launching of the boat on a surfy shore, and the replacing of the stores and cask in her, were managed with some difficulty; and they ran for two islands for shelter late in the afternoon. Finding a landing to be dangerous they again spent the night, cramped, damp, and uncomfortable, in their tossing little eight-foot craft, with their stone anchor dropped under the lee of a tongue of land. Bass could not sleep because, from having for so many hours during the day had his naked body exposed to the burning sun, he was 'one continued blister'. On the third day they took aboard two Aboriginals—'two Indians', Flinders calls them—natives of Botany Bay, who offered to pilot them to a place where they could obtain not only water but also fish and wild duck.

They were conducted to a small stream descending from a lagoon, and rowed up it for about a mile until it became too shallow to proceed. Eight or ten Aboriginals put in an appearance, and Bass and Flinders began to entertain doubts of securing a retreat from these people should they be inclined to be hostile. 'They had the reputation at Port Jackson of being exceedingly ferocious, if not cannibals.'

The powder having become wet and the muskets rusty, Bass and Flinders decided to land in order that they might spread their ammunition in the sun to dry, and clean their weapons. The natives, who increased in number to about twenty, gathered round and watched with curiosity. Some of them assisted Bass in repairing a broken oar. They did not know what the powder was, but, when the muskets were handled, so much alarm was excited that it was necessary to desist. Some of them had doubtless learnt from Aboriginals about Port Jackson of the thunder and lightning made by these mysterious pieces of wood and metal, and had had described to them how blackfellows dropped dead when such things pointed and smoked at them. Flinders, anxious to retain their confidence (because, had they assumed the offensive, they must speedily have annihilated the three whites), hit upon an amusing method of diverting them. The Aboriginals were accustomed to wear their coarse black hair and beards hanging in long, shaggy, untrimmed locks, matted with accretions of oil and dirt. When the two Botany Bay blacks were taken on board the *Tom Thumb* as pilots, a pair of scissors was applied to their abundant and too emphatically odorous tresses. Flinders tells the rest of the story:

> *We had clipped the hair and beards of the two Botany Bay natives at Red Point,*[4] *and they were showing themselves to the others and persuading them to follow their example. Whilst therefore the powder was drying, I began with a large pair of scissors to execute my new office upon the eldest of four or five chins presented to me, and as great nicety was not required, the shaving of a dozen of them did not occupy me long. Some of the more timid were alarmed at a formidable instrument coming so*

[4] Near Port Kembla; named by Cook.

near to their noses, and would scarcely be persuaded by their shaven friends to allow the operation to be finished. But when their chins were held up a second time, their fear of the instrument, the wild stare of their eyes, and the smile which they forced, formed a compound upon the rough savage countenance not unworthy [of] the pencil of a Hogarth. I was almost tempted to try what effect a little snip would produce; but our situation was too critical to admit of such experiments.

Flinders treats the incident lightly, and as a means of creating a diversion while preparing a retreat it was useful; but it can hardly be supposed to have been an agreeable occupation to barber a group of Aboriginals. What the heads were like that received Flinders' ministrations may be gathered from the description by Clarke, the supercargo [an officer in charge of a ship's cargo and the commercial concerns of the voyage] of the wrecked *Sydney Cove*, concerning the natives whom he encountered in the following year (March 1797): 'Their hair is long and straight, but they are wholly inattentive to it, either as to cleanliness or in any other respect. It serves them in lieu of a towel to wipe their hands as often as they are daubed with blubber or shark oil, which is their principal article of food. This frequent application of rancid grease to their heads and bodies renders their approach exceedingly offensive.'

But the adventure, by putting the blacks into a good humour, enabled Bass and Flinders to collect their dried powder, obtain fresh water, and get back to their boat. The natives became vociferous for them to go up to the lagoon, but the natives 'dragged her along down the stream shouting and singing', until the depth of water placed them in safety. Flinders, in his journal, expressed the view that 'we were perhaps considerably indebted for the fear the natives entertained of us to an old red jacket which Mr. Bass wore, and from which they took us to be soldiers, whom they were particularly afraid of; and though we did not much admire our new name, Soja, we thought it best not to undeceive them'.

On 25 March they anchored 'under the innermost of the northern islets … we called these Martin's Isles after our young companion in the boat'.[5]

They were now in the Illawarra district, one of the most prolific in New South Wales;[6] and the observation of Flinders that the land they

---

[5] *Journal.*

[6] McFarlane, *Illawarra and Monaro* (Sydney, 1872), p. 8.

saw was 'probably fertile, and the slopes of the back hills had certainly that appearance', has been richly justified by a century's experience.

The two friends and their boy had to remain on the *Tom Thumb* for a third night; but next afternoon (28 March) they were able to land unmolested, to cook a meal, and to take some rest on the shore. 'The sandy beach was our bed, and after much fatigue and passing three nights of cramp in *Tom Thumb* it was to us a bed of down.'

At about ten o'clock at night, on 29 March, the little craft was in extreme danger of foundering in a gale. The anchor had been cast under the lee of a range of cliffs, but the situation was insecure, so that Bass and Flinders considered it prudent to haul up the stone and run before the wind. The night was dark, the wind burst in a gale, and the adventurers had no knowledge of any place of security to which they could run. The frowning cliffs above them and the smashing of the surf on the rocks, were their guide in steering a course parallel with the coast. Bass held the sheet, Flinders steered with an oar, and the boy bailed out the water which the hissing crests of wind-lashed waves flung into the boat. 'It required the utmost exertion to prevent broaching to [to veer to, windward]; a single wrong movement or a moment's inattention would have sent us to the bottom.'

They drove along for an hour in this precarious situation, hoping for an opening to reveal itself into which they could run for shelter. At last, Flinders, straining his eyes in the darkness, distinguished right ahead some high breakers, behind which there appeared to be no shade of cliffs. So extremely perilous was their position at this time, with the water increasing despite the efforts of the boy, that Flinders, an unusually placid and matter-of-fact writer when dealing with dangers of the sea, declares that they could not have lived ten minutes longer. On the instant he determined to turn the boat's head for these breakers, hoping that behind them, as there were no high cliffs, there might be sheltered water. The boat's head was brought to the wind, the sail and mast were taken down, and the oars were got out. 'Pulling thus towards the reef, through the intervals of the heaviest seas, we found it to terminate in a point, and in three minutes were in smooth water under its lee. A white appearance further back kept us a short time in suspense, but a nearer approach showed it to be the beach of a well-sheltered cove, under which we anchored for the rest of the night.' They called the place of refuge Providential Cove. The native name was Watta-Mowlee (it is now called Wattamolla).

On the following morning, 30 March, the weather having moderated, the *Tom Thumb*'s sail was again hoisted, and she coasted northward.

After a progress of three or four miles, Flinders and Bass found the entrance of Port Hacking, for the exploration of which they had made this cruise. It was a much-indented inlet directly south of Botany Bay, divided from it by a broad peninsula, and receiving at its head the waters of a wide river, besides several small creeks; and was named after Henry Hacking, a pilot who had indicated its whereabouts, having come near it 'in his kangaroo-hunting excursions'. The two young explorers spent the better part of two days in examining the neighbourhood; and anyone who has had the good fortune to traverse that piece of country, with its grassed glades, its timbered hillsides, its exquisite glimpses of sapphire sea and cool silver river, its broken and diversified surface, rich with floral colour—for they saw it in early autumn—can realise how satisfied they must have felt with their work. After a nine-day voyage, they sailed out of Port Hacking early on 2 April, and, aided by a fine wind, drew up alongside the *Reliance* in Port Jackson on the evening of the same day.

The *Reliance* was an old and leaky ship. She had seen much service and was badly in need of repairs. 'She is so extremely weak in her whole frame that it is in our situation a difficult matter to do what is necessary,' wrote Hunter to the Secretary of State. Shipwrights' conveniences could hardly be expected to be ample in a settlement that was not yet ten years old, and where skilled labour was necessarily deficient. But she had to be repaired with the best material and direction available, for she was the best ship which His Majesty's representative had at his disposal. The *Supply* was pretty well beyond renovation. She was American built, and her timbers of black birch were never suitable for service in warm waters. Shortly after the discovery of Port Hacking, Hunter set about the overhauling of the vessel that was at once his principal means of naval defence, his saluting battery, his official inspecting ship, his transport, and his craft of all work. He wanted her especially just now, for a useful piece of colonial service.

The Governor had received intelligence from Major-General Craig, who had commanded the land forces when Admiral Elphinstone occupied the Cape of Good Hope, that a British protectorate had been established at that very important station. As Hunter had himself made the suggestion to the Government that such a step should be taken, the news was especially gratifying to him. Amongst his instructions from the Secretary of State was a direction to procure from South Africa live cattle for stocking the infant colony. He had brought out with him, at Sir Joseph Banks' suggestion, a supply of growing vegetables for transplantation and of seeds for sowing at appropriate seasons. He now set about obtaining the livestock.

The *Reliance* and the *Supply* sailed by way of Cape Horn to South Africa, where they took on board a supply of domestic animals. The former vessel carried 109 head of cattle, 107 sheep and three mares. Some of the officers brought livestock on their own account. Thus Bass had on board a cow and nineteen sheep, and Waterhouse had enough stock to start a small farm; but it does not appear that Flinders brought any animals. 'I believe no ship ever went to sea so much lumbered,' wrote Captain Waterhouse; and the unpleasantness of the voyage can be imagined, apart from that officer's assurance that it was 'one of the longest and most disagreeable passages I ever made'. The vessels left Cape Town for Sydney on 11 April 1797. The *Supply* was so wretchedly leaky that it was considered positively unsafe for her to risk the voyage. But her commander, Lieutenant William Kent, had a high sense of duty, and his courage was guided by the fine seamanship characteristic of the service. Having in view the importance to the colony of the stock he had on board, he determined to run her through. As a matter of fact, the *Supply* arrived in Sydney 41 days before the *Reliance* (16 May), though Hunter reported that she reached port 'in a most distressed and dangerous condition', and would never be fit for sea again. Kent's memory is worthily preserved on the map of Australia by the name (given by Flinders or by Hunter himself) of the Kent group of islands at the eastern entrance of Bass Strait.

The *Reliance*, meeting with very bad weather, made a very slow passage. Captain Waterhouse mentioned that one fierce gale was 'the most terrible I ever saw or heard of', so that he 'expected to go to the bottom every moment'. He wondered how they escaped destruction, but rounded off his description with a seaman's joke: 'possibly I may be intended to be hung in room [instead] of being drowned'. The ship was very leaky all the way, and Hunter reported that she returned to port with her pumps going. She reached Sydney on 26 June.

The unseaworthy condition of the *Reliance* had an important bearing on the share Flinders took in Australian discovery, for it was unquestionably in consequence of his being engaged upon her repair that he was prevented from accompanying his friend Bass on the expedition which led to the discovery of Bass Strait. This statement is proved not only by the testimony of Flinders himself, but by concurrent facts. Waterhouse wrote on the return of the ship to Port Jackson, 'we have taken everything out of her in hopes of repairing her'. This was in the latter part of 1797. A despatch from Hunter to the British Government in January 1798, shows that at that time she was still being patched up. Flinders recorded that 'the great repairs required by the *Reliance* would not allow of my absence', but that 'my friend Mr. Bass, less confined by his duty, made several excursions'. Finally, it was on 3 December 1797, while the refitting was in progress, that Bass started out on the adventurous voyage which led to the discovery of the stretch of water separating Tasmania from the mainland of Australia.

But for the work on the *Reliance*, there cannot be the shadow of a doubt that Flinders would have been with him. Duty had to be done, however; the 'ugly commanded work', in which, as the sage reminds us, genius has to do its part in common with more ordinary mortals, made demands that must take precedence of adventurous cruising along unknown coasts. So it was that the cobbling of a debilitated tub separated on an historic occasion two brave and loyal friends whose names will be thought of together as long as British people treasure the memory of their choice and daring spirits.

VII

THE DISCOVERY OF BASS STRAIT

THE patching-up of the *Reliance* not being surgeon's work, Bass, throbbing with energy, looked about him for some useful employment. The whole of the New South Wales settlement at this time consisted of an oblong—the town of Sydney itself—on the south side of Port Jackson, a few sprawling paddocks on either side of the fang-like limbs of the harbour, some small pieces of cultivated land further west, at and beyond Parramatta, and a cultivable area to the north-west on the banks of the Hawkesbury River. A sketch-map prepared by Hunter, in 1796, illustrates these very small early attempts of the settlement to spread. They show up against the paper like a few specks of lettuce leaf upon a white tablecloth. The large empty spaces are traversed by red lines, principally to the south-west, marking 'country which has been lately walked over'. The red lines end abruptly on the far side of a curve in the course of the River Nepean, where swamps and hills are shown. The map-maker 'saw a bull' near a hill which was called Mount Hunter, and marked it down.

West of the settlement, behind Richmond Hill on the Hawkesbury, the map indicated a mountain range. Bass's first effort at independent exploration was an endeavour to find a pass through these mountains. The need was seen to be imminent. As the colony grew, the limits of occupation would press up to the foot of this blue range, which, with its precipitous walls, its alluring openings leading to stark faces of rock, its sharp ridges breaking to sheer ravines, its dense scrub and timber, defied the energies of successive explorers. Governor Phillip, in 1789, reached Richmond by way of the Hawkesbury. Later in the same year, and in the next, further efforts were made, but the investigators were beaten by the stern and shaggy hills. Captain William Paterson, in 1793, organised an attacking party, consisting largely of Scottish highlanders, hoping that their native skill and resolution would find a path across the barrier; but they proceeded by boat only, and did not go far. In the following year quartermaster Hacking, with a party of hardy men, spent ten days among the mountains, but no path or pass practicable for traffic rewarded his endeavours. Sydney was shut in between the sea and this craggy rampart. What the country on the other side was like no man [European] knew.

In June 1796, before the *Reliance* sailed for South Africa, George Bass made his try. The task was hard, and worth attempting, two qualifications which recommended it strongly to his mind. He collected a small party of men upon whom he could rely for a tough struggle, took provisions for about a fortnight, equipped himself with strong ropes with which to be lowered down ravines, had scaling irons made for his feet, and hooks to fasten on his hands, and set out ready to cut or climb his way over the mountains, determined to assail their defiant fastnesses up to the limits of possibility. It was a stiff enterprise, and Bass and his party did not spare themselves. But the Blue Mountains were a fortress that was not to be taken by storm. Bass's success, as Flinders wrote, 'was not commensurate to the perseverance and labour employed'. After fifteen days of effort, the baffled adventurers confessed themselves beaten, and, their provisions being exhausted, returned to Sydney.

They had pushed research further [made more thorough investigations] than any previous explorers had done, and had marked down the course of the River Grose as a practical result of their work. But Bass now believed the mountains to be hopeless; and, indeed, George Caley, a botanical collector employed by Sir Joseph Banks, having seven years later made another attempt and met with repulse, did not hesitate to tell a committee of the House of Commons, which summoned him to appear as a witness, that the range was impassable. It seemed that Nature had tumbled down an impenetrable bewilderment of rock, the hillsides cracking into deep, dark crevices, and the crests of the mountains showing behind and beyond a massed confusion of crags and hollows, trackless and untraversable. Governor King declared himself satisfied that the effort to cross the range was a task 'as chimerical as useless [as fanciful as it was in vain]', an opinion strengthened by the fact that, as Allan Cunningham had related,[1] the Aboriginals known to the settlement were 'totally ignorant of any pass to the interior'.

It was not, indeed, till 1813 that Gregory Blaxland, with Lieutenant Lawson and William Charles Wentworth (then a youth), as companions,

[1] On 'Progress of Interior Discovery in New South Wales', *Journal of the Royal Geographical Society* (1832), Vol. II, p. 99.

succeeded in solving the problem. The story of their steady, persistent, and desperate struggle being beyond the scope of this biography, it is sufficient to say that after fifteen days of severe labour, applied with rare intelligence and bushcraft, they saw beneath them waving grass-country watered by clear streams, and knew that they had found a path to the interior of the new continent.

Bass's eagerness to explore soon found other scope. In 1797, [a] report was brought to Sydney by shipwrecked mariners that, in traversing the coast, they had seen coal. He at once set off to investigate. At the place now called Coalcliff, about twenty miles south of Botany Bay, he found a vein of coal about twenty feet above the surface of the sea. It was six or seven feet thick, and dipped to the southward until it became level with the sea, 'and there the lowest rock you can see when the surf retires is all coal'. It was a discovery of first-class importance—the first considerable find of a mineral that has yielded incalculable wealth to Australia.[2] He made this useful piece of investigation in August; and in the following month undertook a journey on foot, in company with Williamson, the acting commissary, from Sydney to the Cowpastures, crossing and re-crossing the River Nepean, and thence descending to the sea a few miles south of his old resting place, Watta-Mowlee. His map and notes are full of evidence of his careful observation. 'Tolerably good level ground', 'good pastures', 'mountainous brushy land', and so forth, are remarks scored across his track line. But these were pastimes in comparison with the enterprise that was now occupying his mind, and upon which his fame chiefly rests.

Hunter's despatch to the Duke of Portland, dated 1 March 1798, explains the circumstances of the expedition leading to the discovery of Bass Strait:

> *The tedious repairs which His Majesty's ship* Reliance *necessarily required before she could be put in a condition for going again to sea, having given an opportunity to Mr. George Bass, her surgeon, a young man of a well-informed mind and an active disposition, to offer himself to be employed in any*

---

[2] It is well to remember that the use of coal was discovered in England in very much the same way. Mr Salzmann, *English Industries of the Middle Ages* (1913), p. 3, observes that 'it is most probable that the first coal used was washed up by the sea, and such as could be quarried from the face of the cliffs where the seams were exposed by the action of the waves'. He quotes a sixteenth-century account relative to Durham: 'As the tide comes in it bringeth a small wash sea coal, which is employed to the making of salt and the fuel of the poor fisher towns adjoining.' Hence, originally, coal in England was commonly called sea-coal even when obtained inland.

way in which he could contribute to the benefit of the public service, I enquired of him in what way he was desirous of exerting himself, and he informed me nothing would gratify him more effectually than my allowing him the use of a good boat and permitting him to man her with volunteers from the King's ships. I accordingly furnished him with an excellent whaleboat, well fitted, victualled, and manned to his wish, for the purpose of examining the coast to the southward of this port, as far as he could with safety and convenience go.

It is clear from this despatch that the impulse was Bass's own, and that the Governor merely supplied the boat, provisioned it, and permitted him to select his own crew. Hunter gave Bass full credit for what he did, and himself applied the name to the strait when its existence had been demonstrated. It is, however, but [only] just to Hunter to observe, that he had eight years before printed the opinion that there was either a strait or a deep gulf between Van Diemen's Land and New Holland. In his *Historical Journal of the Transactions at Port Jackson and Norfolk Island* (London, 1793), he gave an account of the voyage of the *Sirius*, in 1789, from Port Jackson to the Cape of Good Hope to purchase provisions. In telling the story of the return voyage he wrote (p. 125):

In passing at a distance from the coast between the islands of Schooten and Furneaux and Point Hicks, the former being the northernmost of Captain Furneaux's observations here, and the latter the southernmost part which Captain Cook saw when he sailed along the coast, there has been no land seen, and from our having felt an easterly set of current and when the wind was from that quarter (north-west), we had an uncommon large sea, there is reason to believe that there is in that space either a very deep gulf or a strait, which may separate Van Diemen's Land from New Holland. There have no discoveries been made on the western side of this land in the parallel I allude to, between 39° 00' and 42° 00' south, the land there having never been seen.

Hunter was, therefore, quite justified, in his despatch, in pointing out that he had 'long conjectured' the existence of the strait. He seems, not unwarrantably, to have been anxious that his own share in the discoveries, as foreseeing them and encouraging the efforts that led to them, should not be overlooked. The *Naval Chronicle* of the time mentioned the subject, and returned to it more than once.[3] But if we may suppose Hunter to have inspired some of these allusions, it must be added that they are scrupulously fair, and claimed no more for him than he was entitled to have remembered. Bass's work is in every instance properly appreciated; and in one article (*Naval Chronicle*, XV, p. 62) he is characterised, probably through Hunter's instrumentality—the language is very like that used in the official despatch—as 'a man of considerable enterprise and ingenuity, a strong and comprehensive mind with the advantage of a vigorous body and healthy constitution'. The boat was 28 feet 7 inches long, head and stern alike, fitted to row eight oars, with banksia timbers and cedar planking.

One error relating to this justly celebrated voyage needs to be corrected, especially as currency has been given to it in a standard historical work. It is not true that Bass undertook his cruise 'in a sailing boat with a crew of five convicts'.[4] His men were all British sailors. Hunter's despatch indicates that Bass asked to be allowed to man his boat 'with volunteers from the King's ships', and that she was 'manned to his wish', and Flinders, in his narrative of the voyage, stated that his friend was 'furnished with a fine whaleboat, and six weeks' provisions by the Governor, and a crew of six seamen from the ships'.

It is, indeed, much to be regretted that, with one exception to be mentioned in a later chapter, the names of the seamen who participated in this remarkable cruise have not been preserved. Bass had no occasion in his diary to mention any man by name, but it is quite evident that they were a daring, enduring, well-matched and thoroughly loyal band, facing the big waters in their small craft with heroic resolution, and never failing to respond when their chief gave a lead. When, after braving foul weather, and with food supplies running low, the boat was at length turned homeward, Bass writes 'we did it reluctantly', coupling his willing little company with himself in regrets that discovery could not be pushed farther than they had been able to pursue it. Throughout his diary he writes in the first person plural, and he records no instance of complaint of the hardships endured or of quailing before the dangers encountered.

It is likely enough that the six British sailors who manned Bass's boat had very little perception that they were engaged upon a task that would shine in history. An energetic ship's surgeon whom everybody liked had called for volunteers in an affair requiring stout arms and hearts. He got

[3] See *Naval Chronicle*, Vol. IV, p. 159 (1800); VI, p. 349 (1801); XV, p. 62 (1806), etc.

[4] *The Royal Navy: a History*, Vol. IV, p. 567.

them, they followed him, did their job, and returned to routine duty. They did not receive any extra pay, or promotion, or official recognition. Neither did Bass, beyond Hunter's commendation in a despatch. He wrote up his modest little diary, a terse record of observations and occurrences, and got ready for the next adventure.

We will follow him on this one.

On the evening of Sunday, 3 December 1797, at six o'clock, Bass's men rowed out of Port Jackson heads and turned south. The night was spent in Little Bay, three miles north of Botany Bay, as Bass did not deem it prudent to proceed further in the darkness, the weather having become cloudy and uncertain, and things not having yet found their proper place in the boat. Nor was very much progress made on the 4th, for a violent wind was encountered, which caused Bass to make for Port Hacking. On the following day, 'the wind headed in flurries', and the boat did not get further than Providential Cove, or Watta-Mowlee, where the *Tom Thumb* had taken refuge in the previous year. On the 7th, Bass reached [the] Shoalhaven, which he named. He remained there three days, and described the soil and situation with some care. 'The country around it is generally low and swampy and the soil for the most part is rich and good, but seemingly much subject to extensive inundation.' One sentence of comment reads curiously now that the district is linked up by railway with Sydney, and exports its butter and other produce to the markets of Europe. 'However capable much of the soil of this country might upon a more accurate investigation be found to be of agricultural improvement, certain it is that the difficulty of shipping off the produce must ever remain a bar to its colonisation. A nursery of cattle might perhaps be carried on here with advantage, and that sort of produce ships off itself.' Bass, a farmer's son, reared in an agricultural centre, was a capable judge of good country, but of course there was nothing when he saw these rich lands to foretell an era of railways and refrigerating machinery.

On 10 December the boat entered Jervis Bay, and on the 18th Bass discovered Barmouth Creek (probably the mouth of the Bega River), 'the prettiest little model of a harbour we had ever seen'. Were it not for the shallowness of the bar, he considered that the opening would be 'a complete harbour for small craft'; but as things were, 'a small boat even must watch her times for going in'. On the 19th, at seven o'clock in the morning, Twofold Bay was discovered. Bass sailed round it, made a sketch of it, and put to sea again, thinking it better to leave the place for further examination on the return voyage, and to take advantage of the fair wind for the southward course. He considered the nautical advantages of the harbour—to become in later years a rather important centre for whaling—superior to those of any other anchorage entered during the voyage. A landmark was indicated by him with a quaint touch: 'It may be known by a red point on the south side, of the peculiar bluish hue of a drunkard's nose.' On the following day at about eleven o'clock in the morning he rounded Cape Howe, and commenced his westerly run. He was now nearing a totally new stretch of coast.

From the 22nd to the 30th bad weather was experienced. A gale blew south-west by west, full in their teeth. The situation must have been uncomfortable in the extreme, for the boat was now entering the strait. The heavy seas that roll under the lash of a south-west gale in that quarter do not make for the felicity of those who face them on a well-found modern steamer. For the seven Englishmen in an open boat, groping along a strange coast, the ordeal was severe. But no doubt they wished each other a merry Christmas, in quite the traditional English way, and with hearty good feeling, on the 25th.

On the last day of the year, in more moderate weather, the boat was coasting the Ninety Mile Beach, behind the sandy fringe of which lay the fat pastures of eastern Gippsland. The country did not look very promising to Bass from the sea, and he minuted his impressions in a few words: 'low beaches at the bottom of heights of no great depth, lying between rocky projecting points; in the back lay some short ridges of lumpy irregular hills at a little distance from the sea'.

Nowhere in his diary did Bass seize upon any picturesque features of scenery, though they are not lacking in the region that he traversed. If he was moved by a sense of the oppressiveness of vast, silent solitudes, or by any sensation of strangeness at feeling his way along a coast hitherto unexplored, the emotion finds scarcely any reflection in his record. Hard facts, dates, times, positions, and curt memoranda, were the sole concern of the diarist. He did not even mention a pathetic, almost tragic, incident of the voyage, to which reference will presently be made. It did not concern the actual exploratory part of his work, and so he passed it by. The one note signifying an appreciation of the singularity of the position is conveyed in the terse words: 'Sunday 31st, a.m. Daylight, got out and steered along to the southward, in anxious expectation, being now nearly come upon an hitherto unknown part of the coast.'

But men are emotional beings after all, and an entry for 'January 1st, 1798' (really the evening of 31 December), bare of the human touch as it is, brings the situation of Bass and his crew vividly before the eye of the reader. The dramatic force of it must have been keenly realised by them. At night there was 'bright moonlight, the sky without a cloud'. A new year was dawning. The seven Englishmen tossing on the waves in this solitary part of the globe would not fail to remember that. They were near enough to the land to see it distinctly; it was 'still low and level'. A flood of soft light lay upon it, and rippled silvery over the sea. They would hear the wash of the rollers that climb that bevelled shore, and pile upon the water-line creaming leagues of phosphorescent foam. And at the back lay a land of mystery, almost as tenantless as the moon herself, but to be the future home of prosperous thousands of the same race as the men in the whaleboat. To them it was a country of weird forms, strange animals, and untutored savages. If ever boat breasted the 'foam of perilous seas in faery lands forlorn', it was this, and if ever its occupants realised the complete strangeness of their situation and their utter aloofness from the tracks of their fellow men, it must have been on this cloudless moonlit summer night. There was hardly a stretch of the world's waters, at all events in any habitable zone, where they could have been farther away from all that they remembered with affection and hoped to see again. About half an hour before midnight a haze dimmed the distinctness of the shore, and at midnight it had thickened so that they could scarcely see land at all. But they crept along in their course, 'vast flights of petrels and other birds flying about us', the watch peering into the mist, the rest wrapped in their blankets sleeping, while the stars shone down on them from a brilliant steel-blue sky, and the Cross wheeled high above the southern horizon.

Cook, on his *Endeavour* voyage in 1770, first sighted the Australian coast at Point Hicks, called Cape Everard on many current maps. His second officer, Lieutenant Zachary Hicks, at six in the morning of 20 April, 'saw ye land making high', and Cook 'named it Point Hicks because Lieutenant Hicks was the first who discovered this land'. Point Hicks is a projection which falls away landward from a peak, backed by a sandy conical hill, but Bass passed it without observing it. The thick haze which he mentions may have obscured the outline. At all events, by dusk on 1 January he found that he had filled up the hitherto unexplored space between Point Hicks 'a point we could not at all distinguish from the rest of the beach', and the high hummocky land further west, which he believed to be that sighted by Captain Tobias Furneaux in 1773. It is, however, to be observed that Flinders pointed out that all Bass's reckonings after 31 December were ten miles out. 'It is no matter of surprise', wrote his friend indicating an error, 'if observations taken from an open boat in a high sea should differ ten miles from the truth; but I judge that Mr. Bass's quadrant must have received some injury during the night of the 31st, for a similar error appears to pervade all the future observations, even those taken under favourable circumstances.' The missing of Point Hicks, therefore, apart from the thick haze, is not difficult to understand.

On Tuesday, 2 January, Bass reached the most southerly point in the continent of Australia, the extremity of Wilson's Promontory. The bold outlines were sighted at seven o'clock in the morning. 'We were surprised by the sight of high hummocky land right ahead, and at a considerable distance.' Bass called it Furneaux Land in his diary, in the belief that a portion of the great granite peninsula had been seen by the captain of the *Adventure* in 1773. Furneaux's name is still attached to the group of islands divided by Banks' Strait from the north-east corner of Tasmania, but the name which Bass gave to the promontory was not retained. It is not likely that Furneaux ever saw land so far west. 'It cannot be the same, as Mr. Bass was afterwards convinced,' wrote Flinders. Governor Hunter, 'at our recommendation', named it Wilson's Promontory, 'in compliment to my friend Thomas Wilson, Esq., of London'. It has been stated that the name was given to commemorate William Wilson, one of the whaleboat crew, who 'jumped ashore first'.[5] Nobody 'jumped ashore first' on the westward voyage, when the discovery was made, because, as Bass twice mentions in his diary, 'we could not land'. Doubly inaccurate is the statement of another writer that 'the promontory was seen and named by Grant in 1800 after Admiral Wilson'.[6] Grant himself, on his chart of Bass Strait, marked down the promontory as 'accurately surveyed by Matthew Flinders, which he calls Wilson's Promontory', and on p. 78 of his *Narrative* wrote that it was named by Bass. The truth is, as related above, that it was named by Hunter on the recommendation of Bass and Flinders; and the two superfluous Wilsons have no proper place in the story. The Thomas Wilson whose name was thus given to one of the principal features of the Australian coast—a form of memorial far more enduring than 'storied urn or animated bust'—is believed to have been a London merchant, engaged partly in the Australian trade. Nothing more definite is known about him. He was as one who 'grew immortal in his own despight'[7] [achieved fame for no particular good reason]. Of the promontory itself Bass wrote—and the words are exceedingly apt—that it was 'well worthy of being the boundary point of a large strait, and a corner stone of this great island New Holland'.

Bass found the neighbourhood of the promontory to be the home of

---

5 *The Coming of the British to Australia*, by Ida Lee (London, 1906), p. 51.

6 Blair, *Cyclopaedia of Australia*, p. 748.

7 Pope, *To Augustus*, l. 69.

vast numbers of petrels, gulls and other birds, as is still the case, and he remarked upon the seals observed upon neighbouring rocks, with 'a remarkably long tapering neck and sharp pointed head'. They were the ordinary Bass Strait seal, once exceedingly plentiful, and still to be found on some of the islands, but unfortunately much fewer in numbers now. The pupping time was passed when Bass sailed through, and many of the females had gone to sea, as is their habit. This cause of depletion accounts for his remark on his return voyage that the number was 'by no means equal to what we had been led to expect'. But, he added, 'from the quantity I saw I have every reason to believe that a speculation on a small scale might be carried on with advantage'.

Foul winds and heavy breaking seas were experienced while the boat was nearing the promontory. To make matters worse, leaks were causing anxiety. Water was gushing in pretty freely near the water-line aft. The crew had frequently remarked in the course of the morning of 3 January how much looser the boat had become during the last few days. Her planks had received no ordinary battering. It had been Bass's intention to strike for the northern coast of Van Diemen's Land, which he supposed to be at no very great distance. He may at this time have been under the impression that he was in a deep gulf. As a matter of fact, the nearest point southward that he could have reached was 130 miles distant. Anxiety about the condition of the boat made him resolve to continue his coasting cruise westward. Water rushed in fast through the boat's side, there was risk of a plank starting [being dislodged], and ploughing through a hollow, irregular sea, the explorers were, as Flinders reviewing the adventure wrote, 'in the greatest danger'. Bass's record of his night of peril is characteristically terse: 'we had a bad night of it, but the excellent qualities of the boat brought us through'. He says nothing of his own careful steering and sleepless vigilance.

It was on the evening of the third day, 3 January, that an incident occurred to which, curiously enough, Bass made no allusion in his diary, presumably because it did not concern the actual work of navigation and discovery, but which throws a dash of tragic colour into the story of his adventure. The boat having returned to the coast of what was supposed to be Furneaux Land, was running along 'in whichever way the land might trend, for the state of the boat did not seem to allow of our quitting the shore with propriety'. The coastline was being scanned for a place of shelter, when smoke was observed curling up from an island not far from the promontory. At first it was thought that the smoke arose from a fire lighted by Aboriginals, but it was discovered, to the amazement of Bass and his crew, that the island was occupied by a party of white men. They were escaped convicts. The tale they had to tell was one of a wild dash for liberty, treachery by confederates, and abandonment to the imminent danger of starvation.

In October of the previous year, a gang of fourteen convicts had been employed in carrying stones from Sydney to the Hawkesbury River settlement, a few miles to the north. Most of them were 'of the last Irish convicts', as Hunter explained in a despatch, part of the bitter fruit of the Irish Mutiny Act of 1796, passed to strike at the movement associated with the names of Lord Edward Fitzgerald and Wolfe Tone, which encouraged the attempted French invasion of Ireland under Hoche. These men seized the boat appointed for the service, appropriated the stores, threatened the lives of all who dared to oppose them, and made their exit through Port Jackson heads. As soon as the Governor heard of the escape he despatched parties in pursuit in rowing boats. The coast was searched 60 miles to the north and 40 to the south but the convicts, with the breeze in their sail and the hope of liberty in their hearts, had all the advantage on their side, and eluded their gaolers.

In April 1797, news had been brought to the settlement of the wreck of the ship *Sydney Cove* on an island to the southward. If the Irish prisoners could reach this island, float the ship on the tide, and repair her rents, they considered that they had an excellent chance of escape. The provisions which they had on their boat, with such as they might find on the ship, would probably be sufficient for a voyage. It was a daring enterprise, but it may well have seemed to offer a prospect of success.

Some of the prisoners at the settlement, as appears from a 'general order' issued by Hunter, had 'picked up somehow or other the idle story of the possibility of travelling from hence to China, or finding some other colony where they expect every comfort without the trouble of any labour'. It may have been the alluring hope of discovering such an earthly paradise that flattered [inspired] these men [with false hope]. As a matter of fact, some convicts did escape from New South Wales and reached India, after extraordinary perils and hardships. They endeavoured to sail up the River Godavery, but were interrupted by a party of sepoys [Indian soldiers in the British army], rearrested, and sent to Madras, whence they were ordered to be sent back to Sydney.[8]

But the party whom Bass found never discovered the place of the wreck upon which they reckoned. Instead, they drifted round Cape Howe, and found themselves off a desolate, inhospitable coast, without knowledge of their whereabouts, and with a scanty, rapidly diminishing stock of food. In fear of starvation seven of them resolved to desert their

---

[8] See *Annual Register*, 1801, p. 15.

companions on this lonely island near Wilson's Promontory, and treacherously sailed away with the boat while the others were asleep. It was the sad, sick, and betrayed remnant of this forlorn hope, that Bass found on that wave-beaten rock on 3 January. For five weeks the wretched men had subsisted on petrels and occasional seals. Small prospect they had of being saved; the postponement of their doom seemed only a prolongation of their anguish. They were nearly naked, and almost starved to death. Bass heard their story, pitied their plight, and relieved their necessities as well as he could from his own inadequate stores. He also promised that on his return he would call again at the island, and do what he could for the party, who only escaped from being prisoners of man to become prisoners of Nature, locked in one of her straitest [most restricted] confines, and fed from a reluctant and parsimonious hand.

Bass kept his word; and it may be as well to interrupt the narrative of his westward navigation in order to relate the end of this story of distress. On 2 February, he again touched at the island. But what could he do to help the fugitives? His boat was too small to enable him to take them on board, and his provisions were nearly exhausted, his men having had to eke out the store by living on seals and sea birds. He consented to take on board two of the seven, one of whom was grievously sick and the other old and feeble. He provided the five others with a musket and ammunition, fishing lines and hooks, and a pocket compass. He then conveyed them to the mainland, gave them a supply of food to meet their immediate wants, and pointed out that their only hope of salvation was to pursue the coastline round to Port Jackson. The crew of the whaleboat gave them such articles of clothing as they could spare. Some tears were shed on both sides when they separated, Bass to continue his homeward voyage, the hapless victims of a desperate attempt to escape to face the long tramp over 500 miles of wild and trackless country, with the prospect of a prolongation of their term of servitude should they ever reach Sydney. 'The difficulties of the country and the possibility of meeting hostile natives are considerations which will occasion doubts of their ever being able to reach us,' wrote Hunter in a despatch reporting the matter to the Secretary of State. It does not appear that one of the five was even seen again [that any of them were ever seen again].[9]

---

[9] What some convicts dared and endured in the effort to escape, is shown in the following very interesting paragraph, printed in a London newspaper of 30 May 1797: 'The female convict who made her escape from Botany Bay, and suffered the greatest hardships during a voyage of three

To return to the discovery cruise: on 5 January, at seven in the evening, Bass's whaleboat turned into Westernport, between the bold granite headland of Cape Wollamai, on Phillip Island, and Point Griffith on the mainland. The discovery of this port, now the seat of a naval base for the Commonwealth, was a splendid crown to a remarkable voyage. 'I have named the place,' Bass wrote, 'from its relative situation to every other known harbour on the coast, Western Port. It is a large sheet of water, branching out into two arms, which end in wide flats of several miles in extent, and it was not until we had been here some days that we found it to be formed by an island, and to have two outlets to the sea, an eastern and western passage.'

Twelve days were spent in the harbour. The weather was bad; and to this cause in the main we may attribute the paucity of the observations made, and the defective account given of the port itself. It contains two islands: Phillip Island, facing the strait, and French Island, the larger of the two, lying between Phillip Island and the mainland. Bass was not aware that this second island was not part of the mainland. Its existence was first determined by the *Naturaliste*, one of the ships of Baudin's French expedition, in 1802.

Bass's men had great difficulty in procuring good water. He considered that there was every appearance of an unusual drought in the country. This may also have been the reason why he saw only three or four blacks, who were so shy that the sailors could not get near them. There must certainly have been fairly large families of blacks on Phillip Island at one time, for there are several extensive middens on the coast, with thick deposits of fishbones and shells; and the author has found there some good specimens of 'blackfellows' knives'—that is, sharpened pieces of flat, hard stone, with which the Aboriginals opened their oysters and mussels—besides witnessing the finding of a few fine stone axes. Bass records the sight of a few brush kangaroos and 'wallabah' [wallabies]; of black swan he observed hundreds, as well as ducks, 'a small but excellent kind', which flew in thousands, and 'an abundance of most kinds of wild fowl'.

---

[9] ***Cont'd.***

thousand leagues [presumably she was a stowaway] and who was afterwards retaken and condemned to death, has been pardoned and released from Newgate. In the story of this woman there is something extremely singular. A gentleman of high rank in the Army visited her in Newgate, heard the details of her life, and for that time departed. The next day he returned, and told the gentleman who keeps the prison that he had procured her pardon, at the same time requesting that she should not be apprized of the circumstances. The next day he returned with his carriage, and took off the poor woman, who almost expired with gratitude.'

By the time the stay in Westernport came to an end, Bass had been at sea a month and two days, and had sailed well into the strait now bearing his name, though he was not yet quite sure that it was a strait. His provisions had necessarily run very low. The condition of the boat, whose repair occupied some time, increased his anxiety. Prudence pointed to the desirableness of a return to Port Jackson with the least possible delay. Yet one cannot but regret that so intrepid an explorer, who was making such magnificent use of means so few and frail, was not able to follow the coast a very few more miles westward. Another day's sail would have brought him into Port Phillip, and he would have been the discoverer of the bay at the head of which now stands the great city of Melbourne. Perhaps if he had done so, his report would have saved Hunter from writing a sentence which is a standing warning against premature judgments upon territory seen at a disadvantage and insufficiently examined. 'He found in general,' wrote the Governor to the Secretary of State, 'a barren, unpromising country, with very few exceptions, and were it even better the want of harbours would render it less valuable.' The truth is that he had seen hardly [only just] the fringe of some of the fairest lands on earth, and was within cannon shot of a harbour wherein all the navies of the world could ride.

Shortly after dawn on 18 January the prow of the whaleboat was 'very reluctantly' turned oceanwards for the home journey. The wind was fresh when they started, but as the morning wore on it increased to a gale, and by noon there were high seas and heavy squalls. As the little craft was running along the coast, and the full force of the south-westerly gale beat hard on her beam, her management taxed the nerve and seamanship of the crew. Bass acknowledged that it was 'very troublesome', and his 'very' means much. This extremely trying weather lasted, with a few brief intervals, for eight days. As soon as possible Bass steered his boat under the lee of Cape Liptrap, not only for safety, but also to salt down for consumption during the remainder of the voyage a stock of birds taken on the islands off Westernport.

On the night of the 23rd the boat lay snugly under the shelter of the rocks, where Bass intended to remain until the weather moderated. But at about one o'clock in the morning the wind shifted to the south, blowing 'stronger than before', and made the place untenable. At daybreak, therefore, another resting place was sought, and later in the morning the boat was beached on the west side of a sheltered cove, 'having passed through a sea that for the very few hours it has been blowing was incredibly high'. When the wind abated the sea went down, so that Bass was able to round the promontory to the east, enter

Sealers' Cove, which he named, and lay in a stock of seal-meat and salted birds.

'The Promontory,' wrote Bass, 'is joined to the mainland by a low neck of sand, which is nearly divided by a lagoon that runs in on the west side of it, and by a large shoal inlet on the east. Whenever it shall be decided that the opening between this and Van Diemen's Land is a large strait, this rapidity of tide and the long S.W. swell that seems continually running in upon the coast to the westward, will then be accounted for.' It is evident, therefore, that at this time Bass regarded the certainty of there being a strait as a matter yet to 'be decided'. He was himself thereafter to assist in the decision.

Though Bass does not give any particulars of Aboriginals encountered at Wilson's Promontory, it is apparent from an allusion in his diary that some were seen. The sentence in which he mentions them is curious for its classification of them with the other animals observed, a classification biologically justifiable, no doubt, but hardly usual. 'The animals,' he wrote, 'have nothing new in them worth mentioning, with these exceptions; that the men, though thieves, are kind and friendly, and that the birds upon Furneaux's Land have a sweetness of note unknown here', *i.e.*, at Port Jackson. He would not, in February, have heard the song-lark, that unashamed rival of an English cousin famed in poetry, and the sharp crescendo of the coach-whip bird would scarcely be classed as 'sweet'. 'The tinkle of the bell-bird in the ranges' may have gratified his ear; but the likelihood is that the birds which pleased him were the harmonious thrush and the mellow songster so opprobiously named the thickhead, for no better reason than that collectors experience a difficulty in skinning it.[10]

The cruise from the promontory eastward was commenced on 2 February. Eight days later, the boat being in no condition for keeping the sea with a foul wind, Bass beached her not far from Ram Head. He had passed Point Hicks in the night. Cape Howe was rounded on the 15th, and on the 25th the boat entered Port Jackson.

Bass and his men had accomplished a great achievement. In an open boat, exposed to the full rigours of the weather in seas that are frequently rough and were on this voyage especially storm-lashed, persecuted persistently by contrary gales, they had travelled 1,200 miles,

---

[10] Mr Chas. L. Barrett, a well known Australian ornithologist, and one of the editors of the *Emu*, knows the promontory well, and he tells me that he has no doubt that the birds which pleased Bass were the grey shrike thrush (*Colluricincla harmonica*) and the white-throated thickhead (*Pachycephala gutturalis*).

principally along an unknown coast, which they had for the first time explored. Hunter in his official despatch commented on Bass's 'perseverance against adverse winds and almost incessant bad weather', and complimented him upon his sedulous examination of inlets in search of secure harbours. But there can be no better summary of the voyage than that penned by Flinders, who from his own experience could adequately appreciate the value of the performance. Writing fifteen years later, when Bass had disappeared and was believed to be dead, his friend said:

> *It should be remembered that Mr. Bass sailed with only six weeks' provisions; but with the assistance of occasional supplies of petrels, fish, seals'-flesh, and a few geese and black swans, and by abstinence, he had been enabled to prolong his voyage beyond eleven weeks. His ardour and perseverance were crowned, in despite of the foul winds which so much opposed him, with a degree of success not to have been anticipated from such feeble means. In three hundred miles of coast from Port Jackson to the Ram Head, he added a number of particulars which had escaped Captain Cook, and will always escape any navigator in a first discovery, unless he have the time and means of joining a close examination by boats to what may be seen from the ship.*
>
> *Our previous knowledge of the coast scarcely extended beyond the Ram Head; and there began the harvest in which Mr. Bass was ambitious to place the first reaping-hook. The new coast was traced three hundred miles; and instead of trending southward to join itself to Van Diemen's Land, as Captain Furneaux had supposed, he found it, beyond a certain point, to take a direction nearly opposite, and to assume the appearance of being exposed to the buffeting of an open sea. Mr. Bass himself entertained no doubt of the existence of a wide strait separating Van Diemen's Land from New South Wales, and he yielded with the greatest reluctance to the necessity of returning before it was so fully ascertained as to admit of no doubt in the minds of others. But he had the satisfaction of placing at the end of his new coast an extensive and useful harbour, surrounded with a country superior to any other harbour in the southern parts of New South Wales.*
>
> *A voyage especially undertaken for discovery in an open boat, and in which six hundred miles of coast, mostly in a boisterous climate, was explored, has not, perhaps, its equal in*

> *the annals of maritime history. The public will award to its high-spirited and able conductor—alas! now no more—an honourable place in the list of those whose ardour stands most conspicuous for the promotion of useful knowledge.*

Bass would have desired no better recognition than this competent appraisement [assessment] of his work by one who, when he wrote these paragraphs, had himself experienced a full measure of the perils of the sea.

Was Bass at the time of his return aware that he had discovered a strait? It has been asserted that 'it is evident that Bass was not fully conscious of the great discovery he had made'.[11] Bass's language, upon which this surmise is founded, was as follows: 'Whenever it shall be decided that the opening between this and Van Diemen's Land is a strait, this rapidity of tide ... will be accounted for.' He also wrote: 'There is reason to believe it [i.e., Wilson's Promontory] is the boundary of a large strait.' I do not think these passages are to be taken to mean that Bass was at all doubtful about there being a strait. On the contrary, the words 'whenever it shall be decided' express his conviction that it would be so decided; but the diarist recognised that the existence of the strait had not yet been proved to demonstration. His reluctance to turn back when he reached Westernport was unquestionably due to the same cause. The voyage in the whaleboat had not proved the strait. It was still possible, though not at all probable, that the head of a deep gulf lay farther westward. The subsequent circumnavigation of Tasmania by Bass and Flinders proved the strait, as did also Grant's voyage through it from the west in the *Lady Nelson* in 1800.

Hunter had no more evidence than that afforded by Bass's discoveries when he wrote, in his despatch to the Secretary of State: 'He found an open ocean westward, and by the mountainous sea which rolled from that quarter, and no land discoverable in that direction, we have much reason to conclude that there is an open strait through.' Hunter's 'much reason to conclude' implies no more doubt about the strait than do the words of Bass, but the phrase does imply a recognition of the want of conclusive proof, creditable to the restrained judgment of both men. Flinders also wrote: 'There seemed to want no other proof of the existence of a passage than that of sailing positively through it,' which is precisely what he set himself to do in Bass's company, as soon as he could secure an opportunity. Still stronger testimony is that of Flinders,

[11] F. M. Bladen, *Historical Records of New South Wales*, III, p. 327, note.

when summing up his account of the discovery: 'The south-westerly swell which rolled in upon the shores of Westernport and its neighbourhood sufficiently indicated to the penetrating Bass that he was exposed to the southern Indian Ocean. This opinion, which he constantly asserted, was the principal cause of my services being offered to the Governor to ascertain the principal cause of it.' Further, although Colonel David Collins was not in Sydney at the time of the discovery, what he wrote in his *Account of the English Colony in New South Wales* (2nd edition, London, 1804), was based on first-hand information; and he was no less direct in his statement: 'There was every appearance of an extensive strait, or rather an open sea'; and he adds that Bass 'regretted that he had not been possessed of a better vessel, which would have enabled him to circumnavigate Van Diemen's Land' (pp. 443–4).

These passages, when compared with Bass's own careful language, leave no doubt that Bass was fully conscious of the great discovery he had made, though a complete demonstration was as yet lacking.[12]

An interesting light is thrown on the admiration felt for Bass among the colonists at Sydney, by François Péron, the historian of Baudin's voyage of exploration. When the French were at Port Jackson in 1802, the whaleboat was lying beached on the foreshore, and was preserved, says Peron, with a kind of 'religious respect'. Small souvenirs were made of its timbers; and a piece of the keel enclosed in a silver frame was presented by the Governor to Captain Baudin, as a memorial of the 'audacieuse navigation' [intrepid navigation]. Baudin's artist, in making a drawing of Sydney, was careful to show Bass's boat stayed up on the sand; and Péron, in his *Voyage de Découvertes aux Terres Australes* [Voyage of Discoveries to the Southern Lands], respectfully described the discovery of 'the celebrated Mr. Bass' as 'precious from a marine point of view'.

[12] The reasons given above appear also to justify me in saying that there is insufficient warrant [basis] for the statement of Sir J. K. Laughton (*Dictionary of National Biography* XLX, p. 326) that 'Bass's observations were so imperfect that it was not until they were plotted after his return that the importance of what he had done was at once apparent.'

VIII

THE VOYAGE OF THE FRANCIS

DURING the absence of Bass in the whaleboat, the repairing of the *Reliance* was finished, and in February 1798, Flinders was able to carry out a bit of exploration on his own account. The making of charts was employment for which he had equipped himself by study and practice, and he was glad to secure an opportunity of applying his abilities in a field where there was original work to do. The schooner *Francis* (a small vessel sent out in frame from England for the use of the colonial government, but now badly decayed) was about to be despatched to the Furneaux Islands—north-east of Van Diemen's Land, and about 480 miles from Sydney—to bring to Sydney what remained of the cargo of the wrecked *Sydney Cove*, and to rescue a few of the crew who had been left in charge. Flinders obtained permission from the Governor to embark in the schooner, 'in order to make such observations serviceable to geography and navigation as circumstances might afford', and instructions were given to the officer in command to forward this purpose as far as possible.

The circumstances of the wreck that occasioned the cruise of the *Francis* were these: The *Sydney Cove*, [under the command of] Captain Guy Hamilton, left Bengal on 10 November 1796, with a speculative cargo of merchandise for Sydney. Serious leakages became apparent on the voyage, but the ship made the coast of New Holland, rounded the southern extremity of Van Diemen's Land, and stood to [set a course to] the northward on 1 February 1797. She encountered furious gales which increased to a perfect hurricane, with a sea described in a contemporary account as 'dreadful'. The condition of the hull was so bad that the pumps could not keep the inrush of water under control, and the vessel became waterlogged. On 8 February she had five feet of water in the well, and by midnight the water was up to the lower deck hatches. She was at daybreak in imminent peril of going to the bottom, so the captain headed for Preservation Island (one of the Furneaux group), sent the longboat ashore with some rice, ammunition and firearms, and ran her in until she struck on a sandy bottom in nineteen feet of water. The whole ship's company was landed safely, tents were rigged up, and as much of the cargo as could be secured was taken ashore.

It was necessary to communicate with Sydney to procure assistance. The longboat was launched, and, under the direction of the first mate, Mr Hugh Thompson, sixteen of the crew started north on 28 February. But fresh misfortunes, as cruel as shipwreck and for most of these men more disastrous, were heaped upon them. They were smitten by a violent storm, terrific seas broke over the boat, and on the morning of 2 March she suddenly shipped enough water to swamp her. The crew with difficulty ran her through the surf that beat on the coast off which they had been struggling, and she went to pieces immediately. The seventeen were cast ashore on the coast of New South Wales, hundreds of miles from the only settlement, which could only be reached by the crossing of a wild, rough, and trackless country, inhabited by tribes of savages. They were without food, their clothing was drenched, and their sole means of defence consisted of a rusty musket, with very little ammunition, a couple of useless pistols, and two small swords.

The wretched band commenced their march along the coast northwards on 25 March. They had to improvise rafts to cross some rivers; once a party of kindly Aboriginals helped them over a stream in canoes; at another time they encountered blacks who hurled spears at them. They lived chiefly on small shellfish. Hunger and exposure brought their strength very low. On 16 April, after over a month of weary tramping, nine of the party dropped from fatigue and had to be left behind by their companions, whose only hope was to push on while sufficient energy lasted. Two days later, three of the remainder were wounded by blacks. At last, in May, three only of the seventeen who started on this heartbreaking struggle for life against distance, starvation and exhaustion, were rescued, 'scarcely alive', by a fishing boat, and taken to Sydney. The others perished by the way.

Captain Hamilton, who had stayed by his wrecked ship, was rescued in July 1797; and, as already stated, in January of the following year, Governor Hunter fitted out the schooner *Francis* to bring away a few Lascar [East Indian] sailors and as much of the remaining cargo as could be saved. 'I sent in the schooner,' wrote the Governor in a despatch, 'Lieutenant Flinders of the *Reliance*, a young man well-qualified, in order to give him an opportunity of making what observations he could among those islands.' The *Francis* sailed on 1 February.

The black shadow of the catastrophe that had overtaken the *Sydney Cove* crossed the path of the salvage party. The *Francis* was accompanied by the ten-ton sloop *Eliza*, [under the command of] Captain Armstrong. But shortly after reaching the Furneaux Islands the two vessels were separated in a storm, and the *Eliza* went down with all hands. Neither the boat nor any soul of her company were ever seen or heard of again.

Flinders had only twelve days available for his own work, from 16 February till the 28th, but he made full and valuable use of that time in exploring, observing and charting. The fruits of his researches were embodied in a drawing sent to the British Government by Hunter, when he announced the discovery of Bass Strait later on in 1798. The principal geographical result was the discovery of the Kent group of islands, which Flinders named 'in honour of my friend' the brave and accomplished sailor, William Kent, who commanded the *Supply*.

The biological notes made by Flinders on this expedition are of unusual interest. Upon the islands he found 'kanguroo' (his invariable spelling of the word), 'womat' (sic), the duck-billed platypus, aculeated ant-eater, geese, black swan, gannets, shags, gulls, red bills, crows, parrakeets, snakes, seals, and sooty petrels, a profusion of wildlife highly fascinating in itself, and, in the case of the animals, affording striking evidence of connection with the mainland at a comparatively recent period. The old male seals were described as of enormous size and extraordinary power.

> *I levelled my gun at one, which was sitting on the top of a rock with his nose extended up towards the sun, and struck him with three musket balls. He rolled over and plunged into the water, but in less than half an hour had taken his former station and attitude. On firing again, a stream of blood spouted forth from his breast to some yards distance, and he fell back senseless. On examination the six balls were found lodged in his breast; and one, which occasioned his death, had pierced the heart. His weight was equal to that of a common ox … The commotion excited by our presence in this assemblage of several thousand timid animals was very interesting to me, who knew little of their manners. The young cubs huddled together in the holes of the rocks and moaned piteously; those more advanced scampered and bowled down to the water with their mothers; whilst some of the old males stood up in defence of their families until the terror of the sailors' bludgeons became too strong to be resisted. Those who have seen a farmyard well stocked with*

pigs, with their mothers in it, and have heard them all in tumult together, may form a good idea of the confusion in connection with the seals at Cone Point. The sailors killed as many of these harmless and not unamiable creatures as they were able to skin during the time necessary for me to take the requisite angles; and we then left the poor affrighted multitude to recover from the effect of our inauspicious visit.

Flinders' observations upon the sooty petrels, or mutton-birds, seen at the Furneaux Islands, are valuable as forming a very early account of one of the most remarkable sea birds in the world:

The sooty petrel, better known to us under the name of sheerwater, frequents the tufted grassy parts of all the islands in astonishing numbers. It is known that these birds make burrows in the ground like rabbits; that they lay one or two enormous eggs in the holes and bring up their young there. In the evening they come in from the sea, having their stomachs filled with a gelatinous substance gathered from the waves, and this they eject into the throats of their offspring, or retain for their own nourishment, according to circumstances. A little after sunset the air at Preservation Island used to be darkened with their numbers, and it was generally an hour before their squabbling ceased and everyone had found its own retreat. The people of the Sydney Cove *had a strong example of perseverance in these birds. The tents were pitched close to a piece of ground full of their burrows, many of which were necessarily filled up from walking constantly over them; yet notwithstanding this interruption and the thousands of birds destroyed (for they constituted a great part of their food during more than six months), the returning flights continued to be as numerous as before; and there was scarcely a burrow less except in the places actually covered by the tents. These birds are about the size of a pigeon, and when skinned and smoked we thought them passable food. Any quantity could be procured by sending people on shore in the evening. The sole process was to thrust in the arm up to the shoulder and seize them briskly; but there was some danger of grasping a snake at the bottom of the burrow instead of a petrel.*

The remark that the egg of the sooty petrel is of enormous size is of course only true relatively to the size of the bird. The egg is about as large as a duck's egg, but longer and tapering more sharply at one end. For the rest the description is an excellent one. The wings of the bird are of great length and strength, giving to it wonderful speed and power of flight. The colour is coal-black. Flinders saw more of the sooty petrel on his subsequent voyage round Tasmania; and it will be convenient to quote here the passage in which he refers to the prodigious numbers in which the birds were seen. It may be added that, despite a century of slaughter by mankind, and after the taking of millions of eggs—which are good food—the numbers of the mutton-birds are still incalculably great.[1] Writing of what he saw off the extreme north-west of Tasmania in December 1798, Flinders said:

> *A large flock of gannets was observed at daylight to issue out of the great bight to the southward; and they were followed by such a number of sooty petrels as we had never seen equalled. There was a stream of from fifty to eighty yards in depth and of three hundred yards, or more, in breadth; the birds were not scattered, but flying as compactly as a free movement of their wings seemed to allow; and during a full hour and a half this stream of petrels continued to pass without interruption at a rate little inferior to the swiftness of a pigeon. On the lowest computation I think the number could not have been less than a hundred millions.*

He explained how he arrived at this estimate, the reliableness of which is beyond dispute, though it may seem incredible to those who have not been in southern seas during the season when the sooty petrels 'most do congregate'. Taking the stream of birds to have been 50 yards deep by 300 in width, and calculating that it moved at the rate of 30 miles[2] an hour, and allowing nine cubic yards for each bird, the number would amount to 151,500,000. The burrows required to lodge this number would be 75,750,000, and allowing a square yard to each burrow they would cover something more than 18½ geographical square miles.

The mutton-bird, it will therefore be allowed, is the most prolific of all avian colonists. It has also played some part in the history of human colonisation. When, in 1790, Governor Phillip sent to Norfolk Island a

---

[1] The author may refer to a paper of his own, 'The Mutton Birds of Bass Strait,' in the *Field*, 18 April 1903, for a study of the sooty petrel during the laying season on Phillip Island. An excellent account of the habits of the bird is given in Campbell's *Nests and Eggs of Australian Birds.*

[2] Flinders is calculating in nautical miles of 2026 2/3 yards each.

company of convicts and marines, and the *Sirius*, the only means of carrying supplies, was wrecked, the population, 506 in all, was reduced to dire distress from want of food. Starvation stared them in the face, when it was discovered that Mount Pitt was honeycombed with mutton-bird burrows. They were slain in thousands. 'The slaughter and mighty havoc is beyond description,' wrote an officer. 'They are very fine eating, exceeding fat and firm, and I think (though no connoisseur) as good as any I ever eat.' Many people who are not hunger-driven profess to relish young mutton-bird, whose flesh is like neither fish nor fowl, but an oily blend of both.

On this cruise Flinders came in sight of Cook's Point Hicks; and his reference to it has some interest because Bass had missed it; because Flinders himself did not on any of his other voyages sail close enough inshore on this part of the coast to observe it, and did not mark it upon his charts; and because the more recent substitution of the name Cape Everard for the name given by Cook, makes of some consequence the allusion of this great navigator to a projection which he saw only once. The *Francis* on 4 February 'was in 38° 16' and (by account) 22' of longitude to the west of Point Hicks. The schooner was kept more northward in the afternoon; at four o'clock a moderately high sloping hill was visible in the N. by W., and at seven a small rocky point on the beach bore N. 50° W. three or four leagues. At some distance inland there was a range of hills with wood upon them, though scarcely sufficient to hide their sandy surface.' That describes the country near Point Hicks accurately.

The largest island in the Furneaux group, now called Flinders Island, was not so named by Flinders. He referred to it as 'the great island of Furneaux'. Flinders never named any of his discoveries after himself, not even the smallest rock or cape. Flinders Island in the Bight (Investigator group) was named after his brother Samuel.

It is a little curious that no allusion to the useful piece of work done by Flinders on this cruise was made by the Governor in his despatches. The omission was not due to lack of appreciation on his part, as the encouragement subsequently given to Bass and Flinders sufficiently showed. But it was, in truth, work very well done, with restricted means and in a very limited time.

The question whether the islands examined lay in a strait or in a deep gulf was occupying the attention of Flinders at just about the same time when his friend Bass, in his whaleboat on the north side of the same stretch of water, was revolving [considering] the same problem in his mind. The reasons given by Furneaux for disbelieving in the existence of a strait did not satisfy Flinders. The great strength of the tides setting westward could, in his opinion, only be occasioned by a passage through to the Indian Ocean, unless the supposed gulf were very deep. There were arguments tending either way; 'the contradictory circumstances were very embarrassing'. Flinders would have liked to use the *Francis* forthwith to settle the question; but, as she was commissioned for a particular service, and not under his command, he had to subjugate his scientific curiosity to circumstances.

Throughout his brief narrative of this voyage we see displayed the qualities which distinguish all his original work. Promptness in taking advantage of opportunities for investigation, careful and cautiously checked observations, painstaking accuracy in making calculations, terse and dependable geographical description, and a fresh quick eye for noting natural phenomena: these were always characteristics of his work. He recorded what he saw of bird and animal with the same care as he noted nautical facts. We may take his paragraph on the wombat as an example. Bass was much interested in the wombats he saw, and with his surgeon's anatomical knowledge gave a description of it which the contemporary historian, Collins, quoted, enunciating the opinion that 'Bass's womb-bat seemed to be very œconomically made'—whatever that may mean. Flinders' description, which must be one of the earliest accounts of the creature, is true [accurate]:

> *Clarke's Island afforded the first specimen of the new animal, called wombat. This little bear-like quadruped is known in New South Wales, and is called by the natives womat, wombat, or womback, according to the different dialects—or perhaps to the different rendering of the wood-rangers who brought the information. It does not quit its retreat till dark; but it feeds at all times on the uninhabited islands, and was commonly seen foraging amongst the sea refuse on the shore, though the coarse grass seemed to be its usual nourishment. It is easily caught when at a distance from its burrow; its flesh resembles lean mutton in taste, and to us was acceptable food.*

The original manuscript containing Flinders' narrative of the expedition to the Furneaux Islands is in the Melbourne Public Library. It is a beautiful manuscript, 22 quarto pages, neat and regular, every letter perfect, every comma and semicolon in place: a portrait in calligraphy of its author.

IX

CIRCUMNAVIGATION OF TASMANIA

FLINDERS arrived in Sydney in the *Francis* about a fortnight after Bass returned in the whaleboat. It was, we may be certain, with delight that he heard from the lips of his friend the story of his adventurous voyage. The eye-sketch of the coastline traversed by Bass was, by the Governor's direction, used by him for the preparation of a chart to be sent to England. He was able to compare notes and discuss the probability of the existence of a strait, and it was but natural that the two men who had so recently been exploring, the one on the north, the other on the south side of the possible strait, should be eager to pursue enquiry to the point of proof. Flinders acknowledged, in relating these events, his anxiety to gratify his desire of positively sailing through the strait and round Van Diemen's Land, and he chafed under the routine duties which postponed the effort. The opportunity did not occur till September.

In the meantime, Flinders had to sail in the *Reliance* to Norfolk Island to take over the surgeon, D'Arcy Wentworth, father of that William Wentworth whose name has already figured in these pages, and who was then a boy of seven. This trip took place in May–July.

In August he sat as a member of the Vice-Admiralty Court of New South Wales to try a case of mutiny on the high seas. Certain members of the New South Wales Corps were accused of plotting to seize the convict ship *Barwell*, on her voyage between the Cape and Australia, and of drinking the toast 'damnation to the King and country'. The court considered the evidence insufficient, and the men were acquitted, after a trial lasting six days.

At last Flinders had an interview with the Governor about completing the exploration of the seas to the southward, and offered his services. Hunter, too, was anxious to have a test made of Bass's contention, which Flinders' own observations supported. On 3 September he wrote to the Secretary of State that he was endeavouring to fit out a vessel 'in which I propose to send the two officers I have mentioned', Bass and Flinders. Later in the month the Governor entrusted the latter with the command of the *Norfolk*, a sloop of 25 tons burthen [capable of carrying cargo of 25 tons], built at Norfolk Island from local pine. She was merely a small decked boat, put together under the direction of Captain Townson of Norfolk Island for establishing communication with Sydney. She leaked; her timbers were poor material for a seaboat in quarters where heavy weather was to be expected; and the accommodation she offered for a fairly extended cruise was cramped and uncomfortable. But she was the best craft the Governor had to offer, and Flinders was too keen for the quest to quarrel with the means. In those days fine seamanship and endurance often had to make up for deficiencies in equipment.

There were not two happier men in the King's service than these fast [firm] friends, when they received the Governor's commission directing them to sail 'beyond Furneaux' Islands, and, should a strait be found, to pass through it, and return by the south end of Van Diemen's Land'. The affection that existed between them is manifest in every reference which Flinders made to Bass in his book, *A Voyage to Terra Australis.* 'I had the happiness to associate my friend Bass in this new expedition,' he wrote of the *Norfolk*'s voyage; and it was a happiness based not only on personal regard, but on kindred feeling for research work [discovery], and a similarity in active, keen and ardent temperament.

The sloop was provisioned for twelve weeks, and 'the rest of the equipment was completed by the friendly care of Captain Waterhouse of the *Reliance*'. A crew of eight volunteers was chosen by Flinders from the King's ships in port. It is likely that some of them were amongst the six who had accompanied Bass to Westernport, and Flinders to the Furneaux and Kent Islands, but their names have not been preserved.

The *Norfolk* sailed on 7 October 1798, in company with a sealing boat, the *Nautilus.*[1] The plan was to make the Furneaux group, then steer westward through the strait till the open ocean was reached on the further side; and, that accomplished, and the fact of the strait's existence conclusively demonstrated, to turn down the western coast of Van Diemen's Land, round the southern extremity, and sail back to Port Jackson up the east coast. This programme was successfully carried out.

---

[1] There are three accounts of the voyage: (1) that of Flinders in diary form, printed in the *Historical Records of New South Wales*, Vol. III, appendix B; (2) that of Flinders in his *Voyage to Terra Australis*, Vol. I, p. cxxxviii ; and (3) that of Bass, embodied in Collins' *Account of New South Wales.* It is probable that Bass's diary was lent to Collins for the purpose of writing his narrative. The original is not known to exist.

An amusing incident, related by Flinders with dry humour, occurred in Twofold Bay, which was entered 'in order to make some profit of a foul wind', Bass undertaking an inland excursion, and Flinders occupying himself in making a survey of the port. An Aboriginal made his appearance.

> *He was of middle age, unarmed, except with a whaddie or wooden scimitar, and came up to us seemingly with careless confidence. We made much of him, and gave him some biscuit; and he in return presented us with a piece of gristly fat, probably of whale. This I tasted; but, watching an opportunity to spit it out when he should not be looking, I perceived him doing precisely the same thing with our biscuit, whose taste was probably no more agreeable to him, than his whale was to me.*

The native watched the commencement of Flinders' trigonometrical operations, 'with indifference, if not contempt', and after a little while left the party, 'apparently satisfied that from people who could thus occupy themselves seriously there was nothing to be apprehended'.

It was not until 1 November that the *Norfolk* sailed from the Furneaux Islands on the flood tide westward. The intervening time had been occupied with detailed exploring and surveying work. Soundings and observations were made, capes, islands and inlets were charted and named. The part of Flinders' narrative dealing with these phases abounds in detail, noted with the most painstaking particularity. Such fullness does not make attractive literature for the reader who takes up a book of travel for amusement. But it was highly important to record these details at the time of the publication of Flinders' book, when the coasts and seas of which he wrote were very little known; and it has to be remembered that he wrote as a scientific navigator, setting down the results of his work with completeness and precision for those interested in his subject, not as a caterer for popular literary entertainment. He preferred the interest in his writing to lie in the nature of the enterprise described and the sincerity with which it was pursued rather than in such anecdotal garniture [adornment] and such play of fancy as can give charm to the history of a voyage. His book was a substantial contribution to the world's knowledge, and it is his especial virtue to have set down his facts with such exactitude that our tests of them, where they are still capable of being tested, earn him credit for punctilious veracity in respect of those observations on wildlife and natural phenomena as to which we have to rely upon his written word. He never succumbs to the common sin of travellers: writing to excite astonishment in the reader, rather than to tell the exact truth as he found it. He was by nature and training an exact man.

On the afternoon of 3 November the sloop entered the estuary of the River Tamar, on which, 40 miles from the mouth, now stands the fine city of Launceston. It was a discovery of first-class importance. Apart from the pleasure which they derived from having made it, the two friends were charmed with the beauty of their surroundings. They derived the most favourable impression of the quality of the land and its suitableness for settlement. They worked up the river for several miles, but time did not permit them to follow it as far as it was navigable. Thus they did not reach the site of the present city, and left the superb gorge and cataract to be discovered by Collins when he entered the Tamar again in 1804. The harbour was subsequently named Port Dalrymple by Hunter, after Alexander Dalrymple, the naval hydrographer.

The extent of the survey, with delays caused by adverse weather, kept the *Norfolk* in the Tamar estuary for a full month. On 3 December her westward course was resumed. From this time forth Bass and Flinders were in constant expectancy of passing through the strait into the open ocean. The northern trend of the coast for a time aroused apprehensions that there was no strait after all, and that the northern shore of Van Diemen's Land might be connected with the coast beyond Westernport. The water was also discoloured, and this led Flinders to think that they might be approaching the head of a bay or gulf. But on 7 December the vigilant commander made an observation of the set of the tide, from which he drew an 'interesting deduction'. 'The tide had been running from the eastward all the afternoon,' wrote Flinders, 'and, contrary to expectation, we found it to be near low water by the shore; the flood therefore came from the west, and not from the eastward, as at Furneaux' Isles. This we considered to be a strong proof, not only of the real existence of a passage betwixt this land and New South Wales, but also that the entrance into the southern Indian Ocean could not be far distant.'

On the following day the deduction was confirmed. After the *Norfolk* had rounded a headland, a long swell was observed to come from the south-west, breaking heavily upon a reef a mile and a half away. This was a new phenomenon; and both Bass and Flinders 'hailed it with joy and mutual congratulation, as announcing the completion of our long-wished-for discovery of a passage into the southern Indian Ocean'. They were now through the strait. What Bass months before had believed to be the case was at length demonstrated to a certainty. 'The direction of the coast, the set of the tides, and the great swell from the S.W., did now completely satisfy us that a very wide strait did really exist betwixt Van Diemen's Land and New South Wales, and also now that we had certainly passed it.'

No time was lost in completing the voyage. The *Norfolk* sped rapidly past Cape Grim and down the western coast of Van Diemen's Land. Amateur-built as she was, and very small for her work in these seas, she was proving a useful boat, and one can enjoy the sailors' pride in a snug craft in Flinders' remark concerning her, that 'upon the whole she performed wonderfully; seas that were apparently determined to swallow her up she rode over with all the ease and majesty of an old experienced petrel'.

The wild and desolate aspect of the west coast, as seen from the ocean, seems to have struck Flinders with a feeling of dread. He so rarely allows any emotion to appear in his writing that the sentences in his diary wherein he refers to the appearance of the De Witt range are striking evidence of his revulsion. 'The mountains which presented themselves to our view in this situation, both close to the shore and inland, were amongst the most stupendous works of nature I ever beheld, and it seemed to me are the most dismal and barren that can be imagined. The eye ranges over these peaks, and curiously formed lumps of adamantine rock, with astonishment and horror.' He acknowledged that he clapped on all sail to get past this forbidding coast. The passage is singular [remarkable]. Flinders was a fenland-bred man, and, passing from the low levels of eastern England to a life at sea in early youth, had had no experience of mountainous country. He had not even seen the mountains at the back of Sydney, except in the blue distance. Now, the De Witt range, though certainly giving to the coast that it dominates an aspect of desolate grandeur, especially when, as is nearly always the case, its jagged peaks are seen under caps of frowning cloud, would not strike a man who had been much among mountains as especially horrid. Flinders' burst of chilled feeling may therefore be noted as a curious psychological fact.[2]

---

[2] The reader will perhaps find it interesting to compare this reference with a passage in Ruskin's *Modern Painters*, Vol. III, chapter 13: 'It is sufficiently notable that Homer, living in mountainous and rocky countries, dwells thus delightedly on all the flat bits; and so I think invariably the inhabitants of mountain countries do, but the inhabitants of the plains do not, in any similar way, dwell delightedly on mountains. The Dutch painters are perfectly contented with their flat fields and pollards: Rubens, though he had seen the Alps, usually composes his landscapes of a hay-field or two, plenty of pollards and willows, a distant spire, a Dutch house with a mast about it, a windmill and a ditch ... So Shakspere never speaks of mountains with the slightest joy, but only of lowland flowers, flat fields, and Warwickshire streams.' Ruskin's citation of the Lincolnshire farmer in *Alton Locke* is apt, with his dislike of 'Darned ups and downs o'hills, to shake a body's victuals out of his inwards'.

The naming of Mounts Heemskerk and Zeehan, the latter since become a mineral centre of vast wealth, were the most noteworthy events of the run down the western coast. They were named by Flinders after the two ships of Tasman, as he took them to be the two mountains seen by that navigator on his discovery of Van Diemen's Land in 1642.

The Derwent, whose estuary is the port of Hobart, was entered on 21 December. Bass's report on the fertility of the soil led to the choice of this locality for a settlement four years later.

On the last day of the year the return voyage was commenced, and on 1 January 1799, the *Norfolk* was making for Port Jackson with her prow set north-easterly. The winds were unfavourable, and prevented Flinders from keeping close inshore, as he would have liked to do in order to make a survey. But the prescribed period of absence having expired, and the provisions being nearly exhausted, it was necessary to make as much haste as possible. On 8 January the Babel Isles were marked down, and named 'because of the confusion of noises made by the geese, shags, penguins, gulls, and sooty petrels'. Anyone who has camped near a rookery of sooty petrels is aware that they are quite capable of maintaining a sufficiently 'babelish confusion'—the phrase is Camden's [presumably William Camden (1551–1623), the famous historian and antiquary]—without any aid from other fowls.

A little later in the month (12 January) the *Norfolk* sailed into harbour, and was anchored alongside the *Reliance.* 'To the strait which had been the great object of research,' wrote Flinders, 'and whose discovery was now completed, Governor Hunter gave at my recommendation the name of Bass Strait. This was no more than a just tribute to my worthy friend and companion for the extreme dangers and fatigues he had undergone in first entering it in the whaleboat, and to the correct judgment he had formed, from various indications, of the existence of a wide opening between Van Diemen's Land and New South Wales.'

Throughout this voyage we find Bass expending his abundant energies in the making of inland excursions whenever an opportunity occurred. To take a boat up rivers, to cut through rough country, to climb, examine soil, make notes on birds and beasts, and exercise his enquiring mind in all directions, was his constant delight.

The profusion of wildlife upon the coasts and islands explored during the voyage astonished the travellers. Seals were seen in thousands, sea birds in hundreds of millions. Flinders' calculation regarding the sooty petrels has already been quoted. Black swans were observed in great quantities. Bass, for example, stated that he saw 300 of these stately birds within a space a quarter of a mile square. The Roman poet Juvenal could think of no better example of a thing of rare occurrence than a black swan:

> *Rara avis in terris, nigroque simillima cygno.*
> [A rare bird on the earth and very like a black swan]

But here black swans could have been cited in a simile illustrating profusion. Bass quaintly stated that the 'dying song' of the swan, so celebrated by poets, 'exactly resembled the creaking of a rusty ale-house sign on a windy day'. The remark is not so pretty as, but far more true than, that of the bard who would have us believe that the dying swan

> *In music's strains breathes out her life and verse,*
> *And, chaunting her own dirge, rides on her watery hearse.*

The couplet of Coleridge is vitiated [rendered invalid] by the same error, but may merit commendation for practical wisdom:

> *Swans sing before they die; 'twere no bad thing*
> *Should certain persons die before they sing.*

Flinders also saw from three to five hundred black swans on the lee side of one point; and so tame were they that, as the *Norfolk* passed through the midst of them, one incautious bird was caught by the neck.

Bass went ashore on Albatross Island to shoot. He was forced to fight his way up the cliffs against the seals, which resented the intrusion; and when he got to the top he was compelled 'to make a road with his club among the albatross. These birds were sitting upon their nests, and almost covered the surface of the ground, nor did they otherwise derange [disturb] themselves for their new visitors than to peck at their legs as they passed by.'

In the Derwent Bass and Flinders encountered Tasmanian Aboriginals, now an [almost] extinct race of men. A human voice was heard coming from the hills. The two leaders of the expedition landed, taking with them a swan as an offering of friendship, and met an Aboriginal man and two women. The women ran off, but the man stayed and accepted the swan 'with rapture'. He was armed with three spears, but his demeanour was friendly. Bass and Flinders tried him with such words as they knew of the dialects of New South Wales and the South Sea Islands, but could not make him understand them, 'though the quickness with which he comprehended our signs spoke in favour of his intelligence'. His hair was either close-cropped or naturally short; but it had not a woolly appearance. 'He acceded to our proposition of going to his hut; but finding from his devious route and frequent stoppings that he sought to tire our patience, we left him delighted with the certain possession of his swan, and returned to the boat. This was the sole opportunity we had of communicating with any of the natives of Van Diemen's Land.'

The results of the cruise of the *Norfolk* were of great importance. From the purely utilitarian point of view, the discovery of Bass Strait shortened the voyage to Sydney from Europe by quite a week. It opened a new highway for commerce. Turnbull, in his *Voyage Round the World* (1814) discussing the advantages of the new route, mentioned that 'already has the whole fleet of China ships, under the convoy of a 64 [under the protection of a 64-gun ship], passed through these Straits without the smallest accident'; and he pointed out that ships which were late in the season for China, and availed themselves of the prevailing winds by taking the easterly route round Australia, were thus enabled to avoid the tempestuous weather which generally faced them to the south of Van Diemen's Land. Governor King, too, writing to the Governor of Bombay in 1802, sent him a chart of the strait, and pointed out that the discovery would 'greatly facilitate the passage of ships from India to this colony'.

The discovery also revealed a fresh and fertile field for the occupation of mankind. Geographically no discovery of such consequence had been made since the noble days of Cook. It brought the names of Bass and Flinders prominently before the scientific world, and the thoroughness with which the latter had done his work won him warm praise from men competent to form a judgment. Intimations concerning the discovery published in the *Naval Chronicle* and other journals valued the work very highly; and it had the advantage of bringing the commander of the *Norfolk* under the notice of Sir Joseph Banks, that earnest and steadfast supporter of all sincere research work, who thus became the firm friend of Flinders, as he had been the friend and associate of Cook 30 years before.

The turbulent state of Europe in and about 1799, with Napoleon Bonaparte rising fast to meridian glory [the peak of his success] on the wings of war, did not incline British statesmen to attach much significance to such events as the discovery of an important strait and the increased opportunities for the development of overseas dominions. Renewed activity in that direction came a little later. There is a letter from Banks to Hunter, written just after the return of the *Norfolk*, but before the news reached England (February 1799), wherein he conveys a concise idea of the perturbation in official circles and the difficulty of getting anything done for Australia. 'The political situation is so difficult,' said Banks, 'and His Majesty's Ministers so fully employed in business of the deepest importance, that it is scarce possible to gain a moment's audience on any subject but those which stand foremost in their minds; and colonies of all kinds, you may be assured, are now put into the background.'

But that was no more than a passing phase. The seeds of a vaster British Empire than had ever existed before had already germinated, and when the years of crisis occurred, the will and power of England were both ready and strong enough to protect the growing plant from the trampling feet of legions. Meanwhile, the work on the *Norfolk* secured for Flinders such useful encouragement and help as enabled him very little later to crown his achievements with a task that at once solidified his title to fame and ultimately ended his life.

X

THE FATE OF GEORGE BASS

IT has been already mentioned that Bass Strait was named by Governor Hunter on the recommendation of Flinders. There is no reason to suppose that George Bass himself made any claim that his name should be applied to his discovery. One derives the impression, from a study of his character as revealed in his words and acts, that he would have been perfectly content had some other name been chosen. He was one of those rare men who find their principal joy in the free exercise of an intrepid and masculine energy, especially in directions affording a stimulus to intellectual curiosity. He did not even write a book or an essay about the work he had done. The whaleboat voyage was tersely recorded in a diary for the information of the Governor; his other material was handed over to Collins for the purposes of his *History of New South Wales*, and Bass went about his business unrewarded, officially unhonoured.

It is curiously significant of the modesty of this really notable man that when, in 1801, he again sailed to Australia, he mentioned quite casually in a letter that he had passed through Bass Strait without any reference to his own connection with the passage. It was not, to him, 'the strait which I discovered', or 'my strait', or 'the strait named after me', but simply Bass Strait, giving it the proper geographical name scored on the map, just as he might have mentioned the name of any other part of the globe traversed during the voyage. The natural pride of the discoverer assuredly would have been no evidence of egotism; but Bass was singularly free from all semblance of human weakness of that kind. The difficulties battled with, the effort joyfully made, the discovery accomplished, he appears hardly to have thought any more about his own part in it. Not only his essential modesty but his affectionate nature and the frank charm of his manner are apparent in such of his letters as have been preserved.

The association of Bass with Flinders was fruitful in achievement, and their friendship was perfect in its manliness; it is pathetic to realise that when they parted, within a few weeks after the return of the *Norfolk* to Sydney, these two men, still young in years and rich in hope, ability and enterprise, were never to meet again.

As from this time Bass disappears from the story of his friend's life, what is known of his later years may be here related. His fate is a mystery that has never been satisfactorily cleared up, and perhaps never will be. He returned to England 'shortly after' the voyage of the *Norfolk.* So wrote Flinders; but 'shortly after' means later than April 1799, for in that month Bass sat on a board of inquiry into the Isaac Nichols case, to be mentioned again hereafter.

In England, Bass married Elizabeth Waterhouse, sister of his old shipmate Henry Waterhouse, the captain of the *Reliance.* With a wife to maintain, he was apparently dissatisfied with his pay and prospects as a naval surgeon. Nor was he quite the kind of man who would, in the full flush of his restless energy, settle down to the ordinary practice of his profession. Confined to a daily routine in some English town, he would have been like a caged albatross pining for regions of illimitable blue.

Within three months of his marriage Bass had become managing owner of a smart little 140-ton brig, the *Venus*, in a venture in which a syndicate of friends had invested £10,890. In the early part of 1801 he sailed in her with a general cargo of merchandise for Port Jackson. The brig, which carried twelve guns—for England was at war, and there were risks to be run—was a fast sailer, teak-built and copper-sheathed, and was described as 'one of the most complete, handsome and strong-built ships in the River Thames, and [which] will suit any trade'. She was loaded 'as deep as she can swim and as full as an egg', Bass wrote to his brother-in-law; and there is the sailor's jovial pleasure in a good ship, with, perhaps, a suggestion of the surgeon's point of view, in his declaration that she was 'very sound and tight, and bids fair to remain sound much longer than any of her owners'.

But the speculation was not an immediate success. The market was 'glutted with goods beyond all comparison', in addition to which Governor King, who succeeded Hunter in 1800, was conducting the affairs of the settlement upon a plan of the most rigid economy. 'Our wings are clipped with a vengeance, but we shall endeavour to fall on our feet somehow or other', wrote Bass early in October 1801.

A contract made with the Governor, to bring salt pork from Tahiti at sixpence per pound, provided profitable employment for the *Venus.* Hogs were plentiful in the Society Islands, and could be procured cheaply. The arrangement commended itself to the thrifty Governor, who had hitherto been paying a shilling per pound for pork, and it kept Bass actively engaged. He was 'tired of civilised life'. There was, too, money to be made, and he sent home satisfactory bills 'to stop a few holes in my debts'. 'That pork voyage,' he wrote to his brother-in-law, 'has been our first successful speculation'; and he spoke again in fond admiration of the *Venus*; 'she is just the same vessel as when we left England, never complains or cries, though we loaded her with pork most unmercifully'. While he was pursuing this trade, the French expedition under Baudin visited Sydney, and they, on their chart of Wilson's Promontory gave the name of Venus Bay to an inlet on the west side of Cape Liptrap. They also bought goods to the extent of £359 10s. from 'Mr. George Basse'.[1]

Bass now secured fishing concessions in New Zealand waters, from which he hoped much. 'The fishery is not to be put in motion till after my return to old England,' he wrote in January 1803. Then, he said playfully, 'I mean to seize upon my dear Bess, bring her out here, and make a *poissarde* [a woman given to coarse expressions] of her, where she cannot fail to find plenty of ease for her tongue. We have, I assure you, great plans in our heads, but, like the basket of eggs, all depends upon the success of the voyage I am now upon.' It was the voyage from which he never returned.

There is another charming allusion to his wife in a letter written from Tahiti: 'I would joke [tease] Bess upon the attractive charms of Tahiti females but that they have been so much belied [misrepresented] in their beauty that she might think me attracted in good earnest. However, there is nothing to fear here.' He speaks of her again in writing to his brother: 'I have written to my beloved wife, and do most sincerely lament that we are so far asunder. The next voyage I have she must make with me, for I shall badly pass it without her.' The pathos of his reference to her in a letter of October 1801, can be felt in its note of manly sympathy, and is deepened by the recollection that the young bride never saw him again. 'Our dear Bess talks of seeing me in eighteen months. Alas! poor Bess, the when is uncertain, very uncertain in everything except its long distances. Turn our eyes where we will, we see nothing but glutted markets around us.'

The pork-procuring ventures continued till 1803. In that year Bass arranged to sail beyond Tahiti to the Chilean coast, to buy other provisions for the use of the colony. Whether he intended to force the

[1] MS. accounts of Baudin, Archives Nationales, BB4. 999.

hand of fortune by engaging in the contraband trade can only be inferred. That there was certainly a large amount of illicit traffic with South America on the part of venturesome captains who made use of Port Jackson as a harbour of refuge, is clear from extant documents.

The position was this. The persistent policy of Spain in the government of her South American possessions was to conserve trade exclusively for Spanish ships and Spanish merchants; and for this purpose several restrictions were imposed upon unauthorised foreign traders. Nevertheless the inhabitants of these colonies urgently required more goods than were imported under such excessive limitations, and wanted to get them much cheaper than was possible while monopoly and heavy taxation prevailed. There was, consequently, a tempting inducement to skippers who were sufficiently bold to take risks, to ship goods for Chile and Peru, and run them in at some place along the immense coastline, evading the lazy eyes of perfunctory Spanish officials, or securing their corrupt connivance by bribes. Contraband trade was, in fact, extensively practised, and plenty of people in the Spanish colonies throve [prospered] on it. As a modern historian writes: 'The vast extent of the border of Spain's possessions made it impossible for her to guard it efficiently. Smuggling could therefore be carried on with impunity, and the high prices which had been given to European wares in America by the system of restriction, constituted a sufficient inducement to lead the merchants of other nations to engage in contraband trade.'[2] The profits from success were great; but the consequences of detection were disastrous.

Now Bass, as already related, had brought out to Sydney in the *Venus* a large quantity of unsaleable merchandise. He could not dispose of it under conditions of glut. He had hoped that the Governor would take the cargo into the Government store and let it be sold even at a 50 per cent reduction. But King declined to permit that to be done. Here, then, was a singularly courageous man, fond of daring enterprises, in command of a good ship, with an unsaleable cargo on his hands. On the other side of the Pacific was a country where such a cargo might, with luck, be sold at a bounding profit. He could easily find out how the trade was done. There was more than one among those with whom he would associate in Sydney who knew a great deal about it.

One or two sentences in Bass's last letters to Henry Waterhouse contain mysterious hints, which to him, with his experience of Port Jackson, would be significant. He explained that he intended taking the

[2] Bernard Moses, *Spanish Rule in America*, p. 289.

Venus to visit the coast of Chile in search of provisions, 'and that they may not in that part of the world mistake me for a contrabandist, I go provided with a very diplomatic-looking certificate from the Governor here, stating the service upon which I am employed, requesting aid and protection in obtaining the food wanted. And God grant you may fully succeed, says your warm heart, in so benevolent an object; and thus also say I; Amen, say many others of my friends.'

But was the diplomatic-looking paper intended rather to serve as a screen than as a guarantee of *bona fides*? 'In a few hours,' wrote Bass at the beginning of February 1803, 'I sail again on another pork voyage, but it combines circumstances of a different nature also'; and at the end of the same letter he added 'Speak not of South America to anyone out of your family, for there is treason in the very name.' What did he mean by that? He spoke of 'digging gold in South America', and clearly did not mean it in the strict literal sense.

It is true that the Governor was anxious to get South American cattle and beef for the settlement in Sydney, but can that have been the only motive for a voyage beyond Tahiti? 'If our approaching voyage proves at all fortunate in its issue, I expect to make a handsome thing out of it, and to be much expedited on my return to old England,' Bass wrote in January. He would not have been likely to make so very handsome a thing out of beef in one voyage, to enable him to expedite his return to England.

The factors of the case are, then, that Bass had on his hands a large quantity of goods which he had failed to sell in Sydney; that there was a considerable and enormously profitable contraband trade with South America at the time; that he expected to make a very large and rapid profit out of the venture he was about to undertake; that he warned Waterhouse against mentioning the matter outside the family circle, 'for there is treason in the very name'; and that he was himself a man distinguished by dash and daring, who was very anxious to make a substantial sum and return to England soon. The inference from his language and circumstances as to the scheme he had in hand is irresistible.

The 'very diplomatic-looking certificate' which the Governor gave him was dated 3 February 1803. It certified that 'Mr. George Bass, of the brigantine *Venus*, has been employed since the first day of November 1801, upon His Britannic Majesty's service in procuring provisions for the subsistence of His Majesty's colony, and still continues using those exertions'; and it went on to affirm that should he find it expedient to resort to any harbour in His Catholic Majesty's dominions upon the west coast of America, 'this instrument is intended to declare my full belief that his sole object in going there will be to procure food, without any view to private commerce or any other view whatsoever'.

Notwithstanding the terms of this certificate, however, there is clear evidence that Governor King was fully aware of the nature of the trade conducted with the Spanish-American colonies by vessels using Port Jackson; and though it may be that Bass did not tell him in so many words what his whole intentions were, King knew that Bass had a large stock of commodities to sell, and could hardly have been ignorant that a considerable portion of them were reshipped on the *Venus* for this voyage. In a later despatch he alluded to vessels which carried goods 'from hence to the coasts of the Spanish possessions on the west side of America', and he observed 'that this must be a forced trade, similar to that carried on among the settlements of that nation and Portugal on the east side of America, and that much risk will attend it to the adventurers'.

Bass sailed from Sydney on 5 February 1803. He never returned, and no satisfactory account of what became of him is forthcoming.[3] Later in 1803 the brig *Harrington*, herself concerned in the contraband trade, reported that the *Venus* had been captured and confiscated by the Spaniards in Peru, and that Bass and the mate, Scott, had been sent as prisoners to the silver mines. In December 1804, Governor King remarked in a despatch to the Secretary of State that he had been 'in constant expectation' of hearing from Bass, 'to whom, there is no doubt, some accident has occurred'. The *Harrington* had reported the capture of the *Venus* before King wrote that. Why did he not mention the circumstance to the British Government? Why did he not allude to the country to which he well knew that Bass intended to sail? It would seem that King carefully avoided referring in his official despatches to an enterprise upon which he had good reason to be aware that Bass had embarked.

War between Great Britain and Spain did not break out till December 1804, after the seizure of the Spanish treasure fleet by British frigates off Cadiz (5 October). But in previous years, while Spain, under pressure from Napoleon, lent her countenance to his aggressive policy, English privateers had freely plundered Spanish commerce in the south Pacific, and some of

---

[3] The writer of the article on Bass in the *Dictionary of National Biography* says that 'except that he left Australia in 1799 to return to England nothing certain is known of Bass's subsequent history'. But we know fairly fully what he was doing up till February 1803, as related above. The Bass mystery commences after that date. The *Encyclopaedia Britannica* (11th edition) finds no space for a separate article on this very remarkable man.

them had brought their prizes to Sydney. That this was done with the knowledge of the authorities cannot be doubted. Everybody knew about it. When the French exploring ships were lying at Sydney in 1802, Péron saw there vessels 'provided with arms, fitting out for the western coast of America, stored with merchandise of various kinds. These vessels were intended to establish, by force of arms, a contraband commerce with the inhabitants of Peru, extremely advantageous to both parties.'

It would not, therefore, be wonderful [surprising] that the Spanish authorities in Chile or Peru should regard Port Jackson as a kind of wasp's nest, and should look with suspicion on any vessel coming thence which might fall into their hands, however much her commander might endeavour to make of his official certificate declaring the Governor's 'full belief' in his lawful intentions. The irritation caused by the use that was being made of Sydney as a privateering and contraband base of operations can be well imagined. As early as December 1799, indeed, Governor Hunter related that a captured Spanish merchant vessel had been brought into port, and he acknowledged that 'this being the second Spanish prize brought hither, we cannot be surprised, should it be known that such captures make a convenience of this harbour, if it should provoke a visit from some of the ships of war from the Spanish settlements on that coast'. The Spaniards would naturally be thirsting for revenge; and a ship sailing direct from the port of which the raiders made a 'convenience' would be liable to feel their ire, should there be the semblance of provocation. The authorities would have been justified in holding up the *Venus* if they suspected that she carried contraband goods; and their treatment of her officers and crew might be expected to reflect the temper of their disposition towards Port Jackson and all that concerned it.

If, as the *Harrington* reported, Bass and his companions were sent to the mines, the Spanish officials managed their act of punishment, or revenge, very quietly. But at that time there was not a formal state of belligerency between England and Spain, though the tension of public feeling in Great Britain concerning Spanish relations with France was acute. If it were considered that such an act as the seizure of the *Venus* would be likely to precipitate a declaration of war, the motive for secrecy was strong. Secrecy, moreover, would have been in complete conformity with Spanish methods in South America. It is not recorded whether the seizure of the *Venus* occurred at Callao, Valparaiso or Valdivia; but a British lieutenant, Fitzmaurice, who was at Valparaiso five years later, heard that a man named Bass had been in Lima some years before.

A friend of the Bass family residing at Lincoln in 1852 wrote a letter to Samuel Sidney, the author of *The Three Colonies of Australia*, stating that Bass's mother last heard of him 'in the Straits of China'. But this was evidently an error of memory. If Bass ever got out of South America, he would have written to his 'dear Bess', to Waterhouse, and to Flinders. The latter, in 1814, wrote of him as 'alas, now no more'. There is on record a report that he was seen alive in South America in that year, but the story is doubtful. He was a man full of affectionate loyalty to his friends, and it is not conceivable that he would have left them without news of him if any channel of communication had been open, as would have been the case had he been at liberty as late as 1814. His father-in-law made enquiries, but failed to obtain news. The report of the *Harrington* was probably true, but beyond that we really have no information upon which we can depend. The internal history of Spanish America has been very scantily investigated, and it is quite possible that even yet some diligent student of archives may find, some day, particulars concerning the fate of this brave and adventurous spirit.

The disappearance of Bass's letters to his mother is a misfortune which the student of Australian history must deplore. He was observant, shrewd, an untiring traveller, and an entertaining correspondent. He probably related to his mother, to whom he wrote frequently, the story of his excursions and experiences, and the historical value of all that he wrote would be very great. The letters, said the Lincoln friend, were long, 'containing full accounts of his discoveries'. His mother treasured them till she died, when they came into the possession of a Miss Calder. She kept them in a box, and used occasionally to amuse herself by reading them. But some time before 1852 Miss Calder went to the box to look at them again, and found that they had disappeared. Whether she had lent them to some person who had failed to return them, or had mislaid them, is unknown. It is possible that they may still be in existence in some dusty cupboard in England, and that we may even yet be gratified by an examination of documents which would assuredly enable us to understand more of the noble soul of George Bass.

It has been mentioned that Flinders and Bass did not meet again after the voyage of the *Norfolk* and Bass's return to England. Though Sydney was the base of both Flinders in the *Investigator* and Bass in the *Venus* in 1802–03, they always had the ill-luck to miss each other. Bass was at Tahiti while Flinders lay in port from 9 May to 21 July 1802. He returned in November, and left once more on his final voyage in February 1803. Flinders arrived in Sydney again, after his exploration of the Gulf of Carpentaria, in June 1803. A farewell letter from him to his friend is quoted in a later chapter.

XI

ON THE QUEENSLAND COAST

Two more incidents in the career of Flinders will concern us before we deal with his important later voyages. The first of these is only worth mentioning for the light it throws upon the character of the man. In March 1799, he sat as a member of a court of criminal judicature in Sydney, for the trial of Isaac Nichols, who was charged with receiving a basket of tobacco knowing it to have been stolen. The case aroused passionate interest at the time. People in the settlement took sides upon it, as upon a matter of acute party politics, and the Governor was hotly at variance with the Judge Advocate, the chief judicial officer.

Nichols had been a convict, but his conduct was good, and he was chosen to be chief overseer of a gang employed in labour of various kinds. On the expiration of his sentence, he acquired a small farm, and by means of sobriety and industry built himself a comfortable house. Through his very prosperity he became 'an object to be noticed', as the Governor wrote, and by reason of his diligent usefulness securing him official employment, 'he stood in the way of others'. In Hunter's opinion, the ruin of Nichols was deliberately planned; and he was convicted on what the Governor believed to be false and malicious evidence.

The striking feature of the trial was that the court (consisting of seven members—three naval officers and three officers of the New South Wales Corps, presided over by the Judge Advocate) was sharply divided in opinion. The three naval men, Flinders, Waterhouse, and Lieutenant Kent, were convinced of the accused man's innocence; the three military men, with the Judge Advocate, voted for his conviction. There was thus a majority against Nichols; but the Governor, believing that an injustice was being done, suspended the execution of the sentence, and submitted the papers to the Secretary of State. Bass came into the matter in the month after the trial, as a member of a Court of Inquiry into the allegation that certain persons had carried the tobacco to Nichols's house with the object of implicating him.

The only point that need concern us here, is that Flinders wrote a memorandum analysing the evidence with minute care, in justification of his belief in the prisoner's innocence. It was a skilfully drawn document, and it exhibits Flinders in a light which enhances our respect for him, as the strong champion of an accused man whom he believed to be wronged. In the result, the Crown granted a pardon to Nichols; but this did not arrive till 1802, so tardy was justice in getting itself done. Apart from Flinders' share in it, the case is interesting as revealing the strained relations existing between the principal officials in the colony at the time. The Judge Advocate was a bitter enemy of the Governor, and the very administration of the law, affecting the liberties of the people, was tinctured [coloured] by these animosities.

It is pleasant to turn from so grimy a subject to the work for which Flinders' tastes and talents peculiarly fitted him. The explorations which he had hitherto accomplished were sufficient to convince Hunter that he had under him an officer from whom good work could be expected, and, the *Reliance* not being required for service, he readily acquiesced when Flinders proposed that he should take the *Norfolk* northward, to Moreton Bay, the 'Glasshouse Bay' of Cook, and Hervey Bay, east of Bundaberg. On this voyage he was accompanied by his younger brother, Samuel Flinders. He also took with him an Aboriginal named Bongaree, 'whose good disposition and manly conduct had attracted [his] esteem'.

He sailed on 8 July. The task did not occupy much time, for the sloop was back in Sydney by 20 August. The results were disappointing. It had been hoped to find large rivers, and by means of them to penetrate the interior of the country; but none were found.

Flinders missed the Clarence, though he actually anchored off its entrance. Nor did he find the Brisbane, though, ascending the Glasshouse Mountains, he saw indications of a river, which he could not enter with the *Norfolk* on account of the intricacy of the channel and the shortness of the time available.

Uneasiness of mind respecting the condition of the sloop must have had much to do with the missing of the rivers. She sprung a leak two days out of Port Jackson, and this was 'a serious cause of alarm', the more so as grains of maize, with which the *Norfolk* had been previously loaded, were constantly choking up the pump. Weather conditions, also, did not favour taking the vessel close inshore on her northward course, and it would have been almost impossible to detect the mouths of the

New South Wales rivers without a close scrutiny of the coastline. Those considerations are quite sufficient, when duly weighed, to account for the omissions. It certainly was a rash statement, after so imperfect an examination, that 'however mortifying the conviction might be, it was then an ascertained fact that no river of importance intersected the east coast between the 24th and 39th degrees of south latitude'. But it is equally certain that he could not have found these rivers with the means at his disposal. They could not well have been observed from the deck of a vessel off the coast.[1] A closer inspection of the shoreline was required. In fact, the rivers were not found by seaward exploration; they were discovered by inland travellers.

The most interesting features of the voyage lay in the meeting with Aboriginals in Moreton Bay. Some of the incidents were amusing, though at one time there seemed to be danger of a serious encounter. Flinders went ashore to meet a party of the natives, and endeavoured to establish friendly relations with them. But as he was leaving, one of them threw a spear. Flinders snatched up his gun and aimed at the offender, but the flint being wet missed fire [misfired]. A second snap of the trigger also failed, but on a third trial the gun went off, though nobody was hurt. Flinders thought that it might obviate future mischief if he gave the blacks an idea of his power, so he fired at a man who was hiding behind a tree; but without doing him any harm. The sound of the gun caused the greatest consternation among the natives, and the small party of white men had no more serious trouble with them while they were in the bay. Flinders was 'satisfied of the great influence which the use of a superior power has in savages to create respect and render their communications friendly'; but he was fortunately able to keep on good terms without resort to severity.

An effort to tickle the Aboriginal sense of humour was a failure. Two of the crew who were Scotch, commenced to dance a reel for the amusement of the blacks. 'For want of music,' it is related, 'they made a very bad performance, which was contemplated by the natives without much amusement or curiosity.' The joke, like Flinders' gun, missed fire [misfired]. There have been, it is often alleged, other occasions when jokes made by Scotsmen have not achieved a shining success; and we do well to respect the intention while we deplore the waste of effort.

An example of cunning which did not succeed occurred shortly after the first landing. Flinders was wearing a cabbage-tree hat, for which a

[1] See Coote, *History of Queensland*, I, p. 7, and Lang, *Cooksland*, p. 17.

native had a fancy. The fellow took a long stick with a hook at the end of it, and, laughing and talking to divert attention from his purpose, endeavoured to take the hat from the commander's head. His detection created much laughter; as did that of another black with long arms, who tried to creep up to snatch the hat, but was afraid to approach too near. The account which Collins, writing from Flinders' notes, gave of the Queensland natives seen at Moreton Bay is graphic but hardly attractive. Two paragraphs about their musical attainments and their general appearance will bear quotation:

> *These people, like the natives of Port Jackson, having fallen to the low pitch of their voices, recommenced their song at the octave, which was accompanied by slow and not ungraceful motions of the body and limbs, their hands being held up in a supplicating posture; and the tone and manner of their song and gestures seemed to bespeak the goodwill and forbearance of their auditors. Observing that they were attentively listened to, they each selected one of our people and placed his mouth close to his ear, as if to produce a greater effect, or, it might be, to teach them the song, which their silent attention might seem to express a desire to learn.*

As a recompense for the amusement they had afforded him Flinders gave them some worsted caps, and a pair of blanket trousers, with which they seemed well pleased. Several other natives now made their appearance; and it was some time before they could overcome their dread of approaching the strangers with the firearms; but, encouraged by the three who were with them, they came up, and a general song and dance was commenced. Their singing was not confined to one air; they gave three.

> *Of those who came last, three were remarkable for the largeness of their heads, and one, whose face was very rough, had much more the appearance of a baboon than of a human being. He was covered with oily soot; his hair matted with filth; his visage, even among his fellows, uncommonly ferocious; and his very large mouth, beset with teeth of every hue between black, white, green and yellow, sometimes presented a smile which might make anyone shudder.*

The *Norfolk* remained fifteen days in Moreton Bay. The judgment that Flinders formed of it was that it was 'so full of shoals that he could not attempt to point out any passage that would lead a ship into it without danger'. The east side was not sounded, and he was of opinion that if a good navigable channel existed it would be found there. His visit to Hervey Bay, further north, did not lead to any interesting observations. He left there on his return voyage on 7 August, and reached Port Jackson at dusk on the 20th.

XII

THE INVESTIGATOR

FLINDERS sailed from Port Jackson for England in the *Reliance* on 3 March 1800. The old ship was in such a bad condition that Governor Hunter 'judged it proper to order her home while she may be capable of performing the voyage'. She carried despatches, which Captain Waterhouse was directed to throw overboard in the event of meeting with an enemy's ship of superior force and being unable to effect his escape. She lived through a tempestuous voyage, making nine or ten inches of water per hour, according to the carpenter's report, and providing plenty of pumping exercise for a couple of convict stowaways who emerged from hiding two days out of Sydney. At St Helena, reached at the end of May, company was joined with four East India ships, and off Ireland HMS *Cerberus* took charge of the convoy till the arrival at Portsmouth on 26 August.

When Flinders left England six years before, he was a midshipman. He passed the examination qualifying him to become lieutenant at the Cape of Good Hope in 1797, and was appointed provisionally to that rank on the return of the *Reliance* to Sydney from the South African voyage in that year. The prompt confirmation of his promotion by the Admiralty he attributed to the kind interest of Admiral Pasley.

When he quitted his ship at Deptford in October 1800, he was a man of mark [a man of some importance]. His name was honourably known to the elders of his profession, whilst he was esteemed by men concerned with geography, navigation, and kindred branches of study, for the importance of the work he had done, and for the thorough scientific spirit manifested in it.

Chief among those who recognised his quality was Sir Joseph Banks, the learned and wealthy squire who was ever ready to be to zealous men of science a friend, a patron, and an influence. Banks was, indeed, memorable for the men and work he helped, rather than for his own original contributions to knowledge. During his presidency of the Royal Society, from 1777 to 1820—a long time for one man to occupy the principal place in the most distinguished learned body in the world—he not only encouraged, but promoted and directed, a remarkable radiation [growth in a wide variety] of research work, and was the accessible friend of every man of ability concerned in extending the bounds of enquiry into phenomena.

Banks took a special interest in the young navigator, who was a native of his own bit of England, Lincolnshire. He knew well what a large field for geographical investigation there was in Australia, and recognised that Flinders was the right man to do the work. Banks had always foreseen the immense possibilities of the country; he was the means of sending out the naturalists George Caley, Robert Brown, and Allan Cunningham, to study its natural products. That he was quick to recognise the sterling capacity of Matthew Flinders constitutes his principal claim to our immediate attention. The spirit of our age is rather out of sympathy with the attitude of patronage, which, as must be confessed, it gratified Banks to assume; but at all events it was, in this instance, patronage of the only tolerable sort, that which helps an able man to fulfil himself and serve his kind.

Before he went to sea again, Flinders was married (April 1801) to Miss Ann Chappell, stepdaughter of the Rev William Tyler, rector of Brothertoft, near Boston. She was a sailor's daughter, her own father having died while in command of a ship out of Hull, engaged in the Baltic trade. It is probable that there was an attachment between the pair before Flinders left England in 1794; for during the *Norfolk* expedition in 1798 he had named a smooth round hill in Kent's group Mount Chappell, and had called a small cluster of islands the Chappell Isles. He does not tell us why they were so named, as was his usual practice. He merely speaks of them as 'this small group to which the name of Chappell Isles is affixed in the chart'. But a tender little touch of sentiment may creep in, even in the making of charts; and we cannot have or wish to have any doubt as to the reason in this case.

In his *Observations*, published in the year of his marriage, Flinders remarks (p. 24) that the hill 'had received the name of Mount Chappell in February, 1798, and the name is since extended to the isles which lie in its immediate neighbourhood'. The fact that the name was given in 1798, indicates that a kindly feeling, to say the least of it, was entertained for Miss Chappell before Flinders left England in 1795. The lover in *As You Like It* carved his lady's name on trees:

O Rosalind, these trees shall be my books,
And in their barks my thoughts I'll character.

Here we find our young navigator writing his lady's name on the map. It is rather an uncommon symptom of a very common complaint.

Miss Chappell and her sister, the sisters of Flinders, and the young ladies of the Franklin family, were a group of affectionate friends who lived in the same neighbourhood, and were constantly together. The boys of the families were brothers to all the girls, who were all sisters to them. Matthew on the *Reliance* wrote to them letters intended to be read by all, addressing them as 'my charming sisters'. In one of these epistles he told the girls: 'never will there be a more happy soul than when I return. O, may the Almighty spare me all those dear friends without whom my joy would be turned into sorrow and mourning.' But that he nourished the recollection of Ann Chappell in his heart with especial warmth is apparent from a letter he wrote to her very shortly after the *Reliance* returned to England (25 September 1800):[1]

> *You are one of those friends whom I consider it indispensably necessary to see. I should be glad to have some little account of your movements, where you reside, and with whom, that my motions may be regulated accordingly.... You see that I make everything subservient to business. Indeed, my dearest friend, this time seems to be a very critical period of my life. I have long been absent—have done services abroad that were not expected, but which seem to be thought a good deal of. I have more and greater friends than before, and this seems to be the moment that their exertions may be most serviceable to me. I may now perhaps make a bold dash forward, or may remain a poor lieutenant all my life.*

And he ended this letter, which Miss Chappell would not fail to read 'between the lines', by assuring 'my dear friend Annette', that 'with the greatest sincerity, I am her most affectionate friend and brother, Matthew Flinders'.

From this point the comforting understanding between the two young people developed in ways as to which there is no evidence in correspondence; but shortly after Flinders received promotion he must have proposed marriage. He wrote a short time afterwards in these terms:

---

[1] Flinders' Papers.

H.M.S. Investigator, *at the Nore,*

My dearest friend, *April 6, 1801.*

Thou hast asked me if there is a possibility *of our living together. I think I see a* probability *of living with a moderate share of comfort. Till now I was not certain of being able to fit myself out clear of the world. I have now done it, and have accommodation on board the* Investigator, *in which as my wife a woman may, with love to assist her, make herself happy. This prospect has recalled all the tenderness which I have so sedulously endeavoured to banish. I am sent for to London, where I shall be from the 9th to the 19th, or perhaps longer. If thou wilt meet me there, this hand shall be thine for ever. If thou hast sufficient love and courage, say to Mr. and Mrs. Tyler*[2] *that I require nothing more with thee than a sufficient stock of clothes and a small sum to answer the increased expenses that will necessarily and immediately come upon me; as well for living on board as providing for it at Port Jackson; for whilst I am employed in the most dangerous part of my duty, thou shalt be placed under some friendly roof there. I need not, nor at this time have I time to enter into a detail of my income and prospects. It will, I trust, be sufficient for me to say that I see a fortune growing under me to meet increasing expenses. I only want a fair start, and my life for it, we will do well and be happy. I will write further to-morrow, but shall most anxiously expect thy answer at 86 Fleet Street, London, on my visit on Friday; and, I trust, thy presence immediately afterwards. I have only time to add that most anxiously I am, Most sincerely thine,*

MATTHEW FLINDERS.

He appended a postscript which covertly alludes to the manner in which Sir Joseph Banks might be expected to regard the marriage on the eve of commencing the new voyage: 'It will be much better to keep this matter entirely secret. There are many reasons for it yet, and I have also a powerful one: I do not know how my great friends might like it.'

But, taking all the risks in this direction, he snatched the first opportunity that presented itself to hurry down to Lincolnshire, get married, and bring his bride up to London, stuffing into his boot, for safe keeping, a roll of banknotes given to him by Mr Tyler at the moment of farewell.

[2] Her mother and stepfather.

In a letter[3] to his cousin Henrietta, he relates how hurriedly the knot matrimonial was at length tied, on 17 April:

> *Everything was agreed to in a very handsome manner, and just at this time I was called up to town and found that I might be spared a few days from thence. I set off on Wednesday evening from town, arrived next evening at Spilsby, was married next morning,[4] which was Friday; on Saturday we went to Donington, on Sunday reached Huntingdon, and on Monday were in town. Next morning I presented myself before Sir Joseph Banks with a grave face as if nothing had happened, and then went on with my business as usual. We stayed in town till the following Sunday, and came on board the* Investigator *next day, and here we have remained ever since, a few weeks on shore and a day spent on the Essex side of the Thames excepted.*

In a letter[5] written to Elizabeth Flinders on the day of the marriage the bride's fluttered [agitated] and mixed emotions were apparent. At this time she believed that she was to make the voyage to Australia in the *Investigator* with her husband, and hardly knew whether the happiness of her new condition or the regretful prospect of a long farewell to her circle of friends prevailed most in her heart.

> *April 17th, 1801.*
>
> *My beloved Betsy,*
>
> *Thou wilt be much surprised to hear of this sudden affair; indeed I scarce believe it myself, tho' I have this very morning given my hand at the altar to him I have ever highly esteemed, and it affords me no small pleasure that I am now a part, tho' a distant one, of thy family, my Betsy. It grieves me much thou art*

---

[3] Flinders' Papers.

[4] Captain F. J. Bayldon, of the Nautical Academy, Sydney, tells me an interesting story about the Flinders–Chappell marriage registration. His father was rector of Partney, Lincolnshire, a village lying two or three miles from Spilsby. When the Captain and his brothers were boys, they found in the rectory a large book, such as was used for parish registers. It was apparently unused. They asked their father if they might have the blank pages for drawing paper, and he gave them permission. But they found upon a single page, a few marriage entries, and one of these was the marriage of Matthew Flinders to Ann Chappell. Captain Bayldon, a student of navigation then as he has been ever since, knew Flinders' name at once, and took the book to his father. The marriage was celebrated at Partney, where the Tylers lived.

[5] Mitchell Library MSS.

so distant from me. Thy society would have greatly cheered me. Thou wilt to-day pardon me if I say but little. I am scarce able to coin one sentence or to write intelligibly. It pains me to agony when I indulge the thought for a moment that I must leave all I value on earth, save one, alas, perhaps for ever. Ah, my Betsy, but I dare not, must not, think [that]. Therefore, farewell, farewell. May the great God of Heaven preserve thee and those thou lovest, oh, everlastingly. Adieu, dear darling girl; love as ever, though absent and far removed from your poor

ANNETTE.

We are afforded a confidential insight into Mrs Flinders' opinion of her husband in a letter from her to another girl friend. It was written after the marriage, and when Matthew was again at sea, prosecuting that voyage from which he was not to return for over nine years. 'I don't admire want of firmness in a man. I love *courage* and *determination* in the male character. Forgive me, dear Fanny, but *insipids* I never did like, and having not long ago tasted such delightful society I have now a greater contempt than in former days for that cast of character.' An 'insipid' Ann Chappell certainly had not married, and she found in Matthew Flinders no lack of the courage and determination she admired.

A second marriage contracted by the elder Matthew Flinders, connecting his family with the Franklins, had an important influence upon the life of another young sailor who had commenced his career in the navy in the previous year. The Franklin family, which sprang from the village of Sibsey (about six miles north-east of Boston), was now resident at Spilsby. At the time of the Flinders–Chappell wedding, young John Franklin was serving on the *Polyphemus*, and had only a few days previously (1 April) taken part in the battle of Copenhagen. In the ordinary course of things he would, there can hardly be a doubt, have followed his profession along normal lines. His virile [vigorous, manly] intellect and resourceful courage would probably have won him eminence, but it is not likely that he would have entered upon that career of exploration which shed so much lustre on his name, and in the end found him a grave beneath the immemorial snows of the frozen north. It was by Flinders that young Franklin was diverted into the glorious path of discovery; from Flinders that he learnt the strictly scientific part of navigation. 'It is very reasonable for us to infer,' writes one of Franklin's biographers,[6] 'that it was in all probability in exploring miles of

[6] Admiral Markham, *Life of Sir John Franklin*, p. 43.

practically unknown coastline, and in surveying hitherto undiscovered bays, reefs, and islands in the southern hemisphere, that John Franklin's mind became imbued with that ardent love of geographical research which formed such a marked and prominent feature in his future professional career. Flinders was the example, and Australian exploration was the school, that created one of our greatest Arctic navigators and one of the most eminent geographers of his day.'

Another matter with which Flinders was occupied during his stay in England was the preparation of a small publication dealing with his recent researches. It was entitled 'Observations on the coasts of Van Diemen's Land, on Bass's Strait and its Islands, and on parts of the coasts of New South Wales, intended to accompany the charts of the late discoveries in those countries, by Matthew Flinders, second lieutenant of His Majesty's ship *Reliance*'. It consisted of 35 quarto pages, issued without a wrapper, and stitched like a large pamphlet. John Nichols, of Soho, was the publisher, but some copies were issued with the imprint of Arrowsmith, the publisher of charts. Very few copies now remain, and the little book, which is one of the rare things of bibliography, is not to be found even in many important libraries.

Flinders dedicated the issue to Sir Joseph Banks. 'Your zealous exertions to promote geographical and nautical knowledge, your encouragement of men employed in the cultivation of the sciences that tend to this improvement, and the countenance you have been pleased to show me in particular, embolden me to lay the following observations before you.' Generally speaking, the *Observations* contain matter that was afterwards embodied in the larger *Voyage to Terra Australis*, and taken from reports that have been used in the preceding pages. The special purpose of the book was to be of use to navigators who might sail in Australian waters, and it is therefore full of particulars likely to guide them. He pointed out that there might be some errors in the longitude records of the *Norfolk* voyage because 'no time-keepers could be procured for this expedition', but he pointed out that the survey was made with great care. 'The sloop was kept close to the shore, and brought back every morning within sight of the same point it had been hauled off during the preceding evening, by which means the chain of angles was never broken.' This was, as will be seen later, the method employed on the more important voyage about to be undertaken.

The task that mainly occupied his attention during these few months in England, was the making of preparations for a voyage of discovery intended to complete the exploration of the coasts of Australia. It has already been remarked that the initiative in regard to the *Francis* and

Norfolk explorations sprang from Flinders' own eager desire, and not from the governing authorities. Precisely the same occurred in the case of the far more important *Investigator* voyage. He did not wait for something to turn up. Immediately after his arrival in England, he formulated a plan, pointed out the sphere of investigation to which attention ought to be directed, and approached the proper authorities. He wrote to Sir Joseph Banks offering his services 'to explore minutely the whole of the coasts, as well those which were imperfectly known as those entirely unknown, provided the Government would provide me with a proper ship for the purpose'. He later recalled: 'I did not address myself in vain to this zealous promoter of science [Banks]; and Earl Spencer, then First Lord of the Admiralty, entering warmly into the views of his friend, obtained the approbation of his Majesty, and immediately set out a ship that could be spared from the present demands of war, which Great Britain then waged with most of the Powers of Europe.'[7]

Lord Spencer's prompt and warm acquiescence in the proposition is not less to be noted than the friendly interest of Banks. His administration of the Admiralty in Pitt's Government was distinguished by his selection of Nelson as the admiral to frustrate the schemes of the French in sea warfare; and it stands as an additional tribute to his sagacity that he at once recognised Flinders to be the right man to maintain the prowess of British seamanship in discovery.

Three reasons made the Government the more disposed to equip an expedition for the purpose. The first was that in June 1800, L. G. Otto, the representative of the French Republic in London, applied for a passport for two discovery ships which were being despatched to the South Seas. French men of science had for many years interested themselves in the investigation of these unknown portions of the globe. The expeditions of La Pérouse (1785–88) and of D'Entrecasteaux (1791–96) were evidence of their concern with the problems awaiting elucidation. The professors of the Museum in Paris were eager that collections of minerals and plants should be made in the southern hemisphere. The Institute of France was led by keen men of science, one of whom, the Comte de Fleurieu, had prepared the instructions for the two previous voyages. They had found a warm friend to research in Louis XVI, and the fall of the monarchy did not diminish their anxiety that France should win honour from pursuing the enquiry. They represented to Napoleon, then First Consul, the utility of undertaking

[7] Flinders' Papers.

another voyage, and his authorisation was secured in May. A passport was granted by Earl Spencer when Otto made the application, but there was a suspicion that the French Government was influenced by motives of policy lying deeper than the ostensible desire to promote discovery.

Secondly, the East India Company was concerned lest the French should establish themselves somewhere on the coast of Australia, and, with a base of operations there, menace the company's trade.

Thirdly, Sir Joseph Banks, after conversations with Flinders and an examination of his charts, saw the importance of the work remaining to be done, and used his influence with the Admiralty to authorise a ship to be detailed for the purpose.

Thus imperial policy, trade interests and scientific ardour combined to procure the equipment of a new research expedition. In view of the fact that the Admiralty became officially aware in June of the intentions of the French, it cannot be said that they were precipitate in making their own plans; for it was not until 12 December that they issued their orders.

The vessel allotted for the employment was a 334-ton sloop, built in the north of England for the merchant service. She had been purchased by the Government for naval work, and, under the name of the *Xenophon*, had been employed in convoying merchant vessels in the English Channel. Her name was changed to the *Investigator*, her bottom was recoppered, the plating being put on 'two streaks higher than before', and she was equipped for a three-year voyage. Flinders took command of her at Sheerness on 25 January 1801. He was promoted to the rank of commander on the 16th of the following month.

The renovated ship was good enough to look at, and she commended herself to Flinders' eye as being the sort of vessel best fitted for the work in contemplation. In form she 'nearly resembled the description of vessel recommended by Captain Cook as best calculated for voyages of discovery'. But, though comfortable, she was old and unsound. Patching and caulking merely plugged up defects which the buffetings of rough seas soon revealed. But she was the best ship the Admiralty was able to spare at the time. Long before she had completed her outward voyage, however, the senility of the *Investigator* had made itself uncomfortably evident. Writing of the leaks experienced on the run down to the Cape, Flinders said:

> *The leakiness of the ship increased with the continuance of the southwest winds, and at the end of a week amounted to five inches of water an hour. It seemed, however, that the leaks were*

> *above the water's edge, for on tacking to the westward they were diminished to two inches. This working of the oakum out of the seams indicated a degree of weakness, which, in a ship destined to encounter every hazard, could not be contemplated without uneasiness. The very large ports, formerly cut in the sides to receive thirty-two pound carronades [muzzle-loading cannons], joined to what I have been able to collect from the dockyard officers, had given me an unfavourable opinion of her strength; and this was now but too much confirmed. Should it be asked why representations were not made and a stronger vessel procured, I answer that the exigencies of the navy were such at that time, that I was given to understand no better ship could be spared from the service; and my anxiety to complete the investigation of the coasts of Terra Australis did not admit of refusing the one offered.*

The history of maritime discovery is strewn with rotten ships. Certainly if the great navigators, before venturing to face the unknown, had waited to be provided with vessels fit to make long voyages, the progress of research would have been much slower than was the case. It sounds like hyperbole to say that, when pitch and planks failed, these gallant seamen stopped their leaks with hope and ardour; but really, something like that is pretty near the truth.

The fitting out of the *Investigator* proceeded busily during January and February 1801. The Admiralty was liberal in its allowances. Indeed, the equipment was left almost entirely to Banks and Flinders. The commander 'obtained permission to fit her out as necessary, [he judged] without reference to the supplies usually allotted to vessels of the same class'. The extent to which the Admiralty was guided by Banks is indicated in a memorandum by the Secretary, Evan Nepean, penned in April. Banks wrote 'Is my proposal for an alteration in the undertaking in the *Investigator* approved?' Nepean replied 'Any proposal you may make will be approved; the whole is left entirely to your decision.'

In addition to plentiful supplies and special provision for a large store of water, the *Investigator* carried an interesting assortment of 'gauds, nick-nacks, trifles', to serve as presents to native peoples with whom it was desired to cultivate friendly relations. The list included useful articles as well as glittering toys, and is a curious document as illustrating [in that it illustrates] a means by which civilisation sought to tickle the barbarian into complaisance [compliance]. Flinders carried for this purpose 500 pocket-knives, 500 looking-glasses, 100 combs, 200 strings of blue, red, white and yellow beads, 100 pairs of ear-rings, 200 finger rings, 1000 yards of blue and red gartering, 100 red caps, 100 small blankets, 100 yards of thin red baize, 100 yards of coloured linen, 1000 needles, five pounds of red thread, 200 files, 100 shoemakers' knives, 300 pairs of scissors, 100 hammers, 50 axes, 300 hatchets, a quantity of other samples of ironmongery, a number of medals with King George's head imprinted upon them, and some new copper coins.

It is a curious assortment, but it may be observed that the materials, as well as the method of ingratiation, were very much the same with the earlier as with the later navigators. An early instance occurs in René Laudonnière's account of his relations with the natives of Florida in 1565:[8] 'I gave them certaine small trifles, which were little knives or tablets of glasse, wherein the image of King Charles the Ninth was drawen very lively ... I recompensed them with certaine hatchets, knives, beades of glasse, combes and looking-glasses.'

The crew of the *Investigator* was selected with particular care. Flinders desired to carry none but young sailors of good character. He was given permission to take men from the *Zealand*, and he explained to those who volunteered the nature of the service, and its probably severe and protracted character. The readiness with which men came forward gave him much pleasure.

> *Upon one occasion, when eleven volunteers were to be received from the* Zealand, *a strong instance was given of the spirit of enterprise prevalent amongst British seamen. About three hundred disposable men were called up, and placed on one part of the deck; and after the nature of the voyage, with the number of men wanted, had been explained to them, those who volunteered were desired to go over to the opposite side. The candidates were no less than two hundred and fifty, most of whom sought with eagerness to be received; and the eleven who were chosen proved, with one single exception, to be worthy of the preference they obtained.*

Of the whole crew (and the total ship's company numbered 83) only two caused any trouble to the commander. As these two 'required more severity in reducing to good order than I wished to exercise in a service of this nature', when the *Investigator* reached the Cape, Flinders arranged with the admiral there, Sir Roger Curtis, to exchange them—as well as two others who from lack of sufficient strength were not

[8] Hakluyt's *Voyages* (edition of 1904), Vol. IX, pp. 31 and 49.

suitable—for four sailors upon the flagship, who made a pressing application to go upon a voyage of discovery. Thus purged of a very few refractories and inefficients, the ship's company was a happy, loyal and healthy crew, of whom the commander was justifiably proud.

The officers and scientific staff were chosen with a view to making the voyage fruitful in utility. The first lieutenant, Robert Fowler, had served on the ship when she was the *Xenophon.* He was a Lincolnshire man, hailing from Horncastle, and had been a schoolfellow of Banks. But it was not through Sir Joseph's influence that he was selected. Flinders made his acquaintance while the refitting of the vessel was in progress, and found him desirous of making the voyage. As his former captain spoke well of him, his services were accepted. Samuel Ward Flinders went as second lieutenant, and there were six midshipmen, of whom John Franklin was one.

Originally it was intended that Mungo Park, the celebrated African traveller, who was at this time in England looking round for employment, should go to Australia on the *Investigator,* and act as naturalist. But no definite engagement was entered into; the post remained vacant, and a Portuguese exile living in London, Correa de Sena, introduced to Banks a young Scottish botanist who desired to go, describing him as one 'fitted to pursue an object with a staunch and a cold mind'. Robert Brown was then not quite 27 years of age. Like the gutsy swashbuckler, Dugald Dalgetty, he had been educated at the Marischal College, Aberdeen. For a few years he served as ensign and assistant surgeon of a Scottish regiment, the Fife Fencibles [Defensibles]. Always a keen botanist, he found a ready friend in Banks, who promised to recommend him 'for the purpose of exploring the natural history, amongst other things'. His salary was £420 a year, and he earned it by admirable service. Brown remained in Australia for two years after the discovery voyage, and his great *Prodromus Florae Novae Hollandiae* [Introduction to the Flora of New Holland], which won the praise of Humboldt, is a classic monument to the extent and value of his researches.

William Westall was appointed landscape and figure draftsman to the expedition at a salary of £315 per annum. The nine fine engravings which adorn the *Voyage to Terra Australis* are his work. He was but a youth of nineteen when he made this voyage. Afterwards he attained repute as a landscape painter, and was elected as Associate of the Royal Academy. One hundred and thirty-eight of his drawings made on the *Investigator* are preserved.

Ferdinand Bauer was appointed botanical draftsman to the expedition at a salary of £315. He was an Austrian, 40 years of age, an enthusiast in his work, and a man of uncommon industry. He made 1,600 botanical drawings which, in Robert Brown's opinion, were 'for beauty, accuracy and completion of detail unequalled in this or in any other country in Europe'. Bauer's *Illustrationes Florae Novae Hollandiae* [Illustrations of the Flora of New Holland], published in 1814, consisted of plates which were drawn, engraved and coloured by his own hand. Flinders formed a very high opinion of the capacity of both Brown and Bauer. 'It is fortunate for science,' he wrote to Banks 'that two men of such assiduity and abilities have been selected; their application is beyond what I have been accustomed to see.'

Peter Good, appointed gardener to the expedition at a salary of £105, was a foreman at the Kew Gardens when he was selected for this service. Brown found him a valuable assistant, and an indefatigable worker. He died in Sydney in June 1803, from dysentery contracted at Timor. Of John Allen, engaged as a miner at a salary of £105, nothing is known.

John Crossley was engaged to sail as astronomer, at a salary of £420, but he did not accompany the *Investigator* further than the Cape of Good Hope, where his health broke down, and he returned to England. The instruments with which he had been furnished by the Board of Longitude were, however, left on board, and Flinders undertook to do his work in co-operation with his brother Samuel, who had been assisting Crossley, and was able to take charge of the astronomical clocks and records.

The interest taken by the East India Company's Court of Directors in the expedition was manifested in their vote of £600 for the table money [extra allowance for food and wine] of the officers and staff.[9] They gave this sum 'from the voyage being within the limits of the Company's charter, from the expectation of the examinations and discoveries proving advantageous, and partly, as they said'—so Flinders modestly observed—'for my former services'. The company's charter gave to it a complete monopoly of trade with the east and the Pacific, and it was therefore interested in the finding of fresh harbours for its vessels in the

[9] The East India Company, through its Court of Directors, actually voted £1,200 in May, 1801; but only £600 of this sum was paid at the commencement of the voyage. The remainder was to be paid to the commander and officers as a reward if they successfully accomplished their task. Flinders' mss. letter-book contains a copy of a letter dated 14 November 1810, wherein he reminds the company of their promise. I have found no record of the payment of the remaining £600, but Flinders' *Journal* shows him to have dined with the directors a few weeks after the letter was sent, and a little later the *Journal* contains a record of a merry evening spent together by Flinders and a party of his old *Investigator* shipmates. It is a fair assumption that the money was divided up on that occasion.

South Seas. But, despite this display of concern, the East India Company had been no friend to Australian discovery and colonisation. In the early years of the settlement at Port Jackson, it resisted the opening of direct trade between Great Britain and New South Wales, with as jealous a dislike as ever the Spanish monopolists at Seville displayed in the sixteenth century concerning all trade with America that did not flow through their hands. Even so recently as 1806 the company opposed—and, strangely enough, successfully—the sale of a cargo of seal-skins and whale oil from Sydney, on the ground 'that the charter of the colony gave the colonists no right to trade, and that the transaction was a violation of Company's charter and against its welfare'. The grant to Flinders was not, therefore, a manifestation of zeal for Australian development, except in the matter of finding harbours, and except, also, that there was an uneasy feeling that the French would be mischievously busy on the north coast. 'I hope the French ships of discovery will not station themselves on the north-west coast of Australia,' wrote C. F. Greville, one of the company's directors.

The instructions furnished to Flinders prescribed the course of the voyage very strictly. They were that he should first run down the coast from 130 degrees of east longitude (that is, from about the head of the Great Australian Bight) to Bass Strait, and endeavour to discover such harbours as there might be. Then, proceeding through the strait, he was to call at Sydney to refresh his company and refit the ship. After that he was to return along the coast and diligently examine it as far as King George's Sound. As the sailing was delayed till the middle of July, Flinders expressed a wish that he should not be ordered to return to the south coast from Port Jackson. 'If my orders do not forbid it, I shall examine the south coast more minutely in my first run along it, and if anything material should present itself, as a strait, gulf, or very large river, shall take as much time in its examination as the remaining part of the summer shall then consist of; for I consider it very material to the success of the voyage and to its early completion that we should be upon the northern coasts in winter and the southern ones in summer.'

This was written to Banks, who, as we have seen, could probably have secured an alteration of the official instructions had he desired to do so. But they were not modified; and about a fortnight later (17 July) Flinders wrote: 'The Admiralty have not thought good to permit me to circumnavigate New Holland in the way that appears to me [underlined] best suited to expedition and safety.' It is probable that, if Banks discussed the proposed alteration with the Admiralty, the more rapid run along the south coast was insisted upon, because that was the field to which the French expedition might be expected to apply itself with most diligence; as, in fact, was actually the case. Governor King had also written to Banks pointing out the importance of a southern survey, 'to see what shelter it affords in case a ship should be taken before she can clear the land to the southward and the western entrance to the Strait'.

The instructions continued that after the exploration of the south of New Holland, the *Investigator* was to sail to the north-west and examine the Gulf of Carpentaria, carefully investigating Torres Strait and the whole of the remainder of the north-west and north-east coasts. After that, the east coast was to be more fully explored; and when the whole programme was finished Flinders was to return to England for further instructions.

The functions of the 'scientific gentlemen' were carefully defined. Flinders was directed to afford facilities for the naturalists to collect specimens and the artists to make drawings. The hand of Banks is apparent in the nice balancing of liberty of independent study with liability to direction from the commander; and his forethought in these particulars was probably inspired by his experience with Cook's expedition many years before.

One other set of instructions from the Admiralty is of great importance in view of what subsequently occurred, and had a bearing upon the expedition as it affected political relations. Great Britain was at war with France, and the *Investigator*, though on a peaceful mission, was a sloop belonging to the British navy. Flinders wrote to the Admiralty (2 July) soliciting instructions as to what he was to do in case he met French vessels at sea, 'for without an order to desist, the articles of war will oblige me to act inimically to them'. The directions that he received were explicit. He was to act towards any French ship 'as if the two countries were not at war; and with respect to the ships and vessels of other powers with which this country is at war, you are to avoid, if possible, having any communication with them; and not to take letters or packets other than such as you may receive from this office or the office of his Majesty's Secretary of State'. The concluding words of the instruction intimately concern the events which, in the next year but one, commenced that long agony of imprisonment which Flinders had to endure in Ile-de-France [Mauritius].

He was also provided with a passport from the French Government, and the terms in which it was couched are of the utmost importance for the understanding of what followed. It was issued for the *Investigator*, commanded by Captain Matthew Flinders, for a voyage of discovery of which the object was to extend human knowledge and promote the progress of nautical science. It commanded all French officers, at sea or on shore, not to interfere with the ship and its officers, but on the contrary to assist them if they needed help. But this treatment was only to be extended as long as the *Investigator* did not announce her intention of committing any act of hostility against the French Republic and her allies, did not render assistance to her enemies, and did not traffic in merchandise or contraband goods. The passport was signed by the French Minister of Marine and Colonies, Forfait, on behalf of the First Consul.[10]

Before the expedition sailed, Flinders became engaged in a correspondence which must have been embarrassing to him, relating to his wife. He was married, as has been stated, in April, after he had been promoted commander, and while the *Investigator* was lying at Sheerness, awaiting sailing orders. As the voyage would in all probability extend over several years, his intention was to take his bride with him to Sydney, and leave her there while he prosecuted his investigations in the south, north and east. He had no reason to think that his doing so would give offence in official quarters, especially as he was aware of cases where commanders of ships had been permitted to take their wives on cruises when their vessels were not protected by passports securing immunity from attack. There are even instances of wives of British naval officers being on board ship during engagements. During Nelson's attack on Santa Cruz, in 1797, Captain Fremantle of the *Seahorse* had with him his wife, whom he had lately married. It was in that engagement that Nelson lost an arm; and when he returned, bleeding and in great pain, he would not go on board the *Seahorse*, saying that he would not have Mrs Fremantle alarmed by seeing him in such a condition, without any news of her husband, who had accompanied the landing. The amputation of the shattered limb was therefore performed on the *Theseus.*

The wisdom of permitting a naval officer to take his wife on a long voyage in a ship of the navy may well be questioned, and the contrary rule is now well established. But it was not invariably observed a century or more ago; and that Flinders acted in perfect good faith in the matter is evident from the correspondence, which, on so delicate a subject, he conducted with a manliness and good taste that display his character in an amiable light.

---

[10] A transcript of Flinders' own copy of the French passport is now at Caen, amongst the Decaen Papers, Vol. 84, p. 133.

In all probability Mrs Flinders would have been allowed to proceed to Port Jackson unchallenged but for the unlucky circumstance that, when the commissioners of the Admiralty paid an official visit of inspection to the ship, she was seen 'seated in the captain's cabin without her bonnet'.[11] They considered this to be 'too open a declaration of that being her home'. Her husband first heard of the matter semi-officially from Banks, who wrote on 21 May:

> *I have but time to tell you that the news of your marriage, which was published in the Lincoln paper, has reached me. The Lords of the Admiralty have heard also that Mrs. Flinders is on board the* Investigator, *and that you have some thought of carrying her to sea with you. This I was very sorry to hear, and if that is the case I beg to give you my advice by no means to adventure to measures so contrary to the regulations and the discipline of the Navy; for I am convinced by language I have heard, that their Lordships will, if they hear of her being in New South Wales, immediately order you to be superseded, whatever may be the consequences, and in all likelihood order Mr. Grant to finish the survey.*

To threaten to supersede Flinders if it were even heard that his wife was in New South Wales was surely an excess of rigour. His reply was written from the Nore, on 24 May 1801:

> *I am much indebted to you, Sir Joseph, for the information contained in your letter of the 21st. It is true that I had an intention of taking Mrs. Flinders to Port Jackson, to remain there until I should have completed the voyage, and to have then brought her home again in the ship, and I trust that the service would not have suffered in the least by such a step. The Admiralty have most probably conceived that I intended to keep her on board during the voyage, but this was far from my intentions. As some vindication of the step I was about to take, I may be permitted to observe that until it was intended to apply for a passport, I not only did not take the step, but did not intend it—which is perhaps a greater attention to that article of the Naval Instructions than many commanders have paid to it. If their Lordships understood this matter in its true light, I should hope that they would have shown the same indulgence*

[11] Flinders' Papers.

to me as to Lieut. Kent of the Buffalo, and many others who have not had the plea of a passport.

If their Lordships' sentiments should continue the same, whatever may be my disappointment, I shall give up the wife for the voyage of discovery; and I would beg of you, Sir Joseph, to be assured that even this circumstance will not damp the ardour I feel to accomplish the important purpose of the present voyage, and in a way that shall preclude the necessity of any one following after me to explore.

It would be too much presumption in me to beg of Sir Joseph Banks to set this matter in its proper light, because by your letters I judge it meets with your disapprobation entirely; but I hope that this opinion has been formed upon the idea of Mrs. Flinders continuing on board the ship when engaged in real service.

Banks promised to lay before the Admiralty the representations made to him, but Flinders a few days later (3 June) wrote another letter in which he conscientiously expressed his determination not to risk a misunderstanding with his superiors by taking his wife:

I feel much obliged by your offer to lay the substance of my letter before the Admiralty, but I foresee that, although I should in the case of Mrs. Flinders going to Port Jackson have been more particularly cautious of my stay there, yet their Lordships will conclude naturally enough that her presence would tend to increase the number of and to lengthen my visits. I am therefore afraid to risk their Lordships' ill opinion, and Mrs. Flinders will return to her friends immediately that our sailing orders arrive.

It can well be believed that 'my Lords' of the Admiralty did not feel very considerate towards ladies just at that time; for one of their most brilliant officers, Nelson, was, while this very correspondence was taking place, gravely compromising himself with Emma Hamilton at Naples. St Vincent and Troubridge, salt-hearted old veterans as they were, were just the men to be suspicious on the score of petticoats fluttering about the decks of the King's ships. It seems that they were inclined unjustly and ungallantly to frown and cry *cherchez la femme* [blame the woman] about small things that went wrong, even when Flinders was in no way to blame for them. They blamed him for some desertions before properly apprehending the circumstances, and when he had merely reported a fact for which he was not responsible.

The next two letters close the whole incident, which gave more annoyance to all parties than ought to have been the case in connection with an officer so sedulously scrupulous in matters concerning the honour and efficiency of the service as Flinders was. Banks, in quite a patron's tone, wrote on 5 June:

> *I yesterday went to the Admiralty to enquire about the* Investigator, *and was indeed much mortified to learn there that you had been on shore in Hythe Bay, and I was still more mortified to hear that several of your men had deserted, and that you had had a prisoner entrusted to your charge, who got away at a time when the quarter-deck was in charge of a midshipman. I heard with pain many severe remarks on these matters, and in defence I could only say that as Captain Flinders is a sensible man and a good seaman, such matters could only be attributed to the laxity of discipline which always takes place when the captain's wife is on board, and that such lax discipline could never again take place, because you had wisely resolved to leave Mrs. Flinders with her relations.*

It was a kindly admonishment from an elderly scholar to a young officer of 27 only recently married; but to attribute affairs for which Flinders was not to blame to the presence of his bride, was a little unamiable. With excellent taste, Flinders, in his answer, avoided keeping his wife's name in the controversy, and he disposed of the allegations both effectively and judiciously:

> *My surprise is great that the Admiralty should attach any blame to me for the desertion of these men from the* Advice *brig, which is the next point in your letter, Sir Joseph. These men were lent, among others, to the brig, by order of Admiral Graeme. From her it was that they absented themselves, and I reported it to the Admiralty. I had been so particular as to send with the men a request to the commanding officer to permit none of them to go on shore, but Lieutenant Fowler pointed out to him such of them as might be most depended on to go in boats upon duty. Nothing more could have been done on our part to prevent desertion, and if blame rests anywhere it must be upon the officers of the* Advice. *The three men were volunteers for this voyage, but having gotten on shore with money in their pockets most probably stayed so long that they became afraid to return.*

On the subject of discipline he said:

> *It is only a duty to myself to assert that the discipline and good order on board the* Investigator *is exceeded in very few ships of her size, and is at least twice what it was under her former commander. I beg to refer to Lieutenant Fowler on this subject, who knows the ship intimately both as the* Xenophon *and* Investigator. *On the last subject I excuse myself from not having thought the occurrence of sufficient consequence to trouble Sir Joseph with, and it was what I least suspected that my character required a defender, for it was in my power to have suppressed almost the whole of those things for which I am blamed; but I had the good of the service sufficiently at heart to make the reports which brought them into light. That the Admiralty have thrown blame on me, and should have represented to my greatest and best friend that I had gotten the ship on shore, had let a prisoner escape, and three of my men run away, without adding the attendant circumstances, is most mortifying and grievous to me; but it is impossible to express so gratefully as I feel the anxious concern with which you took the part of one who has not the least claim to such generosity.*

The last two paragraphs refer to an incident which will be dealt with presently.

Although the *Investigator* was ready to sail in April 1801, the Admiralty withheld orders till the middle of July. Flinders, vexed as he naturally was at having to leave his young wife behind, was impatient at the delay for two good reasons. First, he was anxious to have the benefit of the Australian summer months, between November and February, for the exploration of the south-west, the winter being the better time for the northern work; and secondly, reports had appeared in the journals about the progress of the French expedition, and he did not wish to be forestalled in the making of probably important discoveries. The 'Annual Register' for 1801, for example (p. 33) stated that letters were received from the Isle of France [Ile-de-France] dated 29 April, stating that *Le Naturaliste* and *Le Géographe* had left that station on their voyage to New Holland. While 'my Lords' were warming up imaginary errors in the heat of an excited imagination on account of poor Mrs Flinders, the commander of the *Investigator* was losing valuable time. In May he wrote to Sir Joseph Banks: 'The advanced state of the season makes me excessively anxious to be off. I fear that a little longer delay will lose us a summer and lengthen our voyage at least six months. Besides that, the French are gaining time upon us.'

On 26 May, the *Investigator* left the Nore for Spithead to wait further orders. She was provided, by the Admiralty itself, with a chart published by J. H. Moore, upon which a sandbank known as the Roar, extending from Dungeness towards Folkestone, between 2½ to 4 miles from land, was not marked. On the evening of the 28th, in a perfectly calm sea, and at a time when, sailing by the chart, there was no reason to apprehend any danger, the ship glided on to the bank.

She did not suffer a particle of injury, and in a very short time had resumed her voyage. If Flinders had said nothing at all about the incident, nobody off the ship would have been any the wiser. But as the Admiralty had furnished him with a defective chart, and might do the same to other commanders, who might strike the sand in more inimical circumstances, he considered it to be his duty to the service to report the matter; when lo! the Admiralty, instead of censuring its officials for supplying the *Investigator* with a faulty chart, gravely shook its head, and made those 'severe remarks' about Flinders, which induced Sir Joseph Banks to admonish him so paternally in the letter already quoted. The *Investigator* had, it seemed to be the opinion of their Lordships, struck the sand, not because it was uncharted, but because Mrs Flinders was on board between the Nore and Spithead! Flinders' letter to Banks, dated 6 June, stated his position quite conclusively:

> *Finding so material a thing as a sandbank three or four miles from the shore unlaid down in the chart, I thought it a duty incumbent upon me to endeavour to prevent the like accident from happening to others, by stating the circumstances to the Admiralty, and giving the most exact bearings from the shoal that our situation would enable me to take, with the supposed distance from the land. It would have been very easy for me to have suppressed every part of the circumstance, and thus to have escaped the blame which seems to attach to me, instead of some share of praise for my good intentions. I hope that it will not be thought presumptuous in me to say that no blame ought to be attributed to me ... The Admiralty do not seem to take much into consideration that I had no master appointed, who ought to be the pilot, or that having been constantly employed myself in foreign voyages I cannot consequently have much*

> *personal knowledge of the Channel. In truth, I had nothing but the chart and my own general observations to direct me; and had the former been at all correct we should have arrived here as safe as if we had any number of pilots.*

It is significant of Flinders' truth-telling habit of mind that when he came to write the history of the voyage, published thirteen years later, he did not pass over the incident at the Roar, though he can hardly have remembered as agreeable, an event for which he was blamed when he was not wrong. But perhaps he found satisfaction in being able to write that the circumstance 'showed the necessity there was for a regulation, since adopted, to furnish His Majesty's ships with correct charts'. A natural comment is that it is odd that so obviously sensible a thing was not done until an accident showed the danger of not doing it. The blame temporarily put upon Flinders did no harm to his credit, and was probably merely an oblique form of self-reproach on the part of the Admiralty.

The *Investigator* arrived at Spithead on 2 June, but did not receive final sailing orders till more than another month had elapsed. 'I put an end, I hope, to our correspondence for some months, concluding that you will sail immediately,' wrote Sir Joseph Banks in June, 'and with sincere good wishes for your future prosperity, and with a firm belief that you will, in your future conduct, do credit to yourself as an able investigator, and to me as having recommended you.' The true spirit of friendship breathes in those words, the friendship, too, of a discerning judge of character for a younger man whom he respected and trusted. The trust was nobly justified. Flinders undertook the work with the firm determination to do his work thoroughly. 'My greatest ambition,' he had written some weeks previously (29 April), 'is to make such a minute investigation of this extensive and very interesting country that no person shall have occasion to come after me to make further discoveries.' It was with that downright resolve that Flinders set out, and in that spirit did he pursue his task to its end. It was not for nothing that this man was the nautical grandson of Cook.

Sailing orders arrived from London on 17 July, and on the following day the *Investigator* sailed from Spithead. Mrs Flinders was at this time residing with her friends in Lincolnshire. She had been ill from fretful disappointment when forbidden to sail with her husband, but had recovered before they parted. Many a weary, bitter year was to pass before she would see him again; years of notable things done, and of cruel wrongs endured; and then they were only to be together for a few years—October 1810 to July 1814—till death claimed the brave officer and fine-spirited gentleman who was Matthew Flinders.

From the correspondence of these weeks a few passages may be chosen, as showing the heart-side [emotional side] of a gallant sailor's nature. He wrote to his wife in June: 'The philosophical calmness which I imposed upon thee is fled from myself, and I am just as awkward without thee as one half of a pair of scissors without its fellow,' an image for separation which may be commended to any poet ingenious enough to find a rhyme for 'scissors'. The following is dated 7 July:

> *I should not forget to say that the gentle Mr. Bauer seldom forgets to add 'and Mrs. Flinders' good health' after the cloth is withdrawn, and even the bluff Mr. Bell does not forget you ... Thou wilt write me volumes, my dearest love, wilt thou not? No pleasure is at all equal to that I receive from thy letters. The idea of how happy we* might *be will sometimes intrude itself and take away the little spirits that thy melancholy situation leaves me. I can write no longer with this confounded pen. I will find a better to-morrow. May the choicest blessings of Heaven go with thee, thou dearest, kindest, best of women.*

This one was written from the Cape in November:

> *Write to me constantly; write me pages and volumes. Tell me the dress thou wearest, tell me thy dreams, anything, so do but talk to me and of thyself. When thou art sitting at thy needle and alone, then think of me, my love, and write me the uppermost of thy thoughts. Fill me half a dozen sheets, and send them when thou canst. Think only, my dearest girl upon the gratification which the perusal and reperusal fifty times repeated will afford me, and thou wilt write me something or other every day. Adieu, my dearest, best love. Heaven bless thee with health and comfort, and preserve thy full affection towards thy very own, Matthew Flinders.*

To return from these personal relations to the voyage: some days before the *Investigator* reached Madeira, a Swedish brig was met, and had to receive a lesson in nautical manners during war-time. The incident is reported by seaman Samuel Smith with a pretty mixture of pronouns, genders and tenses: 'At night we was piped all hands in the middle watch to quarters. A brig was bearing down upon our starboard bow. Our

Captn spoke her, but receiving no answer we fired a gun past his stern. Tacked ship and spoke her, which proved to be a Swede.'[12]

Flinders was, it has been said, the nautical grandson of Cook. How thoroughly he followed the example of the great sailor is apparent from the lines upon which he managed his ship and governed his crew. This is what he was able to write of the voyage down to the Cape of Good Hope, reached on 16 October:

> *At this time we had not a single person in the sick list, both officers and men being fully in as good health as when we sailed from Spithead. I had begun very early to put in execution the beneficial plan first practised and made known by the great Captain Cook. It was in the standing orders of the ship, that on every fine day the deck below and the cockpit should be cleaned, washed, aired with stoves, and sprinkled with vinegar. On wet and dull days they were cleaned and aired, without washing. Care was taken to prevent the people from sleeping upon deck or lying down in their wet clothes; and once in every fortnight or three weeks, as circumstances permitted, their beds, and the contents of their chests and bags were opened out and exposed to the sun and air. On the Sunday and Thursday mornings, the ship's company was mustered, and every man appeared clean-shaved and dressed; and when the evenings were fine the drum and fife announced the forecastle to be the scene of dancing; nor did I discourage other playful amusements which might occasionally be more to the taste of the sailors, and were not unseasonable.*
>
> *Within the tropics lime juice and sugar were made to suffice as antiscorbutics; on reaching a higher latitude, sour-krout [sauerkraut] and vinegar were substituted; the essence of malt was served for the passage to New Holland, and for future occasions, on consulting with the surgeon, I had thought it expedient to make some slight changes in the issuing of the provisions. Oatmeal was boiled for breakfast four days in the week, as usual; and at other times, two ounces of portable [in solid form] broth, in cakes, to each man, with such additions of*

---

[12] MS., Mitchell Library: 'Journal of Samuel Smith, Seaman, who served on board the *Investigator*, Captn Flinders, on a voyage of discovery in the South Seas.' The manuscript covers 52 small quarto pages, and is neatly written. Some of Smith's dates are wrong. It may be noted here that Smith, on his return from the voyage, was impressed in the Downs and retained in the navy till 1815. He died at Thornton's Court, Manchester, in 1821, aged 50. He was therefore 30 years of age when he made this voyage.

> *onions, pepper, etc., as the different messes possessed, made a comfortable addition to their salt meat. And neither in this passage, nor, I may add, in any subsequent part of the voyage, were the officers or people restricted to any allowance of fresh water. They drank freely at the scuttled cask, and took away, under the inspection of the officer of the watch, all that was requisite for culinary purposes; and very frequently two casks of water in the week were given for washing their clothes. With these regulations, joined to a due enforcement of discipline, I had the satisfaction to see my people orderly and full of zeal for the service in which we were engaged; and in such a state of health that no delay at the Cape was required beyond the necessary refitment of the ship.*

How wise, considerate, and far-seeing this policy was! It reads like the sageness of a grey-headed veteran. Yet Flinders had only attained his 27th birthday precisely seven months before he reached the Cape on this voyage. He had learnt how men, as well as ships, should be managed. 'It was part of my plan for preserving the health of the people to promote active amusements amongst them,' he said of the jollity on crossing the line; and we can almost see the smile of recollection which played upon his lips when he wrote that 'the seamen were furnished with the means and the permission to conclude the day with merriment'. Seaman Smith, who shared in the fun, tells us what occurred with his own peculiar disregard of correct spelling and grammatical construction: 'we crossd the equinocial line and had the usuil serimony of Neptune and his attendance hailing the ship and coming on board. The greatest part of officers and men was shaved, not having crossd the line before. At night grog was servd out to each watch, which causd the evening to be spent in merriment.'

At the Cape the seams were re-caulked, and the ship gave less trouble on the voyage across the Indian Ocean than she had done on the run south. She left False Bay on 4 November. The run across the Indian Ocean was uneventful, except that the ship ran foul of a whale apparently sleeping on the water, and 'caused such an alarm that he sank as expeditiously as possible'; and that an albatross was captured which, 'being caught with hook and line it had its proper faculties and appeared of a varocious nature'.[13] On 6 December the coast of Australia was sighted near Cape Leeuwin.

---

[13] Smith's journal, Mitchell Library MSS.

XIII

THE FRENCH EXPEDITION

IT will be necessary to devote some attention to the French expedition of discovery, commanded by Nicolas Baudin, which sailed from Havre on 19 October 1800, nearly two months before the British Admiralty authorised the despatch of the *Investigator*, and nine months all but two days before Flinders was permitted to leave England.

The mere fact that this expedition was despatched while Napoleon Bonaparte was First Consul of the French Republic, has led many writers to jump to the conclusion that it was designed to cut out a portion of Australia for occupation by the French; that, under the thin disguise of being charged with a scientific mission, Baudin was in reality an emissary of Machiavellian statecraft, making a cunning move in the great game of world politics. The author has, in an earlier book[1] endeavoured to show that such was not the case. Bonaparte did not originate the discovery voyage. He simply authorised it, as head of the state, when the proposition was laid before him by the Institute of France, a scientific body, concerned with the augmentation of knowledge, and anxious that an effort should be made to complete a task which the abortive expeditions of La Pérouse and D'Entrecasteaux had failed to accomplish.

Moreover, if Bonaparte had wished to acquire territory in Australia, he was not so foolish a person as to fit out an expedition estimated to cost over half a million francs,[2] and which actually cost a far larger sum, when he could have obtained what he wanted simply by asking. The treaty of

---

[1] *Terre Napoléon* (London, 1910). Since that book was published, I have had the advantage of reading a large quantity of manuscript material, all unpublished, preserved in the Archives Nationales and the Bibliothèque Nationale, Paris. It strengthens the main conclusions promulgated in *Terre Napoléon*, but of course amplifies the evidence very considerably. The present chapter is written with the Baudin and other manuscripts, as well as the printed material, in mind.

[2] Report of the Commission of the Institute, mss. Bib. Nat., nouv. acq., France, 9439, p. 139.

Amiens was negotiated and signed while Baudin's ships were at sea. The British Government at that time was very anxious for peace, and was prepared to make concessions—did, in fact, surrender a vast extent of territory won by a woeful expenditure of blood and treasure. It cannot be said that Australia was greatly valued by Great Britain at the time. She occupied only a small portion of an enormous continent, and would certainly not have seriously opposed a project that the French should occupy some other portion of it, if Bonaparte had put forward a claim as a condition of peace. But he did nothing of the kind.

If we are to form sound views of history, basing conclusions on the evidence, we must set aside suspicions generated at a time of fierce racial antipathy, when it was almost part of an Englishman's creed to hate a Frenchman. Neither the published history of Baudin's voyage, nor the papers relating to it which are now available for study—except two documents to which special attention will be devoted hereafter, and which did not emanate from persons in authority—afford warrant [provide grounds] for believing that there was any other object in view than that professed when application for a passport was made to the Admiralty. The confidential instructions of the Minister[3] of Marine to Baudin[4] leave no doubt that the purpose was quite *bona fide.* Forfait wrote:

> *Your labours having for their sole object the perfecting of scientific knowledge, you should observe the most complete neutrality, allowing no doubt to be cast upon your exactitude in confining yourself to the object of your mission, as set forth in the passports which have been furnished. In your relations with foreigners, the glorious success of our arms, the power and wisdom of your government, the grand and generous views of the First Consul for the pacification of Europe, the order that he has restored in the interior of France, furnish you with the means of giving to foreign peoples just ideas upon the real state of the Republic and upon the prosperity which is assured to it.*

The men of science who had promoted the voyage were anxious that not even a similitude [the merest resemblance] of irregularity should be permitted. Thus we find the Comte de Fleurieu, who drew up the itinerary, writing to the Minister urging him to include in the instructions

---

[3] MSS., Archives Nationales, BB4, 999, Marine. I have given an account of this important manuscript, with copious extracts, in the *English Historical Review*, April, 1913.

[4] Fleurieu to Forfait, mss. Bib. Nat., nouv. acq., France, 9439, p. 137.

a paragraph prohibiting the ships from taking on board, under any pretext, merchandise which could give to a scientific expedition the appearance of a commercial venture, 'because if an English cruiser or man-of-war should visit them, and find on board other goods than articles of exchange for dealing with Aboriginal peoples, this might serve as a pretext for arresting them, and Baudin's passport might be disregarded on the ground that it had been abused by being employed as a means of conducting without risk a traffic which the state of war would make very lucrative'.

The question of the origin and objects of the expedition is, however, an entirely different one from that of the use which Napoleon would have made of the information collected, had the opportunity been available of striking a blow at Great Britain through her southern colony. It is also different from the question (as to which something will be said later) of the advantage taken by two members of Baudin's staff of the scope allowed them at Port Jackson, to 'spy out the land' with a view of furnishing information valuable in a military sense to their Government.

The instructions to Baudin were very similar to those which had been given to La Pérouse and D'Entrecasteaux in previous years, being drafted by the same hand, and some paragraphs in an 'instruction particulière' [specific instruction], show that the French were thoroughly up to date with their information, and knew in what parts of the coast fresh work required to be done.[5]

Nicolas Baudin was not a French naval officer. He had been in the merchant service, and, more recently, had had charge of an expedition despatched to Africa by the Austrian Government to collect specimens for the museum at Vienna. War between France and Austria broke out before he returned; and Baudin, feeling less loyal to his Austrian employers than to his own country, handed over the whole collection to the Museum in Paris. This action, which in the circumstances was probably regarded as patriotic, brought him under the notice of Jussieu, the famous French botanist; and when the South Sea expedition was authorised, that scientist recommended Baudin as one who had taken an interest in natural history researches, and who had given 'a new proof of his talent and of his love for science by the choice of the specimens composing his last collection, deposited in the museum'. The Minister of Marine minuted Jussieu's recommendation in the margin: 'No choice

[5] 'Projet d'itinéraire pour le Commandant Baudin; mémoire pour servir d'instruction particulière.' MSS., Archives Nationales, Marine, BB4, 999.

could be happier than that of Captain Baudin,'[6] and so he was appointed. He was by no means the kind of officer whom Napoleon would have selected had his designs been such as have commonly been alleged.

Two ships of the navy were commissioned for the service. Under the names *La Serpente* and *Le Vésuve* they had been built with a view to an invasion of England, contemplated in 1793.[7] They were renamed *Le Géographe* and *Le Naturaliste* on being allotted to a much safer employment. Both were described as solidly built, good sailers, and easy to control; and the officer who surveyed them to determine whether they would be suitable reported that without impairing their sea-going qualities it would be easy to construct upon their decks high poops to hold quantities of growing plants, which it was intended to collect and bring home. On these ships Baudin and his selected staff embarked at Havre, and, a British passport being obtained under the circumstances already related, sailed south in October.

If Baudin had been the keen and capable commander that those who secured his appointment believed him to be, he should have discovered and charted the whole of the unknown southern coast of Australia, before Flinders was many days' sail from England. The fact that this important work was actually done by the English navigator was in no measure due to the sagacity of the Admiralty—whose officials procrastinated in an inexplicable fashion even after the *Investigator* had been commissioned and equipped—but to his own promptness, competence and zeal, and the peculiar dilatoriness of his rivals. Baudin's vessels reached Ile-de-France in March 1801, and lay there for the leisurely space of 40 days. Two-thirds of a year had elapsed before they came upon the Australian coast. But Baudin did not even then set to work where there was discovery to be achieved. Winter was approaching, and sailing in these southern seas would be uncomfortable in the months of storm and cold; so he dawdled up the west coast of Australia, in warm, pleasant waters, and made for Timor, where he arrived in August. He remained in the Dutch port of Kupang till the middle of November—three whole months wasted, nearly eleven months consumed since he had sailed from France. In the meantime, the alert and vigorous captain of the *Investigator* was speeding south as fast as the winds would take him, too eager to lose a day, flying straight to his work like an arrow to its mark, and doing it with the thoroughness and accuracy that were part of his nature.

---

[6] MSS., Bib. Nat., nouv. Acq., France, 9439, p. 121.

[7] MSS., Bib. Nat., nouv. acq., France, 9439, report of de Bruix to the Minister.

The French on board *Le Géographe* and *Le Naturaliste* were as unhappy as their commander was slow. Scurvy broke out, and spread among the crew with virulence. Baudin appeared to have little or no conception of the importance of the sanitary measures which Cook was one of the earliest navigators to enjoin [prescribe], and by which those who emulated his methods were able to keep in check the ravages of this scourge of seafaring men. He neglected common precautions, and paid no heed to the counsel of the ship's surgeons. As a consequence, the sufferings of his men were such that it is pitiful to read about them in the official history of the voyage.

From Timor Baudin sailed for southern Tasmania, arriving there in January 1802, and remaining in the neighbourhood till March. There was no European settlement upon the island at that time, and Baudin described it as a country 'which ought not to be neglected, and which a nation that does not love us does not look upon with indifference'.[8] A severe storm separated *Le Géographe* from her escort on March 7 and 8, in the neighbourhood of the eastern entrance of Bass Strait. *Le Naturaliste* spent some time in Westernport, making a survey of it, and discovering the second island, which Bass had missed on his whaleboat cruise. Her commander, Captain Hamelin, then took her round to Port Jackson, to solicit aid from the Governor of the English colony there. Meanwhile Baudin sailed through the strait from east to west. He called at Waterhouse Island, off the north-east coast of Van Diemen's Land, misled by its name into thinking that he would find fresh water there. The island was named after Captain Henry Waterhouse of the *Reliance*, but Baudin, unaware of this, considered that it belied its name. 'It does not seem,' he wrote, 'to offer any appearance of water being discoverable there, and I am persuaded that it can have been named Water House only because the English visited it at a time when heavy rains had fallen.'[9] Baudin passed Port Phillip, rounded Cape Otway, and coasted along till he came to Encounter Bay, where occurred an incident with which we shall be concerned after we have traced the voyage of Flinders eastward to the same point.

---

[8] Baudin to the Minister of Marine, mss., Archives Nationales, BB4, 995, Marine.

[9] Baudin's Diary, mss. Bibliothèque Nationale: 'Je suis persuadé qu'on ne l'a nommé Wather House que par ce que les Anglais qui l'ont visité y auront eu beaucoup de pluie.'

XIV

SOUTH COAST DISCOVERY

WE now resume the story of Flinders' voyage along the southern coast of Australia, from the time when he made Cape Leeuwin on 6 December 1801.

That part of the coast lying between the south-west corner of the continent and Fowler's Bay, in the Great Australian Bight, had been traversed prior to this time. In 1791 Captain George Vancouver, in the British ship *Cape Chatham*, sailed along it from Cape Leeuwin to King George's Sound, which he discovered and named. He anchored in the harbour, and remained there for a fortnight. He would have liked to pursue the discovery of this unknown country, and did sail further east, as far as the neighbourhood of Termination Island, in longitude 122° 8'. But, meeting with adverse winds, he abandoned the research, and resumed his voyage to north-west America across the Pacific. In 1792, Bruny D'Entrecasteaux, with the French ships *Recherche* and *Espérance*, searching for tidings of the lost La Pérouse, followed the line of the shore more closely than Vancouver had done, and penetrated much further eastward. His instructions, prepared by Fleurieu, had directed him to explore the whole of the southern coast of Australia; but he was short of water, and finding nothing but sand and rock, with no harbour, and no promise of a supply of what he so badly needed, he did not continue further than longitude 131° 38½' east, about two and a half degrees east of the present border line of Western and South Australia. These navigators, with the Dutchman Pieter Nuyts, in the early part of the seventeenth century, and the Frenchman St Alouarn, who anchored near the Leeuwin in 1772, were the only Europeans known to have been upon any part of these southern coasts before the advent of Flinders; and the extent of the voyage of Nuyts is by no means clear.

Flinders, as we have seen, laid it down as a guiding principle that he would make so complete a survey of the shores visited by him as to leave little for anybody to do after him. He therefore commenced his work immediately he touched land, constructing his own charts as the ship slowly traversed the curves of the coast. The result was that many corrections and additions to the charts of Vancouver and D'Entrecasteaux were made before the entirely new discoveries were commenced. In announcing this fact, Flinders, always generous in his references to good work done by his predecessors, warmly praised the charts prepared by Beautemps-Beaupré, 'geographical engineer' of the *Recherche.* 'Perhaps no chart of a coast so little known as this is, will bear a comparison with its original better than this of M. Beaupré,' he said. His own charts were of course fuller and more precise, but he made no claim to superiority on this account, modestly observing that he would have been open to reproach if, after following the coast with an outline of M. Beaupré's chart before him, he had not effected improvements where circumstances did not permit so close an examination to be made in 1792.

Several inland excursions were made, and some of the King George's Sound Aboriginals were encountered. Flinders noted down some of their words, and pointed out the difference from words for the same objects used by Port Jackson and Van Diemen's Land natives. An exception to this rule was the word used for calling to a distance: *cau-wah*! (come here). This is certainly very like the Port Jackson *cow-ee*, whence comes the one Aboriginal word of universal employment in Australia today, the coo-ee of the townsman and the bushman alike, a call entered [which appeared] in the vocabulary collected by Hunter as early as 1790.

The method of research adopted by Flinders was similar to that employed on the *Norfolk* voyage. The ship was kept all day as close inshore as possible, so that water breaking on the shore was visible from the deck, and no river or opening could escape notice. When this could not be done, because the coast retreated far back, or was dangerous, the commander stationed himself at the masthead with a glass [telescope]. All the bearings were laid down as soon as taken, whilst the land was in sight; and before retiring to rest at night Flinders made it a practice to finish up his rough chart for the day, together with his journal of observations. The ship hauled off the coast at dusk, but especial care was taken to come upon it at the same point next morning, as soon after daylight as practicable, so that work might be resumed precisely where it had been dropped on the previous day. 'This plan,' said Flinders, 'to see and lay down everything myself, required constant attention and much labour, but was absolutely necessary to obtaining that accuracy of which I was desirous.' When bays or groups of islands were reached, Flinders went ashore with the theodolite, took his angles, measured, mapped, and made topographical notes. The lead was kept busy, making soundings. The rise and fall of the tides were observed; memoranda on natural phenomena were written; opportunities were given for the naturalists to collect specimens, and for the artist to make drawings. The net was frequently drawn in the bays for examples of marine life. Everybody when ashore kept a look out for plants, birds, beasts, and insects. In short, a keenness for investigation, an assiduity in observation, animated the whole ship's company, stimulated by the example of the commander, who never spared himself in his work, and interested himself in that of others.

As in a drama, 'comic relief' was occasionally interposed amid more serious happenings. The blacks were friendly, though occasionally shy and suspicious. In one scene the mimicry that is a characteristic of the Aboriginal was quaintly displayed. The incident, full of colour and humour, is thus related by Flinders:

> *Our friends, the natives, continued to visit us; and an old man with several others being at the tents this morning, I ordered the party of marines on shore, to be exercised in their presence. The red coats and white crossed belts were greatly admired, having some resemblance to their own manner of ornamenting themselves; and the drum, but particularly the fife, excited their astonishment; but when they saw these beautiful red and white men, with their bright muskets, drawn up in a line, they absolutely screamed with delight; nor were their wild gestures and vociferation to be silenced but by commencing the exercise, to which they paid the most earnest and silent attention. Several of them moved their hands, involuntarily, according to the motions; and the old man placed himself at the end of the rank, with a short staff in his hand, which he shouldered, presented, grounded, as did the marines their muskets, without, I believe, knowing what he did. Before firing, the Indians were made acquainted with what was going to take place; so that the volleys did not excite much terror.*

Seaman Smith was naturally much interested in the Aboriginals, whose features were however to him 'quite awful, having such large mouths and long teeth'. They were totally without clothing, and 'as soon as they saw our tents they run into the bushes with such activity that would pawl any European to exhibit. Because our men would not give them a small tommy-hawk they began to throw pieces of wood at them, which exasperated our men; but orders being so humane towards the natives that we must put up with anything but heaving spears.'

Furthermore, 'they rubbd their skin against ours, expecting some mark of white upon their's, but finding their mistake they appeared surprised'.

Pleasures more immediately incidental to geographical discovery—those pleasures which eager and enterprising minds must experience, however severe the labour involved, on traversing portions of the globe previously unknown to civilised mankind—commenced after the head of the Great Bight was passed. From about the vicinity of Fowler's Bay (named after the first lieutenant of the *Investigator*) the coast was virgin to geographical science. Comparisons of original work with former charts were no longer possible. The ship was entering unnavigated waters, and the coasts delineated were new to the world's knowledge. The quickening of the interest in the work in hand, which touched both officers and men of the expedition, can be felt by the reader of Flinders' narrative. There was a consciousness of having crossed a line separating what simply required verification and amplification, from a totally fresh field of research. Every reach of coastline now traversed was like a cable, long buried in the deep of time, at length hauled into daylight, with its oozy deposits of seaweed, shell and mud lying thick upon it.

Contingent upon discovery was the pleasure of naming important features of the coast. It is doubtful whether any other single navigator in history applied names which are still in use to so many capes, bays and islands, upon the shores of the habitable globe, as Flinders did. The extent of coastline freshly discovered by him was not so great as that first explored by some of his predecessors. But no former navigator pursued extensive new discoveries so minutely, and, consequently, found so much to name; while the precision of Flinders' records left no doubt about the places that he named, when in later years the settlement of country and the navigation of seas necessitated the use of names. Compare, for instance, in this one respect, the work of Cook and Dampier, Vasco da Gama and Magellan, Tasman and Quiros, with that of Flinders. Historically their voyages may have been in some respects more important; but they certainly added fewer names to the map. There are 103 names on Cook's charts of eastern Australia from Point Hicks to Cape York; but there are about 240 new names on the charts of Flinders representing southern Australia and Tasmania. He is the Great Denominator among navigators. He named geographical features after his friends, after his associates on the *Investigator*, after distinguished persons connected with the navy, after places in which he was interested. Fowler's Bay, Point Brown, Cape Bauer, Franklin's Isles, Point Bell, Point Westall, Taylor's Isle, and Thistle Island, commemorate his shipmates. Spencer's Gulf was named 'in honour of the respected nobleman who presided at the Board of Admiralty when the voyage was planned and the ship was put in commission', and Althorp Isles celebrated Lord Spencer's heir.[1] St Vincent's Gulf was named 'in honour of the noble admiral' who was at the head of the Admiralty when the *Investigator* sailed from England, and who had 'continued to the voyage that countenance and protection of which Earl Spencer had set the example'. To Yorke's Peninsula, between the two gulfs, was affixed the name of the Right Hon. C. P. Yorke, afterwards Lord Hardwicke, the First Lord who authorised the publication of Flinders' *Voyage.* Thus, the ministerial heads of the Admiralty in three governments (Pitt's, Addington's and Spencer Perceval's) came to be commemorated. It may be remarked as curious that a naval officer so proud of his service as Flinders was, should nowhere have employed the name of the greatest sailor of his age, Nelson. There is a Cape Nelson on the Victorian coast, but that name was given by Grant.

In Spencer's Gulf we come upon a group of Lincolnshire placenames, for Flinders, his brother Samuel, the mate, Fowler, and Midshipman John Franklin, all serving on this voyage, were Lincolnshire men. Thus we find Port Lincoln, Sleaford Bay, Louth Bay, Cape Donington, Stamford Hill, Surfleet Point, Louth Isle, Sibsey Isle, Stickney Isle, Spilsby Isle, Partney Isle, Revesby Isle, Point Boston, and Winceby Isle. Banks' name was given to a group of islands, and Coffin's Bay must not be allowed to suggest any gruesome association, for it was named after Sir Isaac Coffin, resident naval commissioner at Sheerness, who had given assistance in the equipment of the *Investigator*. A few names, like Streaky Bay, Lucky Bay, and Cape Catastrophe, were applied from circumstances that occurred on the voyage. A poet of the antipodes who should, like Wordsworth, be moved to write 'Poems on the Naming of Places', would find material in the names given by Flinders.

Interest in this absorbing work rose to something like excitement on 20 February, when there were indications, from the set of the tide, that an unusual feature of the coast was being approached. 'The tide from the north-eastward, apparently the ebb, ran more than one mile an hour, which was the more remarkable from no set of the tide worthy to be noticed having hitherto been observed upon this coast.' The ship had rounded Cape Catastrophe, and the land led away to the north, whereas

[1] Cockburn, *Nomenclature of South Australia* (Adelaide, 1909), p. 9, is mistaken in speculating that 'there is a parish of Althorp in Flinders' native country in Lincolnshire which probably accounts for the choice of the name here'. Althorp, which should be spelt without a final 'e,' is not in Lincolnshire, but in Northamptonshire.

hitherto it had trended east and south. What did this mean? Flinders must have been strongly reminded of his experience in the *Norfolk* in Bass Strait, when the rush of the tide from the south showed that the north-west corner of Van Diemen's Land had been turned, and that the demonstration of the strait's existence was complete. There were many speculations as to what the signs indicated. 'Large rivers, deep inlets, inland seas and passages into the Gulf of Carpentaria, were terms frequently used in our conversations of this evening, and the prospect of making an interesting discovery seemed to have infused new life and vigour into every man in the ship.' The expedition was, in fact, in the bell-mouth [bell-shaped mouth] of Spencer's Gulf, and the next few days were to show whether the old surmise was true: that Terra Australis was cloven in twain by a strait from the Gulf of Carpentaria to the southern ocean. It was, indeed, a crisis-time [a turning point] of the discovery voyage.

But before the gulf was examined, a tragedy threw the ship into mourning. On the evening of Sunday, 21 February, the cutter was returning from the mainland, where a party had been searching for water in charge of the Master, John Thistle. She carried a midshipman, William Taylor, and six sailors. Nobody on the ship witnessed the accident that happened; but the cutter had been seen coming across the water, and as she did not arrive when darkness set in, the fear that she had gone down oppressed everybody on board. A search was made, but ineffectually; and next day the boat was found floating bottom uppermost, stove in, and bearing the appearance of having been dashed against rocks. The loss of John Thistle was especially grievous to Flinders. The two had been companions from the very beginning of his career in Australia. Thistle had been one of Bass's crew in the whaleboat; he had been on the *Norfolk* when Van Diemen's Land was circumnavigated; and he had taken part in the cruise to Moreton Bay. His memory lives in the name of Thistle Island, on the west of the entrance to the gulf; and in the noble tribute which his commander paid to his admirable qualities. It would be wrong to deprive the reader of the satisfaction of reading Flinders' eulogy of his companion of strenuous years:

> *The reader will pardon me the observation that Mr. Thistle was truly a valuable man, as a seaman, an officer, and a good member of society. I had known him, and we had mostly served together, from the year 1794. He had been with Mr. Bass in his perilous expedition in the whaleboat, and with me in the voyage round Van Diemen's Land, and in the succeeding expedition to Glass House and Hervey's Bays. From his merit and prudent conduct,*

he was promoted from before the mast to be a midshipman and afterwards a master in His Majesty's service. His zeal for discovery had induced him to join the Investigator *when at Spithead and ready to sail, although he had returned to England only three weeks before, after, an absence of six years.*[2] *Besides performing assiduously the duties of his situation, Mr. Thistle had made himself well acquainted with the practice of nautical astronomy, and began to be very useful in the surveying department. His loss was severely felt by me, and he was lamented by all on board, more especially by his mess-mates, who knew more intimately the goodness and stability of his disposition.*

Taylor's Isle was named after the young midshipman of [lost in] this catastrophe, and six small islands in the vicinity bear the names of the boat's crew. It is a singular fact that only two of the eight sailors drowned could swim. Even Captain Cook never learnt to swim!

Before leaving the neighbourhood, Flinders erected a copper plate upon a stone post at the head of Memory Cove, and had engraved upon it the names of the unfortunates who had perished, with a brief account of the accident. Two fragments of the original plate are now in the museum at Adelaide. In later years it was beaten down by a storm, and the South Australian Government erected a fresh tablet in Memory Cove to replace it.

A thorough survey of Port Lincoln was made while the ship was being replenished with water. Some anxiety had been felt owing to the lack of this necessity, and Flinders showed the way to obtain it by digging holes in the white clay surrounding a brackish marsh which he called Stamford Mere. The water that drained into the holes was found to be sweet and wholesome, though milky in appearance. As the filling of the casks and conveying them to the ship—to a quantity of 60 tons—occupied several days, the surveying and scientific employments were pursued diligently on land.

The discovery of Port Lincoln was in itself an event of consequence, since it is a harbour of singular commodiousness [spaciousness] and beauty, and would, did it but possess a more prolific territory at its back, be a maritime station of no small importance.

---

2 In a letter to Banks from Spithead on 3 June 1801, Flinders had written: 'I am happy to inform you that the *Buffalo* has brought home a person formerly of the *Reliance* whom I wish to have as master. He volunteers, the captain of the ship agrees, and I have made application by to-day's post and expect his appointment by Friday.' The reference was evidently to John Thistle.

Nearly 40 years later, Sir John Franklin, then Governor of Tasmania, paid a visit to Port Lincoln, expressly to renew acquaintance with a place in the discovery of which he had participated in company with a commander whose memory he honoured; and he erected on Stamford Hill, at his own cost, an obelisk in commemoration of Flinders. In the same way, on his first great overland Arctic journey in 1821, Franklin remembered Flinders in giving names to discoveries.

It was on 6 March that the exploration of Spencer's Gulf commenced. As the ship sailed along the western shore, the expectations which had been formed of a strait leading through the continent to the Gulf of Carpentaria faded away. The coast lost its boldness, the water became more and more shallow, and the opposite shore began to show itself. The gulf was clearly tapering to an end. 'Our prospects of a channel or strait cutting off some considerable portion of Terra Australis grew less, for it now appeared that the ship was entering into a gulph.' On the 10th, the *Investigator* having passed Point Lowly, and having on the previous day suddenly come into two-and-a-half fathoms, Flinders decided to finish the exploration in a rowing boat, accompanied by Surgeon Bell. They rowed along the shore till night fell, slept in the boat, and resumed the journey early next morning (11 March). At ten o'clock, the oars touched mud on each side, and it became impossible to proceed further. They had reached the head of the gulf, then a region of mangrove swamps and flat waters, but now covered by the wharves of Port Augusta, and within view of the starting point of the transcontinental railway.

The disappointment was undoubtedly great at not finding even a large river flowing into the gulf. The hope of a strait had been abandoned as the continually converging shores, shallow waters, and diminishing banks made it clear, long before the head was reached, that the theory of a bifurcated Terra Australis was impossible. But as Flinders completed his chart and placed it against the outline of the continent, he might fairly enjoy the happiness of having settled an important problem and of taking one more stride towards completing the map of the world.

The *Investigator* travelled down by the eastern shore, once hanging upon a near bank for half an hour, and by 20 March was well outside. The length of the gulf, from the head to Gambier Island, Flinders calculated to be 185 miles, and its width at the mouth, in a line from Cape Catastrophe, 48 miles. At the top it tapered almost to a point. The whole of it was personally surveyed and charted by Flinders, who was able to write that for the general exactness of his drawing he could 'answer with tolerable confidence, having seen all that is laid down, and, as usual, taken every angle which enters into the construction'.

The next discovery of importance was that of Kangaroo Island, separated from the foot-like southern projection of Yorke's Peninsula by Investigator Strait. The island was named on account of the quantity of kangaroos seen and shot upon it; for a supply of fresh meat was very welcome after four months of salt pork. Thirty-one fell to the guns of the *Investigator*'s men. Half a hundredweight of heads, forequarters and tails were stewed down for soup, and as much kangaroo steak was available for officers and men as they could consume 'by day and night'. It was declared to be a 'delightful regale' [feast].

The place where Flinders is believed to have first landed on Kangaroo Island is now marked by a tall cairn, which was spontaneously built by the inhabitants, the school children assisting, in 1906. An inscription on a faced stone commemorates the event. The white pyramid can be seen from vessels using Backstairs Passage.[3]

A very short stay was made at Kangaroo Island on this first call. On 24 March Investigator Strait was crossed, and the examination of the mainland was resumed. The ship was steered north-west, and, the coast being reached, no land was visible to the eastward. The conclusion was drawn that another gulf ran inland, and the surmise proved to be correct. The new discovery, named St Vincent's Gulf, was penetrated on the 27th, and was first explored on the eastern shore, not on the western as had been the case with Spencer's Gulf. Mount Lofty was sighted at dawn on Sunday, 28 March. The nearest part of the coast was three leagues [approximately nine miles] distant at the time, 'mostly low, and composed of sand and rock, with a few small trees scattered over it; but at a few miles inland, where the back mountains rise, the country was well clothed with forest timber, and had a fertile appearance. The fires bespoke this to be a part of the continent.' The coast to the northward was seen to be very low, and the soundings were fast decreasing. From noon to six o'clock the *Investigator* ran north 30 miles, skirting a sandy shore, and at length dropped anchor in five fathoms.

On the following morning land was seen to the westward, as well as eastward, and there was 'a hummocky mountain, capped with clouds, apparently near the head of the inlet'. Wind failing, very little progress was made till noon, and at sunset the shores appeared to be closing round. The absence of tide gave no prospect of finding a river at the head of the gulf. Early on the morning of the 30th Flinders went out in a boat, accompanied by Robert Brown, and rowed up to the mud-flats at the

[3] See the account of the making of the cairn, by C. E. Owen Smythe, I.S.O., who initiated and superintended the work, South Australian Geographical Society's *Proceedings*, 1906, p. 58.

head of the gulf. Picking out a narrow channel, it was found possible to get within half a mile of dry land. Then, leaving the boat, Flinders and Brown walked along a bank of mud and sand to the shore, to examine the country. Flinders ascended one of the foothills of the range that forms the backbone of Yorke's Peninsula, stretching north and south upwards of 200 miles.

At dawn on 31 March the *Investigator* was got under way to proceed down the eastern side of Yorke's Peninsula. The wind was contrary, and the work could be done only 'partially', though, of course, sufficiently well to complete the chart. The peninsula was described as 'singular in form, having some resemblance to a very ill-shaped leg and foot'. Its length from Cape Spencer to the northern junction with the mainland was calculated to be 105 miles. On 1 April Flinders was able to write that the exploration of St Vincent's Gulf was finished.

The general character of the country, especially on the east, he considered to be superior to that on the borders of Spencer's Gulf; and the subsequent development of the State of South Australia has justified his opinion. He would assuredly have desired to linger longer upon the eastern shore, could he have foreseen that within 40 years of the discovery there would be laid there the foundations of the noble city of Adelaide, with its fair and fruitful olive groves, vineyards, orchards and gardens, and its busy port, whither flow the wheat of vast plains and the wool from a million sheep leagues upon leagues away.

A second visit to Kangaroo Island was necessitated by a desire to make corrections in the *Investigator*'s time-keepers, and on this occasion a somewhat longer stay was made. The ship arrived on 2 April, and did not leave again till the 7th.

Very few Aboriginals were seen upon the shores of the two gulfs, and these only through a telescope. At Port Lincoln some blacks were known to be in the neighbourhood, but the expedition did not succeed in getting into contact with them. Flinders scrupulously observed the policy of doing nothing to alarm them; and his remarks in this relation are characterised by as much good sense as humane feeling. Writing of a small party of natives who were heard calling but did not show themselves, probably having hidden in thick scrub to observe the boat's crew, he said:

> *No attempt was made to follow them, for I had always found the natives of this country to avoid those who seemed anxious for communication; whereas, when left entirely alone, they would usually come down after having watched us for a few days. Nor does this conduct seem to be unnatural; for what, in*

> *such case, would be the conduct of any people, ourselves for instance, were we living in a state of nature, frequently at war with our neighbours, and ignorant of the existence of any other nation? On the arrival of strangers so different in complexion and appearance to ourselves, having power to transplant themselves over, and even living upon, an element which to us was impossible, the first sensation would probably be terror, and the first movement flight. We should watch these extraordinary people from our retreats in the woods and rocks, and if we found ourselves sought and pursued by them, should conclude their designs to be inimical; but if, on the contrary, we saw them quietly employed in occupations which had no reference to us, curiosity would get the better of fear, and after observing them more closely, we should ourselves risk a communication. Such seemed to have been the conduct of these Australians;*[4] *and I am persuaded that their appearance on the morning when the tents were struck was a prelude to their coming down; and that, had we remained a few days longer, a friendly communication would have ensued. The way was, however, prepared for the next ship which may visit this port, as it was to us in King George's Sound by Captain Vancouver and the ship* Elligood; *to whose previous visits and peaceable conduct we were most probably indebted for our early intercourse with the inhabitants of that place. So far as could be perceived with a glass, the natives of this port were the same in personal appearance as those of King George's Sound and Port Jackson. In the hope of conciliating their goodwill to succeeding visitors, some hatchets and various other articles were left in their paths, fastened to stumps of trees which had been cut down near our watering pits.*

More wildlife was seen at Kangaroo Island than in the gulf region. Thirty emus were observed on one day; kangaroos, as has been remarked, were plentiful; and a large colony of pelicans caused the name of Pelican Lagoon to be given to a feature of the island's eastern lobe. The marsupial, the seal, the emu, and the bag-billed bird that nature built in one of her whimsical moods, had held unchallenged possession for tens of thousands of years, probably never visited by any ships, nor even preyed upon by blacks. The reflections of Flinders upon Pelican Lagoon have a tinting of poetic feeling which we do not often find in his solid pages:

---

[4] The only occasion, I think, where Flinders uses this word. He usually called Aboriginals 'Indians'.

> *Flocks of the old birds were sitting upon the beaches of the lagoon, and it appeared that the islands were their breeding places; not only so, but from the number of skeletons and bones there scattered it should seem that they had for ages been selected for the closing scene of their existence. Certainly none more likely to be free from disturbance of every kind could have been chosen, than these inlets in a hidden lagoon of an uninhabited island, situate upon an unknown coast near the antipodes of Europe; nor can anything be more consonant to the feelings, if pelicans have any, than quietly to resign their breath whilst surrounded by their progeny, and in the same spot where they first drew it. Alas, for the pelicans! their golden age is past; but it has much exceeded in duration that of man.*

The picture of the zoological interests of Kangaroo Island is heightened by Flinders' account of the seals and marsupials.

> *Never perhaps has the dominion possessed here by the kangaroo been invaded before this time. The seal shared with it upon the shores, but they seemed to dwell amicably together. It not unfrequently happened that the report of a gun fired at a kangaroo, near the beach, brought out two or three bellowing seals from under bushes considerably further from the water side. The seal, indeed, seemed to be much the more discerning animal of the two; for its actions bespoke a knowledge of our not being kangaroos, whereas the kangaroo not unfrequently appeared to consider us to be seals.*

In the quotation, it may be as well to add, the usual spelling of 'kangaroo' is followed, but Flinders invariably spelt it 'kanguroo'. The orthography of the word was not settled in his time; Cook wrote 'kangooroo' and 'kanguru,' but Hawkesworth, who edited his voyages made it 'kangaroo'.

The quantity of fallen timber lying upon the island prompted the curiosity of Flinders. Trunks of trees lay about in all directions

> *and were nearly of the same size and in the same progress towards decay; from whence it would seem that they had not fallen from age nor yet been thrown down in a gale of wind. Some general conflagration, and there were marks apparently of fire on many of them, is perhaps the sole cause which can be reasonably assigned; but whence came the woods on fire? There were no inhabitants upon the island, and that the natives of the*

continent did not visit it was demonstrated, if not by the want of all signs of such visits, yet by the tameness of the kangaroo, an animal which, on the continent, resembles the wild deer in timidity. Perhaps lightning might have been the cause, or possibly the friction of two dead trees in a strong wind; but it would be somewhat extraordinary that the same thing should have happened at Thistle's Island, Boston Island, and at this place, and apparently about the same time. Can this part of Terra Australis have been visited before, unknown to the world? The French navigator, Lapérouse, was ordered to explore it, but there seems little probability that he ever passed Torres Strait.

Some judgment may be formed of the epoch when these conflagrations happened, from the magnitude of the growing trees; for they must have sprung up since that period. They were a species of eucalyptus, and being less than the fallen tree, had most probably not arrived at maturity; but the wood is hard and solid, and it may thence be supposed to grow slowly. With these considerations, I should be inclined to fix the period at not less than ten, nor more then twenty years before our arrival. This brings us back to Lapérouse. He was in Botany Bay in the beginning of 1788, and, if he did pass through Torres Strait, and come round to this coast, as was his intention, it would probably be about the middle or latter end of that year, or between thirteen and fourteen years before the Investigator. *My opinion is not favourable to this conjecture; but I have furnished all the data to enable the reader to form his own opinion upon the cause which might have prostrated the woods of these islands.*

The passage is worth quoting, if only for the interesting allusion to La Pérouse, whose fate was, at the time when Flinders sailed and wrote, an unsolved mystery of the sea. Captain Dillon's discovery of relics at Vanikoro, in 1826, twelve years after the death of Flinders, informed the world that the illustrious French navigator did not pass through Torres Strait but was wrecked in the Santa Cruz group.[5] The fire, so many signs of which were observed on Kangaroo Island, was in all probability caused naturally in the heat of a dry summer.

Very shortly after leaving Kangaroo Island Flinders met one of the vessels of the French exploring expedition; and the story of that occurrence must occupy our particular consideration in the next chapter.

[5] See the author's *Lapérouse,* Sydney, 1912, pp. 90 *et seq.*

XV

FLINDERS AND BAUDIN IN ENCOUNTER BAY

FLINDERS did not complete the examination of Kangaroo Island. The approach of the winter season, and an apprehension that shortness of provisions might compel him to make for Port Jackson before concluding the discovery of the south coast, induced him to leave the south and west parts of the island, with the intention of making a second visit at a later time. Therefore, in the afternoon of Tuesday, 6 April, the anchor was weighed and he resumed the exploration of the mainland eastward from Cape Jervis, at the extremity of St Vincent's Gulf. Wind and tide made against a rapid passage, and the east end of Kangaroo Island had not been cleared by eight o'clock on the following evening.

At four o'clock on the afternoon of 8 April the sloop was making slow progress eastward, when the man aloft reported that a white rock was to be seen ahead. The attention of everybody on board was at once turned in the direction of the object. Very soon it became apparent that it was not a rock but a ship, which had sighted the *Investigator*, and was making towards her. As no sail had been seen for five months, and it seemed beyond all likelihood that another ship should be spoken [encountered and communicated with] in these uncharted seas, where there was no settlement, no port at which refreshment could be obtained, no possibility of trade, no customary maritime route, it may be imagined that there was a feeling of excitement among the ship's company. Flinders of course knew that the French had a discovery expedition somewhere in Australasian waters, and the fact that it had secured some months' start of him had occasioned a certain amount of anxiety before he left England. He was aware that it was protected by a passport from the British Government. The approaching vessel might be one of Baudin's; but she might by some strange chance be an enemy's ship of war. In any case, he prepared for emergencies: 'we cleared for action in case of being attacked'.

Glasses were turned on the stranger, which proved on closer scrutiny to be 'a heavy-looking ship, without any top-gallant masts up'. The *Investigator* hoisted her colours: the Union Jack, it may be remarked, since that flag was adopted by Great Britain at the beginning of 1801, before the expedition sailed. The stranger put up the tricolour, 'and afterwards an English Jack forward, as we did a white flag'.[1]

It has already been explained (Chapter XI) that *Le Géographe*, commanded by the commodore of the French expedition, separated from *Le Naturaliste* at the eastern entrance to Bass Strait on 7 and 8 March, and that Baudin sailed through the strait westward. We take up the thread again at that point, and will follow Baudin until he met Flinders. He was between Wilson's Promontory and Cape Otway from 28 to 31 March, in very good weather. The most important fact relating to this part of his voyage is that he missed the entrance to Port Phillip. In his letter to the Minister of Marine, he described the promontory and the situation of Westernport, and then proceeded to relate that 'from the 9th to the 11th [of the month Germinal in the French Revolutionary calendar, by which of course Baudin dated events; equivalent to 30 March–1 April] the winds having been very favourable to us, we visited an extensive portion of the coast, where the land is high, well-wooded, and of an agreeable appearance, but does not present any place favourable to debarkation. All the points were exactly determined, and the appearance of the shores depicted.' That describes the Cape Otway country; and the part of the letter which follows refers to the land on the west of the Otway. There is no word of any port being sighted. The letter agrees with what Baudin told Flinders, that 'he had found no ports, harbours or inlets, or anything to interest'; and Flinders was subsequently surprised to find that so large a harbour as Port Phillip had been missed by Baudin, 'more especially as he had fine winds and weather'.[2] Nevertheless, when Péron and Freycinet came to write the history of the French voyage—knowing then of the existence

---

[1] Flinders relates the story of his meeting with Baudin, in his *Voyage to Terra Australis*, I, 188, and in letters to the Admiralty and to Sir Joseph Banks, printed in *Historical Records of New South Wales*, IV, pp. 749 and 755. The official history of the French voyage was written by François Péron, and is printed in his *Voyage de Découvertes aux Terres Australes*, I, p. 324. But Péron was not present at the interviews between Flinders and Baudin. Captain Baudin's own account of the incident is related in his manuscript diary, and in a long letter to the French Minister of Marine, dated 'Port Jackson, 10th November, 1802', both of which are in the Archives Nationales, BB4, 995, Marine. These sources have been compared and used in the writing of this chapter. Baudin's narrative is translated in an appendix.

[2] Flinders to Banks, *Hist. Rec.*, IV, p. 755.

of Port Phillip, and having a chart of it before them—they very boldly claimed that they had seen it, and had distinguished its contours from the masthead,[3] a thing impossible to do from the situation in which they were.

The company on board *Le Géographe* were as excited about the ship sailing eastward, as were the *Investigator*'s men when the reported white rock ahead proved to be the sails of another vessel. The French crew were in a distressingly sick condition. Scurvy had played havoc among them, much of the ship's meat was worm-eaten and stinking, and a large number of the crew were incapacitated. On the morning of 8 April some of Baudin's people had been engaged in harpooning dolphins. They were desperately in need of fresh food, and a shoal of these rapid fish [marine mammals], appearing and playing around the prow, appeared to them 'like a gift from heaven'. Nine large dolphins had been caught, giving a happy promise of enough meat to last a day or two, when the man at the masthead reported that there was a sail in sight. At first Baudin was of opinion that the ship ahead was *Le Naturaliste*, rejoining company after a month's separation. But as the distance between the two ships diminished, and the *Investigator* ran up her ensign, her nationality was perceived, and Baudin hoisted the tricolour.

The situation of the *Investigator* when she hove to [came to a stop] was in 35° 40' south and 138° 58' east. The time was half-past five o'clock in the evening; the position about five miles south-west of the nearest bit of coast, in what Flinders called Encounter Bay, in commemoration of the event. *Le Géographe* passed the English ship with a free wind, and as she did so Flinders hailed her, enquiring 'Are you Captain Baudin?' 'It is he,' was the response. Flinders thereupon called out that he was very glad to meet the French explorer, and Baudin responded in cordial terms, without, however, knowing whom he was addressing. Still the wariness of the English captain was not to be lulled; he records, 'we veered round as *Le Géographe* was passing, so as to keep our broadside to her, lest the flag of truce should be a deception'. But being now satisfied of her good faith, Flinders brought his ship to the wind on the opposite tack, had a boat hoisted out, and prepared to go on board the French vessel.

As Flinders did not speak French, he took with him Robert Brown, who was an accomplished French scholar. On board *Le Géographe* they were received by an officer, who indicated Baudin, and the three passed into the captain's cabin.

---

[3] *Voyage de Découvertes*, I, p. 316, and III, p. 115.

It is curious that Baudin, in his letter to the Minister of Marine, makes no reference to the presence of Brown at this interview, and at a second which occurred on the following morning. He speaks of inviting Flinders to enter his cabin, and proceeds to allude to the conversation which followed when they were 'alone' ('nous trouvant seul'). But Flinders' statement, 'as I did not understand French, Mr. Brown, the naturalist, went with me in the boat; we were received by an officer who pointed out the commander, and by him were conducted into the cabin', can have no other meaning than that Brown was present. He also says, further on in his narrative, 'no person was present at our conversations except Mr. Brown, and they were mostly carried on in English, which the captain spoke so as to be understood'. It may be that Baudin regarded Brown merely as an interpreter, but certainly his presence was a fact.

In the cabin Flinders produced his passport from the French Government, and asked to see Baudin's from the Admiralty. Baudin found the document and handed it to his visitor, but did not wish to see the passport carried by Flinders. He put it aside without inspection.

The conversation then turned upon the two voyages. Flinders explained that he had left England about eight months after the departure of the French ships, and that he was bound for Port Jackson. Baudin related the course of his voyage, mentioning his work in Van Diemen's Land, his passage through Bass Strait, and his run along the coast of what is now the State of Victoria, where he had not found 'any river, inlet or other shelter which afforded anchorage'. Flinders enquired about a large island said to lie in the western entrance to Bass Strait (that is, King Island), but Baudin said he had not seen it, and seemed to doubt whether it existed. Baudin observed in his letter that Flinders appeared to be pleased with this reply, 'doubtless in the hope of being able to make the discovery himself'.

Baudin was very critical about an English chart of Bass Strait, published in 1800. He found fault with the representation of the north side, but commended the drawing of the south side, and of the neighbouring islands. Flinders pointed to a note upon the chart, explaining that it was prepared from material furnished by George Bass, who had merely traversed the coast in a small open boat, and had had no good means of fixing the latitude and longitude; but he added that a rectified chart had since been published, and offered, if Baudin would remain in the neighbourhood during the night, to visit *Le Géographe* again in the morning, and bring with him a copy of this improved drawing, with a memorandum on the navigation of the strait.

He was alluding to his own small quarto book of *Observations*, published before he left England, as related in Chapter XII. Baudin accepted the offer with pleasure, and the two ships lay near together during the night.

The story of the interviews, as related by the two captains, is not in agreement on several points, and the differences are not a little curious. Baudin states that he knew Flinders at the very beginning of the first interview, on 8 April: 'Mr. Flinders, who commanded the ship, presented himself, and as soon as I learnt his name I had no doubt that he, like ourselves, was occupied with the exploration of the south coast of New Holland.' But Flinders affirms that Baudin did not learn his name until the end of the second interview on 9 April: 'At parting ... on my asking the name of the captain of *Le Naturaliste* he bethought himself to ask mine; and finding it to be the same as the author of the chart which he had been criticising, expressed not a little surprise, but had the politeness to congratulate himself on meeting me.' There may well have been some misunderstanding between the two captains, especially as Flinders did not speak French and Baudin only spoke English 'so as to be understood', which, as experience teaches, usually means so as to be misunderstood. It is not very likely that Baudin was unaware of the name of the English captain until the end of the second meeting. While the interview of 8 April was taking place in the cabin, Flinders' boatmen were questioned by some of *Le Géographe*'s company who could speak English, and Péron tells us that the men related the story of the *Investigator*'s voyage.[4] It is difficult to believe that Flinders' name would not be ascertained in this manner; equally difficult to believe that Captain Baudin would sustain two interviews with the commander of another ship without knowing to whom he was talking. In fact, Baudin had the name of Flinders before him on the Bass Strait chart which he had been criticising. It was a chart copied in Paris from an English print, and was inscribed as 'levée par Flinders' [drawn by Flinders]. Baudin in his letter to the Minister observed that he pointed out to Flinders errors in the chart 'that he had given us'. Flinders was of opinion that Baudin criticised the chart without knowing that he was the author of it. Baudin may have been surprised at first to learn that the Captain Flinders with whom he was conversing was the same as he whose name appeared on the chart; but his own statement that he knew the name at the first interview appears credible.

---

[4] Péron, *Voyage de Découvertes*, I, p. 323. Flinders also said that 'some of his officers learnt from my boat's crew that our object was also discovery'.

Again, Baudin was of opinion that at the first interview Flinders was 'reserved'; whilst Flinders, on the other hand, was surprised that Baudin 'made no enquiries concerning my business on this unknown coast, but as he seemed more desirous of communicating information I was happy to receive it'. Reading the two narratives together, it is not apparent either that Flinders wished to be reserved or that Baudin lacked curiosity as to what the *Investigator* had been doing. The probable explanation is that the two men were not understanding each other perfectly.

At half-past six o'clock on the morning of 9 April Flinders again visited *Le Géographe*, where he breakfasted with Baudin.[5] On this occasion they talked freely about their respective voyages, and, said the French commodore, 'he appeared to me to have been happier than we were in the discoveries he had made'. Flinders pointed out Cape Jervis, which was in sight, related the discovery of Spencer's and St Vincent's Gulfs, and described Kangaroo Island, with its abundance of fresh food and water. He handed to Baudin a copy of his little book on Bass Strait and its accompanying chart, related the story of the loss of John Thistle and his boat's crew, and listened to an account which his host gave of a supposed loss of one of his own boats with a number of men on the east coast of Van Diemen's Land. Baudin intimated that it was likely that Flinders, in sailing east, would fall in with the missing *Naturaliste*, and he requested that, should this occur, the captain of that ship might be informed that Baudin intended to sail to Port Jackson as soon as the bad winter weather set in. Flinders himself had invited Baudin to sail to Sydney to refresh [lay in fresh supplies], mentioning that he would be able to obtain whatever assistance he required there. The interview was thoroughly cordial, and the two captains parted with mutual expressions of goodwill. Flinders and Brown returned to the *Investigator* at half-past eight o'clock.

Seaman Smith has nothing new to tell us concerning the Encounter Bay incident, but his brief reference is of some interest as showing how it struck a member of the *Investigator* crew, and may be cited for that purpose.

> *In the morning (9 April) we unmoord and stood for sea between Van Diemen's Land and New Holland. In the afternoon we espied a sail which loomd large. Cleared forequarters, not knowing what might be the consequence. On the ship coming*

[5] Flinders does not mention this circumstance; but as he boarded *Le Géographe* at 6.30 in the morning and did not return to the *Investigator* till 8.30, Baudin's statement is not doubtful.

> *close, our captn spoke her. She proved to be the* Le Geography *[sic] French ship upon investigation. Our boats being lowerd down our captn went on board of her, and soon returnd. Both ships lay to untill the next morning, when our captn went on board of her and soon returnd. We found her poorly mannd, having lost a boat and crew and several that run away. Her acct. was that they had parted compy with the* Naturalizer *[sic] on investigation in a gale of wind. Have been from France 18 months. On the 20th we parted compy. [Smith's dates appear to be at odds with those of Flinders and Péron.]*

Baudin sailed for Kangaroo Island, where his men enjoyed a similar feast to that which had delighted the English sailors a little while before. But the scurvy-stricken condition of his crew made the pursuit of exploration painful, and he did not continue on these coasts beyond another month. On 8 May he abandoned the work for the time being, resolving to pay a second visit to the region of the gulfs after he had refreshed his people. Sailing for Sydney, he arrived there on 20 June, in circumstances that it will be convenient to relate after describing the remainder of the voyage of the *Investigator* up to her arrival in the same port.

XVI

FLINDERS IN PORT PHILLIP

Flinders' actual discovery work on the south coast was completed when he met Baudin in Encounter Bay; for the whole coastline to the east had been found a short while before he appeared upon it, though he was not aware of this fact when completing his voyage. For about 150 miles, from the mouth of the Murray eastward to Cape Banks, the credit of discovery properly belongs to Baudin, and Flinders duly marked his name upon the chart. Further eastward, from Cape Banks to the deep bend of the coast at the head of which lies Port Phillip, the discoverer was Captain Grant of the *Lady Nelson.* His voyage was projected [planned] under the following circumstances.

When Philip Gidley King, who in 1800 succeeded Hunter as Governor of New South Wales, was in England in 1799, he represented to the Admiralty the desirability of sending out to Australia a small, serviceable ship, capable of being used in shallow waters, so that she might explore bays and rivers. One of the Commissioners of the Transport Board, Captain John Schanck, had designed a type of vessel that was considered suitable for this purpose. She was to be fitted with a sliding keel, or centreboard, and was deemed to be a boat of staunch sea-going qualities, as well as being good for close-in coastal service. A 60-ton brig, the *Lady Nelson*, was built to Schanck's plans, and was entrusted to the command of Lieutenant Grant. She was tried in the Downs in January 1800, when Grant reported enthusiastically on her behaviour. She rode out a gale in five fathoms of water without shipping 'even a sea that would come over the sole of your shoe'. Running her into Ramsgate in a heavy sea, Grant wrote of her in terms that, though somewhat crabbed to a non-nautical ear, were a sailor's equivalent for fine poetry: 'though it blew very strong, I found the vessel stand well up under sail, and with only one reef out of the topsails, no jib set, a lee tide going, when close hauled she brought her wake right aft and went at the rate of five knots'.

Grant was ambitious to make discoveries on his own account, and did not lack zeal. He was a skilful sailor, but was lacking in the scientific accomplishment required for the service in which he aspired to shine. When at length he returned from Australia, King summed him up in a sentence: 'I should have been glad if your ability as a surveyor, or being able to determine the longitude of the different places you might visit, was any ways equal to your ability as an officer and a seaman.'

Grant left England early in 1800, intending to sail to Australia by the usual route, making the Cape of Good Hope, and then rounding the south of Van Diemen's Land. But news of the discovery of Bass Strait was received after the *Lady Nelson* had put to sea; and the Admiralty (April 1800) sent instructions to reach him at the Cape, directing him to sail through the strait from the west. This he did. Striking the Australian coast opposite Cape Banks on 3 December 1800, he followed it along past Cape Otway, thence in a line across to Wilson's Promontory and, penetrating the strait, was the first navigator to work through it from the far western side. He attempted no survey, and shortness of water and provisions deterred him from even pursuing the in-and-out curves of the shore; but he marked down upon a rough eye-sketch such prominent features as Mount Gambier, Cape Northumberland, Cape Bridgewater, Cape Nelson, Portland Bay, Julia Percy Island, and Cape Otway. 'I took the liberty of naming the different capes, bays, etc., for the sake of distinction,' he reported to the Governor on his arrival at Sydney on 16 December.

It was in this way that both Baudin and Flinders were anticipated in the discovery of the western half of the coast of Victoria. The *Investigator* voyage had not been planned when the *Lady Nelson* sailed; and when Flinders was commissioned the Admiralty directed that Grant should be placed under his orders, the brig being used as a tender.

The baffling winds that had delayed Flinders' departure from Kangaroo Island on 8 April 1802, continued after he sailed from Encounter Bay, so that he did not pass the 50 leagues [approximately 150 miles] or so first traversed by *Le Géographe* for eight tedious days. On 17 April he reached Grant's Cape Banks; on 18 April passed Cape Northumberland; and on the 19th Capes Bridgewater, Nelson and Grant. But the south-west gale blew so hard during this part of the voyage that, the coast trending south-easterly, it was difficult to keep the ship on a safe course; and Flinders confessed that he was 'glad to miss a small part of the coast'. Thick squally weather prevented the survey being made with safety; and, indeed, it was rarely that the configuration of the land could be distinguished at a greater distance than two miles.

On the 21st Flinders noticed a subsidence of the sea, which made him conclude that he was to the windward of the large island concerning which he had questioned Baudin. He resolved to take advantage of a period when the close examination of the mainland had become dangerous to determine the exact position of this island, of whose whereabouts he had heard from sealers in 1799.

The south part of King Island had been found by the skipper of a sealing brig, named Reid, in 1799, but the name it bears was given to it by John Black, commander of the brig *Harbinger*, who discovered the northern part in January 1801. Flinders was occupied for three days at King Island. On the 24th, the wind having moderated, he made for Cape Otway. But it was still considered imprudent to follow the shore too closely against a south-east wind; and on the 26th the ship ran across the water to Grant's Cape Schanck.

The details of these movements are of some moment, for the ship was nearing the gates of Port Phillip. 'We bore away westward,' Flinders records, 'in order to trace the land round the head of the deep bight.' In view of the importance of the harbour which he was about to enter, we may quote his own description of his approach to it, and his surprise at what he found:

> *On the west side of the rocky point,[1] there was a small opening, with breaking water across it. However, on advancing a little more westward the opening assumed a more interesting aspect, and I bore away to have a nearer view. A large extent of water presently became visible withinside [on the inner side], and although the entrance seemed to be very narrow, and there were in it strong ripplings like breakers, I was induced to steer in at half-past one; the ship being close upon a wind and every man ready for tacking at a moment's warning. The soundings were irregular, between 6 and 12 fathoms, until we got four miles within the entrance, when they shoaled quick to 2¾. We then tacked; and having a strong tide in our favour, worked to the eastward, between the shoal and the rocky point, with 12 fathoms for the deepest water. In making the last stretch from the shoal, the depth diminished from 10 fathoms quickly to 3; and before the ship could come round, the flood tide set her upon a mud bank and she stuck fast. A boat was lowered down to sound; and, finding the deep*

---

[1] Point Nepean.

> *water lie to the north-west, a kedge anchor was carried out; and, having got the ship's head in that direction, the sails were filled, and she drew off into 6 and 10 fathoms; and it being then dark, we came to an anchor.*
>
> *The extensive harbour we had thus unexpectedly found I supposed must be Westernport; although the narrowness of the entrance did by no means correspond with the width given to it by Mr. Bass. It was the information of Captain Baudin, who had coasted along from thence with fine weather, and had found no inlet of any kind, which induced this supposition; and the very great extent of the place, agreeing with that of Westernport, was in confirmation of it. This, however, was not Westernport, as we found next morning; and I congratulated myself on having made a new and useful discovery. But here again I was in error. This place, as I afterwards learned at Port Jackson, had been discovered ten weeks before by Lieutenant John Murray, who had succeeded Captain Grant in the command of the* Lady Nelson. *He had given it the name of Port Phillip, and to the rocky point on the east side of the entrance that of Point Nepean.*

It was characteristic of Flinders that he allowed no expression of disappointment to escape him, on finding that he had been anticipated by a few weeks in the discovery of Port Phillip. Baudin, it will be remembered, observed the satisfaction felt by his visitor in Encounter Bay, when he learnt that *Le Géographe* had not found King Island, because he thought he would have the happiness of being the first to lay it down upon a chart. In this he had been forestalled by Black of the *Harbinger*; and now again he was to find that a predecessor had entered the finest harbour in southern Australia. Disappointment he must have felt; but he was by no means the man to begrudge the success that had accrued to another navigator. He made no remark, such as surely might have been forgiven to him, about the determining accidents of time and weather; though it is but right for us to observe that, had the *Investigator* been permitted to sail from England when she was ready (in April 1801) instead of being delayed by the Admiralty officials till July, Port Phillip, as well as the stretch of coast discovered by Baudin, would have been found by Flinders. That delay was caused by nothing more than a temporary illness of the Secretary of the Admiralty, Evan Nepean, whose name is commemorated in Point Nepean, one of the headlands flanking the entrance to the port.

A perfectly just recognition of the real significance of Flinders in southern exploration has led to his name being honoured and commemorated even with respect to parts where he was not the actual discoverer. It is a function of history to do justice in the large, abiding sense, discriminating the spiritual potency of personalities that dominate events from the accidental connection of lesser persons with them. In that wider sense, Flinders was the true discoverer of the whole of the southern coast of Australia. He, of course, made no such claim; but we who estimate the facts after a long lapse of years can see clearly that it was so. Only the patching up of the old *Reliance* kept him in Sydney while Bass was creeping round the coast to Westernport. Only the illness of an official and other trifling causes prevented him from discovering Port Phillip. It was the completion of his chart of Bass Strait, based upon his friend's memoranda, that led the Admiralty to direct Grant to sail through the strait from the west, and so enabled him to be the first to come upon the coast from Cape Banks to Cape Schanck. It was only the delay before-mentioned and the contrary winds that hindered him from preceding Baudin along the 50 leagues that are credited to that navigator.

Thus it is that although not a league of the coastline of Victoria is in strict verity to be attributed to Flinders as discoverer, he is habitually cited as if he were. Places are named after him, memorials are erected to him. The highest mountain in the vicinity of Port Phillip carries on its summit a tablet celebrating the fact that Flinders entered the port at the end of April 1802; but there is nowhere a memorial to remind anyone that Murray actually discovered it in January of the same year. The reason is that, while it is felt that time and circumstance enabled others to do things which must be inscribed on the historical page, the triumph that should have followed from skill, knowledge, character, preparation and opportunities well and wisely used, was fairly earned by Flinders. The dates, not the merits, prevent their being claimed for him. His personality dominates the whole group of discoveries. We chronicle the facts in regard to Grant, Baudin, Murray, and Bass, but we feel all the time that Flinders was the central man.

Not being aware of Murray's good fortune in January, Flinders treated Port Phillip as a fresh discovery, and examined its approaches with as much thoroughness as his resources would allow. At this time, however, the store of provisions was running low. The *Investigator* was 40 weeks out from England, and re-equipment was fast becoming imperative. Her commander had felt the urgency of his needs before he reached Port Phillip. He had seriously considered whether he should not make for Sydney from King Island. 'I determined, however, to run over to the high land we had seen on the north side of Bass Strait, and to trace as much of the coast from thence eastward as the state of the weather and our remaining provisions could possibly allow.'

As related in the passage quoted above, Flinders at first thought he had reached Westernport, though the narrowness of the entrance did not correspond with Bass's description of the harbour he had discovered four years previously. But Baudin had told him that he found no port or harbour of any kind between Westernport and Encounter Bay. Consequently, it was all the more astonishing to behold this great sheet of blue water broadening out to shores overlooked by high hills, and extending northward further than the eye could penetrate. It was not until the following day, 27 April, that he found he was not in the port which his friend had discovered in the whaleboat. Immediately after breakfast he rowed away from the ship in a boat, accompanied by Brown and Westall, to ascend the bluff mountain on the east side which Murray had named Arthur's Seat. From the top he was able to survey the landscape at a height of 1,000 feet; and then he saw the waters and islands of Westernport lying beneath him only a few miles further to the east, whilst, to his surprise, the curves of Port Phillip were seen to be so extensive 'that even at this elevation its boundary to the northward could not be distinguished'.

Next morning, 28 April, Flinders commenced to sail round the bay. But the wind was slight and progress was slow; with his fast diminishing store of provisions vexing his mind, he felt that he could not afford the time for a complete survey. Besides, the lead showed many shallows, and there was a constant fear of running the ship aground. He therefore directed Fowler to take the *Investigator* back to the entrance, whilst, on the 29th, he went with Midshipman Lacy, in a boat provisioned for three days, to make a rapid reconnaissance of as much as could be seen in that time. He rowed north-east nine miles from Arthur's Seat, reaching about the neighbourhood of Mornington. Then he crossed to the western side of the bay, and on the 30th traversed the opening of the arm at the head of which Geelong now stands.

At dawn on 1 May he landed with three of the boat's crew, for the purpose of ascending the highest point of the You-yang range, whose conical peaks, standing up purple against the evening sky, had been visible when the ship first entered Port Phillip. 'Our way was over a low plain, where the water appeared frequently to lodge. It was covered with small-bladed grass, but almost destitute of wood, and the soil was clayey and shallow. One or two miles before arriving at the feet of the hills, we entered a wood, where an emu and a kangaroo were seen at a distance; and the top of the peak was reached at ten o'clock.'

From the crest of this granite mountain he would command a superb view. Towards the north, in the interior, the dark bulk of Mount Macedon was seen; and all around lay a fertile, promising country, mile after mile of green pastures, as fair a prospect as the eye could wish to rest upon. There can be little doubt that Flinders made his observations from the flat top of a huge granite boulder which forms the apex of the peak. 'I left the ship's name,' he says, 'on a scroll of paper deposited in a small pile of stones upon the top of the peak.' He called it Station Peak, for the reason that he had made it his station for making observations. In 1912 a fine bronze tablet was fastened on the eastern face of the boulder on which Flinders probably stood and worked.[2]

The boat was reached, after the descent of the mountain and the return tramp across the sodden flats, at three o'clock in the afternoon. The party were very weary from this twenty-mile excursion, a feat requiring some power of endurance, as one who has walked along the same route and climbed Station Peak several times can testify; and especially hard on men who were fresh from a long voyage. The party camped for the night at Indented Head, on the west side of the port, and on Sunday, 2 May, they again boarded the *Investigator*.

The ship was anchored under the shelter of the Nepean Peninsula, nearly opposite the present Portsea. On the way back Flinders shot 'some delicate teal', near the piece of water which Murray had called Swan Harbour, and a few black swans were caught.

Port Phillip has since become important as the seat of one of the great cities of the world, and its channels are used by commercial fleets flying every colour known to the trading nations. Scarcely an hour of the day goes by, but the narrow waters dividing the port from the ocean are churned by the propellers of great ships. The imagination sets itself a

---

[2] It is much to be regretted that this very laudable mark of honour to his memory was not effected without doing a thing which is contrary to a good rule and was repugnant to Flinders' practice. The name Station Peak was sought to be changed to Flinders' Peak, and those who so admirably occasioned the erection of the tablet managed to secure official sanction for the alteration by its notification in the Victorian Government *Gazette*. But nobody with any historical sense or proper regard for the fame of Flinders will ever call the mountain by any other name than Station Peak. It was his name; and names given by a discoverer should be respected, except when there is a sound reason to the contrary, as there is not in this instance. As previously observed, Flinders never named any discovery after himself. Honour him by calling any other places after him by all means; the name Flinders for the Commonwealth Naval Base in Westernport is an excellent one, for instance. But his names for natural features should not be disturbed.

task in trying to realise those few days in May 1802, when Flinders called it a 'useful but obscure port' and when the only keels that lay within the bay were those of one small sloop at anchor near the entrance, and one tiny boat in which her captain was rowing over the surface and making a map of the outline. And if it is difficult for us to recapture that scene of spacious solitude, it was quite impossible for Flinders to foresee what a century would bring forth. He recognised that the surrounding country 'has a pleasing and in many places a fertile appearance'. He described much of it as patently fit for agricultural purposes. 'It is in great measure a grassy country, and capable of supporting much cattle, though much better calculated for sheep.' It was, indeed, largely on his report that settlement was attempted at Port Phillip in 1803. But it is quaint, at this time of day [at this point in time], to read his remark that 'were a settlement made at Port Phillip, as doubtless there will be some time hereafter, the entrance could be easily distinguished, and it would not be difficult to establish a friendly intercourse with the natives, for they are acquainted with the effect of firearms, and desirous of possessing many of our conveniences'.

Seaman Smith devotes a paragraph in his journal to the visit to Port Phillip, and it may as well be quoted for its historical interest:

> *On the 28th we came to an anchor in a bay of very large size. Thinking there was a good channel in a passage through, we got aground; but by good management we got off without damadge. Here we caught a Shirk which measured 10 feet 9 inch in length; in girt very large. 29th the captn and boats went to investigate the interior part of the harbr for 3 days, while those on board imploy'd in working ship to get as near the mouth of the harbr as possible. May 2nd our boat and crew came on board. Brought with them 2 swanns and a number of native spears.*

At daylight on 3 May the *Investigator* dropped out of Port Phillip with the tide. Westall, the artist, made a drawing of the heads from a distance of five miles.

At dusk on Saturday, 8 May, she stood seven miles off the entrance to Port Jackson. Flinders was so thoroughly well acquainted with the harbour that he tried to beat up in the night; but the wind was adverse, and he did not pass the heads till one o'clock on the following day. At three o'clock the ship was brought to anchor, and the long voyage of discovery, which had had larger results than any voyage since the great days of Cook, was over. It had lasted nine months and nine days.

The horrors of scurvy were such a customary accompaniment of long voyages in those days that the condition of Flinders' company at the termination of this protracted navigation was healthy almost beyond precedent. But this young captain had learnt how to manage a ship in Cook's school, and had profited from his master's admonitions. Cook, in his *Endeavour* voyage of 1770–01, brought his people through a protracted period at sea with, 'generally speaking', freedom from scurvy, and showed how by scrupulous cleanliness, plenty of vegetable food, and anti-scorbutic remedies the dreadful distemper could be kept at bay. But, fine as Cook's record is in this respect, it is eclipsed by that of Flinders, who entered Port Jackson at the end of this long period aboard ship with an absolutely clean bill of health. There is no touch of pride, but there is a note of very proper satisfaction, in the words which he was able to write of this remarkable record:

> *There was not a single individual on board who was not on deck working the ship into harbour; and it may be averred that the officers and crew were, generally speaking, in better health than on the day we sailed from Spithead, and not in less good spirits. I have said nothing of the regulations observed after we made Cape Leeuwin. They were very little different from those adopted in the commencement of the voyage, and of which a strict attention to cleanliness and a free circulation of air in the messing and sleeping places formed the most essential parts. Several of the inhabitants of Port Jackson expressed themselves never to have been so strongly reminded of England as by the fresh colour of many amongst the* Investigator's *ship's company.*

As soon as the anchor was dropped, Flinders went ashore and reported himself to Governor King, to whom he delivered his orders from the Admiralty. He also reported to Captain Hamelin of *Le Naturaliste*, who had sought refuge in the port and had been lying there since 24 April, the intention of Baudin to bring round *Le Géographe* in due course. Then he set about making preparations for refitting the ship and getting ready for further explorations.

XVII

THE FRENCH AT PORT JACKSON: PÉRON THE SPY

THE condition of *Le Géographe* when she made her appearance outside Port Jackson, on 20 June 1802, was in striking and instructive contrast with that of the *Investigator* on her entry 42 days before. Flinders had not a sick man on board. His crew finished the voyage a company of bronzed, jolly, hearty sailors, fit for any service. Baudin, on the contrary, had not a single man on board who was free from disease. His men were 'covered with sores and putrid ulcers'; the surgeon, Taillefer, found the duty of attending upon them revolting; they lay groaning about the decks in misery and pain, and only four were available for steering and management, themselves being reduced almost to the extremity of debility. 'Not a soul among us was exempt from the affliction,' wrote the commandant in his journal.

The utmost difficulty had been experienced in working the vessel round the south of Van Diemen's Land and up the east coast in tempestuous weather. Baudin obstinately refused, in the teeth of the urgent recommendation of his officers, to sail through Bass Strait, and thus save several days; though, as he had already negotiated the strait from the east, he knew the navigation, and the distressful condition of his people should have impelled him to choose a route which would take them to succour in the briefest period of time. He insisted on the longer course, and in consequence brought his ship to the very verge of disaster, besides intensifying the sufferings of his crew. The voyage from the region of the gulfs to the harbour of refuge was full of pain and peril. Man after man dropped out. The sailors were unable to trim the sails properly; steersmen fell at the wheel; they could not walk or lift their limbs without groaning in agony. It was a plague ship that crept round to Port Jackson Heads in that month of storms:

And as a full field charging was the sea,
And as a cry of slain men was the wind.

All this bitter suffering was caused because, as the official historian of the expedition tells us, Baudin 'neglected the most indispensable precautions relative to the health of the men'. He disregarded instructions which had been furnished with reference to hygiene, paid no heed to the experience of other navigators, and permitted practices which could not but conduce [lead] to disease. His illustrious predecessor, La Pérouse, a true pupil of Cook, had conducted a long voyage with fine immunity from scurvy, and Baudin could have done the same had he possessed valid qualifications for his employment.

There is no satisfaction in dwelling upon the pitiful condition to which Baudin's people were reduced; but it is necessary to set out the facts clearly, because the visit paid by *Le Géographe* and *Le Naturaliste* to Sydney, and what the French officers did there, is of the utmost importance in relation to what happened to Flinders at a later date.

Baudin brought his vessel up to the entrance to the harbour on 20 June, but so feeble were his crew that they could not work her into port. It was reported that a ship in evident distress was outside, and at once a boat's crew of Flinders' men from the *Investigator* was sent down to assist in towing her to an anchorage. 'It was grievous,' Flinders said, 'to see the miserable condition to which both officers and men were reduced by scurvy, there being not more out of one hundred and seventy, according to the Captain's account, than twelve men capable of doing their duty.' Baudin's own journal says they were only four; but, whatever the number may have been, even these were sick, and could only perform any kind of work under the whip of absolute necessity. All the sufferers were attended with 'the most touching activity' by the principal surgeon of the settlement, James Thomson.

The resources of Sydney at that time were slender, but such as they were Governor King immediately placed them at the disposal of the French commodore. The sick were removed to the hospital, permission was given to pitch tents close to where the *Investigator*'s [tents] were erected, at Cattle Point on the east side of Sydney Cove,[1] and everything was done to extend a cordial welcome to the visitors. The Governor wrote to Baudin:

> *Although last night I had the pleasure of announcing that a peace had taken place between our respective countries, yet a continuance of the war would have made no difference in my*

[1] Flinders, Voyage, I, p. 227. The 'Cattle Point' of Flinders is the present Fort Macquarie, or Bennelong Point, behind which Government House stands.

reception of your ship, and affording every relief and assistance in my power; and, although you will not find abundant supplies of what are most requisite and acceptable to those coming off so long a voyage, yet I offer you a sincere welcome. I am much concerned to find from Monsieur Ronsard that your ship's company are so dreadfully afflicted with the scurvy. I have sent the Naval Officer with every assistance to get the ship into a safe anchorage. I beg you would give yourself no concern about saluting. When I have the honour of seeing you, we will then concert means for the relief of your sick.

That was, truly, a letter replete in every word of it with manly gentleness, generous humanity and hospitable warmth. The same spirit was maintained throughout the six months of the Frenchmen's stay at Port Jackson. King even reduced the rations of his own people in order that he might have enough to share with the strangers. Fresh meat was so scarce in the colony that when the *Investigator* arrived Flinders could not buy any for his men; but as soon as the French appeared, King, pitying their plight, at once ordered the slaughtering of some oxen belonging to the Government in order that they might be fed on fresh food. Baudin was daily at the Governor's house,[2] and King entertained his officers frequently. His tact was as conspicuous as his good nature. Baudin was not on good terms with some of his officers, and the Governor was made aware of this fact. He conducted himself as host with a resourceful consideration for the feelings of his quarrelsome guests. And as the Governor comported [conducted] himself towards them, so also did the leading people of Sydney. 'Among all the French officers serving in the division which I command,' wrote Baudin, 'there is not one who is not, like myself, convinced of the indebtedness in which we stand to Governor King and the principal inhabitants of the colony for the courteous, affectionate, and distinguished manner in which they have received us.'

Not only on the social side was this extreme kindness displayed. King did everything in his power to further the scientific purposes of the expedition and to complete the re-equipment of Baudin's ships. *Le Géographe* required to be careened, and to have her copper lining extensively repaired. Facilities were at once granted for effecting these works. Baudin, intending to send *Le Naturaliste* back to France with natural history specimens and reports up to date, desired to purchase a

---

[2] *Historical Records*, IV, p. 952.

small Australian-built vessel to accompany him on the remainder of his voyage. King gave his consent, 'as it is for the advancement of science and navigation', and the *Casuarina*, a locally built craft of between 40 and 50 tons, was acquired for the purpose. The French men of science were assisted in making excursions into the country in prosecution of their researches. Baudin refused the application of his geologist, Bailly, who wished to visit the Hawkesbury River and the mountains to collect specimens and study the natural formation. The British, thereupon, furnished him with boats, guides and even food for the journey, since his own commander declined to supply him. Péron, the naturalist, who afterwards wrote the history of the voyage, was likewise afforded opportunities for travelling in prosecution of his studies, and the disreputable use which he made of the freedom allowed to him will presently appear.

There is no reason to believe that any of the French officers, or the men of science on Baudin's staff, abused the hospitality so nobly extended to them, with two exceptions. The conduct of the crew appears to have been exemplary. Baudin himself won King's confidence, and was not unworthy of it. His demeanour was perfectly frank. '*Entre nous*,' wrote King to Banks in May 1803, 'he showed me and left with me all his journals, in which were contained all his orders from the first idea of the voyage taking place.... He informed me that he knew of no idea that the French had of settling on any part or side of this continent.'

After the departure of the two ships, on 17 November, a rumour came to the Governor's ears that some of the French officers had informed Lieutenant-Colonel Paterson that it was their intention to establish a settlement on D'Entrecasteaux Channel in the south of Van Diemen's Land. The news occasioned grave anxiety to King, who immediately took steps to frustrate any such plans. He sent acting-Lieutenant Robbins in the *Cumberland* in pursuit of Baudin, informing him of what was alleged, and calling upon him for an explanation. Baudin positively denied that he had entertained such an intention; and certainly he had not acted, after leaving Port Jackson, as if he had the design to lay the foundations of a settlement at the place specified, for he had not sailed anywhere near southern Van Diemen's Land. He had made direct for King Island, and was quietly continuing his exploratory work when Robbins found him. This vague and unsubstantial rumour, which Paterson had not even taken the trouble to report officially to the Governor when he heard it, was the only incident with which Baudin was connected that gave King any cause to doubt his perfect good faith; and Baudin's categorical denial of the allegation is fully confirmed by his diary and correspondence—now available for study—which contain no particle of evidence to suggest that the planting of a settlement, or the choice of a site for one, was a purpose of the expedition.

Baudin's gratitude for King's hospitality was expressed in a cordial personal letter, and also in an open letter which he addressed to the Governors of the French colonies of Ile-de-France and Réunion. Twelve copies of the letter were left in King's hands, to be given by him to the captain of any British ships that might have occasion to put in to any port in those colonies. Blanks were left in the letter, to be filled up by King, with the name of the captain to whom he might give a copy and the name of the ship.[3] In this document, it will be noticed, Baudin was bespeaking from [organising] representatives of his country in their own colonies [to show] such consideration as he had experienced from his British hosts at Sydney. The fullness of his obligation could scarcely have been expressed in more thorough terms:

> *The assistance we have found here, the kindness of Governor King towards us, his generous attentions for the recovery of our sick men, his love for the progress of science, in short, everything seemed to have united to make us forget the hardships of a long and painful voyage, which was often impeded by the inclemency of the weather; and yet the fact of the peace being signed was unknown, and we only heard of it when our sick men had recovered, our vessels had been repaired, our provisions shipped, and when our departure was near at hand. Whatever the duties of hospitality may be, Governor King had given the whole of Europe the example of a benevolence which should be known, and which I take a great pleasure in publishing.*
>
> *On our arrival at Port Jackson, the stock of wheat there was very limited, and that for the future was uncertain. The arrival of 170 men was not a happy circumstance at the time, yet we*

[3] Mr F. M. Bladen, in a note appended to a copy of this interesting letter, in the *Historical Records of New South Wales*, Vol. 4, p. 968 says: 'The letter was handed to Governor King by Commodore Baudin, in case it should be required, but was retained by King amongst his papers, and never used. Had it been in the hands of Flinders when forced to touch at the Isle of France it might have prevented any question, real or pretended, as to his *bona fides.* Indeed, it is not unlikely that it was originally intended for Flinders.' But, although the letter was not used by Flinders, Baudin gave a copy of it to General Decaen, Governor of Ile-de-France, when he called there on his homeward voyage. The copy is now among Decaen's manuscripts at Caen, Vol. 84. The blanks are in it, as in King's copy. Decaen was therefore fully aware of the generous treatment accorded to his countrymen at Port Jackson.

Top left: Matthew Flinders' hat. This style of hat was introduced into the Royal Navy between 1795 and 1800.
Top right: Miniature portrait of Matthew Flinders painted in 1801 on a locket which contains a lock of Flinders' hair in the back.
Bottom: Matthew Flinders' cat, the 'faithful, intelligent Trim', who accompanied Flinders on his circumnavigation of Australia.

Top: View of Port Jackson, Sydney, as seen from South Head. Artist William Westall was official landscape and figure draftsman aboard the *Investigator* during its circumnavigation of Australia. Of his drawings made during the voyage, 138 have been preserved. Westall also made the nine engravings which appear in Flinders' *Voyage to Terra Australis*.
Bottom: Seal Island in King George's Sound, Western Australia. While researching the southern coastline, Flinders kept the *Investigator* as close to shore as possible to ensure he did not miss any river opening. Flinders made several inland excursions and encountered some of the Aboriginal people of King George's Sound.

Top: Kangaroo Island was named for the large number of kangaroos seen there. The fresh meat was very welcome to the *Investigator*'s crew after four months of living on salt pork. *Bottom*: When the *Investigator* anchored alongside the largest of Murray's Islands on 29 October 1802, three long Papuan canoes approached. Flinders cautioned his men to arm themselves, but it quickly became clear that the Papuans were interested in bartering rather than fighting.

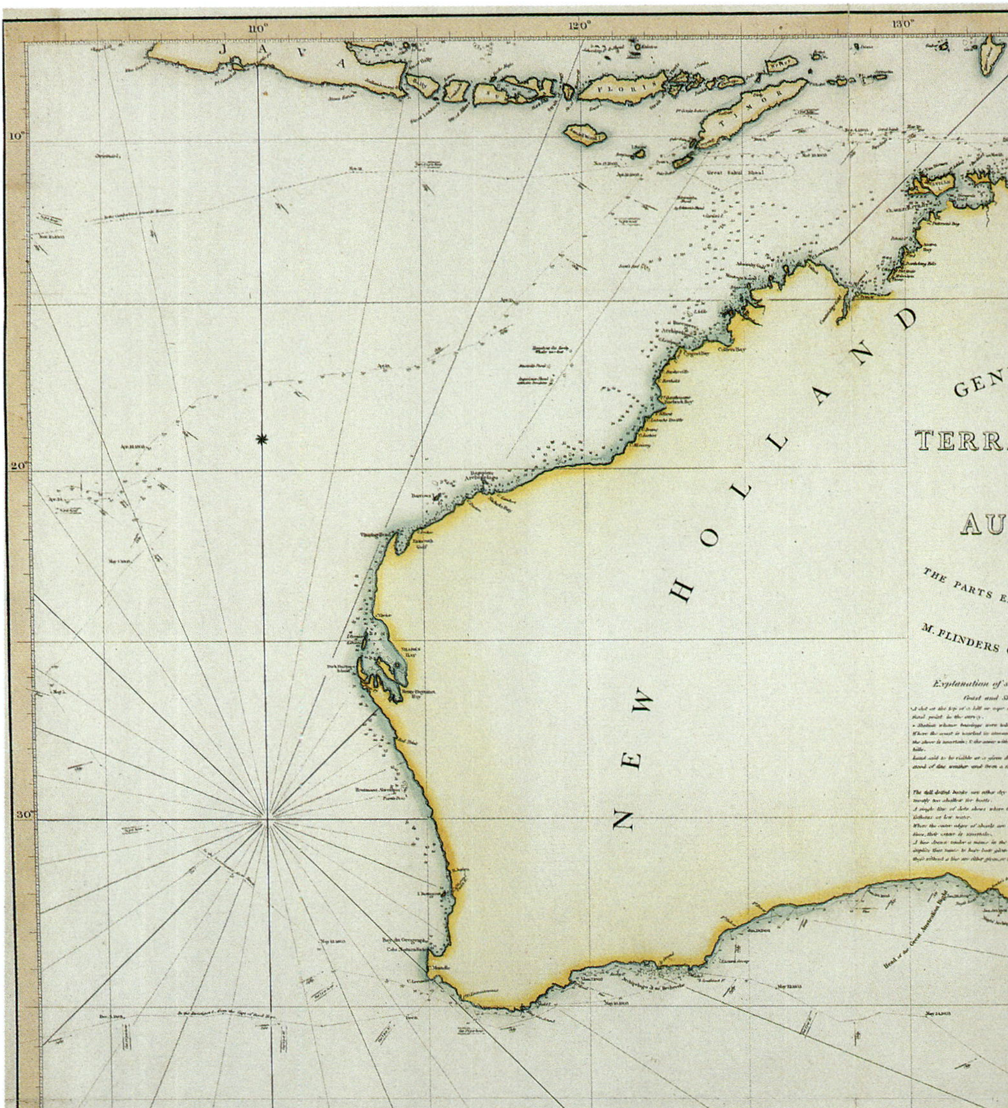

Inset: This marine chronometer, made by Thomas Earnshaw in England, c. 1800, was one of the five used by Matthew Flinders in his circumnavigation of Australia in the *Investigator*. It was the only one still working at the end of that epic voyage.

Above: Flinders' map of Terra Australis is a fine representation of a life devoted to exploration and discovery.

Top: Flinders spent four months exploring the Gulf of Carpentaria, during which time he discovered and named the Sir Edward Pellew group of islands on the south-west of the Gulf. *Bottom*: On its return voyage to England in 1803, the *Porpoise* struck a reef and was wrecked. Flinders set out in the *Porpoise*'s cutter to get help. Six weeks later he returned aboard the *Cumberland*, with the *Rolla* and *Francis*, and the shipwrecked were rescued.

Top left: Bongaree was the first Aboriginal man to circumnavigate Australia, with Flinders in the *Investigator*. *Top right*: George Bass discovered the stretch of water separating Tasmania from the mainland of Australia which now bears his name, and later circumnavigated Tasmania with Flinders. *Above left*: Captain Nicolas Baudin led the French expedition of discovery which was charting the Australian coast at the same time as the *Investigator*. *Above right*: General Charles Mathieu Isidore Decaen was the Governor of Ile-de-France (Mauritius) and responsible for detaining Flinders there for six and a half years.

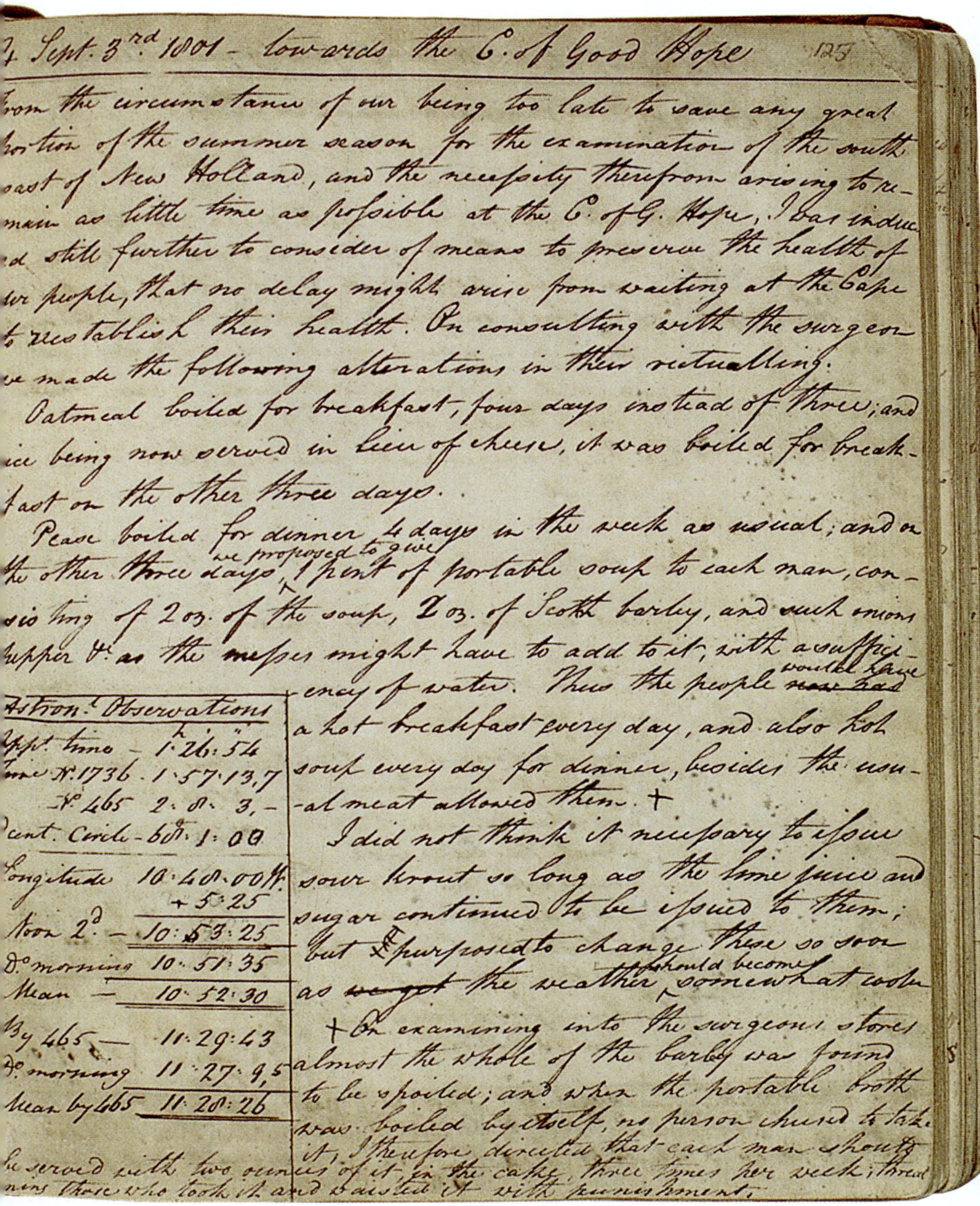

4 Sept. 3rd 1801 – towards the C. of Good Hope 125

From the circumstance of our being too late to save any great portion of the summer season for the examination of the south coast of New Holland, and the necessity therefrom arising to remain as little time as possible at the C. of G. Hope, I was induced still further to consider of means to preserve the health of our people, that no delay might arise from waiting at the Cape to reestablish their health. On consulting with the surgeon we made the following alterations in their victualling.

Oatmeal boiled for breakfast, four days instead of three; and rice being now served in lieu of cheese, it was boiled for breakfast on the other three days.

Pease boiled for dinner 4 days in the week as usual; and on the other three days, we proposed to give 1 pint of portable soup to each man, consisting of 2 oz. of the soup, 2 oz. of Scotch barley, and such onions pepper &c. as the messes might have to add to it, with a sufficiency of water. Thus the people would have a hot breakfast every day, and also hot soup every day for dinner, besides the usual meat allowed them. +

I did not think it necessary to issue sour krout so long as the lime juice and sugar continued to be issued to them; but I purposed to change these so soon as the weather should become somewhat cooler.

+ On examining into the surgeon's stores almost the whole of the barley was found to be spoiled; and when the portable broth was boiled by itself, no person chused to take it, I therefore directed that each man should be served with two ounces of it in the cake, three times per week, threatening those who took it and wasted it with punishment.

Astron.l Observations	
Appt. time –	1:26:54
Time K.1736 –	1:57:13,7
K. 465	2:8:3,–
Cent. Circle –	6d. 1:00
Longitude	10:48:00 W
	+ 5:25
Noon 2d. –	10:53:25
Do. morning	10:51:35
Mean –	10:52:30
By 465 –	11:29:43
Do. morning	11:27:9,5
Mean by 465	11:28:26

Above: A page from Matthew Flinders' journal of the *Investigator* (vol 1, 3 September 1801, p. 88).

were well received; and when our present and future wants were known, they were supplied by shortening part of the daily ration allowed to the inhabitants and the garrison of the colony. The Governor first gave the example. Through those means, which do so great honour to the humane feelings of him who put them into motion, we have enjoyed a favour which we would perhaps have experienced much difficulty in finding anywhere else.

After such treatment, which ought in future to serve as an example for all the nations, I consider it my duty, as much out of gratitude as by inclination, to recommend particularly to you Mr.—— commander of H.M.S.——. Although he does not propose to call at the Isle of France, it may be possible some unforeseen circumstance might compel him to put into port in the colony, the government of which is entrusted to you. Having been a witness of the kind manner with which his countrymen have treated us on every occasion, I hope he will be convinced by his own experience that Frenchmen are not less hospitable and benevolent; and then his mother-country will have over us the advantage only of having done in times of war what happier times enabled us to return to her in time of peace.

That letter has been quoted, and the circumstances attending Baudin's arrival and stay at Sydney have been narrated with some fullness, in order to give particular point to the conduct of two members of his expedition, François Péron and Lieutenant Louis de Freycinet. As will be seen from what follows, both of them used the latitude allowed to them while receiving King's generous hospitality, to spy, to collect information for the purpose of enabling an attack to be made upon Port Jackson, and to supply it with mischievous intent to the military authorities of their nation.

Le Naturaliste returned to Europe from King Island on 8 December. She took with her all the natural history specimens collected up to that time, and reports of the work done. Baudin, with *Le Géographe* and the *Casuarina*, spent six months longer in Australian waters, exploring Spencer's and St Vincent's Gulfs, completing the chart of Kangaroo Island, and making a second voyage along the coast. On 7 July 1803, he determined to return to France. He reached Ile-de-France on 7 August, became seriously ill there, and died on 16 September. The *Casuarina* was dismantled, and *Le Géographe*, which stayed there for three months after her commander's death, arrived in France on 24 March 1804.

The military Governor of Ile-de-France at this time was General Charles Decaen. As a later chapter will be devoted to his career and character, it is only necessary to say here that he was a dogged, strong-willed officer, imbued with a deep-rooted hatred of British policy and power, and anxious to avail himself of any opportunity that might occur of striking a blow at the rival of his own nation. François Péron very soon found that the Governor was eager to get information that might, should a favourable chance present itself, enable him to attack the British colony in Australia, and he lost no time in ministering to the General's belligerent animosity.

On 11 December 1804, four days before *Le Géographe* sailed for Europe, Péron furnished to Decaen a long report on Port Jackson, containing some very remarkable statements.[4] He alleged that the First Consul, Bonaparte, in authorising Baudin's expedition, had given to it a scientific semblance with the object of disguising its real intent from the governments of Europe, and especially from the cabinet of Great Britain. 'If sufficient time were available to me,' said Péron, 'it would be very easy to demonstrate to you that all our natural history researches, extolled with so much ostentation by the Government, were merely the pretext of its enterprise.' The principal object was 'one of the most brilliant and important conceptions', which would, if successful, have made the Government for ever illustrious. The unfortunate circumstance was, however, Péron declared, that after so much had been done to conduce [contribute] to the success of these designs, the execution of them had been confided to a man [Baudin, presumably] utterly unsuited to conduct them to a successful issue.

That there were such designs as those alleged by Péron is disclosed by no word in Napoleon's *Correspondance*; there is no suggestion of anything of the kind in the papers communicated to Baudin by the Minister of Marine, or in Baudin's confidential reports to his Government. It is in the nature of a spy to flavour with his own conjectures the base fruit of his illicit inquisitions, and Péron knew that he was writing to a man greedy to obtain such material as he was ready to supply. There is no word from any other member of the expedition, except Freycinet, written before or after, to support Péron's allegations; and it is extremely unlikely that, if the purpose he indicated had been the real one, he would have been the man to know about it. Péron had not originally been a member of the staff of the expedition. Baudin's ships had been equipped, their complement was complete, and they

[4] MSS., Decaen Papers, Vol. 92. The complete document is translated in appendix B to this volume.

were lying at Havre in October 1800, awaiting sailing orders, when Péron sought employment. He had been a student under Jussieu at the Museum, and to that savant he applied for the use of his influence. Jussieu, with the aid of the biologist, Lacépède, secured an opportunity for Péron to read a paper before the Institute, expounding his views as to research work which might be done in Australasia; the result was that at almost the last moment he obtained appointment.[5] He was not in the confidence of Baudin, with whom he was on bad terms throughout the voyage, and his hatred for whom continued relentlessly after the unfortunate captain's death. On the point in question, therefore, Péron is by no means a trustworthy witness. The very terms in which Baudin wrote of Sydney, in his confidential letter to the Minister of Marine, indicate that he was innocent of any knowledge of a secret purpose. If he had known he would have referred to it here; and if he did not know of one, Péron certainly did not. 'I believe it to be my duty,' wrote Baudin, 'to warn you that the colony of Port Jackson ought to engage the attention of the Government and indeed of other European power also. People in France or elsewhere are very far from imagining that the English, in the space of fourteen years, have been able to build up their colony to such a degree of prosperity, which will be augmented every year by the dispositions of their Government. It seems to me that policy demands [*il me semble que la politique exige*] that by some means the preparations they are making for the future, which foreshadow great projects, ought to be balanced.' That was simply Baudin's personal opinion: 'it seemed to him'. But the statement Péron made to Decaen, as to what he could demonstrate 'if he had time', together with his other assertions, may have had an influence on the general's mind, and may have affected the later treatment of Flinders; and that constitutes its importance for our purpose.

Péron went on to allege that while he was at Port Jackson,

> *I neglected no opportunity of procuring all the information that I foresaw would be of interest. I was received in the house of the Governor with much consideration; he himself and his secretary spoke our language well. Mr. Paterson, the commandant of the New South Wales troops, always treated me with particular regard. I was received in his house, as one may say, like a son. Through him I knew all the officials of the colony. The surgeon, Mr. Thomson, honoured me with his friendship. Mr. Grimes,*

[5] See the biographies of Péron by Deleuze (1811) and Girard (1857).

> *the surveyor-general, Mr. Palmer the commissary-general, Mr. Marsden a clergyman at Parramatta, and a cultivator as wealthy as he was discerning, were all capable of furnishing me with valuable information. My functions permitted me to hazard the asking of a number of questions which would have been indiscreet on the part of another, especially on military matters. I have, in a word, known all the principal people of the colony, in all walks of life, and all of them have furnished me with information as valuable as it is new. Finally, I made in Mr. Paterson's company long journeys into the interior of the country; I have seen the best farms, and I assure you that I have collected everywhere interesting ideas, and have stated them in as exact a form as possible.*

After this illuminating dissertation as to his own value as a spy, and the clever use he had made of his functions as a naturalist to exploit unsuspecting people, Péron proceeded to describe the British establishment in detail. But he omitted to tell Decaen how kindly he and his countrymen had been treated there; not a word had he to say on that subject; no circumstance was mentioned that might tend to withhold an attack if a favourable chance for one should occur. He gave an interesting description of Sydney and its environs, spoke of the growth of its trade, the spread of cultivation, the increase of wealth. Then he gave his views on the designs of the British to extend their power in the Pacific. Their ambitions were not confined to New Holland itself, vast as it was. Their cupidity had been excited by Van Diemen's Land. They did not intend, if they could avoid it, to permit any other nation to occupy that country. They would soon extend their dominion to New Zealand. They were even casting avaricious glances across the Pacific. They had occupied Norfolk Island, and he did not hesitate to say that they were looking for a place further east, whence they might assail Chile and Peru. The British were quite aware of the feebleness of the Spaniards in those regions, and meant to appropriate their possessions in time.

Next Péron gave an account of the transportation system, of which he approved, as making for rapid colonisation, and as having valuable reformatory effects. The climate and productiveness of New South Wales were enthusiastically praised by him, and its eminent suitability for European occupation was extolled. In all that the British had done in Australia [there] were to be recognised great designs for the future. Steps had been taken to convert felons into good colonists, to educate their children, and to train them for useful avocations [employment].

He drew attention to the number of Irish prisoners who had been transported for participation in rebellious movements at home, and to their implacable hatred of Great Britain.

> *The Irish, kept under by an iron sceptre, are quiet to-day; but if ever the Government of our country, alarmed by the rapidly increasing power of that colony, formed the project of taking or destroying it, at the very name of the French the Irish would rise. We had a striking example of what might be expected on our first arrival in the colony. Upon the appearance of the French flag, the alarm became general in the country. The Irish began to flock together from all parts, and if their error had not been speedily dissipated, there would have been a general rising among them. One or two were put to death on that occasion, and several were deported to Norfolk Island.*

The troops at Port Jackson, said Péron, did not number more than 700 or 800 men while the French ships were there, but he believed that as many as 8,000 were expected. He doubted, however, whether Great Britain could maintain a very large force there, in view of the demands upon her resources elsewhere owing to the war; but was of opinion that she would use Port Jackson as a depot for India, on account of the healthiness of the climate. He summed up in eighteen paragraphs the advantage which Great Britain drew, and was likely to draw, from her possession of Port Jackson; and he terminated these by telling Decaen that 'my opinion, and that of all those among us who have been particularly occupied with the organization of that colony, would be that we should destroy it as soon as possible. To-day we can do that easily; we shall not be able to do it in a few years to come.' There followed a postscript in which Péron informed the General that Lieutenant de Freycinet 'has particularly occupied himself with examining all the points on the coast in the neighbourhood of Port Jackson that are favourable for the debarkation of troops. He has made especial enquiries concerning the entry to the port, and if ever the Government thought of putting into execution the project of destroying this freshly set trap of a great Power [This is an odd translation of the French 'ce piège naissant', perhaps 'this newly established place of confinement', is what was in Péron's mind.], that distinguished officer's services would be of precious value in such an operation.' The recommendation of Péron's fellow-spy at the end of the report is interesting, as indicating how the pair worked together. Péron, under the guise of a man of science collecting facts about butterflies and grasshoppers, exploited his hosts for information of a political and military nature; whilst Freycinet, ostensibly examining the harbour in the interest of navigation, made plans of places suitable for landing troops. Both together, having been nourished and nursed in their day of dire calamity by the abundant kindness of the people of Sydney, concocted plans for bringing destruction upon their benefactors, and proffered their services to show the way.

Five days after the arrival of *Le Géographe* in France, on 29 March 1804, Péron wrote to the Minister of Marine[6] in similar terms, relating the valuable opportunities he had had of making himself acquainted with the situation of Port Jackson, and mentioning the names of leading citizens with whom he had associated, and from whom he had collected information.

A second report upon Port Jackson was furnished to General Decaen, giving precise information as to where troops could be landed if an invasion were undertaken. The document is unsigned,[7] but, having regard to Péron's statement concerning Freycinet's investigations, there can be no doubt that the information came from him. The writer described Sydney as 'perhaps the most beautiful port in the world', and observed that, though its natural defences were strong, the English had employed no means to fortify the approaches. Many of the convicts were Irish, and were capable of everything except good.[8] Persons who had played a part in connection with the recent rebellion in Ireland were subject to transportation, and were naturally a disaffected class. England had only 600 troops to maintain order in that 'society of brigands', and discipline was not very well observed amongst them. Particulars were given as to how an invasion could be effected:

> *The conquest of Port Jackson would be very easy to accomplish, since the English have neglected every species of means of defence. It would be possible to make a descent through Broken Bay, or even through the port of Sydney itself; but in the latter case it would be necessary to avoid disembarking troops on the right side of the entrance, on account of the arm of the sea of which I have already spoken.[9] That indentation presents as an obstacle a great fosse [moat], defended by a battery of ten or*

---

[6] *Arch. Nat.*, BB4, 996.

[7] 'Coup d'oeil rapide sur l'establissement des Anglais de la Nouvelle Hollande', mss., Decaen Papers, Vol. 92, p. 74.

[8] 'Ils sont capable de tout, excepté le bien.'

[9] Middle Harbour.

twelve guns, firing from eighteen to twenty-four-pound balls. The left shore of the harbour is undefended, and is at the same time more accessible. The town is dominated by its outlying portions to such an extent, that it might be hoped to reduce the barracks in a little time. There is no battery, and a main road leads to the port of Sydney. Care ought to be taken to organize the invaders in attacking parties. The Aboriginals of the country need not be reckoned with. They make no distinctions between white men. Morever, they are few in numbers. The residence of the Governor, that of the colonel of the New South Wales Regiment, the barracks, and one public building, are the principal edifices. The other houses, to the number of three or four hundred, are small. The chief buildings of the establishment captured, the others would fall naturally into the hands of the conqueror. If the troops had to retreat, they would best do so by the River Oxbury[10] *and thence to Broken Bay. I regret very much that I have not more time to give*[11] *to this slight review of the resources, means of defence of and methods of attack on that colony. I conclude by observing that scarcely any coinage is to be found in circulation there. They use a currency of copper with which they pay the troops, and some paper money.*

There is no need to emphasise the circumstances in which this piece of duplicity was perpetrated. They are made sufficiently clear from the plain story related in the preceding pages. But it should be said in justice to Baudin that there is no reason to associate him with the espionage of Péron. Nor is it the case that the expedition originally had any intention of visiting Port Jackson, for this or any other purpose. As explained in the chapter relating to the Encounter Bay incident, it was Flinders who suggested to Baudin that he should seek the succour he so sorely needed at Sydney; and *Le Naturaliste*, which preceded him thither, was driven by a like severity of need to his own. 'It does not appear by his orders,' wrote King to Banks 'that he was at all instructed to touch here, which I do not think he intended if not obliged by distress.' Such was the case; and it was this very distress, and the generous alleviation of it by the British colonists, that make the singular turpitude of Péron and Freycinet in pursuing nefarious designs of their

[10] i.e., the Hawkesbury; the Frenchman guessed at the spelling from the pronunciation.

[11] Compare Péron's remark concerning the little time at his disposal. Both reports were written only a few days before *Le Géographe* left Ile-de-France for Europe.

own and plotting to rend the breast that fed them. The great war gave rise to many noble acts of chivalry on both sides, deeds which are luminous with a spirit transcending the hatreds of the time, and glorify human nature; but it is happily questionable whether it produced an example to equal that expounded in these pages, of ignoble treachery and ungrateful baseness.

Flinders, when reviewing the unjust account of his own discoveries given by Péron in his *Voyage de Découvertes*, adopted the view that what he wrote was under compulsion from authority. 'How came M. Péron to advance what was so contrary to truth?' he asked. 'Was he a man destitute of all principle? My answer is that I believe his candour to have been equal to his acknowledged abilities; and that what he wrote was from over-ruling authority, and smote him to the heart.' Could Flinders have known what Péron was capable of doing, in the endeavour to advance himself in favour with the rulers of his country, he would certainly not have believed him so blameless.

That Port Jackson was never attacked during these years of war was not due to its own capabilities of defence, which were pitifully weak; nor to reluctance on the part of Napoleon and Decaen; but simply to the fact that the British Navy secured and kept the command of the sea. In 1810 Napoleon directed the equipment of a squadron to 'take the English colony of Port Jackson; where considerable resources will be found'.[12] But it was a futile order to give at that date. Trafalgar had been fought, and the defence of the colony in Australia was maintained effectively wherever British frigates sailed.

Péron's report, then, did no mischief where he intended that it should. But by inflaming Decaen's mind with suspicions it may not have been ineffectual in another unfortunate direction, as we shall presently see.

The action of Péron in trying to persuade Decaen that the object of Baudin's expedition was not truly scientific was all the more remarkable because he himself, as one of its expert staff, did work which earned him merited repute. His papers on marine life, on phosphorescence in the sea, on the zoology of the South Seas, on the temperature of the sea at measured depths, and on other subjects pertaining to his scientific functions, were marked by conspicuous originality and acumen. But he was not content to allow the value of his services to be estimated by researches within his own sphere. He knew the sort of information that would please General Decaen, and evidently considered that espionage

---

[12] Napoleon's *Correspondance*, Vol. XX, document 16, 544.

would bring him greater favour from his Government, at that time, than science.

Nevertheless, it is right to bring out the fact, in justice to the diligent savants who worked under Baudin, that their researches generally were of real importance. Professor Jussieu, one of the foremost men of science in Europe, was deputed to report upon them, and did so in a comprehensive document.[13] 'Of all the collections which have come to us from distant countries at different times,' wrote Jussieu, 'those which *Le Géographe* and *Le Naturaliste* have brought home are certainly the most considerable.' The botanist Leschenault had found over 600 species of plants which were believed to be new to science; and he eulogised the zoological work of Péron, who had succeeded in bringing to France alive seven kinds of kangaroo, an emu, a lyrebird and several black swan. Altogether, 18,414 specimens of Australian fauna had been collected, comprised in 3,872 species, of which 2,592 species were new to the museum. The men of science had 'succeeded beyond all our hopes'. Their task had been perfectly fulfilled, and their services to science deserved to be liberally rewarded by a just and generous government.

It would have been a source of satisfaction if it could be recorded that work so laborious and so well performed had earned for Péron a reputation unstained by such conduct as has been exhibited in the preceding pages.

[13] MSS., Archives of the Museum d'Histoire Naturelle de Paris.

XVIII

AUSTRALIA CIRCUMNAVIGATED

PREPARATIONS for the continuance of researches in the *Investigator* proceeded speedily during June and July 1802. Friendly relations were maintained with the staff of the French ships, who on one occasion dined on board with Flinders, and were received with a salute of eleven guns. A new chart of the south coast was then shown to Baudin, with the part which he had discovered marked with his name. He made no objection to the justice of the limits indicated, though he expressed himself surprised that they were so small; for up to this time he was not aware of the discovery by Grant of the coast eastward from Cape Banks. 'Ah, Captain,' said Freycinet, when he recognised the missed opportunities, 'if we had not been kept so long picking up shells and catching butterflies at Van Diemen's Land, you would not have discovered the south coast before us.'

A glimpse of the social life of the settlement is afforded in a letter to Mrs Flinders, concerning the King's birthday celebrations.[1] Very little is known about the amusements and festivities of Sydney in those early days, but that gaiety and ceremony were not absent from the convict colony is apparent from this epistle, which was dated 4 June 1802:

> *This is a great day in all distant British settlements, and we are preparing to celebrate it with due magnificence. The ship is covered with colours, and every man is about to put on his best apparel and to make himself merry. We go through the form of waiting on His Excellency the Governor at his* levée *[reception], to pay our compliments to him as the representative of majesty; after which, a dinner and ball are given to the colony, at which not less than 52 gentlemen and ladies will be*

[1] Flinders' Papers.

> *present. Amidst all this, how much preferable is such a 'right hand and left' as that we have had at Spilsby with those we love, to that which we shall go through this evening.*

A few alterations were made in the ship, which was re-rigged and overhauled; and a new eight-oar boat was built to replace the one lost in Spencer's Gulf. She cost £30, and was constructed after the model of the boat in which Bass had made his famous expedition to Westernport. She proved, 'like her prototype, to be excellent in a sea, as well as for rowing and sailing in smooth water'.

Fourteen men were required to make up the ship's complement. A new master was found in John Aken of the *Hercules*, a convict transport, and five seamen were engaged; but it was impossible to secure the services of nine others from amongst the free people. Flinders thereupon proposed to the Governor that he should ship nine convicts who could bring 'respectable recommendations'. King concurred, and the number required were permitted to join the *Investigator*, with the promise that they should receive conditional or absolute pardons on their return, 'according to Captain Flinders' recommendation of them'. Several of them were experienced seamen, and proved a great acquisition to the strength of the ship. Flinders also took with him his old friend Bongaree, 'the worthy and brave fellow' who had accompanied him on the *Norfolk* voyage in 1799, and a native lad named Nambaree.

It was determined, after consultation with King, to sail to the north of Australia and explore Torres Strait and the east side of the Gulf of Carpentaria, as well as to examine the north-east coast with more care than Cook had been able to give to it. The *Lady Nelson*, under Murray's direction, was to accompany the *Investigator*; if rivers were found, it was hoped that she would be able to penetrate the country by means of them.

On 21 July the provisioning of the ship was completed, the new boat was hoisted into her place, and the *Investigator* dropped down the harbour to make her course northward.

The *Lady Nelson* proved more of a hindrance than a help to the work of exploration. She was painfully slow, and, to make matters worse, Murray, 'not being much accustomed to make free with the land', hugged the coast, and kept the *Investigator* waiting for him at every appointed rendezvous. In August she bumped on a reef in Port Curtis and lost her sliding keel; in September she ran aground in Broad Sound and injured her main keel. Her capacity for beating to windward was never great, and after she had been repaired her tardiness became irritating. Murray had also lost one anchor and broken another. His ship sailed so ill, in fact, and required so much attention, that she dragged on [impeded] Flinders' vessel; and Murray had given many proofs that he 'was not much acquainted with the kind of service' in which they were engaged. On 18 October, therefore, Flinders sent her back to Sydney, with an expression of regret at depriving Murray, who had shown zeal to make himself useful, of the advantage of continuing the voyage.

On 7 August Port Curtis was discovered, and was named after Sir Roger Curtis, the admiral at the Cape who had been so attentive to the requirements of the *Investigator* on her voyage out from England. In Keppel Bay (discovered by Cook in 1770) the master's mate and a seaman became bogged in a mangrove swamp, and had to pass the night persecuted by clouds of mosquitoes. In the morning their plight was relieved by a party of Aboriginals, who took them to a fire whereat they dried themselves, and fed them on broiled wild duck. Natives were encountered at every landing-place, and were invariably friendly.

Another important discovery was made on 21 August, when Port Bowen was entered. It had not only escaped Cook's notice, but, owing to a change of wind, was nearly missed by Flinders also. He named it after Captain James Bowen of the Royal Navy.

In every bay he entered Flinders examined the refuse thrown up by the sea, with the object of finding any particle of wreckage that might have been carried in. If, as was commonly believed (and was, in fact, the case), La Pérouse had been wrecked somewhere in the neighbourhood of New Caledonia, it was possible that remnants of his vessels might be borne to the Queensland coast by the trade winds. 'Though the hope of restoring La Pérouse or any of his companions to their country and friends could not, after so many years, be rationally entertained, yet to gain some certain knowledge of their fate would do away the pain of suspense.'[2]

The Percy Islands (28 September) were a third discovery of importance on this northern voyage. Flinders now desired to find a passage through the Barrier Reef to the open Pacific, in order that he might make the utmost speed for Torres Strait and the Gulf of

---

[2] In 1861, remains of a small vessel were found at the back of Temple Island not far from Mackay, 150 miles or more north of Flinders' situation when he wrote this passage. The wreckage is believed by some to be part of the craft built by La Pérouse's people at Vanikoro, after the disaster which overtook them there. The sternpost recovered from the wreckage is, I am informed, included among the La Pérouse relics preserved at Paris. See A. C. Macdonald, on 'The Fate of Lapérouse', *Victorian Geographical Journal*, xxvi, p. 14.

Carpentaria. Several openings were tried. At length an opening was found. It is known as Flinders' Passage, in latitude 18° 45' south, longitude 148° 10' east, and is frequently used nowadays. It is about 45 miles north-east from Cape Bowling Green, and is the southernmost of the passages used by shipping through the Barrier Reef. Three anxious days were spent in tacking through the intricacies of the untried passage. The perplexity and danger of the navigation must have recalled to the commander's mind his experiences as a midshipman under Bligh ten years before. It was not until the afternoon of 20 October that a heavy swell from the eastward was felt under the ship, and Flinders knew by that sign that the open sea had been gained. He finished his description of this treacherous piece of reef-ribbed sea by a bit of seaman's advice to brother sailors. A captain who wished to make the experiment of getting through the Barrier Reef 'must not be one who throws his ship's head round in a hurry so soon as breakers are announced from aloft. If he do not feel his nerves strong enough to thread the needle, as it is called, amongst the reefs, while he directs the steerage from the masthead, I would strongly recommend him not to approach this part of the coast.' Strong nerves and seamanship had pulled through in this case, with a few exciting phases; and the *Investigator*, in the open ocean, was headed for Torres Strait.

The strait was entered eight days later, by a passage through the reef which had been found by Captain Edwards of the *Pandora* in 1791, and which Flinders marked on his chart as Pandora's Entrance.[3] He preferred this opening to the one further north, found by Bligh in 1792. The ship was brought to anchor on 29 October under the lee of the largest of Murray's Islands.

Immediately afterwards three long Papuan canoes, carrying about 50 natives, came in sight. Remembering the attacks he had witnessed in the *Providence*, Flinders kept his marines under arms and his guns ready, and warned his officers to watch every movement of the visitors. But the Papuans were merely bent on barter on this occasion, hatchets especially being in demand. Seven canoes appeared on the following morning. 'Wishing to secure the friendship and confidence of these islanders to such vessels as might hereafter pass through Torres Strait, and not being able to distinguish any chief amongst them, I selected the oldest man, and presented him with a handsaw, a hammer and nails, and some other

---

[3] It is generally marked Flinders' Entrance on modern maps; but Flinders himself held to his principle of never calling a place after himself, and of invariably ascribing full credit to his predecessors.

trifles; of all which we attempted to show him the use, but I believe without success; for the poor old man became frightened on finding himself to be so particularly noticed.'

Darwin, in writing his treatise on [entitled] the *Structure and Distribution of Coral Reefs*, in 1842, made use of Flinders' chart and description of the Great Barrier Reef, which extends for more than a 1,000 miles along the east side of the continent, and into the throat of Torres Strait. The hypothesis that as the bed of the ocean subsides the coral polyps go on building steadily upwards, occurred to Darwin more than 30 years after Flinders sailed along the reef; and what the navigator wrote was the result of his own observation and thought. Many absurd and fanciful speculations about coralline formation were current in his day, and have often been repeated since. But the reader who has given any study to Darwin's array of facts and powerful reasoning will be interested in the ideas of the earlier observer:

> *It seems to me, that, when the animalcules which form the corals at the bottom of the ocean cease to live, their structures adhere to each other, by virtue either of the glutinous remains within, or of some property in salt water; and the interstices being gradually filled up with sand and broken pieces of coral washed by the sea, which also adhere, a mass of rock is at length formed. Future races of these animalcules erect their habitations upon the rising bank, and die in their turn, to increase, but principally to elevate, this monument of their wonderful labours. The care taken to work perpendicularly in the early stages would mark a surprising instinct in these diminutive creatures. Their wall of coral, for the most part in situations where the winds are constant, being arrived at the surface, affords a shelter to leeward of which their infant colonies may be safely sent forth; and to their instructive foresight it seems to be owing that the windward side of a reef exposed to the open sea is generally, if not always, the highest part, and rises almost perpendicular, sometimes from the depth of 200, and perhaps many more fathoms. To be constantly covered with water seems necessary to the existence of the animalcules, for they do not work, except in holes upon the reef, beyond low-water mark; but the coral, sand, and other broken remnants thrown up by the sea adhere to the rock, and form a solid mass with it, as high as the common tides reach. That elevation surpassed, the future remnants, being rarely covered,*

lose their adhesive property, and, remaining in a loose state, form what is usually called a key upon the top of the reef. The new bank is not long in being visited by sea-birds; plants take root upon it; a cocoanut, or the drupe of a pandanus is thrown on shore; land-birds visit it and deposit the seeds of shrubs and trees; every high tide, and still more every gale, adds something to the bank; the form of an island is gradually assumed; and last of all comes man to take possession.

The Gulf of Carpentaria was entered on 3 November, and a suitable place was found for careening the ship. As the carpenters proceeded with their work, their reports became alarming. Many of her timbers were found to be rotten, and the opinion was confidently expressed that in a strong gale with much sea running she could hardly escape foundering. She was totally unfit to encounter much bad weather. The formal report to the commander concluded with the depressing warning, 'from the state to which the ship seems now to be advanced, it is our joint opinion that in twelve months there will scarcely be a sound timber in her, but that, if she remain in fine weather and no accident happen, she may run six months longer without much risk'.

Upon receipt of this report Flinders, with much surprise and sorrow, saw that a return to Port Jackson was almost immediately necessary.

My leading object had hitherto been to make so accurate an investigation of the shores of Terra Australis that no future voyage to this country should be necessary; and with this always in view, I had ever endeavoured to follow the land so closely that the washing of the surf upon it should be visible, and no opening, nor anything of interest, escape notice. Such a degree of proximity is what navigators have usually thought neither necessary nor safe to pursue, nor was it always persevered in by us; sometimes because the direction of the wind or shallowness of the water made it impracticable, and at other times because the loss of the ship would have been the probable consequence of approaching so near to a lee shore. But when circumstances were favourable, such was the plan I pursued, and, with the blessing of God, nothing of importance should have been left for future discoverers upon any part of these extensive coasts; but with a ship incapable of encountering bad weather, which could not be repaired if sustaining injury from any of the numerous shoals or rocks upon the coast—which, if constant fine weather could be ensured and all

> *accidents avoided, could not run more than six months—with such a ship I knew not how to accomplish the task.*

Very serious consideration had to be given to the route by which the return voyage should be made. If Flinders returned as he had come, the monsoon season made it certain that storms would be encountered in Torres Strait, and to thread the Barrier Reef in a rotten ship in tempestuous weather was to court destruction. Weighing the probabilities carefully Flinders, with a steady nerve and cool judgment, resolved to continue his exploration of the gulf until the monsoon abated, and then to make for Port Jackson round the north-west and west of Australia—or, if it should appear that the *Investigator* could not last out a winter's passage by this route, to run for safety to the nearest port in the East Indies. In the meantime all that the carpenters could do was to replace some of the rottenest parts of the planking and caulk the bends.

Flinders remained on these coasts, in pursuit of his plan, till the beginning of March, doing excellent work. The Cape Van Diemen of Dutch charts, at the head of the gulf, was found to be not a projection from the mainland but an island, which was named Mornington Island, after the Governor-General of India; and the group of which it is the largest received the designation of Wellesley Islands[4] after the same nobleman. The Sir Edward Pellew group, discovered on the south-west of the gulf, was named after a British admiral who will figure in a later part of this biography.

Traces of the visits of Malays to this part of Australia were found in the form of fragments of pottery, bamboo basket-work, and blue cotton rags, as well as a wooden anchor and three boat rudders. The Cape Maria of Dutch charts was found to be an island, which received the name of Maria Island. In Blue Mud Bay, Morgan, the master's mate, was speared by a native, and died. A seaman shot another native in revenge, and Flinders was 'much concerned' and 'greatly displeased' about the occurrence. His policy throughout was to keep on pleasant terms with all natives, and to encourage them to look upon white men as friendly. Nothing that could annoy them was countenanced by him at any time. The incident was so unusual a departure from his experience on this voyage as to set him conjecturing that the natives might have had differences with Asiatic visitors, which led them to entertain a common enmity towards foreigners.

[4] Richard, Earl of Mornington, afterwards the Marquess Wellesley, was Governor-General of India from 1798 to 1805.

Melville Bay, the best harbour near the gulf, was discovered on 12 February, and on the 17th the *Investigator* moved out of the gulf and steered along the north coast of Australia. Six Malay vessels were sighted on the same day. They hung out white flags as the English ship approached and displayed her colours; and the chief of one of them came on board. It was found that 60 prows from Macassar were at this time on the north coast, in several divisions; they were vessels of about 25 tons, each carrying about twenty men; their principal business was searching for *bêche-de-mer* [sea cucumber], which was sold to the Chinese at Timor.

Arnhem Bay was found marked, but not named, upon an old Dutch chart, and Flinders gave it the name it bears from the conviction that Tasman or some other navigator had previously explored it. In the early part of March he came to the conclusion that it would be imprudent to delay the return to Sydney any longer. Not only did the condition of the ship cause anxiety, but the health of the crew pointed to the urgency of quitting these tropical coasts. Mosquitoes, swarms of black flies, the debility induced by the moist heat of the climate, and the scarcity of nourishing food, made everybody on board anxious to return. Scorbutic ulcers broke out on Flinders' feet, so that he was no longer able to station himself at his customary observation-point, the masthead. Nevertheless, though driven by sheer necessity, it was not without keen regret that he determined to sail away. 'The accomplishment of the survey was, in fact,' he said, 'an object so near to my heart, that could I have foreseen the train of ills that were to follow the decay of the *Investigator* and prevent the survey being resumed, and had my existence depended upon the expression of a wish, I do not know that it would have received utterance; but Infinite Wisdom has, in infinite mercy, reserved the knowledge of futurity to itself.'

Even in face of the troubles facing him, Flinders fought hard to continue his work to a finish. He planned to make for the Dutch port of Kupang, in Timor, and thence send Lieutenant Fowler home in any ship bound for Europe to take to the Admiralty his reports and charts, and a scheme for completing the survey. He hoped then to spend six months upon the north and north-west coasts of Australia, and on the run to Port Jackson, and there to await Fowler's return with a ship fit for the service. But this plan was frustrated. He reached Timor at the end of March, and was courteously received by the Dutch Governor, also renewing acquaintance with Baudin and his French officers, who had put into port to refresh. But no ship bound for England was met. A homeward-bound vessel from India had touched at Kupang ten days before the *Investigator* arrived, but when another one would put in was uncertain. A vessel was due to sail for Batavia in May, and the captain consented to take charge of a packet of letters for transmission to England; but there was no opportunity of sending Fowler. A few days were spent in charting a reef about which the Admiralty had given instructions, and by 16 April the voyage to Port Jackson was being pursued at best speed by way of the west and south coasts. Flinders did not even stay to examine the south of Kangaroo Island, which had not been charted during the visit in 1802, for dysentery made its appearance on board—owing, it was believed, to a change of diet at Timor—and half a dozen men died. Sydney was reached on 9 June, after a voyage of ten months and nineteen days.

Australia had thus been, for the first time, completely circumnavigated by Flinders.

An examination of the *Investigator* showed how perilously near destruction she had been since she left the Gulf of Carpentaria. On the starboard side some of the planks were so rotten that a cane could be thrust through them. By good fortune, when she was running along the south coast the winds were southerly, and the starboard bow, where the greatest weakness lay, was out of the water. Had the wind been northerly, Flinders was of opinion that it would not have been possible to keep the pumps going sufficiently to keep the ship afloat, whilst a hard gale must inevitably have sent her to the bottom.

As Flinders said in a letter to his wife:[5]

> *It was the unanimous opinion of the surveying officers that, had we met with a severe gale of wind in the passage from Timor, she must have crushed like an egg and gone down. I was partly aware of her bad state, and returned sooner to Port Jackson on that account before the worst weather came. For me, whom this obstruction in the voyage and the melancholy state of my poor people have much distressed, I have been lame about four months, and much debilitated in health and I fear in constitution; but am now recovering, and shall soon be altogether well.*

Of the nine convicts who were permitted to make this voyage, one died; the conduct of a second did not warrant Flinders in recommending him for a pardon; the remaining seven were fully emancipated. Four sailed with Flinders on his next voyage; but two of them, no longer having to gain their liberty by good behaviour, conducted themselves ill, and a third was convicted again after he reached England.

[5] Flinders' Papers.

Upon his arrival in port after this voyage Flinders learnt of the death of his father. The occasion called forth a letter to his stepmother, which is especially valuable from the light it throws upon his character.[6] The manly tenderness of his sorrow and sympathy throbs through every sentence of it. In danger, in adversity, in disappointment, in difficulty, under tests of endurance and throughout perilous cruises, we always find Flinders solicitous for the good of others and unsparing of himself; and perhaps there is no more moving revelation of his quality as a man than that made in this letter:

> Investigator, *Port Jackson,*
> *June 10th, 1803.*
>
> *My dearest Mother,*
>
> *We arrived here yesterday from having circumnavigated New Holland, and I received numerous and valuable marks of the friendship of all those whose affection is so dear to me; but the joy which some letters occasioned is dreadfully embittered by what you, my good and kind mother, had occasion to communicate. The death of so kind a father, who was so excellent a man, is a heavy blow, and strikes deep into my heart. The duty I owed him, and which I had now a prospect of paying with the warmest affection and gratitude, had made me look forward to the time of our return with increased ardour. I had laid such a plan of comfort for him as would have tended to make his latter days the most delightful of his life; for I think an increased income, retirement from business, and constant attention from an affectionate son whom he loved, would have done this. Indeed, my mother, I thought the time fast approaching for me to fulfil what I once said in a letter, that my actions should some day show how I valued my father. One of my fondest hopes is now destroyed. O, my dearest, kindest father, how much I loved and reverenced you, you cannot now know!*
>
> *I beg of you, my dear mother, to look upon me with affection, and as one who means to contribute everything in his power to your happiness. Independent of my dear father's last wish, I am of myself desirous that the best understanding and correspondence should exist between us; for I love and*

[6] Flinders' Papers.

reverence you, and hope to be considered by you as the most anxious and affectionate of your friends, whose heart and purse will be ever ready for your services.

I know not who at present can receive my dividend from his legacy to me; but if you can, or either Mr. Franklin or Mr. Hursthouse, I wish the yearly interest to be applied to the education of my young sisters,[7] *in such manner as you will think best. This, my dear Madam, I wish to continue until such time as I can see you and put things upon the footing that they ought to remain.*

Do not let your economy be carried too far. I hope you will continue to visit and see all our good friends, and have things comfortable about you. I should be sorry that my dear mother should lose any of the comforts and conveniences she has been accustomed to enjoy.

I have much satisfaction in hearing both from you and Susan that Hannah[8] *makes so good use of the opportunities she has for improvement. If she goes on cultivating her mind, forming her manners from the best examples before her, and behaves respectfully and kindly to her mother and elder friends, she shall be my sister indeed, and I will love her dearly.*

With great regard for you and my young sisters, I am your anxious and affectionate son,

MATTHEW FLINDERS.

In another vein is a playful letter to his wife written in the same month, June 1803.[9]

If I could laugh at the effusion of thy tenderness, it would be to see the idolatrous language thou frequently usest to me. Thou makest an idol and then worshippest it, and, like some of the inhabitants of the East, thou also bestowest a little castigation occasionally, just to let the ugly deity know the value of thy devotion. Mindest thou not, my dearest love, that I shall be spoiled by thy endearing flatteries? I fear it, and yet can hardly part with one, so dear to me is thy affection in whatever way expressed.

---

[7] His stepsisters.

[8] The elder of his two stepsisters.

[9] Flinders' Papers.

Some account of his companions on the voyage is given in a letter to Mrs Flinders written at this time (25 June 1803).[10] In a letter previously quoted he had referred to being debilitated in health, 'and I fear in constitution'; and in this one he mentions that he, like the ship's cat, Trim, was becoming grey. Such hard unsparing service as he had given was writing its tale on his form and features, and there were worse trials to come:

> *Mr. Fowler is tolerably well and my brother is also well; he is becoming more steady, and is more friendly and affectionate with me since his knowledge of our mutual loss. Mr. Brown is recovering from ill health and lameness. Mr. Bauer, your favourite, is still polite and gentle. Mr. Westall wants prudence, or rather experience, but is good-natured. The two last are well, and have always remained on good terms with me. Mr. Bell*[11] *is misanthropic and pleases nobody. Elder*[12] *continues to be faithful and attentive as before; I like him, and he apparently likes me. Whitewood I have made a master's mate, and he behaves well. Charrington is become boatswain, and Jack Wood is now my coxswain. Trim, like his master, is becoming grey; he is at present fat and frisky, and takes meat from our forks with his former dexterity. He is commonly my bedfellow. The master we have in poor Thistle's place*[13] *is an easy, good-natured man.*

In another letter to his wife[14] he tells her: 'Thou wouldst have been situated as comfortably here as I hoped and told thee. Two better or more agreeable women than Mrs. King and Mrs. Paterson are not easily found. These would have been thy constant friends, and for visiting acquaintances there are five or six ladies very agreeable for short periods and perhaps longer.'

In a previous chapter it was remarked that Flinders and Bass did not meet again after their separation following on the *Norfolk* voyage. Bass was not in Sydney when the *Investigator* lay there, greatly to Flinders' disappointment. 'Fortune seems determined to give me disappointments,' he wrote to Mrs Kent; 'when I came into Port Jackson all the most esteemed of my friends were absent. In the case of Bass I have been twice

---

[10] Flinders' Papers.

[11] The surgeon.

[12] Flinders' servant.

[13] John Aken.

[14] Flinders' Papers.

served this way.'[15] But he left a letter for his friend with Governor King.[16] It was the last word which passed between these two men; and, remembering what they did together, one can hardly read the end of the letter without feeling the emotion with which it was penned:

> *I shall first thank you, my dear Bass, for the two letters left for me with Bishop, and then say how much I am disappointed that the speculation is not likely to afford you a competency so soon as we had hoped. This fishing and pork-carrying may pay your expenses, but the only other advantage you get by it is experience for a future voyage, and this I take to be the purport of your Peruvian expedition.*
>
> *Although I am so much interested in your success, yet what I say about it will be like one of Shortland's letters, vague conjectures only, mingled with* I hope. *Concerning the* Investigator *and myself, there will be more certainty in what I write. In addition to the south coast, we have explored the east coast as far as Cape Palmerston, with the islands and extensive reefs which lie off. These run from a little to the N.W. of Breaksea Spit to those of the Labyrinth. The passage through Torres Straits you will learn as much of here as I can tell you. The newspaper of June 12 last will give you information enough to go through, and it is the best I have (the chart excepted) until the strait is properly surveyed. Should these three ships go through safely, and I do not fear the contrary, the utility of the discovery will be well proved, and the consequences will probably be as favourable to me as the* conclusion *of the voyage might have been without it. I do indeed privately hope that, whether the voyage is or is not further prosecuted, I may attain another step; many circumstances are favourable to this, but the peace and the non-completion of the voyage are against it. To balance these, I must secure the interest of the India House, by means of Sir Joseph, Mr. Dalrymple, and the owner of the* Bridgewater, *Princeps, with whom I am acquainted. I am fortunate in having the attachment of Governor King, who by introductions, favourable reports, and I believe every proper means in his power, has, and is still, endeavouring to assist me; and you are to understand that my going home for another ship is in conformity*

[15] Flinders' Papers.

[16] Flinders' Papers.

to an opinion first brought forward by him. The shores of the Gulf of Carpentaria have undergone a minute examination.

It might appear that the presence of the French upon these coasts would be much against me; but I consider that circumstance as favourable, inasmuch as the attention of the world will be more strongly attracted towards New Holland, and some comparisons will no doubt be found between our respective labours. Now, in the department of geography, or rather hydrography, the only one where the execution rests with me, they seem to have been very vague and inconclusive, even by their own testimony. By comparison, therefore, my charts will rise in value. It is upon these that I wish to rest my credit. You must, however, make the requisite allowance for the circumstances under which each part was examined, and these circumstances I have made the charts themselves explain, I hope to your satisfaction, as you will see on publication.

I shall see your wife, if in London, as well as her family. Accounts speak indifferently of her brother[17] *and his prospects. His sun seems to have passed the meridian, if they speak true. Your good mother I shall endeavour to see too, if my business will anyway fit it.*

God bless you, my dear Bass; remember me, and believe me to be,

Your very sincere and affectionate friend,

MATTHEW FLINDERS.

One other letter of this period may be quoted for the insight it gives into the relations between the Governor and the principal residents of the colony at this time. The urbanity and good sense of Flinders, and the fact that his voyages kept him out of the official circle for prolonged periods, enabled him to avoid offence under such circumstances. The letter was written to Captain Kent's wife, a treasured friend.

The attention of the Governor to me has been indeed very great, as well as that which I have received from my kind friend, Mrs. King. It is a cause of much uneasiness to me that Colonel and Mrs. P——[18]

[17] Captain Henry Waterhouse.

[18] The quarrel between King and Paterson was bitter, and affected the affairs of the colony in many directions.

> *should be upon terms of disagreement with ——. There is now Mrs. K——*[19]*, Mrs. P——*[20] *and Mrs. M——*[21]*, for all of whom I have the greatest regard, who scarcely speak to each other. It is really a miserable thing to split a small society into such small parts. Why do you ladies meddle with politics? But I do not mean you.*

What subsequently happened to the *Investigator*, a ship which had played so memorable a part in discovery, may be chronicled in a few lines. She was used as a store ship in Sydney harbour till 1805. In that year she was patched sufficiently to take her to England. Captain William Kent commanded her on the voyage, leaving Sydney on 24 May. She arrived in Liverpool in a shattered condition on 24 October, having been driven past the Channel in a storm. The Admiralty ordered Kent to take her round to Plymouth. He carried out the order, but not without great difficulty. 'A more deplorably crazy vessel than the *Investigator* is perhaps not to be seen,' Kent informed the Admiralty on reaching Falmouth. She was sold and broken up in 1810. But those rotten planks had played a part in history, and if only a few splinters of them remained today they would be preserved with the tenderest reverence.

---

[19] King.

[20] Paterson.

[21] Marsden.

XIX

THE CALAMITY OF WRECK REEF

THERE was some anxious discussion between King and Flinders as to the best course to follow for the expeditious completion of the survey of the coasts of Australia. The *Investigator* being no longer fit for the service, consideration was given to the qualifications of the *Lady Nelson*, the *Porpoise*, the *Francis*, and the *Buffalo*, all of which were under the Governor's direction. King was most willing to give his concurrence and assistance in any plan that might be considered expedient. He confessed himself convinced of Flinders' 'zealous perseverance in wishing to complete the service you have so beneficially commenced', and cheerfully placed his resources at the explorer's disposal.

Flinders went for a few days to the Hawkesbury settlement, where fresh air, a vegetable diet and medical care promoted his recovery from the ailments occasioned by prolonged ship-life in the tropics; and on his return, at the beginning of July, determined upon a course of action. The *Porpoise* was the best of the four vessels mentioned, but she was by no means a sound ship, and it did not seem justifiable to incur the expense of fitting her for special service only to find her incapable of finishing the task. It was determined, therefore, that she should be sent to England under Fowler's command, and that Flinders should go in her as a passenger, in order that he might lay his charts and journals before the Admiralty, and solicit the use of another vessel to continue his explorations. Brown, the botanist,[1] and Bauer, the botanical draftsman; desired to remain in Port Jackson to pursue their scientific work, but

[1] Brown, in the preface to his *Prodromus* (which, being intended for the elect, was written in Latin), made but one allusion to the discovery voyage whereby his botanical researches became possible. Dealing with the parts of Australia where he had collected his specimens, he spoke of the south coast, 'Oram meridionalem Novæ Hollandiæ, a promontorio Lewin ad promontorium Wilson in Freto Bass, complectentem Lewin's Land, Nuyt's Land et littora Orientem versus, a Navarcho Flinders in expeditione cui adjunctus fui, primum explorata, et paulo post a navigantibus Gallicis

Westall accompanied Flinders, who with 21 of the remainder of the *Investigator*'s company, embarked on the *Porpoise.* She sailed on 10 August, in company with the East India Company's ship *Bridgewater* and the *Cato*, of London, both bound for Batavia. It was intended to go north, and through Torres Strait, in order that further observations might be made there; and Fowler was ordered to proceed 'by the route Captain Flinders may indicate'. Had not Flinders been so eager to take advantage of this as of every other opportunity to prosecute his researches—had he sailed by the Bass Strait and Cape of Good Hope route—the misfortunes that were soon to come upon him would have been averted. But he deliberately chose the Torres Strait course, not only because he considered that a quick passage could be made at that season of the year, but chiefly for the reason that 'it will furnish me with a second opportunity of assuring myself whether that Strait can or cannot become a safe general passage for ships from the Pacific into the Indian Ocean'.

He was destined to see once again the settlement at Sydney, whence had radiated the series of his valuable and unsparing researches; but on the next and final occasion he was 'caught in the clutch of circumstance'.

His leave-taking in August 1803 was essentially his farewell; and his general observations on the country he had served, and which does not forget the service, are, though brief, full of interest. He had seen the little town grow from a condition of dependence to one of self-reliance, few as were the years of his knowledge of it. Part of his early employment had been to bring provisions to Sydney from abroad. In 1803, he saw large herds spreading over the country. He saw forests giving way before the axe, and spreading fields of grain and fruit ripening for the harvest. The population was increasing, the *morale* was improving, 'and that energetic spirit of enterprise which characterises Britannia's children seemed to be throwing out vigorous shoots in this new world'. He perceived the obstacles to progress. The East India Company's charter, which prohibited trade between Sydney and India and the western coasts of America, was one of them. Convict labour was another deterrent. But he had vision, and found in the signs of development which he saw around him phenomena 'highly interesting to the contemplator of the rise of nations'.

Seven days out of Sydney, on 17 August, the *Porpoise* struck a reef and was wrecked.

---

[1] ***Cont'd.***

visa: insulis adjacentibus inclusis'. [I was a member of the expedition to the south coast of New Holland, from Lewin's Promontory to Wilson's Promontory in Bass Strait, including Lewin's Land, Nuyts' Land and the coast towards the east which was first discovered by Captain Flinders and a little later seen by the French navigators, along with the nearby islands.]

The three vessels were running under easy sail, the *Porpoise* leading on what was believed to be a clear course. At half-past nine o'clock at night the look-out man on the forecastle called out 'Breakers ahead'. Aken, the master, who was on watch, immediately ordered the helm to be put down, but the ship answered slowly. Fowler sprang on deck at once; but Flinders, who was conversing in the gun-room, had no reason to think that anything serious had occurred, and remained there some minutes longer. When he went on deck, he found the ship beyond control among the breakers, and a minute later she struck a coral reef and heeled over on her starboard beam ends. 'It was,' says Seaman Smith, 'a dreadful shock.' The reef—now called Wreck Reef—was in latitude 22° 11' south, longitude 155° 13' east, about 200 miles north-east of Hervey Bay, and 739 miles north of Sydney.[2] The wind was blowing fresh, and the night was very dark. The heave of the sea lifted the vessel and dashed her on the coral a second and third time; the foremast was carried away, and the bottom was stove in. It was realised at once that so lightly built and unsound a ship as the *Porpoise* was must soon be pounded to pieces under the repeated shocks.

Anxiety for the safety of the *Cato* and the *Bridgewater* was felt, as they were following the lead of the King's vessel. An attempt was made to fire a gun to warn them, but the heavy surf and the violent motion of the wrecked ship prevented this being done. Before any warning could be given the *Cato* dashed upon the coral about two cables' length [approximately 400 yards] from the *Porpoise*, whose company saw her reel, fall over, and disappear from view. The *Bridgewater* happily cleared the reef.

After the first moments of confusion had passed, Flinders ordered the cutter and the gig [ship's boat] to be launched. He informed Fowler that he intended to save his charts and journals, and to row to the *Bridgewater* to make arrangements for the rescue of the wrecked people. The gig, in which he attempted to carry out this plan, was compelled to lie at a little distance from the ship, to prevent being stove in; so he jumped overboard and swam to her. She leaked badly, and there was nothing with which to

---

[2] Extract from the *Australia Directory*, Vol. II (Published by the Admiralty): 'Wreck Reef, on the central portion of which the ships *Porpoise* and *Cato* were wrecked in 1803, consists of a chain of reefs extending 181 miles and includes 5 sand cays; Bird Islet, the easternmost, is the only one known to produce any vegetation. Of the other four bare cays none are more than 130 yards in extent, or exceed six feet above high water; they are at equal distances apart of about four miles, and each is surrounded by a reef one to one and a half miles in diameter. The passages between these reefs are about two miles wide ... On the northern side of most of them there is anchorage.'

bale her out but the hats and shoes of the ship's cook and two other men who had taken refuge under the thwarts. Flinders steered towards the *Bridgewater*'s lights, but she was standing off, and it was soon seen to be impossible to reach her. It was also unsafe to return to the *Porpoise* through the breakers in the darkness; so that the boat was kept on the water outside the reef till morning, the small party on board being [were] drenched, [and] cold under a sharp south-easter, and wretchedly miserable. Flinders did his best to keep up their spirits, telling them that they would undoubtedly be rescued by the *Bridgewater* at daylight; but he occupied his own mind in devising plans for saving the wrecked company in case help from that ship was not forthcoming.

Meanwhile blue lights had been burnt on the ship every half-hour, as a guide to the *Bridgewater*, whose lights were visible till about two o'clock in the morning. Fowler also occupied time in constructing a raft from the timbers, masts and yards of the *Porpoise*. 'Every breast,' says Smith's narrative, 'was filled with horror, continual seas dashing over us with great violence.' Of the *Cato* nothing could be seen. She had struck, not as the *Porpoise* had done, with her decks towards the reef, but opposed to the full force of the lashing sea. Very soon the planks were torn up and washed away, and the unfortunate passengers and crew were huddled together in the forecastle, some lashed to timber heads, others clinging to any available means of support, and to each other, expecting every moment that the stranded vessel would be broken asunder. In Smith's expressive words, the people were 'hanging in a cluster by each other on board the wreck, having nothing to take to but the unmerciful waves, which at this time bore a dreadful aspect'.

At dawn, Flinders climbed on to the *Porpoise* by the help of the fallen masts. As the light grew, it was seen that about half a mile distant lay a dry sandbank above high-water mark, sufficiently large to receive the whole company, with such provisions as could be saved from the ship. Orders were at once given to remove to this patch, that gave promise of temporary safety, everything that could be of any service; and the *Cato*'s company, jumping overboard and swimming through the breakers with the aid of planks and spars, made for the same spot. All were saved except three lads, one of whom had been to sea on three or four voyages and was wrecked on every occasion. 'He had bewailed himself through the night as the persecuted Jonah who carried misfortune wherever he went. He launched himself upon a broken spar with his captain; but, having lost his hold in the breakers, was not seen afterwards.'

The behaviour of the *Bridgewater* in these distressing circumstances was inhuman and discreditable to such a degree as is happily rare in the history of seamanship. On the day following the wreck (18 August) it would have been easy and safe for her captain, Palmer, to bring her to anchor in one of the several wide and sufficiently deep openings in the reef, and to take the wrecked people and their stores on board. Flinders had the gig put in readiness to go off in her, to point out the means of rescue. A topsail was set up on the highest part of the reef, and a large blue ensign, with the union downwards, was hoisted to it as a signal of distress. But Palmer, who saw the signal, paid no heed to it. Having sailed round the reef, deluding the unfortunates for awhile with the false hope of relief, he stood off and made for Batavia, leaving them to their fate. Worse still, he acted mendaciously as well as with a heartless disregard of their plight; for on his arrival at Tellicherry he sent his third mate, Williams, ashore with an untrue account of the occurrence, reporting the loss of the *Porpoise* and *Cato*, and saying that he had not only found it impossible to weather the reef, but even had he done so it would have been too late to render assistance. Williams, convinced that the crews were still on the reef, and that Palmer's false account had been sent ashore to excuse his own shameful conduct, and 'blind the people', left his captain's narrative as instructed, but only 'after relating the story as contrary as possible' on his own account. He told Palmer what he had done, and his action 'was the cause of many words'. What kind of words they were can be easily imagined. The result of Williams's honest independence was in the end fortunate for himself. Though he left the ship, and forfeited his wages and part of his clothes by so doing, he saved his own life from drowning. The *Bridgewater* left Bombay for London, and was never heard of again. 'How dreadful,' Flinders commented, 'must have been his [Palmer's] reflections at the time his ship was going down.'

On the reef rapid preparations were made for establishing the company in as much comfort as means would allow, and for provisioning them until assistance could be procured. They were 94 men 'upon a small uncertainty'—the phrase is Smith's—nearly 800 miles from the nearest inhabited port. But they had sufficient food for three months, and Flinders assured them that within that time help could be procured. Stores were landed, tents were made from the sails and put up, and a proper spirit of discipline was installed, after a convict-sailor had been promptly punished for disorderly conduct. Spare clothing was served out to some of the *Cato*'s company who needed it badly, and there was some fun at the expense of a few of them who appeared in the uniforms of the King's navy. With good humour came a feeling of hope. 'On the fourth day,' wrote Flinders in a letter,[3]

---

[3] Flinders' Papers.

each division of officers and men had its private tent, and the public magazine contained sufficient provisions and water to subsist us three months. We had besides a quantity of other things upon the bank, and our manner of living and working had assumed the same regularity as on board His Majesty's ships. I had to punish only one man, formerly a convict at Port Jackson; and on that occasion I caused the articles of war to be read, and represented the fatal consequences that might ensue to our whole community from any breach of discipline and good order, and the certainty of its encountering immediate punishment.

The stores available,[4] with the periods for which they would suffice on full allowance, consisted of:

Biscuit	940 lbs.	} 83 days
Flour....................................	9644 „	
Beef in four pounds	1776 pieces	} 94 days
Pork in two pounds	592 „	
Pease....................................	45 bushels	107 days
Oatmeal	50 „	48 days
Rice......................................	1225 lbs.	114 days
Sugar....................................	320 „	} 84 days
Molasses.............................	125 „	
Spirits	225 gallons	} 49 days
Wine	113 „	
Porter	60 „	
Water, 5650 gallons at half a gallon per day		

In addition there were some sauerkraut, essence of malt, vinegar, salt, a new suit of sails, some spars, a kedge anchor, iron-work and an armourer's forge, canvas, twine, various small stores, four-and-a-half barrels of gunpowder, two swivels; and several muskets and pistols, with ball and flints. A few sheep were also rescued. When they were being driven on to the reef under the supervision of young John Franklin, they trampled over some of Westall's drawings. Their hoof-marks are visible on one of the originals, preserved in the Royal Colonial Institute Library, to this day.

As soon as the colony on the reef had been regularly established, a council of officers considered the steps most desirable to be taken to secure relief. It was resolved that Flinders should take the largest of the *Porpoise*'s two six-oar cutters, with an officer and crew, and make his way

---

[4] *Sydney Gazette*, 18 September 1803.

to Port Jackson, where the aid of a ship might be obtained. The enterprise was hazardous at that season of the year. The voyage would in all probability have to be undertaken in the teeth of strong southerly winds, and the safe arrival of the cutter, even under the direction of so skilful a seaman as Flinders, was the subject of dubious speculation. But something had to be done, and that promptly; and Flinders unhesitatingly undertook the attempt. He gave directions for the government of the reef during his absence, and ordered that two decked boats should be built by the carpenters from wreckage, so that in the event of his failure the whole company might be conveyed to Sydney.

By 25 August the cutter had been prepared for her long voyage, and on the following day she was launched and appropriately named the *Hope*. It was a Friday morning, and some of the sailors had a superstitious dread of sailing on a day supposed to be unlucky. But the weather was fine and the wind light. Flinders laughed at those who talked of luck. With Captain Park of the *Cato* as his assistant officer, and a double set of rowers, fourteen persons in all, he set out at once. He carried three weeks' provisions. 'All hands gave them 3 chears, which was returned by the boat's crew,' says Seaman Smith. At the moment when the *Hope* rowed away a sailor sprang to the flagstaff whence the signal of distress had been flying since the morning when help from the *Bridgewater* had been hoped for, and hauled down the blue ensign, which was at once rehoisted with the union in the upper canton [section of a flag]. 'This symbolic expression of contempt for the *Bridgewater* and of confidence in the success of our voyage, I did not see without lively emotion,' Flinders relates.

Leaving the *Hope* to continue her brave course, we may learn from Smith how the 80 men remaining on the reef occupied themselves:

> *From this time our hands are imployd, some about our new boat, whose keel is laid down 32 feet; others imployd in getting anything servisible from the wreck. Our gunns and carriadges we got from the wreck and placed them in a half moon form, close to our flag staf, our ensign being dayly hoisted union downward. Our boats sometimes is imployd in going to an island about ten miles distant; and sometimes caught turtle and fish. This island was in general sand. Except on the highest parts, it produced sea spinage; very plentifully stockd with birds and egs. In this manner the hands are imployd and the month of October is set in. Still no acct. of our Captn's success. Our boat likewise ready for launching, the rigging also fitted over*

her masthead, and had the appearance of a rakish schooner. On the 4th of Octr. we launchd her and gave her name of the Hope.[5] *On the 7th we loaded her with wood in order to take it over to the island before mentiond to make charcoal for our smith to make the ironwork for the next boat, which we intend to build directly. She accordingly saild.*

A letter by John Franklin to his father[6] gives an entertaining account of the wreck and of some other points pertaining to our subject:

Providential Bank,

August 26th, 1803,
Lat. 22° 12', long. 155° 13' (nearly) E.

Dear Father,

Great will be your surprise and sorrow to find by this that the late investigators are cast away in a sandy patch of about 300 yards long and 200 broad, by the wreck of H.M.S. Porpoise *on our homeward bound passage on the reefs of New South Wales. You will then wonder how we came into her. I will explain: The* Investigator *on her late voyage, was found when surveying the Gulf of Carpentaria to be rotten, which obliged us to make our best way to Port Jackson; but the bad state of health of our crew induced Captain Flinders to touch at Timor for refreshment; which being done he sailed, having several men died on the passage of dysentery. On our arrival she was surveyed and condemned as being unfit for service. There being no other ship in Sydney fit to complete her intended voyage, Governor King determined to send us home in the* Porpoise. *She sailed August 10th, 1803, in company with the* Bridgewater, *extra Indiaman, and* Cato, *steering to the N.W. intending to try how short a passage might be made through Torres Straits to England. On Wednesday, 17th, we fell in with reefs,[7] surveyed them, and kept our course, until half-past nine, when I was aroused by the cry of breakers, and before I got on deck the ship struck on the*

---

[5] Smith was in error. The boat built at the reef was named the *Resource.* The *Hope*, as stated above, was the cutter in which Flinders sailed from the reef to Sydney. See *A Voyage to Terra Australis*, II, pp. 315 and 329.

[6] MS., Mitchell Library.

[7] Cato Islet and reefs.

rocks.[8] *Such boats as could be were got out, the masts cut away, and then followed the horrors of ship-wreck, seas breaking over, men downcast, expecting the ship every moment to part. A raft of spars was made, and laid clear, sufficiently large to take the ship's company in case the ship should part; but as Providence ordained she lasted until morning, when happy were we to see this sandbank bearing N.W. quarter of a mile. But how horrible on the other hand to see the* Cato *in a worse condition than ourselves, the men standing forward shouting for assistance, but could get none, when their ship was parting. All except three of them committed themselves to the waves, and swam to us, and are now living on this bank. The* Bridgewater *appeared in sight, and then in a most shameful and inhuman manner left us, supposing probably every soul had perished. Should she make that report on her arrival consider it as false. We live, we have hopes of reaching Sydney. The* Porpoise *being a tough little ship hath, and still does in some measure, resist the power of the waves, and we have been able to get most of her provisions, water, spars, carpenter's tools, and every other necessary on the bank, fortunate spot that it is, on which 94 souls live. Captain Flinders and his officers have determined that he and fourteen men should go to Port Jackson in a cutter and fetch a vessel for the remainder; and in the meantime to build two boats sufficiently large to contain us if the vessels should not come. Therefore we shall be from this bank in six or eight weeks, and most probably in England by eight or nine. Our loss was more felt as we anticipated the pleasure of seeing our friends and relations after an absence of two years and a half. Let me recommend you to give yourselves no anxiety, for there is every hope of reaching England ere long. I received the letters by the* Glatton *and was sorry to find that Captain F. had lost his father. He was a worthy man. You would not dislike to have some account of our last voyage, I suppose. We were 11 months from Sydney, and all that time without fresh meat or vegetables, excepting when we were at Timor, and now and then some fish, and mostly in the torrid zone, the sun continually over our head, and the thermometer at 85, 86, and 89. The ship's company was so weakened by the immense heat that when we were to the southward they were continually ill of the dysentery; nay, nine*

[8] Wreck Reef.

of them died, besides eight we lost on our last cruise. Thus you see the Investigator's *company has been somewhat shattered since leaving England. Our discoveries have been great, but the risks and misfortunes many.*

Have you got the prize money? I see it is due, and may be had by applying at No. 21 Milbank St., Westminster; due July 22, 1802. If you do not, it will go to Greenwich Hospital. I had occasion to draw for necessaries at Sydney this last time £24 from Capt'n. F.

JOHN FRANKLIN.

XX

TO ILE-DE-FRANCE IN THE CUMBERLAND

GOVERNOR KING received the news of the wreck of the *Porpoise* immediately after the arrival of the *Hope* in Port Jackson, on the evening of 8 September. King and his family were at dinner when to his great amazement Flinders was announced. 'A razor had not passed over our faces from the time of the shipwreck,' he records, 'and the surprise of the Governor was not little at seeing two persons thus appear whom he supposed to be many hundred leagues on their way to England; but so soon as he was convinced of the truth of the vision before him, and learned the melancholy cause, an involuntary tear started from the eye of friendship and compassion, and we were received in the most affectionate manner.'

King in an official letter confessed that he could not 'sufficiently commend your voluntary services, and those who came with you, in undertaking a voyage of 700 miles in an open boat to procure relief for our friends now on the reef'. It was, indeed, an achievement of no small quality in itself.

Plans for the relief of the wrecked people were immediately formed. Captain Cumming of the *Rolla*, a 438-ton merchant ship, China-bound, agreed to call at the reef, take some of them on board, and carry them to Canton, whilst the *Francis*, which was to sail in company, was to bring the remainder back to Sydney. Flinders himself was to take command of the *Cumberland*, a 29-ton schooner, and was to sail in her to England with his charts and papers as rapidly as possible.

The *Cumberland* was a wretchedly small vessel in which to traverse 15,000 miles of ocean. She was 'something less than a Gravesend passage boat' and hardly better suited for the effort than a canal barge. But, given anything made of wood that would float and steer, inconvenience and difficulty never baffled Matthew Flinders when there was service to perform. She was the first vessel that had been built in Australia. Moore, the Government boat-builder, had put her together for colonial service, and she was reputed to be strong, tight, and well behaved in a sea; but of course she was never designed for long ocean voyages. However, she was the only boat available; and though Flinders regretted that the meagre accommodation she afforded would prevent him from working at his charts while making the passage, he was too eager to accomplish his purpose to hesitate about accepting the means. '*Fortuna audaces juvat*' might at any time have been his motto; fortune helpeth them that dare. An unavoidable delay of thirteen days caused some anxiety. 'Every day seemed a week', until he could get on his way towards the reef. But, at length, on 21 September, the *Cumberland* in company with the *Rolla* and *Francis* sailed out of Port Jackson. The crew consisted of a boatswain and ten men.

On Friday, 7 October, exactly six weeks after the *Hope* had left Wreck Reef, the ensign on the flagstaff was sighted from the masthead of the *Rolla.* At about the same time a seaman who was out with Lieutenant Fowler, in a new boat that had been constructed from the wreckage, saw a white object in the distance against the blue of the sky. At first he took it for a sea bird; but, looking at it more steadfastly, he suddenly jumped up, exclaiming, 'damn my blood, what's that?' It was, in truth, the top-gallant sail of the *Rolla.* Everybody looked at it; a sail indeed it was; Flinders had not failed them, and rescue was imminent. A shout of delight went up, and the boat scurried back to the reef to announce the news.

At about two o'clock in the afternoon, Flinders anchored under the lee of the bank. The shell of the *Porpoise* still lay on her beam side high up on the reef, but, her carronades having been landed, the happy people welcomed their deliverers with a salute of eleven guns. 'Every heart was overjoyed at this unexpected delivery,' as seaman Smith's narrative records; and when Flinders stepped ashore, he was long and loudly cheered. Men pressed around him to shake his hands and thank him, and tears of joy rolled down the hard, weather-worn faces of men not over-given to a display of feeling. For his own part 'the pleasure of rejoining my companions so amply provided with the means of relieving their distress made this one of the happiest moments of my life'.

In singular contrast with the pleasure of everyone else was the cool demeanour of Samuel Flinders. A letter previously cited contains a reference to him, which suggests that he was not always quite brotherly or generally satisfactory. On this occasion he was oddly stiff and uncordial. Flinders relates the incident:

Lieutenant Flinders, then commanding officer on the bank, was in his tent calculating some lunar distances, when one of the young gentlemen ran to him calling, 'Sir, sir, a ship and two schooners in sight.' After a little consideration, Mr. Flinders said he supposed it was his brother come back, and asked if the vessels were near. He was answered, not yet; upon which he desired to be informed when they should reach the anchorage, and very calmly resumed his calculations. Such are the varied effects produced by the same circumstances upon different minds. When the desired report was made, he ordered the salute to be fired, and took part in the general satisfaction.

After the welcoming was over, Flinders assembled all the people and informed them what his plans were. Those who chose might go to Sydney in the *Francis*; the others, with the exception of ten, would sail in the *Rolla* to Canton and others take ship for England. To accompany him in the *Cumberland* he chose John Aken, who had been master of the *Investigator*, Edward Charrington, the boatswain, his own servant, John Elder, and seven seamen. Their names are contained in the log-book which General Decaen detained at Ile-de-France. They were George Elder, who had been carpenter on the *Porpoise*, John Woods, Henry Lewis, Francis Smith, N. Smith, James Carter, and Jacob Tibbet, all picked men.

Young Franklin went in the *Rolla*. As he explained in a letter to his mother[1]: 'The reason I did not accompany Captain Flinders was the smallness of the vessel and badness of accommodation, he having only taken the master with him.' The young sailor's application had won the commendation of the commander, who was a hero to him throughout his adventurous life. We find Flinders writing to his wife[2]: 'John Franklin approves himself worthy of notice. He is capable of learning everything that we can show him, and but for a little carelessness I would not wish to have a son otherwise than he is.'

At noon on 11 October, four days after the arrival of the relieving ships at the reef, they parted company, with cheers and expressions of good will. The *Rolla* accomplished her voyage to China safely, and in the following year Lieutenant Fowler, Samuel Flinders, John Franklin, and the remainder of the old *Investigator*'s company who sailed in her

---

[1] MSS., Mitchell Library.

[2] Flinders' Papers.

returned to England. On their return voyage they participated in as remarkable a comedy as the history of naval warfare contains. Their ship was one of a company of 31 sail, all richly laden merchantmen, under the general command of the audacious Commodore Nathaniel Dance; and he, encountering a French squadron under Rear-Admiral Linois, succeeded by sheer, impudent 'bluff' in making him believe that they were convoyed by British frigates, and deterred him from capturing or even seriously attacking them.[3]

From the very commencement of the voyage the little *Cumberland* caused trouble and anxiety. She leaked to a greater extent than had been reported, and the pumps were so defective that a fourth part of every day had to be spent at them to keep the water down. They became worse with constant use, and by the time Timor was reached, on 10 November, one of them was nearly useless. At Kupang no means of refitting the worn-out pump or of pitching the leaky seams in the upper works of the boat were obtainable; and Flinders had to face a run across the Indian Ocean with the prospect of having to keep down the water with an impaired equipment.

When discussing the route with Governor King before leaving Sydney, Flinders had pointed out that the size of the *Cumberland*, and the small quantity of stores and water she could carry, would oblige him to call at every convenient port; and he mentioned that the places which he contemplated visiting were Kupang in Timor, Ile-de-France (Mauritius), the Cape of Good Hope, St Helena, and one of the Canaries. But King took exception to a call being made at Ile-de-France, partly because he did not wish to encourage communication between Port Jackson and the French colony, and partly because he understood that hurricane weather prevailed in the neighbourhood at about the time of the year when the *Cumberland* would be in the Indian Ocean. To respect King's wishes, Flinders on leaving Kupang set a course direct for the Cape of Good Hope. But when 23 days out from Timor, on 4 December, a heavy south-west groundswell combined with a strong eastern following sea caused the vessel to labour exceedingly, and to ship such quantities of water that the one effective pump had to be kept working day and night continually. If anything went wrong with this pump, a contingency to be feared from its incessant employment, there was a serious risk of foundering.

---

[3] Lieutenant Fowler was presented with a sword valued at 50 guineas for his part in this action, which took place on 14 February 1804, off Polo Aor, Malacca Strait. See the author's *Terre Napoléon*, p. 16.

After enduring two days of severe shaking, Flinders came to the determination that considerations of safety compelled him to make for Ile-de-France. On 6 December, therefore, he altered the *Cumberland*'s course for that island.

When he wrote his *Voyage to Terra Australis*, he had not his journal in his possession, and worked from notes of his recollections. In telling the story now, the author has before him not only what Flinders wrote in this way, but also a copy of the French translation of the journal which Decaen had prepared for his own use, and several letters written by Flinders, wherein he related what passed in his mind when he resolved to alter his course.

The first and most imperative reason was the necessity for repairing the ship and refitting the pumps. Secondly, rations had had to be shortened, and victuals and water were required. Thirdly, Flinders had come to the conclusion that the *Cumberland* was unfit to complete the voyage to England, and he hoped to be able to sell her, and procure a passage home in another ship. 'I cannot write up my journal unless the weather is extremely fine,' he wrote. Fourthly, he desired 'to acquire a knowledge of the winds and weather at the island of the actual state of the French colony, of what utility it and its dependencies in Madagascar, might be to Port Jackson, and whether the colony could afford me resources in my future voyages'.[4]

When he sailed from Port Jackson there was, as far as he knew, peace between England and France. But there was a possibility that war had broken out again. In that event, the thought occurred to him that it would be safer to call at the French colony than at the Cape, since he had a passport from the French Government, but not from the Dutch, who would probably be involved in hostilities against England. He did not forget that the passport was made out for the *Investigator*, not for the *Cumberland.*

> *But I checked my suspicions by considering that the passport was certainly intended to protect the voyage and not the* Investigator *only. A description of the* Investigator *was indeed given in it, but the intention of it could be only to prevent imposition. The* Cumberland *was now prosecuting the voyage, and I had come in her for a lawful purpose, and upon such an occasion as the passport allowed me to put into a French port. The great desire also that the French nation has long shown to promote*

[4] Journal.

> *geographical researches, and the friendly treatment that the* Géographe *and the* Naturaliste *had received at Port Jackson, rose up before me as guarantees that I should not be impeded, but should receive the kindest welcome and every assistance.*[5]

He had no chart of Ile-de-France, but a description in the third edition of the *Encyclopaedia Britannica* informed him that the principal harbour, Port Louis, was on the north-west side, and thither he intended to steer.

On 15 December the peaks of the island showed up against the morning sky. At noon the *Cumberland* was running along the shore, close enough to be observed, and made a signal for a pilot from the fore-topmast head. A small French schooner came out of a cove, and Flinders, wishing to speak with her to make enquiries, followed her. She ran on, and entered a port, which proved to be Baye du Cap (now Cape Bay) on the south-west coast. Flinders steered in her wake, thinking that she was piloting him to safety. The truth was that the French on board thought they were being pursued by an English fighting ship, which meant to attack them; and immediately they came to anchor, without even waiting to furl sails, they hurried ashore in a canoe and reported accordingly. Thus from the very beginning of his appearance at Ile-de-France, was suspicion cast on Flinders. So began his years of sore trouble.

It was evident from the commotion on shore that the arrival of the *Cumberland* had aroused excitement. Flinders saw the people from the schooner speaking to a soldier, who, from the plumes in his hat, appeared to be an officer. Presently some troops with muskets appeared in sight. Apparently orders had been given to call out the guard. Flinders concluded that a state of war existed, and hastened to inform the authorities by sending Aken ashore in a boat, that he had a passport, and was free from belligerent intentions.

Aken returned with an officer, Major Dunienville, to whom the passport was shown, and the necessities of the *Cumberland* explained. He politely invited Flinders to go on shore and dine with him. It was pointed out that the immediate requirements were fresh water and a pilot who would take the ship round to Port Louis, as repairs could not be effected at Baye du Cap. The pilot was promised for the next day, and Major Dunienville at once sent a boat for the *Cumberland*'s empty casks.

---

[5] Flinders to Fleurieu; copy in Record Office, London. An entry in his journal shows that only when he was informed that the war had been renewed did it occur to Flinders that the French authorities would interpret literally the fact that the passport was granted to the *Investigator*.

As soon as he got ashore again, Dunienville wrote a report of what had occurred to the Captain-General, or Military Governor of the island, General Decaen, and sent it off by a special messenger. In this document[6] he related that a schooner flying the English flag had chased a coastal schooner into the bay; that the alarm had been given that she was a British privateer; that he had at once called out the troops; and that, expecting an attack, he had ordered the women and children to retire to the interior, and had given orders for cattle and sheep to be driven into the woods! 'Happily,' he proceeded, 'all these precautions, dictated by circumstances, proved to be unnecessary.' The English captain had explained to him that he had merely followed the coastal boat because he had no pilot, and wished to enter the bay to solicit succour; 'adding that he did not know of the war, and consequently had no idea that he would spread alarm by following it'.

Later in the afternoon Dunienville returned to the *Cumberland* with the district commandant, Etienne Bolger, and an interpreter. The passport was again examined, when Bolger pointed out that it was not granted to the *Cumberland* but to the *Investigator*, and that the matter must be dealt with by the Governor personally. At first he desired to send the passport to him, but Flinders objected to allowing it to leave his possession, as it constituted his only guarantee of protection from the French authorities. Then it was arranged that he should travel overland to Port Louis, while Aken took round the ship. But finally Bolger allowed Flinders to sail round in the *Cumberland*, under the guidance of a pilot. He was hospitably entertained at dinner by Major Dunienville, who invited a number of ladies and gentlemen to meet him; and on the morning of 16 December he sailed, with the major on board, for Port Louis, where he was to confront General Decaen.

The character and position of the Captain-General of Ile-de-France are so important in regard to the remainder of Flinders' life, that it will be desirable to devote a chapter to some account of him.

[6] Decaen Papers, Vol. 84.

XXI

GENERAL DECAEN

CHARLES MATHIEU ISIDORE DECAEN was born at Caen, the ancient and picturesque capital of Normandy, on 13 April 1769. Left an orphan at the age of twelve, his education was superintended by a friend of his father, who had been a public official. At the end of his schooldays he studied law under an advocate of local celebrity, M. Lasseret. Though his juristic training was not prolonged, the discipline of the office gave a certain bent to his mind, a certain lawyer-like strictness and method to his mode of handling affairs, that remained characteristic during his military career, and was exceedingly useful to him while he governed Ile-de-France. Very often in perusing his *Mémoires*[1] the reader perceives traces of the lawyer in the language of the soldier. Thus, when during the campaign of the Rhine he found that his superior officer, General Jourdan, was taking about with him as his aide-de-camp a lady in military attire, Decaen, with a solemnity that seems a little un-French under the circumstances, condemned the breach of the regulations as conduct 'which was not that of a father of a family, a legislator and a general-in-chief'. As for the lady, 'les charmes de cette maussade créature' [the charms of that sullen creature] merely evoked his scorn. It does not appear that Jourdan's escapade produced any ill effects in a military sense, but it was against the regulations, and Decaen was as yet as much lawyer as soldier.

---

[1] *The Mémoires et Journaux du Général Decaen* were prepared for publication by himself, and the portion up to the commencement of his governorship has been printed, with notes and maps, by Colonel Ernest Picard, Chief of the Historical Section of the Staff of the French Army (2 vols., Paris, 1910). Colonel Picard informed me that he did not intend to print the remainder, thinking that the ground was sufficiently covered by Professor Henri Prentout's admirable book *L'Ile de France sous Decaen.* I have, therefore, had the section relating to Flinders transcribed from the manuscript, and used it freely for this book.

When the revolutionary wars broke out, and France was ringed round by a coalition of enemies, the voice of 'la patrie en danger' [the homeland in danger] rang in the ears of the young student like a call from the skies. He was 22 years of age when two deputies of the Legislative Assembly came down to Caen and made an appeal to the manhood of the country to fly to arms. Decaen, fuming with patriotic indignation, threw down his quill, pitched his calf-bound tomes on to their shelf, and was the first to inscribe his name upon the register of the fourth battalion of the regiment of Calvados, an artillery corps. He was almost immediately despatched to Mayence on the Rhine, where Kléber (who was afterwards to serve with distinction under Bonaparte in Egypt) hard pressed by the Prussians, withdrew the French troops into the city (March 1793) and prepared to sustain a siege.

Decaen rose rapidly, by reason not merely of his bulldog courage and stubborn tenacity, but also of his intelligence and integrity. He received his 'baptism of fire' in an engagement in April, when Kleber sent a detachment to chase a Prussian outpost from a neighbouring village and to collect whatever forage and provisions might be obtained. He was honest enough to confess—and his own oft-proved bravery enabled him to do so unashamed—that, when he first found the bullets falling about him, he was for a moment afraid. 'I believe,' he wrote, 'that there are few men, however courageous they may be, who do not experience a chill, and even a feeling of fear, when for the first time they hear around them the whistling of shot, and above all when they first see the field strewn with killed and wounded comrades.'[2] But he was a sergeant-major by this time, and remembered that it was his duty to set an example; so, screwing up his courage to the sticking-place by an effort of will, and saying to himself that it was not for a soldier of France to quail before a ball, he deliberately wheeled his horse to the front of a position where a regiment was being shaken by the enemy's artillery fire, and by his very audacity stiffened the wavering troops and saved the situation.

After the capitulation of Mayence in July 1793, Decaen fought with distinction in the war in La Vendée. In this cruel campaign he displayed unusual qualities as a soldier, and attained the rank of adjutant-general. Kléber gave him a command calling for exceptional nerve, with the comment, 'It is the most dangerous position, and I thought it worthy of your courage.' It was Decaen, according to his own account, who devised the plan of sending out a number of mobile columns to strike at the rebels swiftly and unexpectedly. But though he was succeeding in a

---

[2] *Mémoires*, I, p. 13.

military sense, these operations against Frenchmen, while there were foreign foes to fight beyond the frontiers, were thoroughly distasteful to him. The more he saw of the war in La Vendée, and the more terribly the thumb of the national power pressed upon the throat of the rebellion, the more he hated the service. It was at his own solicitation, therefore, that he was transferred to the army of the Rhine in January 1795.

Here he served under the ablest general, saving only Bonaparte himself, whom the wars of the Revolution produced to win glory for French arms, Jean Victor Moreau. His bravery and capacity continued to win him advancement. Moreau promoted him to the command of a brigade, and presented him with a sword of honour for his masterly conduct of a retreat through the Black Forest, when, in command of the rearguard, he fought the Austrians every mile of the road to the Rhine.

He became a general of division in 1800. At the battle of Hohenlinden, where Moreau concentrated his troops to give battle to the Austrians under the Archduke John, Decaen performed splendid service; indeed it was he who chose the position, and recommended it as a favourable place for taking a stand.[3] Moreau knew him well by now, and on the eve of the fight (2 December) when he brought up his division to the plateau in the forest of Ebersberg, where the village of Hohenlinden stands, and presented himself at headquarters to ask for orders, the commander-in-chief rose to greet him with the welcome, 'Ah, there is Decaen, the battle will be ours to-morrow.' It was intended for a personal compliment, we cannot doubt, though Decaen in his *Mémoires* (II, p. 136) interpreted it to mean that the general was thinking of the 10,000 troops whose arrival he had come to announce.

Moreau's plan was this. He had posted his main force strongly fronting the Austrian line of advance, on the open Hohenlinden plateau. The enemy had to march through thickly timbered country to the attack. The French general instructed Decaen and Richepance to manoeuvre their two divisions, each consisting of 10,000 men, through the forest, round the Austrian rear, and to attack them there, as soon as they delivered their attack upon the French front. The Archduke John believed Moreau to be in full retreat, and hurried his army forward from Haag, east of Hohenlinden, amid falling snow.

By torch and trumpet fast array'd
Each horseman drew his battle-blade,
And furious every charger neigh'd

---

[3] *Mémoires*, II, p. 89.

To join the dreadful revelry.
Then shook the hills with thunder riven;
Then rush'd the steed, to battle driven,
And louder than the bolts of Heaven
Far flashed the red artillery.

Decaen's division marched at five o'clock on the morning of 3 December, and shortly before eight the boom of the Austrian cannon was heard. His troops pressed forward in a blinding snowstorm. An officer said that the guns seemed to show that the Austrians were turning the French position. 'Ah, well,' said Decaen, 'if they turn ours, we will turn theirs in our turn.' It was one of the few jokes he made in his whole life, and it exactly expressed the situation. The Austrian army was caught like a nut in a nut-cracker. Battered from front and rear, their ranks broke, and fugitives streamed away east and west, like the crumbled kernel of a filbert [the nut of the cultivated hazel tree]. Decaen threw his battalions upon their rear with a furious vigour, and crumpled it up; and almost at the very moment of victory the snow ceased to fall, the leaden clouds broke, and a brilliant sun shone down upon the scene of carnage and triumph. Ten thousand Austrians were killed, wounded, or taken prisoners, whilst 80 guns and about 200 baggage waggons fell as spoils to the French. In this brilliant victory Decaen's skill and valour, rapidity and verve, had been of inestimable value, as Moreau was prompt to acknowledge.

The quick soldier's eye of Bonaparte recognised him at once as a man of outstanding worth. The Consulate had been established in December 1799, and the First Consul was anxious to attach to him strong, able men. In 1802 Decaen ventured to use his influence with the Government regarding an appointment to the court of appeal at Caen, for which Lasseret, his old master in law, was a candidate; and we find Bonaparte writing to Cambacérès, who had charge of the law department, that 'if the citizen possesses the requisite qualifications I should like to defer to the wishes of General Decaen, who is an officer of great merit'.[4]

He saw much of Bonaparte in Paris during 1801 and 1802; when the part he had to play was an extremely difficult one, demanding the exercise of tact and moral courage in an unusual measure. The *Mémoires* throw a vivid light on the famous quarrel between Moreau and Napoleon, which in the end led to the exile of the victor of Hohenlinden.

---

[4] Napoleon's *Correspondance*, Document 5596.

Moreau was Decaen's particular friend, the commander who had given him opportunities for distinction, one whom he loved and honoured as a man and a patriot. But he [Moreau] was jealous of Napoleon's success, was disaffected towards the consular government, and was believed to be concerned in plots for its overthrow. On the other hand, Napoleon was not only the head of the State, but was the greatest soldier of his age. Decaen's admiration of him was unbounded, and Napoleon's attitude towards Decaen was cordial. He tried to reconcile these two men whom he regarded with such warm affection, but failed. One day, when business was being discussed, Napoleon said abruptly, 'Decaen, General Moreau is conducting himself badly; I shall have to denounce him.' Decaen was moved to tears, and insisted that Napoleon was ill informed. 'You are good yourself,' said the First Consul, 'and you think everybody else is like you. Moreau is corresponding with Pichegru,' whose conspiracy was known to the Government. 'It is not possible.' 'But I have a letter which proves it.' Moreover, Moreau was openly disrespectful to the Government. He had presented himself out of uniform on occasions when courtesy demanded that he should wear it. If Moreau had anything to complain about, he did not make it better by associating with malcontents. 'He has occupied a high position, which gives him influence, and a bad influence upon public opinion hampers the work of the Government. I have not fallen here out of the sky, you know; I follow my glory. France wants repose, not more disturbance.' Decaen manfully championed his friend, 'I am persuaded,' he said, 'that if you made overtures to Moreau you would easily draw him towards you.' 'No,' said Napoleon 'he is a shifting sand.' Moreau said to Decaen, 'I am too old to bend my back'; but the latter was of opinion that the real source of the mischief was that Moreau had married a young wife, and that she and his mother-in-law considered they were entitled to as much attention as Madame Bonaparte received. Pride, jealousy and vanity, he declared, were the real source of the quarrel. Decaen, indeed, has a story that when Madame Moreau once called upon Josephine at Malmaison, she returned in an angry state of mind because she was not at once admitted, bidding a servant tell her mistress that the wife of General Moreau was not accustomed to be kept waiting. The simple explanation was that Josephine was in her bath!

Decaen came to be appointed Governor of Ile-de-France in this way. One day, after dining with Napoleon at Malmaison, the First Consul took a stroll with him, and in the course of conversation asked him what he wanted to do. 'I have my sword for the service of my country,' said Decaen. 'Very good,' answered Napoleon, 'but what would you like to do now?' Decaen then mentioned that he had been reading the history of the exploits of La Bourdonnaye and Dupleix in India, and was much attracted by the possibilities for the expansion of French power there. 'Have you ever been to India?' enquired Napoleon. 'No, but I am young, and, desiring to do something useful, I should like to undertake a mission which I believe would not be likely to be coveted by many, having regard to the distance between France and that part of the world. And even if it were necessary to spend ten years of my life awaiting a favourable opportunity of acting against the English, whom I detest because of the injury they have done to our country, I should undertake the task with the utmost satisfaction.' Napoleon merely observed that what he desired might perhaps be arranged.

A few months later Decaen was invited to breakfast with Napoleon at Malmaison. He was asked whether he was still inclined to go to India, and replied that he was. 'Very well, then, you shall go.' 'In what capacity?' 'As Captain-General. Go and see the Minister of Marine, and tell him to show you all the papers relative to the expedition that is in course of being fitted out.'

Under the treaty of Amiens, negotiated in 1802, Great Britain agreed to restore to the French Republic and its allies all conquests made during the recent wars except Trinidad and Ceylon. From the British point of view it was an inglorious peace. Possessions which had been won in fair fight, by the ceaseless activity and unparalleled efficiency of the navy, and by the blood and valour of British manhood, were signed away with a stroke of the pen. The surrender of the Cape was especially lamentable, because upon security at that point depended the safety of India and Australia. But the Addington ministry was weak and temporising, and was alarmed about the internal condition of England, where dear food, scarcity of employment and popular discontent, consequent upon prolonged warfare, made the King's advisers nervously anxious to put an end to the struggle. The worst feature of the situation was that everybody thoroughly well understood that it was a mere parchment peace. Cornwallis called it 'an experimental peace'. It was also termed 'an armistice' and 'a frail and deceptive truce'; and though Addington declared it to be 'no ordinary peace but a genuine reconciliation between the two first nations of the world', his flash of rhetoric dazzled nobody but himself. He was the Mr Perker of politics [a character in Dickens's *Pickwick Papers*], an accommodating attorney rubbing his hands and exclaiming 'My dear sir!' while he bartered the interests of his client for the delusive terms of a brittle expediency.

Decaen was to go to India to take charge of the former French possessions there, under the terms of the treaty, and from Pondicherry was also to control Ile-de-France (Mauritius) which the English had not taken during the war. Napoleon's instructions to him clearly indicated that he did not expect the peace to endure. Decaen was 'to dissimulate the views of the Government as much as possible'; 'the English are the tyrants of India, they are uneasy and jealous, it is necessary to behave towards them with suavity, dissimulation and simplicity'. He was to regard his mission primarily as one of observation upon the policy and military dispositions of the English. But Napoleon informed him in so many words that he intended some day to strike a blow for 'that glory which perpetuates the memory of men throughout the centuries'. For that, however, it was first necessary 'that we should become masters of the sea'.[5]

Decaen sailed from Brest in February 1803. Lord Whitworth, the British Ambassador to Paris, watched the proceedings with much care, and promptly directed the attention of his Government to the disproportionate number of officers the new Captain-General was taking with him. The Government passed the information on to the Governor-General of India, Lord Wellesley, who was already determined that, unless absolutely ordered so to do, he would not permit a French military force to land. Before Decaen arrived at Pondicherry, indeed, in June 1803, Wellesley had received a despatch from Lord Hobart, Secretary of State for War and the Colonies, warning him that, notwithstanding the treaty of Amiens, 'certain circumstances render desirable a delay in the restitution of their possessions in India' to the French, and directing that territory occupied by British troops was not to be evacuated by them without fresh orders. Great Britain already perceived the fragility of the peace, and, in fact, was expediting preparations for a renewal of war, which was declared in May 1803.

When, therefore, the French frigate *Marengo*, with Decaen on board, arrived at Pondicherry, the British flag still flew over the Government buildings, and he soon learnt that there was no disposition to lower it. Moreover, *La Belle Poule*, which had been sent in advance from the Cape to herald the Captain-General's coming, was anchored between two British ships of war, which had carefully ranged themselves alongside her. Decaen grasped the situation rapidly. A few hours after his arrival, the French brig *Bélier* appeared. She had left France on 25 March, carrying a despatch informing the Captain-General that war was anticipated, and directing him to land his troops at Ile-de-France, where he was to assume the governorship.

Rear-Admiral Linois, who commanded the French division, wanted

[5] *Mémoires*, II, p. 310.

to sail at once. Decaen insisted on taking aboard some of the French who were ashore, but Linois pointed to the strong British squadron in sight, and protested that he ought not to compromise the safety of his ships by delaying departure. Linois was always a very nervous officer. Decaen stormed, and Linois proposed to call a council of his captains. 'A council!' exclaimed Decaen, 'I am the council!' It was worthy of what Voltaire attributed to Louis XIV: *'l'état, c'est moi.'* [I am the State.] After sunset Decaen visited the ships of the division in a boat, and warned their captains to get ready to follow the *Marengo* out of the roadstead [a protected anchorage] of Pondicherry in the darkness. He considered that it would be extremely embarrassing if the British squadron, suspecting their intentions, endeavoured to frustrate them. At an appointed hour the *Marengo* quietly dropped out of the harbour, cutting the cable of one of her anchors rather than permit any delay.

On 15 August Decaen landed at Port Louis, Ile-de-France, and on the following day he took over the government. He had therefore been in command exactly four months when Matthew Flinders, in the *Cumberland*, put into Baye du Cap on 15 December.

For his conduct in the Flinders affair Decaen has been plentifully denounced. 'A brute', 'a malignant tyrant', 'vindictive, cruel and unscrupulous'—such are a few shots from the heavy artillery of language that have been fired at his reputation. The author knows of one admirer of Flinders who had a portrait of Decaen framed and hung with its face to the wall of his study. It is, unfortunately, much easier to denounce than to understand; and where resonant terms have been flung in freest profusion, it does not appear that an endeavour has been made to study what occurred from the several points of view, and to examine Decaen's character and actions in the light of full information. A postponement of epithets until we have ascertained the facts is in this, as in so many other cases, extremely desirable.

No candid reader of Decaen's *Mémoires*, and of Prentout's elaborate investigation of his administration, can fail to recognise that he was a conspicuously honest man. During his governorship he handled millions of francs. Privateers from Ile-de-France captured British merchant ships, to a value, including their cargo, of over £3,000,000 sterling,[6] a share of

---

6 Prentout, p. 509, estimates the value of captures at £2,000,000, but Mr H. Hope informed Flinders in 1811, that insurance offices in Calcutta had actually paid £3,000,000 sterling on account of ships captured by the French at Mauritius. Flinders, writing with exceptional opportunities for forming an opinion, calculated that during the first sixteen months of the war the French captures of British merchant ships brought to Ile-de-France were worth £1,948,000 (*Voyage* II, p. 416).

which it would have been easy for Decaen to secure. But his financial reputation is above suspicion. His management was economical and efficient. He ended his days in honourable poverty.

He was blunt and plain-spoken; and though he could be pleasant, was when ruffled by no means what Mrs Malaprop [a character in Sheridan's play *The Rivals,* notorious for her misuse of words] called 'the very pineapple of politeness'. His quick temper brought him into continual conflict with superiors and subordinates. He quarrelled repeatedly with generals and ministers; with Admiral Linois, with Soult, with Decrès, with Barras, with Jourdan, and with many others. When General Lecourbe handed him a written command during the Rhine campaign, he says himself that, 'when I received the order I tightened my lips and turned my back upon him'. He speaks of himself in one place as being 'of a petulant character and too free with my tongue'. That concurs with Flinders' remark, after bitter experience of Decaen, that he possessed 'the character of having a good heart, though too hasty and violent'.

Decaen's military capacity was much higher than his historical reputation might lead one to suppose. During the fierce wars of the Napoleonic Empire, whilst Ney, Oudinot, Murat, Junot, Augereau, Soult, St Cyr, Davoust, Lannes, Marmont, Masséna and Suchet were rendering brilliant service under the eye of the great captain, and were being converted into dukes and princes, Decaen was shut up in a far-off isle in the Indian Ocean, where there was nothing to do but hold on under difficulties, and wait in vain for the turn of a tide that never floated a French fleet towards the coveted India. Colonel Picard, than whom there is hardly a better judge, is of opinion that had Decaen fought with the Grand Army in Europe, his military talents would have designated him for the dignity of a marshal of the Empire. On his return he did become a Comte, but then the Napoleonic régime was tottering to its fall.

Such then was the man—stubborn, strong-willed, brusque, honest, irritable, ill-tempered, but by no means a bad man at heart—with whom Matthew Flinders had to do [deal]. We may now follow what occurred.

XXII

THE CAPTIVITY

AT four o'clock in the afternoon of 17 December the *Cumberland* entered Port Louis, where Flinders learnt that *Le Géoqraphe* had sailed for France on the previous day. As soon as he could land he went ashore to present himself to the Governor, whom he found to be at dinner. To occupy the time until an interview could be arranged, he joined a party of officers who were lounging in a shady place, and gossiped with them about his voyage, about Baudin's visit to Port Jackson, about the English settlement there, 'and also concerning the voyage of Monsieur Flindare, of whom, to their surprise, I knew nothing, but afterwards found it to be my own name which they so pronounced'.

In a couple of hours he was conducted to Government House, where, after a delay of half an hour, he was shown into a room. At a table stood two officers. One was a short, thick man in a gold-laced mess jacket, who fixed his eyes sternly on Flinders, and at once demanded his passport and commission. This was General Decaen. Beside him stood his aide-de-camp, Colonel Monistrol. The General glanced over the papers, and then enquired 'in an impetuous manner', why Flinders had come to Ile-de-France in the *Cumberland*, when his passport was for the *Investigator*. The necessary explanation being given, Decaen exclaimed impatiently, 'You are imposing on me, sir! It is not probable that the Governor of New South Wales should send away the commander of a discovery expedition in so small a vessel.' Decaen's own manuscript *Mémoires* show that when this story was told to him, he thought it 'very extraordinary that he should have left Port Jackson to voyage to England in a vessel of 29 tons'; and, in truth, to a man who knew nothing of Flinders' record of seamanship it must have seemed unlikely. He handed back the passport and commission, and gave some orders to an officer; and as Flinders was leaving the room 'the Captain-General said something in a softer tone about my being well treated, which I could not comprehend'.

It is clear that Decaen's brusque manner made Flinders very angry. He did not know at this time that it was merely the General's way, and that he was not at all an ill-natured man if discreetly handled. On board the *Cumberland*, in company with the interpreter and an officer, who were very polite, he confesses having 'expressed my sentiments of General Decaen's manner of receiving me', adding 'that the Captain-General's conduct must alter very much before I should pay him a second visit, or even set my foot on shore again'. It is very important to notice Flinders' state of mind, because it is apparent that a whole series of unfortunate events turned upon his demeanour at the next interview. His anger is perfectly intelligible. He was a British officer, proud of his service; he had for years been accustomed to command, and to be obeyed; he knew that he was guiltless of offence; he felt that he had a right to protection and consideration under his passport. Believing himself to have been affronted, he was not likely to be able to appreciate the case as it presented itself at the moment to this peppery general; that here was the captain of an English schooner who, as reported, had chased a French vessel into Baye du Cap, and who gave as an explanation that he had called to seek assistance while on a 16,000 mile voyage, in a 29-ton boat. Surely Flinders' story, as Decaen saw it at this time, was not a probable one; and at all events he, as Governor of Ile-de-France, had a duty to satisfy himself of its truth. We can well understand Flinders' indignation; but can we not also appreciate Decaen's doubt?

The officers, acting under instructions, collected all the charts, papers, journals, letters, and packets, found on board, and put them in a trunk which, says Flinders, 'was sealed by me at their desire'. They then requested him to go ashore with them, to a lodging at an inn, which the General had ordered to be provided for him. In fact, they had orders to take him there. 'What! I exclaimed in the first transports of surprise and indignation, I am then a prisoner!' The officers expressed the hope that the detention would not last more than a few days, and assured him that in the meantime he should want for nothing. Flinders, accompanied by Aken, went ashore, and the two were escorted to a large house in the middle of the town, the Café Marengo, where they were shown into a room approached by a dark entry up a dirty staircase, and left for the night with a sentry on guard in the passage outside.

That Flinders had no doubt that he would soon be released, is shown by the fact that he wrote from the tavern the following letter to the captain of the American ship *Hunter*, then lying in Port Louis: 'Sir, understanding that you are homeward bound, I have to represent to you that I am here with an officer and nine men belonging to His Britannic Majesty's ship

Investigator, lately under my command, and if I am set at liberty should be glad to get a passage on board your vessel to St Helena, or on any other American who does not touch at the Cape of Good Hope[1] and may be in want of men. I am, Sir, etc., etc., MATTHEW FLINDERS.

'If it is convenient for you to call upon me at the tavern where I am at present confined, I shall be glad to see you as soon as possible.'

Early in the afternoon of the following day Colonel Monistrol came to the inn to take Flinders and Aken before the General, who desired to ask certain questions. The interrogatories [questions] were read from a paper, as dictated by Decaen, and Flinders' answers were translated and written down. In the document amongst Decaen's papers the French questions and answers are written on one side of the paper, with the English version parallel; the latter being signed by Flinders. The translation is crude (the scribe was a German with some knowledge of English) but is printed below literally:

> *Questions made to the commanding officier of an English schooner anchored in Savanna Bay, at the Isle of France, on the 24th frimaire 12th year [on 17 December 1803] chasing a coaster, which in consequence of the declaration of war between the French Republic and Great Britain, had intention to avoid the poursuit of said schooner. Said schooner carried the next day in the harbour of Port North-West, where she anchored under cartel colours [under a flag of truce], the commanding officer having declared to the officer of the health boat that his name was Matthew Flinders, and his schooner the Cumberland.*
> *Demanded: The Captain's name?*
> *Answered: Matthew Flinders.*
> *D.: From what place the Cumberland sailed?*
> *A.: From Port Jackson.*
> *D.: At what time?*
> *A.: The Captain does not recollect the date of his departure. He thinks it is on the 20th of September.*
> *D.: What is the purpose of his expedition?*
> *A.: His only motive was to proceed on to England as soon as possible, to make the report of his voyages and to request a ship to continue them.*

[1] He did not wish to call at the Cape, because if he got clear of the French frying pan he did not want to jump into the Dutch fire.

D.: What can be the reason which has determined Captain Flinders to undertake a voyage on board of the so small a vessel?
A.: To avoid losing two months on proceeding by China, for a ship sailing from Port Jackson was to put in China.
D.: Does not Port Jackson offer frequent opportunities for Europe?
A.: There are some, as he has observed it above, but that ship putting in China is the reason which determined him not to proceed that way.
D.: At what place had the Cumberland *put in?*
A.: At Timor.
D.: What could be the reason of her putting in at Timor?
A.: To take fresh provision and water. He has left Timor 34 days ago.
D.: What passports or certificates has he taken in that place?
A.: None.
D.: What has been his motive for his coming at the Isle of France?
A.: The want of water. His pumpers [sic] are bad, and his vessel is very leaky.
D.: To what place does Captain Flinders intend to go to from this island?
A.: Having no passport for the Dutch Government, he cannot put in the Cape, according to his wishes, and will be obliged to stop at St. Helena.
D.: What can be the reason of his having none of his officiers, naturalis [sic], or any of the other persons employed in said expedition?
A.: Two of these gentlemen have remained in Port Jackson to repair on board of the ship Captain Flinders expected to obtain in England,[2] and the rest have proceeded on to China.
D.: What reason induced Captain Flinders to chase a boat in sight of the island?
A.: Being never to this island, he was not acquainted with the harbour. Seeing a French vessel he chased her[3] for the only

[2] 'Pour s'embarquer sur le vaisseau que le Cap. Flinders a espoir d'obtenir en Angleterre,' in the French [In order to embark on the vessel which Captain Flinders had hoped to obtain in England]. That is to say, Brown and Bauer remained behind till Flinders came out again with another ship.

[3] It is singular that Flinders did not take exception to this word 'chased' in the translation when he signed it. The French version of his statement is correct: 'il forca de voile, *non pour luy appuyer chasse* mais pour luy demander un pilote.' [He put on sail, not to give chase but in order to request a pilot.] The German translator boggled between the French and the English.

purpose of obtaining a pilot, and seeing her entering a bay he followed her.
D.: What reason had he to make the land to leewards, the different directories pointing out the contrary route to anchor in the harbour?
A.: He came to windwards, but the wind shifting contrary he took to leewards and perceiving said vessel he followed her and anchored in the same bay. He has no chart of the island.
D.: Why has he hoisted cartel colours [a flag of truce]?
A.: He answers that it is the custom, since Captain Baudin coming to Port Jackson hoisted the colours of both nations.
D.: Was he informed of the war?
A.: No.
D.: Has he met with any ship either at sea or in the different ports where he put in?
A.: He met one ship only, by the 6° or 7° to the east of the Isle of France. He did not speak her, though desirous of so doing, being prevented by the night. He met with no ship at Timor.

In consequence of the questions made to Captain Flinders respecting to his wreck, he declares that after putting in at Port Jackson with the ship under his command, he was through her bad condition obliged to leave her, being entirely decayed. The Governor at that time furnished him with a ship thought capable of transporting him to Europe. He had the misfortune to wreck on the east coast of New Holland by the 22° 11' of latitude south on some rock distant 700 miles from Port Jackson, and 200 miles from the coast. He embarked in the said ship's boat, taking with him 14 men, and left the remainder of his crew on a sand bank. He lost on this occasion three charts respecting his voyages and particularly Golph Carpentary. After 14 days' passage he arrived at Port Jackson. After tarrying in said place 8 or 9 days, the Governor furnished him with the small vessel he is now in, and a ship to take the remainder of the crew left on the bank. This vessel not being a government ship and bound to China, proceeded on her intended voyage with the officers and the crew which had been left on the bank.

Captain Flinders declares that of the two boxes remitted by him one contains despatches directed to the Secretary of State and the other was entrusted to him by the commanding officer of the troops in Port Jackson, and that he is ignorant what they contain.

Captain Mw. Flinders to ascertain the legality of this expedition and the veracity of what he expose,[4] *has opened in our presence a trunk sealed by him containing the papers having a reference to his expedition, and to give us a copy by him certified of the passport delivered to him by the First Consul and His Majesty King of Great Britain; equally the communication of his journal since the condemnation of his ship* Investigator.

Port North-West, Ile of France, the 26th frimaire 12th year of the French Republic [answering to 19 December 1803].

(Signed) MATTW. FLINDERS.

Flinders corroborates the statement regarding the taking of papers from the trunk, stating that they consisted of the third volume of his rough log-book, which contained 'the whole of what they desired to know', respecting his voyage to Ile-de-France. He told Decaen's secretary to make such extracts as were considered requisite, 'pointing out the material passages'. 'All the books and papers, the third volume of my rough log-book excepted, were then returned into the trunk, and sealed as before.' It is important to notice that at no time were papers taken from the trunk without Flinders' knowledge and concurrence, because the charge has frequently been made, even by historical writers of authority,[5] that his charts were plagiarised by the cartographers of Baudin's expedition. Flinders himself never made any such allegation, nor is there any foundation for it. On the contrary, as will be made clear hereafter, neither Decaen and his officers, nor any of the French, ever saw any of Flinders' charts at any time.

Immediately after the examination the General, on behalf of Madame Decaen, sent Flinders an invitation to dine, dinner being then served. At this point, one cannot help feeling, he made a tactical mistake. It is easily understood, and allowance can be made for it, but the consequences of it were serious. He was angry on account of his detention, irritated by the treatment to which he had been subjected, and unable in his present frame of mind to appreciate the Governor's point of view. He refused to go, and said he had already dined. The officer who bore the invitation pressed him in a kindly manner, saying that at all events he had better go

---

[4] 'La verité de son exposé', i.e., the truth of his statement.

[5] In the *Cambridge Modern History*, for instance (ix, p. 739): 'The French authorities at Mauritius having captured and imprisoned the explorer Flinders on his passage to England, attempted by the use of his papers to appropriate for their ships the credit of his discoveries along the south coast of Australia.'

to the table. Flinders replied that he would not; if the General would first set him at liberty he would accept the invitation with pleasure, and be flattered by it. Otherwise he would not sit at table with Decaen. 'Having been grossly insulted both in my public and private character, I could not debase the situation I had the honour to hold.'

The effect of so haughty a refusal upon an inflammatory temper like that of Decaen may be readily pictured. Presently an aide-de-camp returned with the message that the General would renew the invitation when Captain Flinders was set at liberty. There was a menace in the cold phrase.

Now, had Flinders bottled up his indignation and swallowed his pride—had he frankly recognised that he was in Decaen's power—had he acknowledged that some deference was due to the official head of the colony of a foreign nation with whom his country was at war—his later troubles might have been averted. An opportunity was furnished of discussing the matter genially over the wine and dessert. He would have found himself in the presence of a man who could be kind-hearted and entertaining when not provoked, and of a charming French lady in Madame Decaen. He would have been assisted by the secretary, Colonel Monistrol, who was always as friendly to him as his duty would permit. He would have been able to hold the company spellbound with the story of the many adventures of his active, useful life. He would have been able to demonstrate his *bona fides* completely. It is a common experience that the humane feelings of men of Decaen's type are easily touched; and his conduct regarding the Napoleon–Moreau quarrel has been related above with some fullness for the purpose of showing that there was milk as well as gunpowder in his composition. But Flinders was angry; justifiably angry no doubt, but unfortunately angry nevertheless, since thereby he lost his chance.

He learnt afterwards that 'some who pretended to have information from near the fountain-head hinted that, if his invitation to dinner had been accepted, a few days would have been the whole' of his detention.[6] That seems probable. He had no better friend than Sir Joseph Banks; and he learnt to his regret that Banks 'was not quite satisfied with his conduct to the Government of Mauritius, thinking he had treated them perhaps with too much haughtiness'. His comment upon this was, 'should the same circumstances happen to me again I fear I should follow nearly the same steps'.[7] That is the sort of thing that strong-willed

[6] Flinders, *Voyage* II, p. 398.

[7] Flinders' Papers.

men say; but a knowledge of the good sense and good feeling that were native to the character of Matthew Flinders enables one to assert with some confidence that if, after this experience, the choice had been presented to him, on the one hand of conquering his irritation and going to enjoy a pleasant dinner in interesting company with the prospect of speedy liberation; on the other of scornfully disdaining the olive branch, with the consequence of six-and-a-half years of heartbreaking captivity; he would have chosen the former alternative without much reluctance. There is a sentence in one of his own letters which indicates that wisdom counted for more than obstinacy in his temperament: 'After a misfortune has happened, we all see very well the proper steps that ought to have been taken to avoid it; to be endowed with a never-failing foresight is not within the power of man.'

That the view presented above is not too strong is clear from a passage in an unpublished portion of Decaen's *Mémoires.* He stated that after the examination of Flinders, 'I sent him an invitation from my wife[8] to come to dine with us, although he had given me cause to withhold the invitation on account of his impertinence; but from boorishness, or rather from arrogance, he refused that courteous invitation, which, if accepted, would indubitably have brought about a change favourable to his position, through the conversation which would have taken place.'[9] Here it is distinctly suggested that if the invitation had been accepted, and a pleasant discussion of the case had ensued, the detention of the *Cumberland* and her commander would probably not have been prolonged.

Further light is thrown on these regrettable occurrences by a manuscript history of Ile-de-France, written by St Elme le Duc,[10] a friend of Decaen, who possessed intimate knowledge of the General's feelings. It is therein stated that Decaen received Flinders 'in uniform, the head uncovered', but that 'Captain Flinders presented himself with arrogance, his hat upon his head; they had to ask him to remove it'. The same writer alleges that Flinders disregarded all the rules of politeness. It is fair to state these matters since the candid student must always wish to

---

[8] Flinders does not state that the invitation came from Madame Decaen. He may not have understood. But the refusal of it would on that account have been likely to make the General all the more angry.

[9] Decaen Papers, Vol. 10. Decaen said in his despatch to the Minister: 'Captain Flinders imagined that he would obtain his release by arguing, by arrogance, and especially by impertinence; my silence with regard to his first letter led him to repeat the offence.'

[10] Bibliothéque Nationale, nouveaux acquisitions, France, No. 1, 775.

see a case presented from several points of view. But it must be said that only an intense feeling of resentment could have unhinged the courteous disposition which was habitual with Flinders. A gentler man in his relations with all could hardly have been found. He was not more respectful to authority than he was considerate to subordinates; and throughout his career a close reading of his letters and journals, and of documents relating to him, can discover no other instance of even temporary deviation from perfect courtesy. Even in this case one can hardly say that he was to blame. There was sufficient in what occurred to make an honest man angry. But we wish to understand what occurred and why it occurred, and for that reason we cannot ignore or minimise the solitary instance wherein a natural flame of anger fired a long train of miserable consequences.

What, then, did Decaen intend to do with Flinders, at the beginning? He never intended to keep him six-and-a-half years. He simply meant to punish him for what he deemed to be rudeness; and his method of accomplishing that object was to report to Paris, and allow the case to be determined by the Government, instead of settling it himself forthwith. Here again Flinders was well informed. His journal for 24 May 1806 contains the following entry:[11] 'It has been said that I am detained a prisoner here solely because I refused the invitation of General Decaen to dine; that to punish me he referred the judgment of my case to the French Government, knowing that I should necessarily be detained twelve months before an answer arrived.' Or, as he stated the matter in his published book (II, p. 489): 'My refusal of the intended honour until set at liberty so much exasperated the Captain-General that he determined to make me repent it.' It will be seen presently that the term of detention, originally intended to endure for about a year, was lengthened by circumstances that were beyond Decaen's control; that the punishment which sprang from the hasty ire of a peppery soldier increased, against his own will, into what appeared to all the world, and most of all to the victim, to be a piece of malevolent persecution. The ball kicked off in a fit of spleen rolled on and on beyond recovery.

There was, it must be admitted, quite enough in the facts brought under Decaen's notice to warrant a reference to Paris, if he chose to be awkward. In the first place, Flinders was carrying on board the *Cumberland* a box of despatches from Governor King for the Secretary of State. As pointed out in Chapter XII, the Admiralty instructions for the *Investigator* voyage cautioned him 'not to take letters or packets

[11] Flinders' Papers.

other than those such as you may receive from this office or the office of His Majesty's Secretary of State'. Governor King was well aware of this injunction. Yet he entrusted to Flinders this box of despatches, containing material relative to military affairs. It is true that a state of war was not known to exist at the time when the *Cumberland* sailed from Port Jackson in September 1803, although as a matter of fact it had broken out in the previous May. But it was well known that war was anticipated. It is also true that Flinders knew nothing of the contents of the despatches. But neither, as a rule, does any other despatch carrier in war-time. When the *Cumberland*'s papers were examined by Decaen's officers, and these despatches were read and translated, there was at once a *prima facie* ground for saying, 'this officer is not engaged on purely scientific work; he is the bearer of despatches which might if delivered have an influence upon the present war'. Flinders himself, writing to Banks,[12] said:

> *I have learnt privately that in the despatches with which I was charged by Governor King, and which were taken from me by the French General, a demand was made for troops to be sent out to Port Jackson for the purpose of annoying Spanish America in the event of another war, and that this is considered to be a breach of my passport. 'Tis pity that Governor King should have mentioned anything that could involve me in the event of a war, either with the French at Mauritius, or the Dutch at Timor or the Cape; or that, having mentioned anything that related to war, he did not make me acquainted in a general way with the circumstances, in which case I should have thrown them overboard on learning that war was declared; but as I was situated, having little apprehension of being made a prisoner, and no idea that the despatches had any reference to war, since it was a time of peace when I left Port Jackson, I did not see the necessity of throwing them overboard at a hazard. To be the bearer of any despatches in time of peace cannot be incorrect for a ship on discovery more than for any other; but with a passport, and in time of war, it certainly is improper.*

With characteristic straightforwardness, Flinders did not hesitate to tell King himself that the despatches had cast suspicion on him:[13]

---

[12] *Historical Records*, VI, p. 49.

[13] *Historical Records*, VI, p. 105.

> *I have learned privately that in your despatches to the Secretary of State there is mention of Spanish America, which rendered me being the bearer, criminal with respect to my passport. 'Tis pity I had not known anything of this, for on finding myself under the necessity of stopping at the Isle of France, and learning the declaration of war, I should have destroyed the despatches; but leaving Port Jackson in time of peace, and confiding in my passport, I did not think myself authorised to take such a step, even after I knew of the war, having no idea there was anything in the despatches that could invalidate my passport; neither, indeed, is it invalidated in justice, but it is said to be the under-plea against me.*

These despatches of King are preserved among Decaen's papers,[14] and an examination of them reveals that they did contain material of a military character. In one of them, dated 7 August 1803, King referred to the possibility in any future war

> *of the Government of the Isle of France annoying this colony, as the voyage from hence may be done in less than seven weeks; and on the same idea this colony may hereafter annoy the trade of the Spanish settlements on the opposite coast. But to defend this colony against the one, and to annoy the other, it would be necessary that some regard should be had to the military and naval defences. The defences of the port may be made as strong as in any port I know of. By the return of cannon and batteries your Lordship will observe that those we have are placed in the best situation for annoying an enemy. Still, a small establishment of artillery officers and men are wanted to work those guns effectually in case of necessity.*

King went on to make recommendations for the increase of the military strength in men, officers, and guns. The originals of those despatches, which could furnish the French Government with valuable information concerning Port Jackson and the Flinders affair, are endorsed, 'letters translated and sent to France'; and Decaen commented upon them that in his opinion the despatches alone afforded a sufficient pretext for detaining Flinders. 'Ought a navigator engaged in discovery, and no longer possessing a passport for his ship, to be in time of war in

---

[14] Decaen Papers, Vols. 84 and 105.

command of a despatch-boat,[15] especially when, having regard to the distance between the period of the declaration of war and his departure from Port Jackson he could have obtained there the news that war had broken out?'

In reporting to his Government Decaen related the story of the *Cumberland*'s arrival from his point of view at considerable length. He expressed himself as satisfied that her commander really was Captain Flinders of the *Investigator*, to whom the French Government had issued a passport; detailed the circumstances of the examination; and complained of Flinders' 'impertinence' and 'arrogance'. Then he proceeded to describe 'several motives which have caused me to judge it to be indispensable to detain Captain Flinders'.

The first motive alleged was 'the conduct of the English Government in Europe, where she has violated all treaties, her behaviour before surrendering the Cape of Good Hope, and her treatment of our ships at Pondicherry'. In no way could it be pretended that Flinders was connected with these events.

The second motive was 'the seizing of *Le Naturaliste*, as announced by the newspapers'. Decaen was here referring to the fact that, when *Le Naturaliste* was on her homeward voyage from Port Jackson, conveying the natural history collections, she was stopped by the British frigate *Minerva* and taken into Portsmouth. But no harm was done to her. She was merely detained from 27 May 1803 till 6 June, when she was released by order of the Admiralty. In any case Flinders had nothing to do with that.

The third motive was that Captain Flinders' log-book showed an intention to make an examination of Ile-de-France and Madagascar, from which Decaen drew the inference that, if the English Government received no check, they would extend their power, and would seize the French colony. Herein the General did a serious injustice to Flinders. His log-book did indeed indicate that he desired 'to acquire a knowledge of the winds and weather periodically encountered at Ile-de-France, of the actual state of the French colony, and of what utility it and its dependencies in Madagascar might be to Port Jackson, and whether that island could afford resources to myself in my future voyages'. But information of this description was such as lay within the proper province of an explorer; and the log-book contained no hint, nor was there a remote intention, of acquiring information which, however used, could be inimical to the security of the French colony.

---

[15] 'Devait-il en temps de guerre conduire un paquebot?'

Decaen's mind had been influenced by reading François Péron's report to him concerning the expansive designs of the British in the Pacific and Indian Oceans. 'There is no doubt,' he informed his Government, 'that the English Government have the intention to seize the whole trade of the Indian Ocean, the China Seas and the Pacific, and that they especially covet what remains of the Dutch possessions in these waters.' He derived that extravagant idea from Péron's inflammatory communication, as will be seen from a perusal of that interesting document.

By these strained means, then, did Decaen give a semblance of public policy to his decision to detain Flinders. It would have been puerile to attempt to justify his action to his superiors on the personal ground that the English captain had vexed him; so he hooked in these various pretexts, though ingenuously acknowledging that they would have counted for nothing if Flinders had dined with him and talked the matter over conversationally!

On the day following the examination and the refusal of the invitation, Flinders was again conducted on board the *Cumberland* by Colonel Monistrol and the official interpreter, who 'acted throughout with much politeness, apologising for what they were obliged by their orders to execute'. On this occasion all remaining books and papers, including personal letters, were collected, locked up in a second trunk, and sealed. The document noting their deposition and sealing was signed by Flinders,[16] who was ordered to be detained in the inn under guard. It was, Decaen reported, the best inn in the island, and orders were given to furnish the prisoner with all that he could want; but Flinders described it as an exceedingly dirty place.

On his return to the inn from the ship Flinders wrote a letter to the Governor, recounting the history of his explorations, and making two requests: that he might have his printed books ashore, and that his servant, John Elder, might be permitted to attend him. On the following day Elder was sent to him. On the 22nd he wrote again, soliciting 'that I may be able to sail as soon as possible after you shall be pleased to liberate me from my present state of purgatory'.[17] On Christmas Day he sent a letter suffused with indignant remonstrance, wherein he alleged that 'it appears that your Excellency had formed a determination to stop the *Cumberland* previously even to seeing me, if a specious pretext were wanting for it', and reminded Decaen that 'on the first evening of my

[16] Decaen Papers.

[17] Decaen Papers.

arrival … you told me impetuously that I was imposing on you'. He continued, in a strain that was bold and not conciliatory:

I cannot think that an officer of your rank and judgment to act either so ungentlemanlike or so unguardedly as to make such a declaration without proof; unless his reason had been blinded by passion, or a previous determination that it should be so, nolens volens *[whether one liked it or not]. In your orders of the 21st last it is indeed said that the Captain-General has acquired the conviction that I am the person I pretend to be, and the same for whom a passport was obtained by the English Government from the First Consul. It follows then, as I am willing to explain it, that I* am not *and* was not *an imposter. This plea was given up when a more plausible one was thought to be found; but I cannot compliment your Excellency upon this alteration in your position, for the first, although false, is the more tenable post of the two.*

Decaen's reply was stiff and stern. He attributed 'the unreserved tone' of Flinders to 'the ill humour produced by your present situation', and concluded: 'This letter, overstepping all the bounds of civility, obliges me to tell you, until the general opinion judges of your faults or of mine, to cease all correspondence tending to demonstrate the justice of your cause, since you know so little how to preserve the rules of decorum.'

Flinders in consequence of this snub forbore to make [refrained from making] further appeals for consideration; but three days later he preferred [put forward] a series of requests, one of which related to the treatment of his crew:

To his Excellency Captain-General Decaen,
Governor in Chief, etc., etc., etc., Isle of France.
From my confinement, Dec. 28th, 1803.

Sir,

Since you forbid me to write to you upon the subject of my detainer I shall not rouse the anger or contempt with which you have been pleased to treat me by disobeying your order. The purpose for which I now write is to express a few humble requests, and most sincerely do I wish that they may be the last I shall have occasion to trouble your Excellency with.

1st. I repeat my request of the 23rd to have my printed books on shore from the schooner.

2nd. I request to have my private letters and papers out of the two trunks lodged in your secretariat, they having no connection with my Government or the voyage of discovery.

3rd. I beg to have two or three charts and three or four manuscript books out of the said trunks, which are necessary to finishing the chart of the Gulf of Carpentaria and some parts adjacent. It may be proper to observe as an explanation of this last request that the parts wanting were mostly lost in the shipwreck, and I wish to replace them from my memory and remaining materials before it is too late. Of these a memorandum can be taken, or I will give a receipt for them, and if it is judged necessary to exact it I will give my word that nothing in the books shall be erased or destroyed, but I could wish to make additions to one or two of the books as well as to the charts, after which I shall be ready to give up the whole.

4th. My seamen complain of being shut up at night in a place where not a breath of air can come to them, which in a climate like this must be not only uncomfortable in the last degree, but also very destructive to European constitutions; they say, further, that the people with whom they are placed are much affected with that disagreeable and contagious disorder the itch; and that the provisions with which they are fed are too scanty, except in the article of meat, the proportion of which is large but of bad quality. Your Excellency will no doubt make such an amendment in their condition as circumstances will permit.

A compliance with the above requests will not only furnish me with a better amusement in this solitude than writing letters to your Excellency, but will be attended with advantages in which the French nation may some time share. This application respecting the charts is not altogether made upon a firm persuasion that you will return everything to me, for if I could believe that they were never to be given to me or my Government I should make the same request.

Your prisoner,

MATTHEW FLINDERS.

On the day when the letter was despatched, Colonel Monistrol called, and promised that the books and papers requested should be supplied; and, in fact, the trunk containing them was without delay brought to the inn. The Colonel courteously expressed his regret that

Flinders had adopted such a tone in his letters to the General, thinking 'that they might tend to protract rather than terminate' his confinement. The complaint respecting the seamen was attended to forthwith, and they were treated exactly on the same footing as were French sailors on service.[18]

The first thing Flinders did, when he received the trunk, was to take out his naval signal-book and tear it to pieces. Next day he was conducted to Government House, and was allowed to take from the second trunk all his private letters and papers, his journals of bearings and observations, two log-books, and such charts as were necessary to complete his drawings of the Gulf of Carpentaria. All the other books and papers 'were locked up in the trunk and sealed as before'.

Until the end of March 1804, Flinders was kept at the inn, with a sentry constantly on guard over the rooms. St Elme le Duc, in the manuscript history already cited, declares that 'Captain Flinders was never put in prison', and that his custom of addressing letters 'from my prison' was an 'affectation'. But a couple of inn rooms wherein a person is kept against his will, under the strict surveillance of a military custodian, certainly constitute a prison. It is true that the Governor allotted 450 francs per month for his maintenance, sent a surgeon to attend to him when scorbutic sores broke out upon his body, and gave him access to the papers and books he required in order that he might occupy his time and divert his mind with the work he loved. But it is surely quibbling to pretend that even under these conditions he was not a prisoner. Even the surgeon and the interpreter were not admitted without a written order; and when the interpreter, Bonnefoy, took from Flinders a bill, which he undertook to negotiate, the sentry reported that a paper had passed between the two, and Bonnefoy was arrested, nor was he liberated until it was ascertained that the bill was the only paper he had received. The bill was the subject of an act of kindness from the Danish consul, who negotiated it at face value at a time when bills upon England could only be cashed in Port Louis at a discount of 30 per cent. This liberal gentleman sent the message that he would have proffered his assistance earlier but for the fear of incurring the Governor's displeasure.

An attempt was made in February to induce Decaen to send his prisoner to France for trial. It was submitted in the following terms:[19]

[18] St Eleme le Duc's MS. History.

[19] Decaen Papers.

Sir,

Having waited six weeks with much anxiety for your Excellency's decision concerning me, I made application for the honour of an audience, but received no answer; a second application obtained a refusal. It was not my intention to trouble the Captain-General by recounting my grievances, but to offer certain proposals to his consideration; and in now doing this by letter it is my earnest wish to avoid everything that can in the most distant manner give offence; should I fail, my ignorance and not intention must be blamed.

1st. If your Excellency will permit me to depart with my vessel, papers, etc., I will pledge my honour not to give any information concerning the Isle of France, or anything belonging to it, for a limited time, if it is thought that I can have gained any information; or if it is judged necessary, any other restrictions can be laid upon me. If this will not be complied with I request—

2nd, to be sent to France.

3rd. But if it is necessary to detain me here, I request that my officer and my people may be permitted to depart in the schooner. I am desirous of this as well for the purpose of informing the British Admiralty where I am, as to relieve our families and friends from the report that will be spread of the total loss of the two ships with all on board. My officer can be laid under what restrictions may be thought necessary, and my honour shall be a security that nothing shall be transmitted by me but what passes under the inspection of the officer who might be appointed for that purpose.

If your Excellency does not think proper to adopt any of these modes, by which, with submission, I conceive my voyage of discovery might be permitted to proceed without any possible injury to the Isle of France or its dependencies, I then think it necessary to remind the Captain-General that since the shipwreck of the Porpoise, *which happened now six months back, my officers and people as well as myself have been mostly confined either on a very small sandbank in the open sea, or in a boat, or otherwise on board the small schooner* Cumberland, *where there is no room to walk, or been kept prisoners as at present; and also, that previous to this time I had not recovered from a scorbutic and very debilitated state arising from having been eleven months exposed to great fatigue, bad climates and salt provisions. From the scorbutic sores which have again troubled me since my arrival in this port the surgeon who dressed them saw that a vegetable diet and exercise were necessary to correct the diseased state of the blood and to restore my health; but his application through your Excellency's aide-de-camp for me to walk out, unfortunately for my health and peace of mind, received a negative. The Captain-General best knows whether my conduct has deserved, or the exigencies of his Government require, that I should continue to remain closely confined in this sickly town and cut off from all society.*

With all due consideration, I am,
Your Excellency's prisoner,

MATTHEW FLINDERS.

To this petition Decaen returned no reply. Feeling therefore that his detention was likely to be prolonged, Flinders, weary of confinement, and longing for human fellowship, applied to be removed to the place where British officers, prisoners of war, were kept. It was a large house with spacious rooms standing in a couple of acres of ground, about a mile from the tavern, and was variously called the Maison Despeaux, or the Garden Prison. Here at all events fresh air could be enjoyed. The application was acceded to immediately, and Colonel Monistrol himself came, with the courtesy that he never lost an opportunity of manifesting, to conduct Flinders and Aken and to assist them to choose rooms. 'This little walk of a mile,' Flinders recorded, 'showed how debilitating is the want of exercise and fresh air, for it was not without the assistance of Colonel Monistrol's arm that I was able to get through it. Conveyances were sent in the evening for our trunks, and we took possession of our new prison with a considerable degree of pleasure, this change of situation and surrounding objects producing an exhilaration of spirits to which we had long been strangers.'

XXIII

THE CAPTIVITY PROLONGED

WE shall now see how a detention which had been designed as a sharp punishment of an officer who had not comported [conducted] himself with perfect respect, and which Decaen never intended to be prolonged beyond about twelve months, dragged itself into years, and came to bear an aspect of obstinate malignity.

Decaen's despatch arrived in France during the first half of the year 1804. Its terms were not calculated to induce the French Government to regard Flinders as a man entitled to their consideration, even if events had been conducive to a speedy determination. But the departments, especially those of Marine and War, were being worked to their full capacity upon affairs of the most pressing moment. Napoleon became Emperor of the French in that year (May), and his immense energy was flogging official activities incessantly. War with England mainly absorbed attention. At Boulogne a great flotilla had been organised for the invasion of the obdurate country across the Channel. A large fleet was being fitted out at Brest and at Toulon, the fleet which Nelson was to smash at Trafalgar in the following year. Matters relating to the isolated colony in the Indian Ocean did not at that moment command much interest in France.

There were several other pieces of business, apart from the Flinders affair, to which Decaen wished to direct attention. He sent one of his aides-de-camp, Colonel Barois, to Paris to see Napoleon in person, if possible, and in any case to interview the Minister of Marine and the Colonies, Decrès. Decaen especially directed Barois to see that the Flinders case was brought under Napoleon's notice, and he did his best.[1] He saw Decrès and asked him whether Decaen's despatches had been well received. 'Ah,' said the Minister pleasantly, in a voice loud enough to be heard by the circle of

---

[1] Prentout, p. 392.

courtiers, 'everything that comes from General Decaen is well received.' But there was no spirit of despatch. Finally Barois did obtain an interview with Napoleon, through the aid of the Empress Josephine. He referred to 'l'affaire Flinders', of which Napoleon knew little; but 'he appeared to approve the reasons invoked to justify the conduct of Decaen'. The Emperor had no time just then for examining the facts, and his approval simply reflected his trust in Decaen. As he said to the General's brother Réné, at a later interview, 'I have the utmost confidence in Decaen.' But meanwhile no direction was given as to what was to be done. It will be seen later how it was that pressure of business delayed the despatch of an intimation to Ile-de-France of a step that was actually taken.

That at this time Decaen was simply waiting for an order from Paris to release Flinders is clear from observations which he made, and from news which came to the ears of the occupant of the Garden Prison. In March 1804, he told Captain Bergeret of the French Navy, who showed Flinders friendly attentions, to tell him to 'have a little patience, as he should soon come to some determination on the affair'. In August of the same year Flinders wrote to King that Decaen had stated that 'I must wait until orders were received concerning me from the French Government.'[2] A year later (November 1805) he wrote: 'I firmly believe that, if he had not said to the French Government, during the time of his unjust suspicion of me, that he should detain me here until he received their orders, he would have gladly suffered me to depart long since.'[3] Again, in July 1806,[4] he wrote: 'General Decaen, if I am rightly informed, is himself heartily sorry for having made me a prisoner,' but 'he remitted the judgment of my case to the French Government, and cannot permit me to depart or even send me to France, until he shall receive orders'.

The situation was, then, that Decaen, having referred the case to Paris in order that the Government might deal with it, could not now, consistently with his duty, send Flinders away from the island until instructions were received; and the department concerned had too much pressing business on hand at that moment to give attention to it. Flinders had to wait.

His health improved amidst the healthier surroundings of his new abode, and he made good progress with his work. His way of life is described in a letter of 18 May 1804:[5]

---

[2] *Historical Records*, VI, p. 411.

[3] ibid, VI, p. 737.

[4] ibid, VI, p. 106.

[5] Flinders' Papers.

My time is now employed as follows: Before breakfast my time is devoted to the Latin language, to bring up what I formerly learnt. After breakfast I am employed in making out a fair copy of the Investigator*'s log in lieu of my own, which was spoiled at the shipwreck. When tired of writing I apply to music, and when my fingers are tired with the flute, I write again till dinner. After dinner we amuse ourselves with billiards until tea, and afterwards walk in the garden till dusk. From thence till supper I make one at Pleyel's quartettes; afterwards walking half an hour, and then sleep soundly till daylight, when I get up and bathe.*

A letter to his stepmother, dated 25 August of the same year, comments on his situation in a mood of courageous resignation:[6]

I have gone through some hardships and misfortunes within the last year, but the greatest is that of having been kept here eight months from returning to my dear friends and family. My health is, however, good at this time, nor are my spirits cast down, although the tyranny of the Governor of this island in treating me as a spy has been grievous. I believe my situation is known by this time in England, and will probably make some noise, for indeed it is almost without example. The French inhabitants even of this island begin to make complaints of the injustice of their Governor, and they are disposed to be very kind to me. Four or five different people have offered me any money I may want, or any service that they can do for me, but as they cannot get me my liberty their services are of little avail. I have a companion here in one of my officers, and a good and faithful servant in my steward, and for these last four months have been allowed to walk in a garden. The Governor pretends to say that he cannot let me go until he receives orders from France, and it is likely that these will not arrive these four months. I am obliged to call up all the patience that I can to bear this injustice; my great consolation is that I have done nothing to forfeit my passport, or that can justify them for keeping me a prisoner, so I must be set at liberty with honour when the time comes, and my country will, I trust, reward me for my sufferings in having supported her cause with the spirit becoming an Englishman.

[6] Flinders' Papers.

A letter to Mrs Flinders (24 August 1804) voices the yearning of the captive for the solace of home:[7]

> *I yesterday enjoyed a delicious piece of misery in reading over thy dear letters, my beloved Ann. Shall I tell thee that I have never before done it since I have been shut up in this prison? I have many friends, who are kind and much interested for me, and I certainly love them. But yet before thee they disappear as stars before the rays of the morning sun. I cannot connect the idea of happiness with anything without thee. Without thee, the world would be a blank. I might indeed receive some gratification from distinction and the applause of society; but where could be the faithful friend who would enjoy and share this with me, into whose bosom my full heart could unburthen itself of excess of joy? Where would be that sweet intercourse of soul, the fine seasoning of happiness, without which a degree of insipidity attends all our enjoyments?... I am not without friends even among the French. On the contrary. I have several, and but one enemy, who unfortunately, alas, is all-powerful here; nor will he on any persuasion permit me to pass the walls of the prison, although some others who are thought less dangerous have had that indulgence occasionally.*

'When my family are the subject of my meditation,' he said in a letter to his stepmother, 'my bonds enter deep into my soul.'

His private opinion of Decaen is expressed in a letter written at this period:[8]

> *The truth I believe is that the violence of his passion outstrips his judgment and reason, and does not allow them to operate; for he is instantaneous in his directions, and should he do an injustice he must persist in it because it would lower his dignity to retract. His antipathy, moreover, is so great to Englishmen, who are the only nation that could prevent the ambitious designs of France from being put into execution, that immediately the name of one is mentioned he is directly in a rage, and his pretence and wish to be polite scarcely prevent him from breaking out in the presence even of strangers. With all this he has the credit of having a good heart at the bottom.*

---

[7] Flinders' Papers.

[8] Flinders' Papers.

The captain of a French ship, M. Coutance, whom Flinders had known at Port Jackson, saw Decaen on his behalf, and reported the result of the interview. 'The General accused me of nothing more than of being *trop vive* [too bold]; I had shown too much independence in refusing to dine with a man who had accused me of being an impostor, and who had unjustly made me a prisoner.'

Meanwhile two playful sallies penned at this time show that his health and appetite had mended during his residence at the Maison Despeaux:[9] 'My appetite is so good that I believe it has the intention of revenging me on the Governor by occasioning a famine in the land. Falstaff says, "Confound this grief, it makes a man go thirsty; give me a cup of sack." Instead of thirsty read hungry, and for a cup of sack read mutton chop, and the words would fit me very well.'

The second passage is from his private journal, and may have been the consequence of too much mutton chop: 'Dreamt that General Decaen was sitting and lying upon me, to devour me; was surprised to find devouring so easy to be borne, and that after death I had the consciousness of existence. Got up soon after six much agitated, with a more violent headache than usual.'

Flinders lost no opportunity of appealing to influential Frenchmen, relating the circumstances of his detention. He offered to submit himself to an examination by the officers of Admiral Linois's squadron, and that commander promised to speak to Decaen on the subject, adding that he should be 'flattered in contributing to your being set at liberty'. Captain Halgan, of *Le Berceau*, who had been in England during the short peace, and had heard much of Flinders' discoveries, visited him several times and offered pecuniary assistance if it were required. Flinders wrote to the French Minister of the Treasury, Barbé-Marbois, urging him to intercede, and to the Comte de Fleurieu, one of the most influential men in French scientific circles, who was particularly well informed concerning Australian exploration.

The flat roof of the Maison Despeaux commanded a view of Port Louis harbour; and, as Flinders was in the habit of sitting upon the roof in the cool evenings, enjoying the sight of the blue waters, and meditating upon his work and upon what he hoped still to do, Decaen thought he was getting to know too much. In June 1804, therefore, the door to the roof was ordered to be nailed up, and telescopes were taken away from the imprisoned officers. At this time also occurred an incident which shows that Flinders' proud spirit was by no means broken by captivity.

---

[9] Flinders' Papers.

The sergeant of the guard demanded the swords of all the prisoners, that of Flinders among the rest. It was an affront to him as an officer that his sword should be demanded by a sergeant, and he promptly refused. He despatched the following letter to the Governor:[10]

To His Excellency Captain-General Decaen,
Governor-in-Chief, etc., etc., etc.

Sir,—The sergeant of the guard over the prisoners in this house has demanded of me, by the order of Captain Neuville, my sword, and all other arms in my possession.

Upon this subject I beg leave to represent to Your Excellency that it is highly inconsistent with my situation in His Britannic Majesty's service to deliver up my arms in this manner. I am ready to deliver up to an officer bearing your Excellency's order, but I request that that officer will be of equal rank to myself.

I have the honour to be,
Your Excellency's most obedient servant and prisoner,

MATTW. FLINDERS.

Maison Despeaux, June 2, 1804.

In a few days Captain Neuville called to apologise. It was, he said, a mistake on the part of the sergeant to ask for the sword. Had the Governor required it, an officer of equal rank would have been sent, 'but he had no intention to make me a prisoner until he should receive orders to that effect'. Not a prisoner! What was he, then? Certainly not, said Captain Neuville; he was merely 'put under surveillance for a short period'. Inasmuch as Flinders was being treated with rather more strictness than those who were confessedly prisoners of war, the benefit of the distinction was hard to appreciate.

Flinders considered that he had been treated rather handsomely in the matter of the sword. But about three months later a junior officer, who behaved with much politeness, came under the orders of Colonel D'Arsonville, the town major, to demand it. D'Arsonville had been instructed by Decaen to take possession of it, but had been unable to come himself. Flinders considered that under the circumstances he had better give up the sword to save further trouble, and did so. The significance of the incident is that, having received no orders from France, Decaen from this time regarded Flinders as a prisoner of war in

---

[10]Decaen Papers, Vol. 84.

the technical sense. He felt bound to hold him until instructions arrived, and could only justifiably hold him as a prisoner.

December 1804 arrived, and still no order of release came. On the anniversary of his arrest, Flinders wrote the following letter to Decaen:[11]

> *Maison Despeaux, Dec. 16, 1804.*
> *General,*
>
> *Permit me to remind you that I am yet a prisoner in this place, and that it is now one year since my arrestation [arrest]. This is the anniversary of that day on which you transferred me from liberty and my peaceful occupations to the misery of a close confinement.*
>
> *Be pleased, sir, to consider that the great occupations of the French Government may leave neither time nor inclination to attend to the situation of an Englishman in a distant colony, and that the chance of war may render abortive for a considerable time at least any attempts to send out despatches to this island. The lapse of one year shows that one or other of these circumstances has already taken place, and the consequence of my detainer until orders are received from France will most probably be, that a second year will be cut out of my life and devoted to the same listless inaction as the last, to the destruction of my health and happiness, and the probable ruin of all my further prospects. I cannot expect, however, that my private misfortunes should have any influence upon Your Excellency's public conduct. It is from being engaged in a service calculated for the benefit of all maritime nations; from my passport; the inoffensiveness of my conduct; and the probable delay of orders from France. Upon these considerations it is that my present hope of receiving liberty must be founded.*
>
> *But should a complete liberation be so far incompatible with Your Excellency's plan of conduct concerning me as that no arguments will induce you to grant it; I beg of you, General, to reflect whether every purpose of the most severe justice will not be answered by sending me to France; since it is to that Government, as I am informed, that my case is referred for decision.*
>
> *If neither of these requests be complied with, I must prepare to endure still longer this anxious tormenting state of suspense,*

[11] Decaen Papers.

this exclusion from my favourite and, I will add, useful employment, and from all that I have looked forward to attain by it. Perhaps also I ought to prepare my mind for a continuance of close imprisonment. If so, I will endeavour to bear it and its consequences with firmness, and may God support my heart through the trial. My hopes, however, tell me more agreeable things, that either this petition to be fully released with my people, books and papers will be accorded, or that we shall be sent to France, where, if the decision of the Government should be favourable, we can immediately return to our country, our families and friends, and my report of our investigations be made public if it shall be deemed worthy of that honour.

My former application for one of these alternatives was unsuccessful, but after a year's imprisonment and a considerable alteration in the circumstances, I hope this will be more fortunate.

With all due consideration I have the honour to be, Your Excellency's most obedient humble servant.

MATTW. FLINDERS.

To this appeal the General vouchsafed no response.

The return of the hot weather aggravated a constitutional internal complaint from which Flinders suffered severely. The principal physician of the medical staff visited him and recommended a removal to the highlands in the interior of the island. John Aken, the companion of his captivity, also became very ill, and his life was despaired of. In May 1805, having somewhat recovered, he applied to be allowed to depart with several other prisoners of war who were being liberated on parole. Very much to his surprise the permission was accorded. Aken left on 20 May in an American ship bound for New York, the captain of which gave him a free passage; taking with him all the charts which Flinders had finished up to date, as well as the large general chart of Australia, showing the extent of the new discoveries, and all papers relating to the *Investigator* voyage. There was at this time a general exchange of prisoners of war, and by the middle of August the only English prisoners remaining in Ile-de-France were Flinders, his servant, who steadfastly refused to avail himself of the opportunity to leave, and a lame seaman.

XXIV

THE CAPTIVITY MODIFIED

FLINDERS continued to reside at the Garden Prison till August 1805. In that month he was informed that the Governor was disposed to permit him to live in the interior of the island, if he so desired. This change would give him a large measure of personal freedom, he would no longer be under close surveillance, and he would be able to enjoy social life. He had formed a friendship with an urbane and cultivated French gentleman, Thomas Pitot, whom he consulted, and who found for him a residence in the house of Madame D'Arifat at Wilhelm's Plains.

Here commenced a period of five years and six months, of detention certainly, but no longer of imprisonment. In truth, it was the most restful period of Flinders' whole life; and, if he could have banished the longing for home and family, and the bitter feeling of wrong that gnawed at his heart, and could have quietened the desire that was ever uppermost in his mind to continue the exploratory work still remaining to be done, his term under Madame D'Arifat's roof would have been delightfully happy.

Those twenty months in Port Louis had made him a greatly changed man. Friends who had known him in the days of eager activity, when fatigues were lightly sustained, would scarcely have recognised the brisk explorer in the pale, emaciated, weak, limping semi-invalid who took his leave of the kind-hearted sergeant of the guard on 19 August, and stepped feebly outside the iron gate in company with his friend Pitot. A portrait of him, painted by an amateur some time later, crude in execution though it is, shows the hollow cheeks of a man who had suffered, and conveys an idea of the dimmed eyes whose brightness and commanding expression had once been remarked by many who came in contact with him.

But at all events over five years of fairly pleasant existence were now before him. The reason why the period was so protracted will be explained in the next chapter. This one can be devoted to the life at Wilhelm's Plains.

A parole [an undertaking] was given, by which Flinders bound himself not to go more than two leagues from his habitation, and to conduct himself with that degree of reserve which was becoming in an officer residing in a colony with whose parent state his nation was at war.

The interior of Mauritius is perhaps as beautiful a piece of country as there is in the world. The vegetation is rich and varied, gemmed [adorned] with flowers and plentifully watered by cool, pure, never-failing streams. To one who had been long in prison [imprisoned] pent, the journey inland was a procession of delights. Monsieur Pitot, who was intimate with the country gentlemen, made the stages easy, and several visits were paid by the way. The cultivated French people of the island were all very glad to entertain Flinders, of whom they had heard much, and who won their sympathy by reason of his wrongs, and their affection by his own personality. Charming gardens shaded by mango and other fruit trees, cool fishponds, splashing cascades and tumbling waterfalls, coffee and clove plantations, breathing out a spicy fragrance, stretches of natural forest—a perpetual variety in beauty—gratified the traveller, as he ascended the thousand feet above which stretched the plateau whereon the home of Madame D'Arifat stood.

In the garden of the house were two comfortable pavilions. One of these was to be occupied by Flinders, the other by his servant, Elder, and the lame seaman who accompanied him. Madame D'Arifat hospitably proposed that he should take his meals with her family in the house, and his glad acceptance of the invitation commenced a pleasant and profitable friendship with people to whom he ever after referred with deep respect.

A note about the kindness of these gentle friends is contained in a letter to his wife:[1]

> *Madame and her amiable daughters said much to console me, and seemed to take it upon themselves to dissipate my chagrin by engaging me in innocent amusement and agreeable conversation. I cannot enough be grateful to them for such kindness to a stranger, to a foreigner, to an enemy of their country, for such they have a right to consider me if they will, though I am an enemy to no country in fact, but as it opposes*

[1] Flinders' Papers.

> *the honour, interest, and happiness of my own. My employment and inclinations lead to the extension of happiness and of science, and not to the destruction of mankind.*

The kindly consideration of the inhabitants was unfailing. Their houses were ever open to the English captain, and they were always glad to have him with them, and hear him talk about the wonders of his adventurous life. He enjoyed his walks, and restored health soon stimulated him to renewed mental activity.

He studied the French language, and learnt to speak and write it clearly. He continued to read Latin, and also studied Malay, thinking that a knowledge of this tongue would be useful to him in case of future work upon the northern coasts of Australia and the neighbouring archipelagoes. He never lost hope of pursuing his investigations in the field where he had already won so much distinction. To his brother Samuel, in a letter of October 1807, he wrote:[2] 'You know my intention of completing the examination of Australia as soon as the Admiralty will give me a ship. My intentions are still the same, and the great object of my present studies is to render myself more capable of performing the task with reputation.' He cogitated [devised] a scheme for exploring the interior of Australia 'from the head of the Gulf of Carpentaria to the head of the great gulf on the south coast', i.e., Spencer's Gulf. 'In case of being again sent to Australia I should much wish that this was part of my instructions.' Much as he longed to see his friends in England, work, always work, scope for more and more work, was his dominating passion. 'Should a peace speedily arrive,' he told Banks (March 1806), 'and their Lordships of the Admiralty wish to have the north-west coast of Australia examined immediately, I will be ready to embark in any ship provided for the service that they may choose to send out. My misfortunes have not abated my ardour in the service of science.' If there was work to do, he would even give up the chance of going home before commencing it. 'In the event of sending out another *Investigator* immediately after the peace, probably Lieutenant Fowler or my brother might be chosen as first lieutenant to bring her out to me.' He spoke of directing researches to the Fiji Islands and the South Pacific. Rarely has there been a man so keen for the most strenuous service, so unsparing of himself, so eager to excel.

Occasionally in the letters and journals appear lively descriptions of life at Wilhelm's Plains. The following is a tinted vignette of this kind:

---

[2] Flinders' Papers.

In the evening I walked out to visit my neighbour, whom I had not seen for near a week. I met the whole family going out in the following order: First, Madame, with her youngest daughter, about six years old, in a palankin [a covered litter] with M. Boistel walking by the side of it. Next, Mademoiselle Aimée, about 16, mounted astride upon an ass, with her younger sister, about 7, behind her, also astride. Third, Mademoiselle her sister, about 15, mounted upon M. Boistel's horse, also astride; and two or three black servants carrying an umbrella, lanthorn, etc., bringing up the rear. The two young ladies had stockings on to-day,[3] *and for what I know drawers also; they seemed to have occasion for them. Madame stopped on seeing me, and I paid my compliments and made the usual enquiries. She said they were taking a promenade, going to visit a neighbour, and on they set. I could perceive that the two young ladies were a little ashamed of meeting me, and were cautious to keep their coats well down to their ankles, which was no easy thing. I stood looking after and admiring the procession some time; considering it a fair specimen of the manner in which the gentry of the island, who are not very well provided with conveyances, make visits in the country. I wished much to be able to make a sketch of the procession. It would have been as good, with the title of 'Going to See our Neighbour' under it, as the Vicar of Wakefield's family 'Going to Church'.*

He was much interested in an inspection of the Mesnil estate, where La Pérouse had resided when as an officer of the French navy he had visited Ile-de-France, and which in conjunction with another French officer he purchased. It was here, though Flinders does not seem to have been aware of the romantic fact, that the illustrious navigator fell in love with Éléanore Broudou, whom, despite family opposition, he afterwards married.[4] 'I surveyed the scene,' wrote Flinders, 'with mingled sensations of pleasure and melancholy; the ruins of his house, the garden he had laid out, the still blooming hedgerows of China roses, emblems of his reputation, everything was an object of interest and curiosity.' Flinders continued:

This spot is nearly in the centre of the island, and upon the road from Port Louis to Port Bourbon. It was here that the man

[3] On a previous day, mentioned in the journal, they had worn none.

[4] The charming love-story of La Pérouse has been related in the author's *La Pérouse* (Sydney, 1912).

lamented by the good and well-informed of all nations, whom science illumined, and humanity, joined to an honest ambition, conducted to the haunts of remote savages, in this spot he once dwelt, perhaps little known to the world, but happy; when he became celebrated he had ceased to exist. Monsieur Airolles promised me to place three square blocks of stone, one upon the other, in the spot where the house of this lamented navigator had stood; and upon the uppermost stone facing the road to engrave 'Lapérouse'.

Investigations made in later years by the Comité des Souvenirs Historiques of Mauritius, show that Airolles carried out his promise to Flinders, and erected a cairn in the midst of what had been the garden of La Pérouse. But the stones were afterwards removed by persons who had little sentiment for the associations of the place. In the year 1897, the Comité des Souvenirs Historiques obtained from M. Dauban, then the proprietor of the estate, permission to erect a suitable memorial, such as Flinders had suggested. This was done. The inscription upon the face of the huge conical rock chosen for the purpose copies the words used by Flinders. It reads:

LAPÉROUSE
ILLUSTRE NAVIGATEUR
A acheté ce terrain en Avril 1775 et l'a habité.
Le CAPITAINE FLINDERS dit:
'In this spot he once dwelt, perhaps little known to the world, but happy.'
(Comité des Souvenirs Historiques.—*1897.*)
[The renowned navigator La Pérouse purchased this land in April 1775 and resided on it. Captain Flinders said:]

Flinders' pen was very busy during these years. Access to his charts and papers, printed volumes and log-books (except the third log-book, containing details of the *Cumberland*'s voyage), having been given to him, he wrote up the history of his voyages and adventures. By July 1806, he had completed the manuscript as far as the point when he left the Garden Prison. An opportunity of despatching it to the Admiralty occurred when the French privateer *La Piémontaise* captured the richly laden China merchantman *Warren Hastings* and brought her into Port Louis as a prize. Captain Larkins was released after a short detention, and offered to take a packet to the Admiralty. Finished charts were also sent; and Sir John Barrow, who wrote the powerful *Quarterly Review* article of 1810, wherein Flinders' cause was valiantly championed, had resort to this material. A valuable paper by Flinders, upon the use of the marine barometer for predicting changes of wind at sea, was also the fruit of his enforced leisure. It was conveyed to England, read before the Royal Society by Sir Joseph Banks, and published in the *Transactions* of that learned body in 1806.

The friendship of able and keen-minded men was not lacking during these years. There existed in Ile-de-France a Société d'Emulation, formed to promote the study of literary and philosophical subjects, whose members, learning what manner of man Flinders was, addressed a memorial to the Institute of France relating what had happened to him, and eulogising his courage, his high character, his innocence, and the worth of his services. They protested that he was a man into whose heart there had never entered a single desire, a single thought, the execution of which could be harmful to any individual, of whatever class or to whatever nation he might belong. 'Use then, we beg of you,' they urged, 'in favour of Captain Flinders the influence of the first scientific body in Europe, the National Institute, in order that the error which has led to the captivity of this learned navigator may become known; you will acquire, in rendering this noble service, a new title to the esteem and the honour of all nations, and of all friends of humanity.'

The Governor-General of India, Lord Wellesley, took a keen interest in Flinders' situation, and in 1805 requested Decaen's 'particular attention' to it, earnestly soliciting him to 'release Captain Flinders immediately, and to allow him either to take his passage to India in the *Thetis* or to return to England in the first neutral ship'. Rear-Admiral Sir Edward Pellew, commander-in-chief of the British naval forces in the East Indies, tried to effect an exchange by the liberation of a French officer of equal rank. But in this direction nothing was concluded.

Under these circumstances, with agreeable society, amidst sympathetic friends, in a charming situation, well and profitably employed upon his own work, Flinders spent over five years of his captivity. He never ceased to chafe under the restraint, and to move every available influence to secure his liberty, but it cannot be said that the chains were oppressively heavy. Decaen troubled him very little. Once (in May 1806) the General's anger flamed up, in consequence of a strong letter of protest received from Governor King of New South Wales. King's affection for Flinders was like that of a father for a son, and on receipt of the news about the *Cumberland* his indignation poured itself out in this letter to Decaen, with which he enclosed a copy of Flinders' letter to him. It happened that, at the time of the arrival of the letter in Ile-de-France, Flinders was on a visit to Port Louis, where he had been permitted to come for a few days. The result of King's intervention was that Decaen ordered him to return to Wilhelm's Plains, and refused the application he had made to be allowed to visit two friends who were living on the north-east side of the island.

John Elder, Flinders' servant, remained with him until June 1806. He might have left when there was a general exchange of prisoners in August 1805, and another opportunity of quitting the island was presented in April 1806, when the lame seaman departed on an American ship bound for Boston. But Elder was deeply attached to his master, and would have remained till the end had not his mind become somewhat unhinged by frequent disappointments and by his despair of ever securing liberation. When his companion, the lame seaman, went away, Elder developed a form of melancholy, with hallucinations, and appeared to be wasting away from loss of sleep and appetite. Permission for him to depart was therefore obtained, and from July 1806, Flinders was the only remaining member of the *Cumberland*'s company.

Throughout the period of detention Flinders was placed on half-pay by the Admiralty. It cannot be said that he was treated with generosity by the Government of his own country at any time. He was not a prisoner of war in the strict sense, and the rigid application of the ordinary regulations of service in his peculiar case seems to have been a rather stiff measure. Besides, the Admiralty had evidence from time to time, in the receipt of new charts and manuscripts, that Flinders was industriously applying himself to the duties of the service on which he had been despatched. But there was the regulation, and someone in authority ruled that it had to apply in this most unusual instance. There is some pathos in a letter written by Mrs Flinders to a friend in England (August 1806): 'The Navy Board have thought proper to curtail my husband's pay, so it behoves me to be as careful as I can; and I mean to be very economical, being determined to do with as little as possible, that he may not deem me an extravagant wife.'

XXV

THE ORDER OF RELEASE

THE several representations concerning the case of Flinders that were made in France, the attention drawn to it in English newspapers, and the lively interest of learned men of both nations, produced a moving effect upon Napoleon's Government. Distinguished Frenchmen did not hesitate to speak plainly. Fleurieu, whose voice was attentively heard on all matters touching geography and discovery, declared publicly that 'the indignities imposed upon Captain Flinders were without example in the nautical history of civilised nations'. Malte-Brun, a savant of the first rank, expressed himself so boldly as to incur the displeasure of the authorities. Bougainville, himself a famous navigator, made personal appeals to the Government. Sir Joseph Banks, whose friendly relations with French men of science were not broken by the war, used all the influence he could command. He had already, 'from the gracious condescension of the Emperor', obtained the release of five persons who had been imprisoned in France,[1] and had no doubt that if he could get Napoleon's ear he could bring about the liberation of his *protégé*.

At last, in March 1806, the affair came before the Council of State in Paris, mainly through the instrumentality of Bougainville. Banks wrote to Mrs Flinders:[2] 'After many refusals on the part of Bonaparte to applications made to him from different quarters, he at last consented to order Captain Flinders' case to be laid before the Council of State.'

On 1 March an order was directed to be sent to Decaen, approving his previous conduct, but informing him that, moved 'by a sentiment of generosity, the Government accord to Captain Flinders his liberty and the restoration of his ship'. Accompanying the despatch was an

---

[1] Banks to Flinders, *Historical Records*, V, 646.

[2] Flinders' Papers.

extract from the minutes of the Council of State, dated 1 March 1806, recording that:

> *The Council of State, which, after the return of His Majesty the Emperor and King, has considered the report of its Marine section on that of the Minister of Marine and the Colonies concerning the detention of the English schooner* Cumberland *and of Captain Flinders at Ile-de-France (see the documents appended to the report), is of opinion that the Captain-General of Ile-de-France had sufficient reason for detaining there Captain Flinders and his schooner; but by reason of the interest that the misfortunes of Captain Flinders has inspired, he seems to deserve that His Majesty should authorise the Minister of Marine and the Colonies to restore to him his liberty and his ship.*

This document was endorsed 'Approuvé au Palais des Tuileries, le onze Mars, 1806. NAPOLEON'.

The terms of the despatch with which the order was transmitted contained a remarkable statement. Decrès informed Decaen that he, as Minister, had on 30 July 1804—nearly one year and nine months before the order of release—brought Flinders' case under the notice of the Council of State. But nothing was done: the Emperor had to be consulted, and at that date Napoleon was not accessible. He was superintending the army encamped at Boulogne, preparing for that projected descent upon England which even his magnificent audacity never dared to make. He did not return to St Cloud, within hail of Paris, till 12 October.[3] Then the officials surrounding him were kept busy with preparations for crowning himself and the Empress Josephine, a ceremony performed by Pope Pius VII, at Notre Dame, on 2 December. The consequence was that this piece of business about an unfortunate English captain in Ile-de-France—like nearly all other business concerned with the same colony at the time—got covered up beneath a mass of more urgent affairs, and remained in abeyance until the agitation stimulated by Banks, Fleurieu, Bougainville, Malte-Brun and others forced the case under the attention of the Emperor and his ministers.

Even then the despatch did not reach Ile-de-France till July 1807, sixteen months after the date upon it; and it was then transmitted, not by a French ship, but by an English frigate, the *Greyhound*, under a flag of truce. The reason for that was unfortunate for Flinders as an individual,

---

[3] The movements of Napoleon day by day can be followed in Schuerman's *Itinéraire Général de Napoléon.*

but entirely due to the efficiency of the navy of which he was an officer. In 1805 the British fleet had demolished the French at Trafalgar, and from that time forward until the end of the war, Great Britain was mistress of the ocean in full potency. Her frigates patrolled the highways of the sea with a vigilance that never relaxed. In January 1806, she took possession of the Cape of Good Hope for the second time, and has held it ever since. The consequences to Decaen and his garrison were very serious. With the British in force at the Cape, how could supplies, reinforcements and despatches get through to him in Ile-de-France? He saw the danger clearly, but was powerless to avert it. Of this particular despatch four copies were sent from France on as many ships. One copy was borne by a French vessel which was promptly captured by the British; and on its contents becoming known the Admiralty sent it out to Admiral Pellew, in order that he might send a ship under a flag of truce to take it to Decaen. The Secretary to the Admiralty, Marsden, wrote to Pellew (December 1806) that the despatch 'has already been transmitted to the Isle of France in triplicate, but as it may be hoped that the vessels have been all captured you had better take an opportunity of sending this copy by a flag of truce, provided you have not heard in the meantime of Flinders being at liberty'. As a fact, one other copy did get through, on a French vessel.

Pellew lost no time in informing Flinders of the news, and the captive wrote to Decaen in the following terms:[4]

> *July 24, 1807.*
>
> *General,*
>
> *By letters from Rear-Admiral Sir Edward Pellew, transmitted to me yesterday by Colonel Monistrol, I am informed that orders relating to me have at length arrived from His Excellency the Marine Minister of France, which orders are supposed to authorize my being set at liberty.*
>
> *Your Excellency will doubtless be able to figure to yourself the sensations such a communication must have excited in me, after a detention of three years and a half, and my anxiety to have such agreeable intelligence confirmed by some information of the steps it is in Your Excellency's contemplation to take in consequence. If these letters have flattered me in vain with the hopes [inspired me with false hopes] of returning to my country*

[4] Decaen Papers.

and my family, I beg of you, General, to inform me; if they are correct, you will complete my happiness by confirming their contents. The state of incertitude in which I have so long remained will, I trust, be admitted as a sufficient excuse for my anxiety to be delivered from it.

I have the honour to be, Your Excellency's most obedient humble servant,

MATTW. FLINDERS.

His Excellency the Captain-General Decaen.

In reply Decaen transmitted to Flinders a copy of the despatch of the Minister of Marine, and informed him through Colonel Monistrol 'that, so soon as circumstances will permit, you will fully enjoy the favour which has been granted you by His Majesty the Emperor and King'.

But now, having at length received orders, countersigned by Napoleon himself, that Flinders should be liberated, Decaen came to a decision that on the face of it seems extremely perplexing. We have seen that in August 1805, Flinders, well informed by persons who had conversed with Decaen, believed that the General 'would be very glad to get handsomely clear of me', and that in November of the same year he made the assertion that Decaen 'would have gladly suffered me to depart long since' but for the reference of the case to Paris. We have direct evidence to the same effect in a letter from Colonel Monistrol regarding Lord Wellesley's application for Flinders' release.[5] The Colonel desired 'with all [his] heart' that the request could be acceded to, but the Captain-General could not comply until he had received a response to his despatch. Yet, when the response was received, and Flinders might have been liberated with the full approbation of the French Government, Decaen replied to the Minister's despatch in the following terms (20 August 1807):

I have the honour to inform Your Excellency that by the English frigate Greyhound, *which arrived here on July 21st under a flag of truce, in the hope of gathering information concerning His British Majesty's ships* Blenheim *and* Java, *I have received the fourth copy of Your Excellency's despatch of March 21st, 1806, no. 8, relative to Captain Flinders. Having thought that the favourable decision that it contains regarding that officer had been determined at a time when the possibility of some renewal*

[5] *Historical Records*, V, 651.

> *of friendliness with England was perceived, I did not consider that the present moment was favourable for putting into operation that act of indulgence on the part of His Majesty. I have since received the second copy of the same despatch; but, the circumstances having become still more difficult, and that officer appearing to me to be always dangerous, I await a more propitious time for putting into execution the intentions of His Majesty. My zeal for his service has induced me to suspend the operations of his command. I trust, Monsieur, that that measure of prudence will obtain your Excellency's approbation. I have the honour to be, etc., etc., etc., DECAEN.*[6]

It will be observed that in this despatch Decaen describes the circumstances of the colony he governed as having become 'more difficult', and Flinders as appearing to him to be 'always dangerous'. We must, then, examine the circumstances to ascertain why they had become so difficult, and why he considered that it would now be dangerous to let Flinders go.

It is easy enough to attribute the General's refusal to obstinacy or malignity. But his anger had cooled down by 1807; his prisoner was a charge on the establishment to the extent of 5,400 francs a year, and Decaen was a thrifty administrator; why, then, should he apparently have hardened his heart to the extent of disobeying the Emperor's command? The explanation is not to be found in his temper, but in the military situation of Ile-de-France, and his belief that Flinders was accurately informed about it; as was, indeed, the case.

At this time Decaen was holding Ile-de-France by a policy fairly describable as one of 'bluff'. The British could have taken it by throwing upon it a comparatively small force, had they known how weak its defences were. But they did not know; and Decaen, whose duty it was to defend the place to the utmost, did not intend that they should if he could prevent information reaching them. After the crushing of French naval power at Trafalgar and the British occupation of the Cape, Decaen's position became untenable, though a capitulation was not forced upon him till four years later. He constantly demanded reinforcements and money, which never came to hand. The military and financial resources of France were being strained to prosecute Napoleon's wars in Europe. There were neither men nor funds to spare for the colony in the

[6] This despatch was originally published by M. Albert Pitot in his *Esquisses Historiques de l'Ile-de-France.* (Port Louis, 1899).

Indian Ocean. Decaen felt that his position was compromised.[7] He addressed the Emperor personally 'with all the sadness of a wounded soul', but nothing was done for Ile-de-France. There was not enough money to repair public buildings and quays, which fell into ruins. There was no timber, no sailcloth to refit ships. Even nails were lacking. A little later (1809) he complained in despatches of the shortness of flour and food. There was little revenue, no credit. Now that the British had asserted their strength, and held the Cape, prizes were few. Above all he represented [set forth earnestly] 'the urgent need for soldiers'. He felt himself abandoned. But still, with a resolute tenacity that one cannot but admire, he hung on to his post, and maintained a bold front to the enemy.

Did Flinders know of this state of things? Unquestionably he did; and Decaen knew that he knew. He could have informed the British Government, had he chosen to violate his parole; but he was in all things a scrupulously honourable man, and, as he said, 'an absolute silence was maintained in my letters'. He was constantly hoping that an attack would be made upon the island, and 'if attacked with judgment it appeared to me that a moderate force would carry it'.[8] But all this while the British believed that Ile-de-France was strong, and that a successful assault upon it would require a larger force than they could spare at the time. Even after Flinders had returned to England, when he was asked at the Admiralty whether he thought that a contemplated attack would succeed, his confident assurance that it would was received with doubt. Decaen's 'bluff' was superb.

On one point, if we may believe St Elme le Duc, Decaen did Flinders a grave injustice. It was believed, says that writer's manuscript, that Flinders had several times managed to go out at night, that he had made soundings along the coast, and had transmitted information to Bengal which was of use when ultimately the colony was taken by the English. For that charge there is not a shadow of warrant [the slightest justification]. There is not the faintest ground for supposing that he did not observe his parole with the utmost strictness. Had he supplied information, Ile-de-France would have passed under British rule long before 1810.[9]

---

[7] 'Il sentait sa position compromise.' Prentout, p. 521; who gives an excellent account of the situation.

[8] *Voyage to Terra Australis*, II, p. 419.

[9] The belief that Flinders took soundings appears to have been common among the French inhabitants of Port Louis. In the *Proceedings* of the South Australian Branch of the Royal Geographical Society, 1912–13, p. 71, is printed a brief account of the detention of Flinders, by a contemporary, D'Epinay, a lawyer of the town. Here it is stated: 'It is found out that at night he

A few passages written for inclusion in the *Voyage to Terra Australis*, but for some reason omitted, may be quoted to show how rigorously visiting ships were treated lest information should leak out.[10]

> *It may not be amiss to mention the rules which a ship is obliged to observe on arriving at Port North-West, since it will of itself give some idea of the nature of the Government. The ship is boarded by a pilot one or two miles from the entrance to the port, who informs the commander that no person must go on shore, or any one be suffered to come on board until the ship has been visited by the officer of health, who comes soon after the ship has arrived at anchor in the mouth of the port, accompanied with an officer from the captain of the port, and, if it is a foreign ship, by an interpreter. If the health of the crew presents no objection, and after answering the questions put to him concerning the object of his coming to the island, the commander goes on shore in the French boat, and is desired to take with him all papers containing political information, and all letters, whether public or private, that are on board the vessel; and although there should be several parcels of newspapers of the same date, they must all go. On arriving at the Government House, to which he is accompanied by the officer and interpreter, and frequently by a guard, he sooner or later sees the Governor, or one of his aides-de-camp, who questions him upon his voyage, upon political intelligence, the vessels he has met at sea, his intentions in touching at the island, etc.; after which he is desired to leave his letters, packets, and newspapers, no matter to whom they are addressed. If he refuse this, or to give all the information he knows, however detrimental it may be to his own affairs, or appears to equivocate, if he escapes being imprisoned in the town he is sent back to his ship under a guard, and forbidden all communication with the shore. If he gives satisfaction, he is conducted from the General to the Prefect, to answer his questions, and if he satisfies him also, is then left at liberty to go to his consul and transact his business. The letters and packets left with the General, if not addressed to persons obnoxious to the*

---

[9] ***Cont'd.***

takes soundings off the coast and has forwarded his notes to India.' Those who gave credence to this wild story apparently never reflected that Flinders had no kind of opportunity for taking soundings.

[10] MS., Mitchell Library.

Government, are sent unopened, according to their direction. I will not venture to say that the others are opened and afterwards destroyed, but it is much suspected. If the newspapers contain no intelligence but what is permitted to be known, they are also sent to their address. The others are retained; and for this reason it is that all the copies of the same paper are demanded, for the intention is not merely to gain intelligence, but to prevent what is disagreeable from being circulated.

Decaen's conduct in refusing to liberate Flinders when the order reached him need not be excused, but it should be understood. To impute sheer malignity to him does not help us much, nor does it supply a sufficient motive. What we know of his state of mind, as well as what we know of the financial position of the colony, induce the belief that he would have been quite glad to get rid of Flinders in 1807, had not other and stronger influences intervened. But he was a soldier, placed in an exceedingly precarious situation, which he could only maintain by determining not to lose a single chance. War is an affliction that scourges a larger number of those who do not fight than of those who do; and Flinders, with all his innocence, was one of its victims. He was thought to know too much. That was why he was 'dangerous'. A learned French historian[11] stigmatises Decaen's conduct as 'maladroit and brutal, but not dishonest'. Dishonest he never was; as to the other terms we need not dispute so long as we understand the peculiar twist of circumstances that intensified the maladroitness and brutality that marked the man, and without which, indeed, he would not perhaps have been the dogged, tough, hard-fighting, resolute soldier that he was.

Flinders could have escaped from Ile-de-France on several occasions, had he chosen to avail himself of opportunities. He did not, for two reasons, both in the highest degree honourable to him. The first was that he had given his parole [his word not to escape], and would not break it; the second that escape would have meant sacrificing some of his precious papers. In May 1806, an American captain rejoicing in the name of Gamaliel Matthew Ward called at Port Louis, and hearing of Flinders' case, actually made arrangements for removing him. It was Flinders himself who prevented the daring skipper from carrying out his plan. 'The dread of dishonouring my parole,' he wrote, 'made me contemplate this plan with a fearful eye.'[12] In December of the same year he wrote to

[11] Prentout, p. 661.

[12] Flinders' Papers.

John Aken: 'Since I find so much time elapse, and no attention paid to my situation by the French Government, I have been very heartily sorry for having given my parole, as I could otherwise have made my escape long ago.' Again, he wrote to his wife: 'Great risks must be run and sacrifices made, but my honour shall remain unstained. No captain in His Majesty's Navy shall have cause to blush in calling me a brother officer.'

As time went on, and release was not granted, he several times thought of surrendering his parole, which would have involved giving up the pleasant life at Wilhelm's Plains, and being again confined in Port Louis. But escape would have meant the loss of many of his papers, the authentic records of his discoveries; and he could not bring himself to face that.

Consequently the captivity dragged itself wearily out for three years after the order of release was received. The victim chafed, protested, left no stone unturned, but Decaen was not to be moved. Happily depression did not drag illness in its miserable train. 'My health sustains itself tolerably well in the midst of all my disappointments,' he was able to write to Banks in 1809.

XXVI

THE RELEASE

FROM June 1809, the British squadron in the Indian Ocean commenced to blockade Ile-de-France.[1] Decaen's fear of Flinders' knowledge is revealed in the fact that he ordered him not for the future to go beyond the lands attached to Madame D'Arifat's habitation. Flinders wrote complying, and henceforth declined invitations beyond the immediate neighbourhood of the plantation. He amused himself by teaching mathematics and the principles of navigation to the two younger sons of the family, and by the study of French literature.

After October the blockade increased in strictness, under Commodore Rowley. Decaen's situation was growing desperate. Fortunately for him, the French squadron brought in three prizes in January 1810, slipping past Rowley's blockade, much to that enterprising officer's annoyance. The situation was temporarily relieved, but the assistance thus afforded was no better than a plaster on a large wound. Here again we find Flinders accurately and fully informed: Decaen did not underrate his 'dangerous' potentialities.

> *The ordinary sources of revenue and emolument were nearly dried up, and to have recourse to the merchants for a loan was impossible, the former bills upon the French treasury, drawn it was said for three millions of livres, remaining in great part unpaid; and to such distress was the Captain-General reduced for ways and means that he had submitted to ask a voluntary contribution in money, wheat, maize, or any kind of produce from the half-ruined colonists. It was even said to have been promised that, if pecuniary succour did not arrive in six months, the Captain-General would retire and leave the inhabitants to govern themselves.*

---

[1] Flinders to Banks, *Historical Records*, VII, 202.

Decaen, in fact, saw clearly that the game was up. His threat to retire in six months did not mean that he would not have given the British a fight before he lowered the tricolour. He was not the man to surrender quite tamely; but he knew that he could no longer hold out for more than a measurable period, the length of which would depend upon the enemy's initiative.

There was, therefore, no longer any purpose in prolonging the captivity of the prisoner who was feared on account of his knowledge of the situation; and Decaen availed himself of the first opportunity presented in 1810 to grant Flinders his longed-for release. In March, Mr Hugh Hope was sent to Ile-de-France by Lord Minto (who had become Governor-General of India in 1807) to negotiate for the exchange of prisoners. This gentleman had done his best to secure Flinders' release on a former occasion, and had been refused. But now Decaen realised that the end was drawing near, and there was no sound military purpose to serve in keeping the prisoner any longer. It is quite probable that he would have been glad if information had been conveyed to the British which would expedite the inevitable fight and the consequent fall of French power in Mauritius.

On 15 March Flinders received a letter from Mr Hope informing him that the Governor had consented to his liberation. A fortnight later came official confirmation of the news in a letter from Colonel Monistrol, who assured him of the pleasure he had in making the announcement. His joy was great. At once he visited his French friends in the neighbourhood to give them the news and bid them farewell; next day he took an affectionate leave of the kind family who had been his hosts for four years and a half; and as soon as possible he departed for Port Louis, where he stayed with his friend Pitot until he went aboard the cartel [the ship employed to effect the exchange of prisoners]. At the end of the month a dinner was given in his honour by the president of the Société D'Emulation, to which a large number of English men and women were invited. When Flinders arrived in Ile-de-France, more than six years before, he could speak no French and could only decipher a letter in that language with the aid of a dictionary; but now, when he found himself again in the company of his own countrymen, he experienced a difficulty in speaking English.

On 13 June, Flinders' sword was restored to him. He was required to sign a parole [an undertaking], wherein he pledged himself not to act in any service which might be considered as directly or indirectly hostile to France or her allies during the present war. On the same day the cartel *Harriet* sailed for Bengal. Flinders was free: 'after a captivity of six years five months and twenty-seven days I at length had the inexpressible pleasure of being out of the reach of General Decaen'.

Rowley's blockading squadron was cruising outside the port, and the *Harriet* communicated with the commodore. It was ascertained that the sloop *Otter* was running down to the Cape with despatches on the following day, and Flinders had no difficulty in securing a passage in her. After dining with Rowley he was transferred to the *Otter.* He was delayed for six weeks at the Cape, but in August embarked in the *Olympia*, and arrived in England on 23 October, after an absence of nine years and three months.

News of his release had preceded him, and his wife had come up from Lincolnshire to meet him. He speaks in a letter to a friend of the meeting with the woman whom he had left a bride so many years before:[2] 'I had the extreme good fortune to find Mrs. Flinders in London, which I owe to the intelligence of my liberty having preceded my arrival. I need not describe to you our meeting after an absence of nearly ten years. Suffice it to say I have been gaining flesh ever since.' John Franklin, then a midshipman on the *Bedford*, had come up to London to welcome his old commander, and, much to his disturbance, witnessed the meeting of Flinders and his wife, as we find from a letter written by him: 'Some apology would be necessary for the abrupt manner in which I left you, except in the peculiar circumstances wherein my departure was taken. I felt so sensibly the affecting scene of your meeting Mrs. Flinders that I would not have remained any longer in the room under any consideration.'

The capture of Ile-de-France by the British, when ultimately an attack was made (on 3 December 1810), gave peculiar pleasure to naval officers and Anglo-Indians. 'It is incredible,' Mr Hope wrote to Flinders, 'the satisfaction which the capture of that island has diffused all over India, and everyone is now surprised that an enterprise of such importance should never have been attempted before.' When the change of rulers took place, some of the French inhabitants objected to take the oath of allegiance to the British Crown, and a letter on the subject was sent to Napoleon. His comment was pithy: 'I should like to see anybody refuse me the oath of allegiance in any country I conquered!'[3]

It will be convenient to deal at this point with the oft-repeated charge, to which reference has been made previously, that charts were taken from Flinders during his imprisonment, and were used in the

---

[2] Flinders' Papers.

[3] Flinders' Papers.

preparation of the atlas to Péron and Freycinet's *Voyage de Découvertes aux Terres Australes.*

The truth is that no charts were at any time taken from the trunks wherein they were deposited in 1803, except by Flinders himself, nor was a single one of his charts ever seen by any French officer unless he himself showed it. He never made any such charge of dishonesty against his enemy, Decaen, or against the General's countrymen. He had, as will be seen, a cause of grievance against Freycinet, who was responsible for the French charts, and gave voice to it; but plagiarism was neither alleged nor suspected by him.

On each occasion when Flinders applied to Decaen to be supplied with papers from the trunks, he gave a formal receipt for them. The first occasion when papers were removed was on 18 December 1803, when Flinders took from one of his trunks his *Cumberland* log-book, in order that Decaen might ascertain from it his reasons for calling at Ile-de-France. It was never restored to him. Mr Hope made application for it in 1810, when he was set free, but Decaen did not give it up; and in 1813 Decrès was still demanding it unavailingly. This book and the box of despatches were the only papers of Flinders that Decaen ever saw. When it was handed over, all other books and papers were replaced in the trunk, 'and sealed as before'. The second occasion was on 27 December 1803, when the trunk containing printed books was restored to Flinders at his request in order that he might employ himself in confinement at the Port Louis tavern. The third occasion was on 29 December, when he was conducted to Government House, and was allowed to take out of the sealed trunk there his private letters and journals, two log-books, and other memoranda necessary to enable him to construct a chart of the Gulf of Carpentaria. All other papers were 'locked up in the trunk and sealed as before'. The fourth occasion was in July 1804, when Flinders was allowed to take out of the same trunk a quantity of other books, papers and charts, which he required for the pursuit of his work. For these also a receipt was duly given. In that instance Flinders was especially vigilant. He had received a private warning that some of his charts had been copied, but when the seals were broken and he examined the contents he was satisfied that this was not true. He asked Colonel Monistrol, an honourable gentleman who was always of friendly disposition, whether the papers had been disturbed, and 'he answered by an unqualified negative'. The fifth occasion was in August 1807, when all the remaining papers, except the log-book and the despatches, were restored to him. He then gave the following receipt:[4]

[4] Decaen Papers.

Received from Colonel Monistrol, chef d'état-major général of the Isle of France, one trunk containing the remainder of the books, papers, etc., which were taken from me in Port North-West on December 16th, 1803, and December 20th of the same year, whether relating to my voyage of discovery or otherwise; which books and, papers, with those received by me at two different times in 1804, make up the whole that were so taken; with the following exceptions: 1st, Various letters and papers, either wholly or in part destroyed by rats, of which the remains are in the trunk. 2nd, The third volume of my rough log-books, containing the journal of my transactions and observations on board the Investigator, *the* Porpoise, *the* Hope *cutter, and the* Cumberland *schooner, from some time in June, 1803, to December 16th, 1803, of which I have no duplicate. 3rd, Two boxes of despatches; the one from his Excellency Governor King of New South Wales, addressed to His Majesty's principal Secretary of State for the Colonies; the other from Colonel Paterson, Lieutenant-Governor at Port Jackson, the address of which I do not remember. In truth of which I hereunto sign my name at Port Napoleon, Isle of France this 24th day of August, 1807.*

MATTW. FLINDERS,

Late commander of H.M. Sloop the Investigator, *employed on discoveries to the South Seas, with a French passport.*

The papers which the rats had destroyed were not described; but there is a letter of Flinders to the Admiralty, written after his return to England (8 November 1810), which informs us what they were.[5] In this letter he explained that, when the trunk containing the papers was restored, 'I found the rats had gotten into the trunk and made nests of some of them. I transmitted the whole from the Isle of France in the state they then were, and now find that some of the papers necessary to the passing of my accounts as commander and purser of His Majesty's sloop *Investigator* are wanting. I have therefore to request you will lay my case before their Lordships and issue an order to dispense with the papers which from the above circumstances it is impossible for me to produce.' It is apparent, therefore, that none of the navigation papers or charts were destroyed. Had any been abstracted [removed] Flinders, who was a punctiliously exact man, would have missed them. His intense feeling

[5] Flinders' Papers.

of resentment against Decaen would have caused him to call attention to the fact if any papers whatever had been disturbed.

The *Quarterly Review* pointed out the circumstance that the French charts were '*very like*' those of Flinders, giving sinister emphasis to the words in italics. They were very like in so far as they were good. It is evident that if two navigators sail along the same piece of coast, and each constructs a chart of it, those charts will be 'very like' each other to exactly the degree in which they accurately represent the coast charted. Freycinet, who did much of the hydrographical work on Baudin's expedition, was an eminently competent officer. Wherever we find him in charge of a section, the work is well done. His atlas contained some extremely beautiful work. There is no reason whatever for suggesting that it was not his own work. He certainly saw no chart of Flinders, except the one shown to him at Port Jackson, until the atlas to the *Voyage to Terra Australis* was published.

Moreover, the reports and material prepared by Baudin's cartographers, upon which Freycinet worked, are in existence. The reports[6] to the commander give detailed descriptions of sections of the Australian coast traversed and charted, and show conclusively that some parts were examined with thoroughness. For regions in which Baudin's expeditions sailed, Freycinet had no need to resort to Flinders' material. He had enough of his own. The papers of Flinders which Freycinet might have wished to see were those relating to the Gulf of Carpentaria, Torres Strait, and the Queensland coast, which Baudin's vessels did not explore. But the French maps contain no new features in respect to these parts. They present no evidence that Freycinet was acquainted with the discoveries made there by Flinders.

The accusation of plagiarism arose partly from the intense animosity felt against Frenchmen by English writers in a period of fierce national hatred; partly from natural resentment of the treatment accorded to Flinders; partly from the circumstance that, while he was held in captivity, French maps were published which appeared to claim credit for discoveries made by him; and partly from a misunderstanding of a charge very boldly launched by an eminent French geographer. Malte-Brun, in his *Annales des Voyages* for 1814 (Vol. XXIII, p. 268) made an attack upon the French atlas. He detested the Napoleonic régime, and published his observations while Napoleon was in exile at Elba. He

[6] I have read the whole of these reports from copies of the originals in the Dépot de la Marine, Service Hydrographique, Paris, but have not thought it necessary to make further use of them in this book.

pointed out the wrong done to Flinders in labelling the southern coast of Australia 'Terre Napoléon', and in giving French names to geographical features of which Flinders, not Baudin, was the discoverer. He continued: 'the motive for that species of national plagiarism[7] is evident. The Government wished to create for itself a title for the occupation of that part of New Holland.' Malte-Brun should have known Napoleon better than that. When he wanted territory, and was strong enough to take it, he did not 'create titles'. He took: his title was the sword.

But the point of importance is that Malte-Brun did not allege 'plagiarism' against the authors of the French maps. His charge was made against the Government. It was not that Freycinet had plagiarised Flinders' charts, but that the Government had plagiarised his discoveries by, as Malte-Brun thought, ordering French names to be strewn along the Terre Napoléon coasts. In a later issue of the *Annales des Voyages*[8] Malte-Brun testified to having seen Freycinet working at the material upon which his charts were founded. But his former use of the word 'plagiat' had created a general impression that Flinders' charts had been dishonestly taken from him in Mauritius, and used by those responsible for the French maps; a charge which Malte-Brun never meant to make, and which, though still very commonly stated and believed, is wholly untrue.

The really deplorable feature of the affair is that Péron and Freycinet, in their published book and atlas, gave no credit to Flinders for discoveries which they knew perfectly [well] that he had made. They knew where he was while they were working up their material. It does not appear that either of them ever moved in the slightest degree to try to secure his liberation. Péron died in December 1810. Malte-Brun, who saw him frequently after the return of Baudin's expedition, says that in conversation on the discoveries of Flinders, Péron 'always appeared to me to be agitated by a secret sorrow, and has given me to understand that he regretted not being at liberty to say in that regard all that he knew'. Flinders also believed Péron to be a worthy man who acted as he did 'from overruling authority'. Those who have read the evidence printed in this book, exhibiting the detestable conduct of both Péron and Freycinet in repaying indulgence and hospitality by base espionage, will hardly be precipitate in crediting either of them with immaculate motives. There is no evidence that authority was exercised to induce them to name the southern coasts Terre Napoléon, or to give the name

[7] 'Le motif de cette espèce de plagiat national ...'

[8] Vol. XXIV, 273.

Golfe Bonaparte to the Spencer's Gulf of Flinders, that of Golfe Josephine to his St Vincent's Gulf, that of Ile Decrès to his Kangaroo Island, that of Detroit de Lacépède to his Investigator Strait, and so forth. They knew that Flinders had made these discoveries before their own ships appeared in the same waters; they knew that only the fact of his imprisonment prevented his charts from being published before theirs. The names with which they adorned their maps were a piece of courtiership and a means of currying favour with the great and powerful, just as their espionage, and their supply of illicitly obtained and flavoured information to Decaen in Mauritius, were essays [endeavours] to advance their own interests by unworthy services.

Freycinet's anxiety to get his maps out before Flinders had time to publish is curiously exhibited in a letter from him to the Minister of Marine (29 August 1811). Flinders was then back in England, hard at work upon his charts. A volume of text, and one thin book of plates, containing only two maps, had been published at Paris in 1807. Then delay occurred, and in 1811 the engravers, not having been paid for their work, refused to continue. Freycinet appealed to the Minister in these terms:[9]

> *Very powerful reasons, Monsieur, appear to demand that the atlas should be published with very little delay, and even before the text which is to accompany it. Independently of the advantages to me personally as author, of which I shall not speak, the reputation of the expedition ordered by His Majesty appears to me to be strongly involved. I have the honour to remind your Excellency that Captain Flinders was sent on discovery to Terra Australis a short while after the French Government had despatched an expedition having the same object. The rival expeditions carried out their work in the same field, but the French had the good fortune to be the first to return to Europe. Now that Flinders is again in England, and is occupied with the publication of the numerous results of his voyage, the English Government, jealous on account of the rivalry between the two expeditions, will do all it can for its own. The conjectures I have formed acquire a new force by the recent announcement made by the newspapers, that Captain Flinders' voyages in the South Seas are to be published by command of the Lords of the Admiralty. If the English publish*

[9] MSS., Archives Nationales, Marine, BB4, 996.

> *before the French the records of discoveries made in New Holland, they will, by the fact of that priority of publication, take from us the glory which we have a right to claim. The reputation of our expedition depends wholly upon the success of our geographical work, and the more nearly our operations and those of the English approach perfection, and the more nearly our charts resemble each other, the more likelihood there is of our being accused of plagiarism, or at all events of giving rise to the thought that the English charts were necessary to aid us in constructing ours; because there will be no other apparent motive for the delay of our publication.*

Here, it will be seen, Freycinet anticipated the charge of plagiarism, but thought it would spring from the prior publication of Flinders' charts. He had no suspicion at this time that the accusation would be made that he used charts improperly taken from Flinders when he was under the thumb of Decaen; and when this unjust impeachment was launched a few years later he repudiated it with strong indignation. In that he was justified; and our sympathy with him would be keener if his own record in other respects had been brighter.

XXVII

LAST YEARS AND DEATH OF FLINDERS

ONE of the first matters which occupied Flinders after his arrival in England was the use of his influence with the Admiralty to secure the release of a few French prisoners of war who were relatives of his friends in Mauritius. In a letter he pointed out that these men were connected with respectable families from whom he himself and several other English prisoners had received kindness.[1] His plea was successful. There was, surely, a peculiar beauty in this act of sympathy on the part of one who had so recently felt the pain and distress of captivity.

Flinders was anxious for news about his old *Investigator* shipmates. The faithful Elder, he found, had secured an appointment as servant to Admiral Hollowell, then on service in the Mediterranean, and was a great favourite. Franklin was able to enlighten him as to some of the others. Purdie, who had been assistant-surgeon, was surgeon on the *Pompey.* Inman, who had been sent out to act as astronomer during the latter part of the voyage, was a professor at the Naval College, Portsmouth. Lacy and Sinclair, midshipmen, were dead. Louth was a midshipman on the *Warrior.* Olive was purser on the *Heir Apparent*, and Matt, the carpenter, filled that post on the *Bellerophon.* Of Dr Bell Franklin knew nothing. 'The old ship,' he said, 'is lying at Portsmouth, cut down nearly to the water's edge.'

In naval and scientific circles Flinders was the object of much honour and interest. He was received 'with flattering attention' at the Admiralty. We find him visiting Lord Spencer, who, having authorised the *Investigator* voyage, was naturally concerned to hear of its eventful history. Banks took him to the Royal Society and gave a dinner in his honour. The Duke of Clarence, afterwards William IV, himself a sailor, wished to meet him and inspect his charts, and he was taken to see the

---

[1] Flinders' Papers.

Prince by Bligh. In 1812 he gave evidence before a Committee of the House of Commons on the penal transportation system.[2] What he had to say related principally to the nature of the country he had examined in the course of his explorations. 'Were you acquainted with Port Dalrymple?' the chairman asked him. 'I discovered Port Dalrymple.' 'Were you ever at the Derwent?' 'I was, and from my report, I believe, it was that the first settlement was made there.' He was one of the few early explorers of Australia whose vision was hopeful; and experience has in every instance justified his foreseeing [prescient] optimism.

But save for a few social events, and for some valuable experiments with the magnetic needle, to be referred to in the final chapter, his time and energies were absorbed by work upon his charts. He laboured incessantly. 'I am at my voyage,' he said in a letter, 'but it does by no means advance according to my wishes. Morning, noon and night I sit close at writing, and at my charts, and can hardly find time for anything else.' He was a merciless critic when the proofs came from the engravers. One half-sheet contains 92 corrections and improving marks in his handwriting. Such directions as 'make the dot distinct', 'strengthen the coast-line', 'make this track a fair equal line', 'points wanting', are abundant. As we turn over the great folio which represents so much labour, so much endurance, so much suffering, it is good to remember that these superb drawings are the result of the ceaselessly patient toil of perhaps the most masterly cartographer who has ever adorned the British naval service.

He took similar pains with the text of *A Voyage to Terra Australis.* It was never meant to be a book for popular reading, though there is no lack of entertainment in it. It was a semi-official publication, in which the Admiralty claimed and retained copyright, and its author was perhaps a little hampered by that circumstance. Bligh asked that it should be dedicated to him, but 'the honour was declined'.[3] The book was produced under the direction of a committee appointed by the Admiralty, consisting of Banks, Barrow, and Flinders himself.

It abounds in exact data concerning the latitude and longitude of coastal features. The English is everywhere clear and sound; but the book which Flinders could have written had he lived a few years longer, if it had been penned with the freedom which made his conversation so delightful to his friends, might have been one of the most entertaining pieces of travel literature in the language. At first he was somewhat

[2] House of Commons Papers, 1812; the evidence was given on 25 March.

[3] Flinders' Papers.

apprehensive about authorship, and thought of calling in the aid of a friend; but the enforced leisure of Ile-de-France induced him to depend upon his own efforts. Before he left England in 1801, he had suggested that he might require assistance. In a letter to Willingham Franklin, John's brother, a fellow of Oriel College, Oxford, and afterwards a judge in Madras, he wrote (27 November 1801):[4]

> *You must understand that this voyage of ours is to be written and published on our return. I am now engaged in writing a rough account, but authorship sits awkwardly upon me. I am diffident of appearing before the public unburnished by an abler hand. What say you? Will you give me your assistance if on my return a narration of our voyage should be called for from me? If the voyage be well executed and well told afterwards I shall have some credit to spare to deserving friends. If the door now open suits your taste and you will enter, it should be yours for the undertaking. A little mathematical knowledge will strengthen your style and give it perspicuity. Arrangement is the material point in voyage-writing as well as in history. I feel great diffidence here. Sufficient matter I can easily furnish, and fear not to prevent anything unseamanlike from entering into the composition; but to round a period well and arrange sentences so as to place what is meant in the most perspicuous point of view is too much for me. Seamanship and authorship make too great an angle with each other; the further a man advances upon one line the further distant he becomes from any point on the other.*

It did not prove so in Flinders' own case, for his later letters and the latter part of his book are written in an easier, more freely flowing style than marks his earlier writings. He solicited no assistance in the final preparation of his work. He preferred to speak to his public in his own voice, and was unquestionably well advised in so doing. It is a plain, honest sailor's story; that of a cultivated man withal [as well].

Intense application to the work in hand brought about a recurrence of the constitutional internal trouble which had occasioned some pain in Mauritius. The illness became acute at the end of 1813. He was only 39 years of age, but Mrs Flinders wrote to a friend that he had aged so much that he looked 70, and was 'worn to a skeleton'. He mentioned in his journal that he was suffering much pain. Yet he was never heard

---

[4] Flinders' Papers.

to complain, and was never irritable or troublesome to those about him. He was full of kindness and concern for his friends. We find him attending sittings of the Admiralty Court, where his friend Pitot had a suit against the British Government, and he interested himself in the promotion of two of his old *Investigator* midshipmen. He urged upon the Admiralty with all his force that his own branch of the naval service was as honourable and as deserving of official recognition as war service. The only inducement for young officers to join a voyage of discovery, and forgo the advantages arising from prizes and active service, was the reasonable certainty of promotion on their return. 'This,' he observed, 'certainly has been relied upon and fulfilled in expeditions which returned in time of peace, when promotion is so difficult to be obtained; whereas I sailed and my officers returned during a war in which promotion was never before so liberally bestowed. Yet no one of my officers, so far as I have been able to ascertain, has received promotion for their services in that voyage, although it has been allowed the service was well executed.'[5]

The illness increased during 1814, while the *Voyage* and its accompanying atlas were passing through the press. He never saw the finished book. The first copy of it came from the publishers, G. and W. Nicol, of Pall Mall, on 18 July, on the day before he died; but he was then unconscious. His wife took the volumes and laid them upon his bed, so that the hand that fashioned them could touch them. But he never understood. He was fast wrapped in the deep slumber that preceded the end. On the 19th he died. His devoted wife stood by his pillow, his infant daughter (born 1 April 1812) was in an adjoining room, and there was one other friend present. Just before the brave life flickered out, he started up, and called in a hoarse voice for 'my papers'. Then he fell back and died.

Upon the manuscript of the friend who wrote an account of his death, there is pencilled a brief memorandum, which chronicles a few words muttered some time before death touched his lips. The pencil-writing is rubbed and only partly decipherable, but the letters 'Dr' are distinct. I take the meaning to be that the doctor attending him heard him murmur the words. They are: 'But it grows late, boys, let us dismiss!' One can easily realise the kind of picture that floated before the mind of the dying navigator. It was, surely, a happy vision of a night among friends and companions, who had listened with delight to the vivid talk of him who had seen and done so much in his wonderful 40 years of life. In such a

---

[5] Flinders' Papers.

company his mates would not be the first to wish to break the spell, so he gave the word: '[But] it grows late, boys, let us dismiss.'

Flinders died at 14 London Street, Fitzroy Square, and was buried in the graveyard of St James's, Hampstead Road, which was a burial ground for St James's, Piccadilly. No man now knows exactly where his bones were laid.[6] A letter written years later by his daughter, Mrs Petrie, says: 'Many years afterwards my aunt Tyler went to look for his grave, but found the churchyard remodelled, and quantities of tombstones and graves with their contents had been carted away as rubbish, among them that of my unfortunate father, thus pursued by disaster after death as in life.'

On the 25th of the same month died Charles Dibdin, who wrote the elegy of the perfect sailor:

Here a sheer hulk lies poor Tom Bowling,
The darling of our crew,
No more he'll hear the tempest howling
For death has broached him to.

During his last years in London, Flinders lodged in six houses successively, and it may be as well to enumerate them. They were: 16 King Street, Soho, from 5 November 1810; 7 Nassau Street, Soho, from 19 January 1811; 7 Mary Street, Brook Street, from 30 September 1811; 45 Upper John Street, Fitzroy Square, from 30 March 1813; 7 Upper Fitzroy Street, from 28 May 1813; and 14 London Street, Fitzroy Square, from 28 February 1814.

A letter from the widow to her husband's French friend Pitot, evidently in answer to a message of sympathy, is poignant:

You who were in a measure acquainted with the many virtues and inestimable qualities he possessed, will best appreciate the worth of the treasure I have lost, and you will easily imagine that, were the whole universe at my command, it could offer no compensation; and even the tenderest sympathy of the truest friend avails but little in a case of such severe trial and affliction. You will not be surprised when I say that sorrow continually circles round my heart and tears are my daily companion. 'Tis true the company of my little girl soothes and

[6] The vicar of St James's, Piccadilly, who examined the burial register in response to an enquiry by Mr George Gordon McCrae of Melbourne, in 1912, states that the entry was made, by a clerical error, in the name of Captain Matthew Flanders, aged 40.

cheers many an hour that would otherwise pass most wearily away, but life has lost its chief charm, and the world appears a dreary wilderness to me.

An unpleasant feature of the subject, which cannot be overlooked, relates to the Admiralty's ungenerous treatment of Flinders and his widow. When he returned from Mauritius, the First Lord was Mr C. P. Yorke after whom Flinders named Yorke's Peninsula, who was inclined to recognise that the special circumstances of the case demanded special treatment. He at once promoted Flinders to the rank of post-captain. But in consequence of his long detention Flinders had lost the opportunity for earlier promotion. It was admitted that if he had returned to England in 1804 he would at once have been rewarded for his services by promotion to post-captain's rank. Indeed, Lord Spencer had definitely promised him a step in rank. It was therefore urged in his behalf that, as he had not been a prisoner of war in the ordinary sense, his commission should be ante-dated [backdated] to 1804. Yorke appeared to think the claim reasonable. The Admiralty conceded that he had not been a prisoner of war, and he was not brought before a court martial, although the *Cumberland*, left to rot in Port Louis, had been lost to the service. The First Lord directed that the commission should be ante-dated to the time of the release, but it was not considered that more could be done without an Order in Council. This could not be obtained at the moment, because King George III was mentally incapacitated. When the Regency was established (1811) an application did not meet with a sympathetic response. 'The hinge upon which my case depends,' said Flinders in a letter, 'is whether my having suffered so long and unjustly in the Isle of France is a sufficient reason that I should now suffer in England the loss of six years' rank.' The response of the Admiralty officials was that the case was peculiar; there was 'no precedent' for ante-dating a promotion.

Flinders asked that he might be put on full pay, while he was writing the *Voyage*, which would make up the difference in the expense to which he would be put by living in town instead of in the country; but Barrow assured him that the Admiralty would object 'for want of a precedent'. He showed that he would be £500 or £600 out of pocket, to say nothing of the loss of chances of promotion by remaining ashore. It was to meet this position that the Admiralty granted him £200; but as a matter of fact he was still £300 out of pocket,[7] and was put out of health irrecoverably

[7] Flinders' Papers.

by intense application to the task. His friend, Captain Kent, then of the *Agincourt*, advised him to abandon the work. 'I conjure [implore] you,' he wrote 'to give the subject your serious attention, and do not suffer yourself to be involved in debt to gratify persons who seem to have no feeling.' But to have abandoned his beloved work at this stage would have appeared worse to him than loss of life itself. The consequence was that his expenses during this period, even with the strictly economical mode of living which he adopted, entrenched upon [cut into] the small savings which he was able to leave to his widow. He was compelled to represent [make the case] that, unless a concession were made, he would have to choose between abandoning his task or reducing his family to distress; and it was for this reason that the Admiralty granted a special allowance of £200, in supplement of his half-pay. This, with £500 'in lieu of compensation' on account of his detention in Ile-de-France was the entire consideration that he received.

When he died, application was made to the Admiralty to grant a special pension to Mrs Flinders. The widow of Captain Cook had been granted a pension of £200 a year. (Mrs Cook, by the way, was still living in England at this time; she did not die till 1835.) Stout old Sir Joseph Banks declared that he would not die happy unless something were done for the widow and child of Matthew Flinders. But his influence with the Admiralty was not so great as it had been in Lord Spencer's time, and his efforts were ineffectual. The case was at a later date brought under the notice of William IV, who said that he saw no reason why the widow of Captain Flinders should not receive the same treatment as the widow of Captain Cook. The King mentioned the subject to Lord Melbourne; he, however, was unsympathetic, and nothing whatever was done. Mrs Flinders was paid only the meagre pension of a post-captain's widow until she died in 1852. No official reward of any kind was granted by the British Government for the truly great services and discoveries of Flinders. The stinginess of a rich nation is a depressing subject to reflect upon in a case of this kind.

A gratifying contrast is afforded by the voluntary action of two Australian colonies. It was learnt, to the surprise of many, some time after 1850, that the widow of the discoverer and her married daughter were living in England, and were not too well provided for. The Colonies of New South Wales and Victoria thereupon (1853) voted a pension of £100 a year each to Mrs Flinders, with reversion to Mrs Petrie. The news of this decision did not reach England in time to please the aged widow, but the spirit of the grant gave unfeigned satisfaction to Flinders' daughter. 'Could my beloved mother have lived to receive this announcement,' she wrote,[8] 'it would indeed have cheered her last days to know that my father's long-neglected services were at length appreciated. But my gratification arising from the grant is extreme, especially as it comes from a quarter in which I had not solicited consideration; and the handsome amount of the pension granted will enable me to educate my young son in a manner worthy of the name he bears, Matthew Flinders.'[9]

A Voyage to Terra Australis, it may be mentioned, was originally sold for eight or twelve guineas, according to whether or not the atlas was bought with the two quarto volumes. A copy today [1914], with the folio atlas, sells for about ten guineas.

---

[8] New South Wales Parliamentary Papers, 1854, I, 785.

[9] 'My young son' refers to Professor W. Matthew Flinders Petrie.

XXVIII

CHARACTERISTICS

MATTHEW FLINDERS was a short, neatly-built, very lithe and active man. He stood five feet six inches in height.[1] His figure was slight and well proportioned. When he was in full health, his light, buoyant step was remarked upon by acquaintances. Neither of the two portraits of him conveys a good impression of his alert, commanding look. His nose was 'rather aquiline', and his lips were customarily compressed. 'He had a noble brow, hair almost black, eyes dark, bright, and with a commanding expression, amounting almost to sternness.' So his friend records.

Mrs Flinders was not satisfied with the engraved portrait published in the *Naval Chronicle* in 1814, nor with the miniature from which it was reproduced. In a letter to Captain Stuart she wrote: 'In the portrait you will not be able to trace much of your departed friend. The miniature from which it was taken is but an indifferent likeness, and the engraver has not done justice to it. He has given the firmness of the countenance but not the intelligence or animation.' It is quite certain that a rapid, piercing, commanding expression of eye and features was characteristic of him. During his captivity, the look in his eyes forbad all approach to familiarity. There is record of an occasion—in all probability connected with the sword incident—when he was addressed in terms that appeared to him to be wanting in respect; and the unlucky Frenchman who ventured thus far was so astonished at the sternness of countenance that immediately confronted him, that he started back some paces. He had been accustomed to command from an early age, and had exercised authority on service of a kind that compelled him to demand ceaseless vigilance and indefatigable vigour from himself and those under him. In a passage written in Mauritius[2] he makes allusion to

---

[1] These particulars are from the MSS. sketch by a friend, previously cited; Flinders' Papers.

[2] Flinders' Papers.

the stern element in his character; and surely what he says here is worthy of being well pondered by all whose duty demands the exercise of power over other men:

> *I shall learn patience in this island, which will perhaps counteract the insolence acquired by having had unlimited command over my fellow men. You know, my dearest, that I always dreaded the effect that the possession of great authority would have upon my temper and disposition. I hope they are neither of them naturally bad; but, when we see such a vast difference between men dependent and men in power, any man who has any share of impartiality must fear for himself. My brother will tell you that I am proud, unindulgent, and hasty to take offence, but I doubt whether John Franklin will confirm it, although there is more truth in the charge than I wish there were. In this land, those malignant qualities are ostentatiously displayed. I am made to feel their sting most poignantly. My mind has been taught a lesson in philosophy, and my judgment has gained an accession of experience that will not soon be forgotten.*

That is a fairly rigorous piece of self-analysis; but there are abundant facts to show that he exercised authority with a kindly and friendly disposition, and did not surpass the limits of wisdom. Men like a commander who can command; the weak inspire no confidence. Flinders had the art of attracting people to him. His servant, the faithful John Elder, willingly endured imprisonment with him, and would not leave him until his own health gave way. John Thistle, who had served under him before 1800, returned to England shortly before the *Investigator* sailed, and at once volunteered for service under him again. He ruled his crews by sheer force of mind and unsparing example, and though the good of the service in hand was ever his first thought, there is plenty of evidence to prove that the happiness of the men under him was constantly in his mind.

In hours of relaxation he was genial, a lively companion, a warm friend. An intimate friend records: 'He possessed the social virtues and affections in an eminent degree, and in conversation he was particularly agreeable, from the extent of his general information and the lively acuteness of his observations. His integrity, uprightness of intention, and liberality of sentiment were not to be surpassed.'

A scrap of dialogue written for insertion in the *Voyage to Terra Australis*, but cancelled with other matter, enables us to realise that he could recall an incident with some dramatic force. Bonnefoy, an interpreter in Ile-de-France, told him a story of an American skipper under examination by one of General Decaen's officers, and he wrote it down as follows:

> *I was amused with his account of a blunt American captain who, having left a part of his people to collect seal-skins upon the island Tristan d'Acuna, had come in for provisions, and to get his vessel repaired. This honest man did not wish to tell where he was collecting his cargo, nor did he understand all the ceremony he was required to go through. The dialogue that passed between the old seaman and the French officers of the port was nearly thus:*
>
> *Off.: 'From whence do you come, Sir?'*
>
> *'From whence do I come? Haugh! why, Monsieur, I come from the Atlantic Ocean.'*
>
> *Off.: 'But, pray, Sir, from what port?'*
>
> *'Port? You will find that out from my papers, which I suppose you want to see?'*
>
> *Off.: 'It appears, Sir, that you have not above half your crew on board. Be so good as to inform me where are the rest?'*
>
> *'O, my crew? Poor fellows, yes, why, Sir, we met with an island of ice on the road, and I left them there a-basket-making.'*
>
> *Off.: 'Making baskets on an island of ice? This is a very strange answer, Sir; and give me leave to tell you such will not do here; but you will accompany me to the Captain-General, and we shall then see whether you will answer or not.'*
>
> *'Ay, we shall see indeed. Why, look ye, Monsieur: as to what I have been about, that is nothing to anybody. I am an honest man, and that's enough for you; but if you want to know why I am come here, it is to buy provisions and to lie quiet a little bit. I am not come to beg or steal, but to buy, and I fancy good bills upon M——— of Salem will suit you very well, eh, Monsieur? Convenient enough?'*
>
> *Off.: 'Very well, Sir, you will come with us to the General.'*
>
> *'To the General? I have nothing to do with Generals! They don't understand my business. Suppose I don't go?'*
>
> *Off.: 'You will do as you please, Sir; but if you do not, you will soon .... '*

The sheet on which the continuation of this vigorous bit of dialogue was written[3] is unfortunately missing, so that we are deprived of the joy of

[3] MS., Mitchell Library.

reading the conclusion of the comedy. But as the passage stands it presents a truly dramatic picture.

We get a glimpse of the way in which genial spirits regarded him in a jolly letter from Madras, from Lieutenant Fitzwilliam Owen, who had been a prisoner with him in Mauritius, and was on the cartel [ship] on which he sailed from that island. 'You cannot doubt how much our society misses you. We toasted you, Sir, like Englishmen. We sent the heartiest good wishes of your countrymen, ay, and women too, to Heaven for your success, in three times three loud and manly cheers, dictated by that sincerity which forms the glorious characteristic of our rough-spun English. Nay, Waugh got drunk for you, and the ladies did each take an extra glass to you.'[4]

A pleasant playful touch makes the following letter to his wife's half-sister worth quoting. He was hungry for home letters in Ile-de-France, and thus gently chid the girl:

> *There is indeed a report among the whales in the Indian Ocean that a scrap of a letter from you did pass by for Port Jackson, and a flying fish in the Pacific even says he saw it; but there is no believing these travellers. If you will take the trouble to give it under your own hand I will then believe that you have written to me. A certain philosopher being informed that his dear friend was dead, replied that he would not believe it without having it certified under his own hand; a very commendable prudence this, and worthy of imitation in all intricate cases. As I have a fund of justice at the bottom of my conscience, which will not permit me to exact from others more than I would perform myself, I do hereby certify that I have this day addressed a letter to my well-beloved sister Isabella Tyler, spinster, in which letter I do desire for her all manner of blessings, spiritual and temporal; that she may speedily obtain a husband six feet high, if it so pleases her, with the wishing cap of Fortunatus. [Fortunatus was a hero of medieval legend who had an inexhaustible purse and a magical cap capable of conferring fulfilment of one's wishes.]*

The strictness of the man's conduct, in his relations with superiors and subordinates alike, sprang from his integrity of heart. Everybody trusted him. A memoir published by a contemporary commented upon the fidelity of his friendships. 'He was faithful to the utmost in

[4] Flinders' Papers.

the performance of a promise, whether important or trifling in its consequences.'

Some of the best friends he ever made were among the French in Ile-de-France; and he became so much attached to them that, even when he secured his longed-for freedom, he could not part from them without a pang of regret. They saw in him not only a wronged man, but a singularly high-minded one. Pitot, writing to Bougainville to urge him to do his utmost to secure Flinders' release, repudiated, in these terms, the idea that he could be a spy:[5] 'No, Monsieur Flinders is not capable of such conduct; his pure and noble character would never permit him to descend to the odious employment of a spy.' One wonders whether by any chance Bougainville had occasion to show that letter to Messieurs Péron and Freycinet!

A touching and beautiful example of his gentleness occurred in connection with a wounded French officer whom he visited at Port Louis. Lieutenant Charles Baudin des Ardennes had sailed as a junior officer on *Le Géographe* under Baudin (to whom he was not related) and Flinders had known him at Port Jackson. In 1807 he was serving as a lieutenant on *La Sémillante*, in the Indian Ocean. He was badly wounded in a sharp engagement with the British ship *Terpsichore* in March 1807, and was brought into Port Louis, where his shattered right arm was amputated. Flinders, full of compassion for the young man, visited him, and, as oranges were required for the sufferer, bought up the whole stock of a fruiterer, 53 of them. Upon his return to Wilhelm's Plains, he wrote Baudin a letter of sympathy and encouragement, bidding him reflect that there were other branches of useful service open to a sailor than that of warfare. He had commenced his naval career with discovery; he now knew what the horrors of war were. Which was the worthier branch of the two? Flinders continued:

> *No, my friend, I cannot contemplate this waste of human life to serve the cause of restless ambition without horror. Never shall my hands be voluntarily steeped in blood, but in the defence of my country. In such a cause every other sentiment vanishes. Also, my friend, if ever you have thought my actions worthy of being imitated, imitate me in this. You have, like me, had just sufficient experience to learn what the commander of a voyage of discovery ought to be, and what he ought to know Adieu,*

[5] MSS., Mitchell Library; letter dated 19 Vendémiaire, an XIII (11 Oct. 1804).

> *my dear friend. May the goodness of God speedily restore you to perfect health, and turn your thoughts from war to peace.*

Young Baudin, it may be added, was not compelled by the loss of his arm to leave the service. He became an admiral in 1839, and lived till 1854.

Flinders endeavoured to exert a stimulating influence upon young officers. Writing to his brother (6 December 1806) he said:[6]

> *Remember that youth is the time in which a store of knowledge, reputation and fortune must be laid in to make age respectable. Imitate, my dear Samuel, all that you have found commendable in my proceedings, manners, and principles, and avoid the rest. Study is necessary, as it gives theory. I need not speak to you now upon this, but active exertion is still more necessary to a good sea officer. From both united it is that perfection is attained. Neither would I have you neglect politeness, and the best society to which circumstances may permit your admission; though not the basis that constitutes a good officer or valuable member of society, the manners thereby acquired are yet of infinite service to those who possess them.*

There could hardly be a sounder piece of advice to a young officer from an elder than is contained in a letter written by Flinders to John Franklin's father. It was intended for the youth's eye, beyond a doubt. It is dated 10 May 1805:[7]

> *I hope John will have got into some active ship to get his time completed before I go out [on] another voyage, and learn the discipline of the service. I have no doubt of being able to get him a lieutenant's commission if it should be agreeable to him to sail with me again. He may rest confident of my friendship, although I believe he had some fears on that head when we parted, on account of a difference between him and my brother. He has ability enough, but he must be diligent, studious, active in his duty, not over-ready to take offence at his superior officers, nor yet humbling too much to them; but in all things should make allowances for difference of disposition and ways of thinking and should judge principally from the intention.*

---

6 Mr Charles Bertie, of the Municipal Library, Sydney, has kindly supplied me with this letter, which was obtained from Professor Flinders Petrie.

7 MSS., Mitchell Library.

> *Above all things he should be strict in his honour and integrity, for a man who forfeits either cannot be independent or brave at all times; and he should not be afraid to be singular, for, if he is, the ridicule of the vicious would beat him out of his rectitude as well as out of his attention to his duty. I do not speak this from my fear of him [because I have any doubt about him], but from my anxiety to see him the shining character which I am sure he is capable of being.*

In a similar strain is a letter to John Franklin (14 January 1812) regarding a lad named Wiles, the son of a Jamaica friend, who had lately been put on the *Bedford* as a midshipman:

> *I will thank you to let me know from time to time how he goes on. Pray don't let him be idle. Employ him in learning to knot and splice under a quartermaster; in working under observation, in writing his journal, and in such studies as may be useful to him. Make it a point of honour with him to be quick in relieving the deck, and strict in keeping his watch; and when there are any courts martial endeavour either to take him with you or that he may attend when it can be done. In fine, my dear John, endeavour to make a good officer and a good man of him, and be sure I shall always entertain a grateful sense of your attention to him.*

Active-minded himself, he encouraged study among those who came in contact with him. It gave him pleasure to teach mathematics to Madame D'Arifat's sons at Wilhelm's Plains. He mastered French so as to speak it with grace and write with ease. He worked at Malay because he thought it would be useful on future voyages. From the early days, when he taught himself navigation amidst the swamps of his native Lincolnshire, until his last illness laid him low, he was ever an eager student. Intelligent curiosity and a desire to know the best that the best minds could teach were a basic part of his character. We find him counselling Ann Chappell, at about the time when he became engaged to her:[8] 'Learn music, learn the French language, enlarge the subjects of thy pencil, study geography and astronomy and even metaphysics, sooner than leave thy mind unoccupied. Soar, my Annette, aspire to the heights of science. Write a great deal, work with thy needle a great deal, and read every book that comes in thy way, save trifling novels.'

[8] Flinders' Papers.

Flinders read widely, and always carried a good library with him on his voyages. His acquaintance with the literature of navigation was very extensive. Some of his books were lost in the *Porpoise* wreck; the remainder he took with him in the *Cumberland*, and, when he was imprisoned, his anxiety to secure his printed volumes manifested the true book-lover's hunger to have near him those companions of his intellectual life. He derived great pleasure from the French literature which he studied in Mauritius. A letter to his wife dated March 1803, when he was upon the north coast of Australia in the *Investigator*, reveals him relieving his mind, amid anxieties about the condition of the ship, by reading Milton's *Paradise Lost.* 'The elevation and, also, the fall of our first parents,' he comments, 'told with such majesty by him whose eyes lacked all of what he threw so masterly o'er the great subject, dark before and intricate—these with delight I perused, not knowing which to admire most, the poet's daring, the subject, or the success with which his bold attempt was crowned.' He somewhat quaintly compares his wife with Eve: 'But in thee I have more faith than Adam had when he, complying with Eve's request of separation in their labours, said "Go, thou best, last gift of God, go in thy native innocence." But how much dearer art thou here than our first mother! Our separation was not sought by thee, but thou borest it as a vine whose twining arms when turned from round the limb lie prostrate, broken, life scarcely left enough to keep the withered leaf from falling off.' We should especially have welcomed notes from such a pen on a few passages in Milton which must have stirred his deepest interest, as for example the majestic comparison of Satan's flight:

As when far off at sea a fleet descried
Hangs in the clouds, by equinoctial winds
Close sailing from Bengala, or the isles
Of Ternate or Tidore, whence merchants bring
Their spicy drugs; they on the trading flood,
Through the wide Ethiopian to the Cape,
Ply stemming nightly towards the pole: so seemed
Far off the flying Fiend.'

To these characteristics may be added a passage illustrating the view of our navigator concerning the marriage state. It must be confessed that when he wrote it (30 June 1807) his experience was not extensive. He left England when he had been a husband only a few weeks; but the passage is interesting as conveying to his wife what his conception of the ideal relation was:

> *There is a medium between petticoat government and tyranny on the part of the husband, that with thee I think to be very attainable; and which I consider to be the summit of happiness in the marriage state. Thou wilt be to me not only a beloved wife, but my most dear and most intimate friend, as I hope to be to thee. If we find failings, we will look upon them with kindness and compassion, and in each other's merits we will take pride, and delight to dwell upon them; thus we will realise, as far as may be, the happiness of heaven upon the earth. I love not greatness nor desire great riches, being confident they do not contribute to happiness, but I desire to have enough for ourselves and something to assist our friends in need. I think, my love, this is also thy way of thinking.*

In the few concluding months of her husband's life, Mrs Flinders had him beside her under circumstances that were certainly far from easy. Their somewhat straitened means, consequent upon the Admiralty's niggard [mean] construction of regulations, the prolonged severity of his employment, and the last agonised weeks of illness, must have gone far to detract from perfect felicity in domestic conditions. The six changes of residence in four and a half years point to the same conclusion. Nevertheless we find Mrs Flinders writing to a friend in these terms, wherein her own happiness is clearly mirrored:

> *I am well persuaded that very few men know how to value the regard and tender attentions of a wife who loves them. Men in general cannot appreciate properly the delicate affection of a woman, and therefore they do not know how to return it. To make the married life as happy as this world will allow it to be, there are a thousand little amenities to be rendered on both sides, and as many little shades of comfort to be attended to. Many things must be overlooked, for we are all such imperfect beings; and to bear and forbear is essential to domestic peace. You will say that I find it easy to talk on this subject, and that precept is harder than practice. I allow it, my dear friend, in the practical part I have only to return kind affection and attention for uniform tenderness and regard. I have nothing unpleasant to call forth my forbearance. Day after day, month after month passes, and I neither experience an angry look nor a dissatisfied word. Our domestic life is an unvaried line of peace and comfort; and O, may Heaven continue it such, so long as it shall permit us to dwell together on this earth.*

XXIX

THE NAVIGATOR

NOT only is Flinders to be regarded as a discoverer whose researches completed the world's knowledge of the last extensive region of the habitable globe remaining in his time to be revealed; not only as one whose work was marked by an unrivalled exactitude and fineness of observation; but also as one who did very much to advance the science of navigation in directions calculated to make seafaring, safer, more certain, with better means and methods at disposal. Malte-Brun declared, when he [Flinders] died, that 'the geographical and nautical sciences have lost in the person of Flinders one of their most brilliant ornaments',[1] and that criticism, coming from a foreign critic than whom there was no better informed savant in Europe, was no mere piece of obituary rhetoric.

In 1805 he wrote a paper on the marine barometer, based upon observations made during his Australian voyages. The instrument employed was one which had been used by Cook; Flinders always kept it in his cabin. He was the first to discover, and this essay was the first attempt to show, the connection between the rise and fall of the barometer and the direction of the wind. Careful observation showed him that where his facts were collected the mercury of the barometer rose some time before a change from landbreeze to seabreeze, and fell before the change from seabreeze to landbreeze. Consequently a change of wind might generally be predicted from the barometer. The importance of these observations was at once recognised by men connected with navigation. As the *Edinburgh Review* wrote, dealing with Flinders' paper when presented before the Royal Society on 27 March 1806:[2] 'It is very easy for us, speculating in our closet upon the theory of winds and their

---

[1] *Annales des Voyages*, XXIII, p. 268.

[2] *Edinburgh Review*, January, 1807; Flinders' Paper 'Observations on the Marine Barometer', was published in the *Philosophical Transactions* of the Royal Society, Part II, 1806.

connection with the temperature, to talk of drawing a general inference on this subject with confidence. But when the philosopher chances to be a seaman on a very dangerous coast, it will be admitted that the strength of this confidence is put to a test somewhat more severe; and we find nevertheless that Captain Flinders staked the safety of his ship and the existence of himself and his crew on the truth of the above proposition.' Nowadays, indeed, the principal use of a barometer to a navigator aboard ship is to enable him to anticipate changes of wind.

Not less important were his experiments and writings upon variations of the compass aboard ship. The fact that the needle of a compass showed deviations on being moved from one part of a ship to another had been observed by navigators in the eighteenth century, but Flinders was the first to experiment systematically to ascertain the cause and to invent a remedy.[3]

He observed not only that the direction of the needle varied according to the part of the ship where it was placed, but also that a change in the direction of the ship's head made a difference. Further, he found that in northern latitudes (in the English Channel, for instance) the north end of the needle was attracted towards the bow of the ship; whilst in southern latitudes, in Bass Strait, there was an attraction towards the stern; and at the equator there was no deviation. He came to the conclusion that these results were due to the presence of iron in the ship. When he returned to England in 1810, he wrote a memorandum on the subject to the Admiralty, and requested that experiments might be made upon ships of the navy, with the object of verifying a law which he had deduced from a long series of observations. His conclusion was that 'the magnetism of the earth and the attraction forward in the ship must act upon the needle in the nature of a compound force, and that errors produced by the attraction should be proportionate to the sines of the angles between the ship's head and the magnetic meridian'. Experiments were made at Sheerness, Portsmouth, and Plymouth on five vessels. He took a keen personal interest in them; and the result was his invention of the Flinders' bar, which is now used in every properly equipped ship in the world. The purpose of the bar, which is a vertical rod of soft iron, placed so that its upper end is level with or slightly above the compass needle, is to compensate for the effect of the vertical soft iron in the ship.[4] Flinders'

---

[3] For the history of the matter see Alexander Smith's Introduction to W. Scoresby's *Journal of a Voyage to Australia for Magnetic Research* (1859).

[4] See the excellent chapter entitled 'Compasses' in Vol. II of the British Admiralty's *Manual of Seamanship.*

work upon this technical subject was important even in the days of wooden ships. In this era of iron and steel ships it is regarded by every sailor as of the utmost value.

In Flinders' day the delicacy of the compass, its liability to error, the nature of the magnetic force to which it responds, and the necessity for care in its handling, were very little appreciated. 'Among the nautical instruments taken to sea there are not any so ill-constructed, nor of which so little care is taken afterwards, as the compass,' he did not hesitate to write.[5] Compasses were supplied to the Admiralty by contract, and were not inspected. They were stowed in storehouses without any regard to the attraction to which the needles might be exposed. They might be kept in store for a few years; and they were then sent on board ships without any re-touching, 'for no magnets were kept in the dockyards, and probably no person there ever saw them used'. When a compass was sent aboard a ship of the navy, it was delivered into the charge of the boatswain and put into his store or sailroom. Perhaps it was put on a shelf with his knives and forks and a few marline-spikes. Flinders urged that spare compasses should be preserved carefully in officers' cabins. Magnets for re-touching were not kept in one ship in a hundred. Under these circumstances, he asked,

> *can it be a subject of surprise that the most experienced navigators are those who put the least confidence in the compass, or that ships running three or four days without an observation should be found in situations very different from what was expected, and some of them lost? The currents are easily blamed, and sometimes with reason. Ships coming home from the Baltic and finding themselves upon the shores of the Dutch coast, when they were thought to be on the English side, lay it to the currents; but the same currents, as I am informed, do not prevail when steering in the opposite direction.*

The last is a neat stroke of irony. Flinders strongly recommended that the Admiralty should appoint an inspector of compasses, that there should be at every dockyard an officer for re-touching compasses, and that a magnet for re-touching should be carried on each flagship. The recommendations may seem like a counsel of elementary precautions today, but they involved an important reform of method in 1810.

---

[5] MS., 'Chapter in the History of Magnetism'; Flinders' Papers; another copy was sent to the Admiralty.

Flinders also wrote on the theory of the tides; a set of notes on the magnetism of the earth exists in manuscript; a manuscript of 106 pages, consisting of a treatise on spheric trigonometry, is illustrated by beautifully drawn diagrams, and includes an account of eight practical methods of calculating latitude and five of calculating longitude. In Mauritius he read all he could obtain about the history of the island, and wrote a set of notes on Grant's *History*.

He was eager to praise the work of previous navigators. La Pérouse was especially a hero of his, and he wrote in French for the Société d'Emulation of Ile-de-France an account of the probable fate of that celebrated sailor. In an eloquent passage in this essay, speaking of the wreck, he cried:

> *O, Lapérouse, my heart speaks to me of the agony that rent yours. Ah, your eyes beheld the hapless companions of your dangers and your glory fall one after another exhausted into the sea. Ah, your eyes saw the fruit of vast and useful labours lost to the world. I think of your sorrowing family. The picture is too painful for me to dwell upon it; but at least when all human hope abandoned you, then—the last blessing that God gives to the good—a ray of consolation shone upon your eyes, and showed you that beyond those furious waves which broke upon your vessels and swept away from you your companions another refuge was opened to your virtues by the angel of pity.*

Knowing the extreme difficulties attaching to navigation, even when in the public interest he had to make a correction in the work of others, he was anxious to cause no irritation. He sent to the editor of the *Naval Chronicle* a correction in Horsburgh's *Directions for Sailing to and from the East Indies*, but requested the editor to submit it first to the author of that work, and to suppress publication if Horsburgh so desired. He never expressed a tinge of regret that he had chosen a field of professional employment wherein promotion and reward were not liberally bestowed. Entering the navy under influential auspices, in a period when active service provided plentiful scope for advancement, he deliberately preferred the explorer's hard lot. The only prizemoney he ever won was £10 after Lord Howe's victory in 1794. 'I chose a branch,' he said in a letter to Banks, 'which though less rewarded by rank and fortune is yet little less in celebrity. If adverse fortune does not oppose me, I will succeed.' He succeeded beyond all he could have hoped.

The excellence of his charts was such that to this day the Admiralty charts for those portions of the Australian coast where he did original work bear upon them the honoured name of Matthew Flinders; and amongst the seamen who habitually traverse these coasts, no name, not even that of Cook, is so deeply esteemed as his. Flinders is not a tradition; the navigators of our own time count him a companion of the watch.

XXX

THE NAMING OF AUSTRALIA

THE name Australia was given to the great southern continent by Flinders. When and why he gave it that name will now be shown.

In the first place a common error must be set right. It is sometimes said that the Spanish navigator, Pedro Fernandez de Quiros, named one of the islands of the New Hebrides group, in 1606, Australia del Espiritu Santo. This is not the case. The narrative of his voyage described 'all this region of the south as far as the Pole which from this time shall be called Austrialia del Espiritu Santo', from 'His Majesty's title of Austria'. The word 'Austrialia' is a punning name. Quiros's sovereign, Philip III, was a Habsburg; and Quiros, in compliment to him, devised the name 'Austrialia' as combining the meaning 'Austrian land', as well as 'southern land'.[1]

In 1756 the word 'Australasia' was coined. Charles de Brosses, in his *Histoire des Navigations aux Terres Australes*, wanted a word to signify a new division of the globe. The maps marked off Europe, Asia, Africa and America, but the vast region to the south of Asia required a name likewise. De Brosses simply added 'Austral' to 'Asia', and printed 'Australasia' upon his map.

The earliest use of the word 'Australia' that I have been able to find, occurs in the index to the Dutch *Generale Beschrijvinge van Indien* (General Description of the Indies) published at Batavia in 1638. The work consists mainly of accounts of voyages by Dutch vessels to the East Indies. Among them is a history of the 'Australische Navigatien' of Jacob Le Maire and Willem Cornelisz Schouten, made in 1615–17. They sailed through the Straits of Magellan, crossed the Pacific, touched at the Solomon Islands, and thence made their way round by the north of New Guinea to Java. The word 'Australia' does not occur anywhere in the

---

[1] See Markham, *Voyages of Quiros* (Hakluyt Society), Vol. I, p. xxx.

black-letter text of the narrative, and the word 'Australische' in the phrase 'Australische Navigatien', simply means southern. There are references in the book to 'Terra Australis', but Le Maire and Schouten knew not Australia. Nor does the narrative make any allusion to the continent which we know by that name. The Terra Australis of these Dutch navigators was land of the southern hemisphere in general. But, curiously, the indexer of the *Generale Beschrijvinge* made four entries, in which he employed the word 'Australia'. Thus, his entry 'Australia Incognita Ondeckt' (Australia Incognita Discovered) referred to passages in Le Maire and Schouten's voyage relating to the southern lands they had seen. But it did not refer to the Australia of modern geography. It is very strange that the Dutch indexer in Batavia should have hit upon the word and employed it when he did not find it in the text of the book itself.

The use of 'Australia' in an English book of 1693 is also extremely curious. In 1676 Gabriel de Foigny, under the assumed name of Jacques Sadeur, published at Vannes a quaint little duodecimo [24-page] volume, purporting to give a description of an unknown southern land. He called his book *La Terre Australe connue; c'est à dire, la description de ce pays inconnu jusqu'ici.* [The known South Land, that is to say, the description of that country unknown until now.] It was a 'voyage imaginaire', a pure piece of fancy. In 1693 it was translated into English, and published in London, by John Dunton, under the title *A New Discovery of Terra Incognita, or the Southern World, by James Sadeur, a Frenchman, who being cast there by a shipwreck, lived 35 years in that country and gives a particular description of the manners, customs, religion, laws, studies and wars of those southern people, and of some animals peculiar to that place; with several other rarities.* In the original French the word Australia does not occur. But in the English translation Foigny's phrase 'continent de la Terre Australe', is rendered 'Australia'. Foigny's ingenious piece of fiction drew its 'local colour' from the South American region, not from any supposed land in the neighbourhood of the Australian continent. The instance is all the more interesting from the possibility that the book may have given a hint to Swift in the writing of *Gulliver's Travels.*[2]

In 1770–71 Alexander Dalrymple published *An Historical Collection of Voyages and Discoveries in the South Pacific Ocean.* In the preface to that work he used the word 'Australia' as 'comprehending the

---

[2] See the *Cambridge History of English Literature*, IX, p. 106; where, however, the English translation is erroneously cited as *Journey of Jacques Sadour to Australia.*

discoveries at a distance from America to the eastward'.[3] He did not intend it to include the present Australia at all. De Brosses had used the three names Magellanica, Polynesia and Australasia, which Dalrymple accepted; but he thought there was room for a fourth for the area east of South America. The part of the Australian continent known when Dalrymple published his book—only the west and northern coasts—was included within the division which De Brosses called Australasia.

Here we have three instances of the use of the word 'Australia' in the seventeenth and eighteenth centuries, but without reference to the continent which now bears that name.

In 1793, G. Shaw and J. E. Smith published in London a *Zoology and Botany of New Holland.* Here the word Australia was used in its modern sense, as applied to the southern continent. The authors wrote of 'the vast island, or rather continent, of Australia, Australasia, or New Holland, which has so lately attracted the particular attention of European navigators and naturalists'.

The word was not therefore of Flinders' devising. But it may be taken to be certain that he was unacquainted with the previous employment of it by the Dutch indexer, by Foigny's English translator, or by Shaw and Smith. It is doubtful whether he had observed the previous use of it by Dalrymple. Undoubtedly he had read that author's book. He may have had the volumes in his cabin library. But he was so exact and scrupulous a man that we can say with confidence that, had he remembered the occurrence of the word in Dalrymple, he would have mentioned the fact. The point is not material, however, because, as already observed, Dalrymple did not apply 'Australia' to this continent, but to a different region. The essential point is that 'Australia was reinvented by Flinders'.[4]

Flinders felt the need of a single word that would be a good name for the island which had been demonstrated by his own researches to be one great continent. It will be remembered that he had investigated the whole extent of the southern coasts, had penetrated to the extremities of the two great gulfs found there, had proved that they did not open into a passage cutting Terra Australis in two, and had thoroughly examined the Gulf of Carpentaria, finding no inlet southward there. The country was clearly one immense whole. But what was it to be called? Terra Australis, Southern Land, was too long, was cumbrous [cumbersome], was Latin. That would not be a convenient name for a country that was

[3] p. xv of the 1780 edition of Dalrymple.

[4] Morris, *Dictionary of Austral English*, p. 10.

to play any part in the world. The Dutch had named the part which they found New Holland. But they knew nothing of the east. Cook called the part which he had discovered New South Wales. But Cook knew nothing of the west. Neither the Dutch nor Cook knew anything of the south, a large part of which Flinders himself had discovered.

We find him for the first time using the word 'Australia' in a letter written to his brother Samuel on 25 August 1804.[5] He was then living at Wilhelm's Plains: 'I call the whole island Australia, or Terra Australis. New Holland is properly that portion of it from 135° of longitude westward; and eastward is New South Wales, according to the Governor's patent.'

Flinders' first public use of the word was not in English, but in French. In the essay on the probable fate of La Pérouse, written for the Société d'Emulation in Ile-de-France (1807), he again stated the need for a word in terms which I translate as follows:

> *The examination of the eastern part was commenced in 1770 by Captain Cook, and has since been completed by English navigators.*[6] *The first (i.e., the west) is New Holland properly so called, and the second bears the name of New South Wales. I have considered it convenient to unite the two parts under a common designation which will do justice to the discovery rights of Holland and England, and I have with that object in view had recourse to the name Austral-land or Australia. But it remains to be seen whether the name will be adopted by European geographers.*[7]

After 1804 Flinders repeatedly used the word 'Australia' in his correspondence. Before that date he had invariably written of 'New Holland'. But in a letter to Banks (31 December 1804) he referred to 'my general chart of Australia';[8] in March 1806, he wrote of 'the north-west coast of Australia';[9] in July 1806, writing to the King he underlined the word in the phrase 'my discoveries in Australia';[10] in July 1807, he spoke

---

[5] Flinders' Papers.

[6] By himself; but in this paper he modestly said nothing of his own researches.

[7] 'Il reste a savoir si ce nom sera adopté par des géographes européens.' The paper was printed in the *Annales des Voyages* by Malte-Brun (Paris, 1810). Flinders kept a copy, and his manuscript is now in the Melbourne Public Library. It is an exquisite piece of calligraphy, perhaps the most beautifully written of all his manuscripts.

[8] *Historical Records*, V, 531.

[9] ibid, VI, 50.

[10] ibid, VI, 107.

of 'the north coast of Australia';[11] in February 1809, of 'the south coast of Australia';[12] and the same phrase was employed in January 1810.[13] It is therefore apparent that before his return to England he had determined to use the name systematically and to make its employment general as far as he could. We do not find it occurring in any other correspondence of the period.

When he reached England in 1810 and commenced to work upon his book, he wished to use the name 'Australia', and brought the subject forward at a meeting at Sir Joseph Banks' house. But Banks was not favourable, and Arrowsmith, the chart-publisher, 'did not like the change' because his firm had always used the name New Holland in their charts. A Major Rennell was present at one of the meetings, when Flinders thought he had converted Sir Joseph. But afterwards he found Banks disinclined to sanction the name, and wrote to Major Rennell asking whether he remembered the conversation. The Major replied (15 August 1812):[14] 'I certainly think that it was as you say, that Australia was the proper name for the continent in question; and for the reason you mention. I suppose I must have been of that opinion at the time, for I certainly think so now. It wants a collective name.'

Two days after the receipt of Major Rennell's letter Flinders wrote to Banks, reminding him that he was the first person consulted about the name 'Australia'; and that he had understood that it was generally approved. Bligh had not objected to it. When part of the manuscript of the *Voyage* was submitted to Mr Robert Peel, Under-Secretary for the Colonies (afterwards Sir Robert Peel and Prime Minister of England), and to Lord Liverpool, the principal Secretary of State, there had been some discussion respecting the inclusion of the Gulf of Carpentaria as part of New South Wales, and it was accordingly erased. But no objection was raised to the name 'Australia'. Flinders fought hard for his word, but did not succeed completely. Captain Burney suggested that Terra Australis was a name 'more familiar to the public'. Banks on 19 August withdrew his objection to 'the propriety of calling New Holland and New South Wales by the collective name of Terra Australis', and accordingly as *A Voyage to Terra Australis* his book ultimately went forth. The work being published under the aegis of the Admiralty, he had to conform to the opinion of those who were less sensible of the need for

---

[11] ibid, VI, 274.

[12] ibid, VII, 52.

[13] ibid, VII, 275.

[14] Flinders' Papers.

an innovation than he was, and it was only in a modest footnote that he used the name he preferred. The passage in the book wherein he discussed the question may be quoted, together with his footnote:

> *The vast regions to which this voyage was principally directed comprehend, in the western part, the early discoveries of the Dutch, under the name of New Holland; and in the east the coasts explored by British navigators, and named New South Wales. It has not, however, been unusual to apply the first appellation to both regions; but to continue this would be almost as great an injustice to the British nation, whose seamen have had so large a share in the discovery as it would be to the Dutch were New South Wales to be so extended. This appears to have been felt by a neighbouring, and even rival, nation; whose writers commonly speak of these countries under the general term of Terres Australes. In fact, the original name, used by the Dutch themselves until some time after Tasman's second voyage in 1644, was Terra Australis, or 'Great South Land;' and, when it was displaced by 'New Holland,' the new term was applied only to the parts lying westward of a meridian line passing through Arnhem's Land on the north, and near the isles of St. Francis and St. Peter on the south; all to the eastward, including the shores of the Gulf of Carpentaria, still remained as Terra Australis. This appears from a chart published by Thevenot in 1663; which, he says 'was originally taken from that done in inlaid work upon the pavement of the new Stadt-House at Amsterdam.' The same thing is to be inferred from the notes of Burgomaster Witsen in 1705 of which there will be occasion to speak in the sequel.*
>
> *It is necessary, however, to geographical precision, that so soon as New Holland and New South Wales were known to form one land, there should be a general name applicable to the whole; and this essential point having been ascertained in the present voyage, with a degree of certainty sufficient to authorise the measure, I have, with the concurrence of opinions entitled to deference, ventured upon the adoption of the* original Terra Australis; *and of this term I shall hereafter make use when speaking of New Holland and New South Wales in a collective sense; and when using it in the most extensive signification, the adjacent isles, including that of Van Diemen, must be understood to be comprehended.*

> *There is no probability that any other detached body of land, of nearly equal extent, will ever be found in a more southern latitude; the name Terra Australis will, therefore, remain descriptive of the geographical importance of this country, and its situation on the globe, it has antiquity to recommend it; and, having no reference to either of the two claiming nations, appears to be less objectionable than any other which could have been selected.*

Then comes the footnote in which the name Australia is suggested: 'Had I permitted myself any innovation upon the original term, it would have been to convert it into Australia; as being more agreeable to the ear, and an assimilation to the names of the other great portions of the earth.'

The name came into general use after the publication of Flinders' book, though it was not always adopted in official documents. Governor Macquarie, of New South Wales, in a despatch in April 1817, expressed the hope that the name would be authoritatively sanctioned.[15] As already noted, the officials of 1849 drew a distinction between New Holland, the mainland, and Australia, which included the island of Tasmania; and so Sir Charles Fitzroy, Governor of New South Wales, was styled 'Governor-General of Australia', in a commission dated 1851. The proudest of all places wherein this name is used is in the forefront of the majestic instrument cited as 63 and 64 Vict., cap. XII.—'An Act to constitute the Commonwealth of Australia'.

---

[15] See M. Phillips, *A Colonial Autocracy* (London, 1909) p. 2, note.

APPENDICES

APPENDIX A
BAUDIN'S ACCOUNT OF ENCOUNTER BAY

[In a long letter of about 30,000 words, written to the French Minister of Marine from Port Jackson in 1802, Captain Baudin described his explorations in Australian waters up to that date. The manuscript is in the Archives Nationales, Paris, BB4, 995, Marine. It has never been published. In this appendix, which relates to Chapter XIV of the book, I translate the portion of the letter concerning the meeting of the *Investigator* and *Le Géographe* in Encounter Bay, with a few notes.]

> *'On the 18th,*[1] *continuing to follow the coast and the various coves upon it, we sighted towards the northeast a long chain of high mountains, which appeared to terminate at the border of the sea. The weariness we had for a long time experienced at seeing coasts which for the most part were arid, and offered not the slightest resource, was dissipated by the expectation of coming upon a more promising country. A little later, a still more agreeable object of distraction presented itself to our view. A square-sailed ship was perceived ahead. Nobody on board had any doubt that it was* Le Naturaliste. *As she was tacking south and we were tacking north, we approached each other. But what was our astonishment when the other vessel hoisted a white flag on the mainmast. It was beyond doubt a signal of recognition, to which we responded. A little later, that signal was hauled down, and an English ensign and pennant were substituted.*[2] *We replied by hoisting our colours; and we*

[1] That is, the 18th Germinal in the French revolutionary calendar; 8 April by the Gregorian calendar.

[2] Flinders says: 'Our colours being hoisted, she showed a French ensign, and afterwards an English jack forward, as we did a white flag'.

continued to advance towards each other. The manoeuvre of the English ship indicating that she desired to speak to us, we stood towards her.[3] *When we got within hail, a voice enquired what ship we were. I replied simply that we were French. 'Is that Captain Baudin?' 'Yes, it is he.' The English captain then saluted me graciously, saying 'I am very glad to meet you.' I replied to the same effect, without knowing to whom I was speaking; but, seeing that arrangements were being made for someone to come on board, I brought the ship to.*

Mr. Flinders, who commanded the English vessel, presented himself. As soon as I learnt his name, I no longer doubted that he, like ourselves, was occupied with the exploration of the south coast of New Holland; and, in spite of the reserve that he showed upon that first visit, I could easily perceive that he had already completed a part of it. Having invited him to come into my cabin, and finding ourselves alone there, the conversation became freer.[4]

He informed me that he had left Europe about eight months after us, and that he was bound for Port Jackson, having previously refreshed at the Cape of Good Hope.

I had no hesitation about giving him information concerning what we had been doing upon the coast until that moment. I pointed out to him defects which I had observed in the chart which he had published[5] *of the strait separating New Holland from Van Diemen's Land, etc., etc.*

Mr. Flinders observed to me that he was not unaware that the chart required to be checked, inasmuch as the sketch from which it was prepared had been drawn from uncertain information, and that the means employed when the discovery was made did not conduce to securing exact results.[6] *Finally, becoming less circumspect than he had hitherto been, he told*

---

[3] Flinders' own explanation of his manoeuvring is: 'We veered round as *Le Géographe* was passing so as to keep our broadside to her lest the flag of truce should be a deception.'

[4] 'Nous trouvant seul, la conversation devint plus libre.' Flinders says that Brown accompanied him, and went into the cabin with him. 'No person was present at our conversations except Mr. Brown.'

[5] 'la carte qu'il nous a donné des détroits'. From this it appears that Baudin knew Flinders as the author of the chart, even while pointing out its defects. Flinders had the impression that Baudin did not know him till he was about to leave *Le Géographe* at the end of the second interview.

[6] Flinders: 'On my pointing out a note upon the chart, explaining that the north side of the strait was seen only in an open boat by Mr. Bass, who had no good means of fixing either latitude or longitude, he appeared surprised, not having before paid attention to it.'

me that he had commenced his work at Cape Leeuwin, and had followed the coast to the place where we were met. He suggested that our ships should pass the night near together, and that early on the following morning he should come on board again, and give me some particulars which would be useful to me. I accepted his proposition with pleasure, and we tacked about at a short distance from each other during the night. It was seven o'clock in the evening when he returned to his ship.[7]

On the 19th[8] *Mr. Flinders came on board at six o'clock in the morning. We breakfasted together,*[9] *and talked about our respective work. He appeared to me to have been happier than we had been with respect to the discoveries he had made. He told me about a large island, about a dozen or fifteen leagues away, which had been visited by him. According to his account, he stayed there six weeks to prepare a chart of it;*[10] *and with the aid of a corvette*[11] *had explored two deep gulfs, the direction of which he sketched for me, as well as of his Kangaroo Island, which he had so named in consequence of the great quantity of those quadrupeds found there. The island, though not far from the continent, did not appear to him to be inhabited.*

An accident like that which had unfortunately happened to us on the coast of Van Diemen's Land had overtaken Mr. Flinders.[12] *He had lost a boat and eight men. His ship was also short of stores, and he was not without uneasiness as to what would happen.*

---

[7] Flinders: 'I told him that some other and more particular charts of the strait and its neighbourhood had since been published; and that if he would keep company until next morning I would bring him a copy with a small memoir belonging to them. This was agreed to.'

[8] 9 April.

[9] Flinders does not mention this incident.

[10] A mistake; Flinders was at Kangaroo Island only six days.

[11] Péron also had the erroneous impression that the *Investigator* had been accompanied by a corvette, which foundered in Spencer's Gulf, and so wrote in his *Voyage de Découvertes.* Baudin must have confused what Flinders told him about the drowning of Thistle and the boat's crew, with an idea of his own that this boat was a consort of the *Investigator* as *Le Naturaliste* was of *Le Géographe.*

[12] Baudin was referring to a boat party of his own, consisting of Boullanger, one of his hydrographers, a lieutenant and eight sailors. They had gone out in a boat to chart a portion of the coast which *Le Géographe* could not reach. They did not return, and Baudin supposed them to have been lost. But they were in fact picked up by the sealing brig *Snow-Harrington* from Sydney, which afterwards sighted *Le Naturaliste*, and handed the men over to her.

Before we separated the Captain asked me if I had any knowledge of an island which was said to exist to the north of the Bass Strait islands. I replied that I had not, inasmuch as, having followed the coast fairly closely after leaving the Promontory as far as Westernport, I had not met with any land placed in the position which he indicated.[13] *He appeared to be well pleased with my response, doubtless in the hope of being the first to discover it. Perhaps* Le Naturaliste, *in searching for us in the Strait, will have discovered it.*[14] *At the moment of his departure, Mr. Flinders presented me with several new charts, published by Arrowsmith, and a printed memoir by himself, dealing with discoveries in the strait, the north coast of Van Diemen's Land, the east coast, etc., etc. He also invited me to sail, like himself, for Port Jackson, the resources of which he perhaps exalted too highly, if I had to remain long in these seas. At eight o'clock we*[15] *separated. He sailed south and we went to the west.*

[13] What Flinders asked Baudin was whether he had any 'knowledge concerning a large island said to lie in the western entrance of Bass Strait. But he had not seen it and seemed to doubt much of its existence.' The reference was to King Island. Baudin marked on his chart, in consequence of this enquiry, an island 'believed to exist', guessing at its situation and placing it wrongly; though he subsequently stayed at King Island himself.

[14] This sentence is interesting, as showing that Baudin wrote this part of his letter to the Minister at the time, not at Port Jackson weeks later. If the sentence had been written later, he would not have said that *Le Naturaliste* would perhaps sight the island. He by then knew that she did not.

[15] Flinders: 'I returned with Mr. Brown on board the *Investigator* at half-past-eight in the morning and we then separated from *Le Géographe*; Captain Baudin's course being directed to the north-west and ours to the southward.'

APPENDIX B
PÉRON'S REPORT ON PORT JACKSON

[The following is a fairly literal translation of Péron's report on Port Jackson, furnished to General Decaen at Ile-de-France.]

Port N.-O., 20th Frimaire,
Year 12[1]
Citizen Captain-General,

Fifteen years ago England transported, at great expense, a numerous population to the eastern coast of New Holland. At that time this vast continent was still almost entirely unknown. These southern lands and the numerous archipelagoes of the Pacific were invaded by the English, who had solemnly proclaimed themselves sovereign over the whole dominion extending from Cape York to the southern extremity of New Holland, that is to say, from 10° 37' S., to 43° 39' S. latitude. In longitude their positions had been fixed as reaching from 105° W. of Greenwich to the middle of the Pacific Ocean, including all the archipelagoes with which it is strewn.[2]

Note especially in this respect that in the formal deed of annexation no exact boundary was fixed on the Pacific Ocean side. This omission seems to have been the result of astute policy; the English Government thus prepared for itself an excuse for claiming, at the right time and place, all the islands which in the future may be, or actually are, occupied by the Spaniards—who thus find themselves England's next-door neighbours.

---

[1] i.e., Port North-West (Port Louis), 11 December 1802.

[2] This is a literal translation of Péron's statement, which is obviously confused and wrong. 105° W. long. is east of Easter Island, as well as being an 'exact boundary' in the Pacific, which, Péron goes on to say, did not exist. The probability is that he gives here a muddled reproduction of the boundaries actually fixed by Phillip's commission—'westward as far as the 135th degree of east longitude ... including all the islands adjacent in the Pacific Ocean.' [Mr. Jose's note.]

So general a project of encroachment alarmed, as it must, all the nations of Europe. The sacrifices made by England to maintain this colony redoubled their suspicions. The Spanish expedition of Admiral Malaspina[3] *had not fulfilled the expectations of its Government. Europe was still ignorant of the nature of the English settlement; its object was unknown; its rapid growth was not even suspected.*

Always vigilant in regard to whatever may humiliate the eternal rival of our nation, the First Consul, soon after the revolution of the 18th Brumaire,[4] *decided upon our expedition.*[5] *His real object was such that it was indispensable to conceal it from the Governments of Europe, and especially from the Cabinet of St. James's. We must have their unanimous consent; and that we might obtain this, it was necessary that, strangers in appearance to all political designs, we should occupy ourselves only with natural history collections. Such a large expenditure had been incurred to augment the collections of the Museum of the Republic that the object of our voyage could not but appear to all the world as a natural consequence of the previous action of our Government. It was far from being the case, however, that our true purpose had to be confined to that class of work; and if sufficient time permitted it would be very easy for me, citizen Captain-General, to demonstrate to you that all our natural history researches, extolled with so much ostentation by the Government, were merely a pretext for its enterprise, and were intended to assure for it the most general and complete success. So that our expedition, so much criticised by faultfinders, so much neglected by the former administrators of this colony, was in its principle, in its purpose, in its organization, one of*

---

[3] Two Spanish ships, commanded by Don Alexandro Malaspina, visited Sydney in April 1793. They had left Cadiz on an exploring and scientific expedition in July 1789.

[4] It was on the 18th Brumaire (9 November 1799) that Bonaparte overthrew the Directory by a coup-d'état, and became First Consul of the French Republic.

[5] Péron's statement is quite wrong. The matter of despatching an expedition to Australia had been considered and proposed to the Government by the professors of the Museum two years before the coup-d'état of Brumaire: before therefore Bonaparte had anything to do with the Government. Their letter to the Minister, making this proposal, is dated 12th Thermidor, year 6—that is, 31 July 1797. Bonaparte was then a young general commanding the army of Italy. The project was taken up by the Institute of France, and Bonaparte, as First Consul, sanctioned the expedition in May 1800. There is no evidence that he ever gave a thought to the matter until it was brought before him by the Institute.

those brilliant and important conceptions which ought to make our present Government for ever illustrious. Why was it that, after having done so much for the success of these designs, the execution of them was confided to a man utterly unfitted in all possible respects to conduct them to their proper issue?

You have asked me, General, to communicate to you such information as I have been able to procure upon the colony of Port Jackson. A work of that kind would be as long as it would be important; and, prepared as I conceive it ought to be, and as I hope it will be when presented to the French Government, it would fix our attention to some useful purpose upon that growing snare of a redoubtable power. Unfortunately, duty has made demands upon me until to-day, and now that I find myself a little freer our departure is about to take place. Moreover, all the information we have collected upon the regions in question is deposited in the chest which has to be forwarded, sealed, to the Government, and without access to this the notes that I should desire to furnish to you cannot be completed. Nevertheless, in order to contribute as far as possible to your enlightenment on the subject, I take the liberty of furnishing you with some particulars of the new establishment. In asking you to excuse, on account of the circumstances, faults both of style and of presentation, I venture to assure you, General, that you can rely upon my jealous exactitude in fulfilling as far as was in my power the intention of the Government of my country. I have neglected no means of procuring all the information that as far as I could foresee would be of interest. I was received in the house of the Governor with much consideration. He and his secretary spoke our language well. The commandant of the troops of New South Wales, Mr. Paterson, a member of the Royal Society of London, a very distinguished savant, *always treated me with particular regard. I was received in his house, as one might say, as a son. I have through him known all the officials of the colony. The surgeon, a distinguished man, Mr. Thompson, honoured me with his friendship. Mr. Grimes, the surveyor of the colony, Mr. Palmer the commissary-general of the Government, Mr. Marsden, a clergyman of Parramatta, and a cultivator as wealthy as he is discerning, were all capable of furnishing me with valuable information. My functions on board permitted me to hazard the asking of a large number of questions which would have been indiscreet on the part of another, particularly on the part of soldiers. I have, in a word, known at Port Jackson all the principal people of the colony, in all vocations, and each of them has furnished, unsuspectingly, information as valuable as it is new. Finally, I made with Mr. Paterson very long excursions into the interior of the country. I saw most of the best farms, and I assure you that I have gathered everywhere interesting ideas upon things, which I have taken care to make exact as possible.*

1ST—PRESENT ESTABLISHMENTS OF THE ENGLISH.

Whilst in Europe they are spoken of as the colony of Botany Bay, as a matter of fact there is no establishment there. Botany Bay is a humid, marshy, rather sterile place, not healthy, and the anchorage for vessels is neither good nor sure.

Port Jackson, thirteen leagues from Botany Bay, is unquestionably one of the finest ports in the world. It was in these terms that Governor Phillip spoke of it, and certainly he did not exaggerate when he added that a thousand ships of the line could easily manoeuvre within it. The town of Sydney has been founded in the heart of this superb harbour. It is already considerable in extent, and, like its population, is growing rapidly. Here reside the Governor and all the principal Government officers. The environs of Sydney are sandy and not very fertile; in almost all of them there is a scarcity of water during the hot summer months.

Parramatta is the largest town founded by the English. It is in the interior of the country, about six leagues from Sydney, from which it can be reached by a small river called the Parramatta River. Small vessels can proceed close to the town; larger ones have to discharge some distance away. A very fine road leads overland from Sydney to Parramatta. Some very good houses have been built here and there along the road. Already people who have made considerable fortunes are to be found there. The land around Parramatta is of much better quality than that at Sydney. The country has been cleared to a considerable extent; and grazing in particular presents important advantages.

Toongabbie, further inland, three or four leagues from Parramatta, is still more fertile. Its pasture are excellent. It is there that the flocks belonging to the Government have been established.

Hawkesbury, more than 60 miles from Sydney, is in the vicinity of the Blue Mountains. It is the richest and most fruitful of the English establishments. It may be regarded as the granary of the colony, being capable by itself of supplying nearly all the wants of the settlement. The depth of soil in some parts is as much as 80 feet; and it is truly prodigious in point of fertility. These incalculable advantages are due to the alluvial deposits of the Hawkesbury River, which descends in cascades from the summits of the Blue Mountains, and precipitates itself upon the plain loaded with a thick mud of a quality eminently suitable for promoting vegetable growth. Unfortunately with benefits such as are conferred by the Nile it unites its inconveniences. It is subject to frightful floods, which overwhelm everything. Houses, crops, and flocks—everything is destroyed unless men and animals save themselves by very rapid flight. These unexpected floods are sometimes so prodigious that the water has been known to rise 60 and even 80 feet above the normal level. But what gives a great importance to the town of Hawkesbury is the facility with which large ships can reach it by the river of which I have just spoken. This part of New Holland will be a source of rapid and very large fortunes.

Castle Hill is a new establishment in the interior of New Holland, distant 21 miles from Parramatta, from which it is reached by a superb road, which traverses thick forests. Allotments of land are crowded round this place, and the clearances are so considerable that for more than a league all round the town we could see the forest grants being burnt off.

Richmond Hill, towards the Hawkesbury, is a more considerable place than the last mentioned, and is in a fertile situation.

So, General, it will be seen that this colony, which people in Europe still believe to be relegated to the muddy marshes of Botany Bay, is daily absorbing more and more of the interior of the continent. Cities are being erected, which, at present in their infancy, present evidences of future grandeur. Spacious and well-constructed roads facilitate communication with all parts, whilst important rivers render access by water still more convenient and less expensive.

But the English Government is no longer confining its operations to the eastern coast of New Holland. Westernport, on the extreme south, beyond Wilson's Promontory, is already engaging its attention. At the time of our departure a new establishment there was in contemplation. The Government is balancing the expediency of founding a new colony there or at Port Phillip, to the north.[6] *In any case, it is indubitable, from what I have heard the Governor say—it is indubitable, I say, that such a step will soon be taken. Indeed, whatever advantage Port Jackson may possess, it suffers from a grave disadvantage in the narrowness of its entry. Two frigates could by themselves blockade the most numerous fleet within. Westernport would in certain eventualities offer an advantageous position. Moreover, the navigation of Bass Strait is very dangerous. The winds there are terrible. Before negotiating the strait, ships from Europe, fatigued by a long voyage, require succour and shelter. The new establishment will be able to accommodate them. A third reason, and no doubt the most important, is that the English in spite of all their efforts, in spite of the devotion of several of their citizens, in spite of the sacrifices made by the Government, have not yet been able to traverse the redoubtable barrier of the Blue Mountains and to penetrate into the west of New Holland. An establishment on the part of the coast that I have just mentioned would guarantee them success in their efforts in that direction. At all events it is indubitable that the establishment to which I have referred will be immediately founded, if indeed such is not already the case, as appears very probable from the letter which the Governor wrote to our commandant in that regard a few days after our departure from Port Jackson.*

So then, the English, already masters of the eastern coast of New Holland, now wish to occupy the immense extent of the west and south-west coasts which contain very fine harbours, namely, that which they call Westernport, Port Phillip, Port Flinders[7] *at the head of one of the great gulfs of the south-west, Port Esperance, discovered by D'Entrecasteaux, King George's Sound, etc.*

---

[6] 'Le Port Phillip dans le nord de ce dernier.' Péron's information was correct. King had in May, 1802, made a recommendation to the British Government that a settlement should be founded at Port Phillip. The reasons, also, are stated accurately by him.

[7] Péron probably meant the present Port Augusta in Spencer's Gulf; but the name Port Flinders was his own.

But still more, General, their ambition, always aspiring, is not confined to New Holland itself, vast as it may be. Van Diemen's Land, and especially the magnificent D'Entrecasteaux Channel, have excited their cupidity. Another establishment has probably been founded there since our departure from Port Jackson. Take a glance at the detailed chart of that part of Van Diemen's Land. Look at the cluster of bays and harbours to be found there, and judge for yourself whether it is likely that that ambitious nation will permit any other power to occupy them. Therefore, numerous preparations had been made for the occupation of that important point. The authorities were only awaiting a frigate, the Porpoise,[8] *to transport colonists and provisions. That establishment is probably in existence to-day.*[9] *Several reasons will have determined it; 1st.—The indispensable necessity, for the English, of keeping away from their establishments in that part of the world rivals and neighbours as redoubtable as the French; 2nd.—The desire of removing from occupation by any other nation those impregnable ports whence their important trade with New Zealand might be destroyed and their principal establishment itself be eventually shaken; 3rd.—The fertility of the soil in that part of Van Diemen's Land, and above all the hope of discovering in the vast granite plateaux, which seems here to enclose the world, mines of precious metals or some new substance unknown to the stupid Aboriginals of the country.*

I will not refer in detail to the Furneaux and Hunter's Islands, to King Island and Maria Island. Everywhere the British flag is flown with pride. Everywhere profitable fisheries are established. Seals of various species, to be found upon these islands, open up a new source of wealth and power, to the English nation.

But New Zealand is especially advantageous to them in that regard. There is the principal seat of the wealth of their new colony. Thence a large number of ships sail annually for Europe laden with whale oil. Never, as the English themselves acknowledge, was a fishery so lucrative and so easy. The number

---

[8] Péron spells the name as it sounded to him, *La Poraperse.*

[9] Again, Péron's information was correct. A settlement on the Derwent, close to D'Entrecasteaux Channel, was ordered to be founded in March 1803, and the *Porpoise*, with the *Lady Nelson* as tender, was employed to carry colonists and supplies thither.

of vessels engaged in it is increasing rapidly. Four years ago there were but four or five. Last year there were seventeen.[10] *I shall have occasion to return to this subject.*

Let us sum up what has been said concerning the English establishments in this part of the world. Masters of the east coast of New Holland, we see them rapidly penetrating the interior of the country, clearing pressed forward on all sides, towns multiplying. Everywhere there is hope of abundance of great agricultural wealth. The south coast is menaced by coming encroachments, which, perhaps, are by now effected. All the ports of the south-west will be occupied successively, and much sooner than is commonly thought. Van Diemen's Land and all the neighbouring islands either are to be occupied or already are so. New Zealand offers to them, together with excellent harbours, an extraordinarily abundant and lucrative fishery. In a word, everything in these vast regions presents a picture of unequalled activity, unlimited foresight, swollen ambition, and a policy as deep as it is vigilant.

Well then—come forward now to the middle of these vast seas, so long unknown; we shall see everywhere the same picture reproduced, with the same effects. Cast a glance over that great southern ocean. Traverse all those archipelagoes which, like so many stepping-stones, are scattered between New Holland and the west coast of America. It is by their means that England hopes to be able to stretch her dominion as far as Peru. Norfolk Island has for a long time been occupied. The cedar that it produces, coupled with the great fertility of the soil, render it an important possession. It contains already between 1,500 and 1,800 colonists. No settlement has as yet been founded in any of the other islands, but researches are being pursued in all parts. The English land upon all the islands and establish an active commerce, by means of barter, with the natives. The Sandwich Islands, Friendly Islands, Loyalty Islands,[11] *Navigator Islands,*[12] *Marquesas and Mendore Islands all furnish excellent salt provisions. Ships, employed in trade, frequently arrive at Port Jackson; and it increases every day, proof positive of the advantage that is derived from it.*

[10] It will be remembered that Bass intended to engage in the New Zealand fishery. Cf. Chapter IX.

[11] New Caledonian Group.

[12] Samoan Group.

The Government is particularly occupied with endeavouring to discover upon some one of these archipelagoes a strong military post, a species of arsenal, nearer to the coasts of Peru and Chile.[13] *It is towards these two points that the English Government appears to be especially turning its eyes. They are quite aware of the feebleness of the Spaniards in South America. They are above all aware that the unconquered Chileans are constantly making unexpected attacks, that like so many Bedouins they appear unawares with a numerous cavalry upon places where the Spaniards are most feeble, committing robberies and outrages in all directions before sufficient forces have been collected to repulse them. Then they retire with a promptitude which does not permit of their being followed to their savage fastnesses, which are unknown to the Spaniards themselves—retreats whence they very soon reappear, to commit fresh massacres. (See the Voyage of La Pérouse.) The English, to whom nothing that occurs in those important regions is unknown, are equally aware that it is simply a deficiency in arms and ammunition which prevents the redoubtable Chileans from pushing much farther their attacks against the Spaniards. It is to the furnishing of these means that the English Government are at the present moment confining their enterprise. A very active contraband trade is calculated to enable them to carry out their perfidious ends, whilst at the same time providing a profitable market for the produce of their manufacturers. Another manner in which they torment the Spaniards of Peru is by despatching a swarm of pirates to these seas. During the last war very rich prizes were captured by simple whaling vessels, and you can judge what attacks of this kind will be like when they are directed and sustained by the English Government itself.*

Their hopes in regard to the Spanish possessions are heightened, and their projects are encouraged, by the general direction of the winds in these seas. A happy experience has at length taught the English that the prevailing wind, that which blows strongest and most constantly, is the west wind. Determined by these considerations (would you believe it, General?) the English nowadays, instead of returning to Europe from Port Jackson by traversing Bass Strait and

[13] This statement was entirely false.

doubling the Cape of Good Hope, turn their prows eastwards, abandon themselves to their favourite wind, traverse rapidly the great expanse of the South Seas, double Cape Horn, and so do not reach England until they have made the circuit of the globe! Consequently those voyages round the world, which were formerly considered so hazardous, and with which are associated so many illustrious names, have become quite familiar to English sailors. Even their fishing vessels accomplish the navigation of the globe just as safely as they would make a voyage from Europe to the Antilles. That circumstance is not so unimportant as may at first appear. The very idea of having circumnavigated the globe exalts the enthusiasm of English sailors. What navigation would not seem to them ordinary after voyages which carry with them great and terrible associations? Anyhow—and this is a most unfortunate circumstance for the Spaniards—it is indubitable that the fact of the constancy of the west wind must facilitate extraordinarily projects of attack and invasion on the part of the English, and everything sustains the belief that they will count for much in the general plan of the establishment in New Holland. Therefore the English Government appears day by day to take more interest in the colony. It redoubles sacrifices of all kinds. It endeavours in every way to increase the population as much as possible. Hardly a month passes but there arrives some ship freighted by it, laden with provisions, goods, and above all with men and women, some transported people, who have to serve practically as slaves, others free immigrants, cultivators, to whom concessions will be granted. Perhaps at first you will be astonished to learn that honest men voluntarily transport themselves with their families to the extremity of the world, to live in a country which is still savage, and which was originally, and is still actually, occupied by brigands who have been thrust from the breast of society. But your astonishment will cease when you learn under what conditions such individuals consent to exile themselves to these shores, and what advantages they are not slow in deriving from a sacrifice which must always be painful.

In the first place, before their departure from Europe, a sufficient sum is allowed to each individual to provide for the necessities of a long voyage. On board the vessel which transports them to Sydney a price is fixed for the sustenance of the immigrant and his family, if he has any. Upon his landing at Port Jackson concessions are granted to him in proportion to the number of individuals comprised in his family. A number of convicts (that is the name they give the transported persons), in proportion to the extent of the concessions granted, are placed at his disposal. A house is constructed for him; he is provided with all necessary furniture and household utensils, and all the clothes he needs; they grant him all the seed he needs to sow his land, all the tools he needs to till it, and one or more pairs of all domestic animals and several kinds of poultry. Besides, they feed him, his family, and his assigned servants during eighteen months. He is completely sustained during that period; and for the next twelve months half rations are allowed to him. At the end of that time the produce of his land is, with reason, expected to be sufficient for his requirements, and the Government leave him to his own resources.

During five years he remains free of all contribution, accumulating the produce of land all the more prolific because it is virgin. At the end of that time a slight repayment is required by the Government. This gradually and slightly increases as time goes on. But mark here, General, the profound wisdom of the English Government, that enlightened policy which guides all their enterprises and assures them success. If the new immigrant during these five years has shown himself to be a diligent and intelligent cultivator; if his clearings have been well extended and his stock is managed with prudence; if the produce of his land has increased rapidly—then, so far from finding himself a debtor to the Government, his holding is declared to be his own, and, as a recompense, fresh concessions are made to him, additional servants are assigned to him, his immunity from contributions is prolonged, and additional assistance of all sorts is extended to him. It is to these extensive and well-considered sacrifices that it is necessary to attribute the fine farms that daily increase in number in the midst of what was recently wild and uncultivated forest. Activity, intelligence and application conduce here more rapidly than elsewhere to fortune; and already several of the earlier immigrants have become very wealthy proprietors. Emulation of the noblest kind is stimulated everywhere. Experiments of all kinds are made and multiplied. The Government encourages them, and generously recompenses those who have succeeded.

What still further proves the particular interest which the English Government takes in the colony is the enormous expense incurred in procurring commodities for the new colonists. Nearly everything is furnished by the Government. Vast depots are filled with clothes and fabrics of all kinds and qualities, from the commonest to the finest. The simplest furniture and household goods are to be found alongside the most elegant. Thus the inhabitants are able to buy, at prices below those ruling in England,[14] *everything necessary to not only the bare wants of life, but also its comforts and pleasures.*

Anxious to maintain the settlement on a firm and unshakeable basis, it is to agriculture, the source of the true wealth of nations, that the English Government endeavours to direct the tastes of the inhabitants of the new colony. Different kinds of cattle have been imported, and all thrive remarkably well. The better kinds, so far from losing quality, gain in size and weight. But the improvement in sheep is especially astonishing. Never was there a country so favourable to these animals as the part of New Holland now occupied by the British. Whether it be the effect of the climate or, as I think, the peculiar quality of the herbage (almost wholly aromatic), certain it is that the flocks of sheep have multiplied enormously. It is true that the finest breeds have been imported by the Government. At first, the choicest kinds of English and Irish sheep were naturalised. Then breeds from Bengal and the Cape of Good Hope were introduced. Finally, the good fortune which seems to have conspired with the enterprise of our rivals furnished them with several pairs of merinos from Spain, which the Spanish Government at great expense were sending to the Viceroy of Peru, upon a ship which was captured upon the coast of that country by an English vessel out of Port Jackson, and which were brought thither, much to the satisfaction of the Governor, who neglected nothing to derive the fullest possible advantage from a present valuable to the colony. His endeavours have not been in vain. This species, like the others, has improved much, and there is reason to believe that in a few years Port Jackson will be able to supply valuable and abundant

[14] This statement is surprising, but probably true of part of the period when Péron was in Sydney. There was then a glut of goods, as Bass found to his cost. He had to sell commodities brought out in the *Venus* at 50 per cent below their proper values.

material for the manufacturers of England. What is most astonishing is that the Indian sheep, which naturally produce short, coarse hair instead of wool, in the course of three or four generations in this country produce a wool that can hardly be distinguished from that furnished by English breeds, or even Spanish. I have seen at the Governor's house an assortment of these different kinds of wool, which were to be sent to Lord Sydney, and I assure you that it would be difficult to find finer samples. In my excursions with Mr. Paterson, Mr. Marsden and Mr. Cox, I have seen their flocks, and really one could not but admire in that regard the incalculable influence of the industry of man, so long as it is encouraged and stimulated by enlightened and just administrators.

Another source of production which appears to offer great advantages to the English is that of hemp. In this country it is as fine in quality as it is abundant, and several persons whose testimony is beyond suspicion have assured me that New Holland, before many years have passed, will herself be able to furnish to the British Navy all the hemp that it requires, thus freeing England from the considerable tribute that she pays at present in that regard to the north of Europe.

The climate also appears to be favourable to the cultivation of the vine. Its latitude, little different from that of the Cape of Good Hope, combined with its temperature, lead the Government to hope for great advantages from the introduction of this plant to the continent of New Holland. Furthermore, French vignerons *have been introduced at great expense to promote this object. It is true that their first attempts have not been very happy, but the lack of success is due entirely to the obstinacy of the English Governor, who, in spite of the representations of these men, compelled them to make their first plantations upon the side of a small, pleasant terrace forming a kind of semi-circle round Government House at Parramatta. This was, unfortunately, exposed to the north-west winds, burning winds like the mistral of Italy and Provence, the khamsin of Egypt, etc. The French* vignerons *whom I had occasion to see at Parramatta, in company with the Lieutenant-Governor, Mr. Paterson, assured me that they had found a piece of country very favourable to their new plantations, and that they hoped for the greatest success from their fresh efforts. Choice plants had been imported from Madeira and the Cape.*

In all the English establishments on these coasts traces of grand designs for the future are evident. The mass of the people, being originally composed of the unfortunate and of wrong-doers, might have propagated immorality and corruption, if the Government had not taken in good time means to prevent such a sad result. A house was founded in the early days of the settlement for the reception of young girls whose parents were too poor and too constrained in their circumstances at the commencement of their sojourn there to be able to devote much care to them; while if parents, when emancipated, so conduct themselves that their example or their course of life is likely to have an evil effect on their offspring, the children are taken from them and placed in the home to which I have referred. There they pursue regular studies; they are taught useful arts appropriate to their sex; they are instructed in reading, writing, arithmetic, sewing, etc. Their teachers are chosen with much care, and the wife of the Governor himself is charged with the supervision of that honourable establishment, a supervision in which she is assisted by the wife of the commandant of the troops. Each or both of them visit every day their young family, as they themselves call it. They neglect nothing to ensure the maintenance of good conduct, the soundness of the education and the quality of the provisions. I have several times accompanied these admirable ladies to the establishment, and have on every occasion been moved by their anxious solicitude and their touching care.

When these young girls arrive at marriageable age they are not abandoned by the Government. The following is the sagacious and commendable manner in which their establishment in life is provided for. Among the free persons who come to Port Jackson are many men who are not yet married. The same is the case with some of those who by good conduct have earned their freedom. When one of those young men wishes to take a worthy wife, he presents himself to the Governor's wife, who, after having obtained information concerning his character, permits him to visit her young flock. If he fixes his choice upon someone, he informs the Governor's wife, who, after consulting the tastes and inclinations of the young person, accords or refuses her consent. When a marriage is arranged, the Government endows the young girl by means of concessions, assigned servants, etc.; and these unions have already become the nursery of a considerable number of good and happy homes. It is undoubtedly an admirable policy, and one which has amply rewarded the English Government for the sacrifices made to support it.

The defence of the country has not up to the present been very formidable, and has not needed to be, on account of the ignorance which prevails in Europe respecting the nature of this colony. The English Government is at the present moment directing men's minds towards agriculture. It has not, however, neglected to provide what the physical condition of the land and the nature of its establishment demand. Two classes of men are much to be feared at present: first, the criminals, condemned for the most part to a long servitude, harshly treated, compelled to the roughest and most fatiguing labour. That infamous class, the vile refuse of civilised society, always ready to commit new crimes, needs to be ceaselessly restrained by force and violence. The English Government therefore maintains a strong police. It is so efficient that in the midst of that infamous canaille *[mob] the most perfect security reigns everywhere, and—what may appear paradoxical to those who do not know the details of the administration of the colony—fewer robberies are committed than in a European town of equal population. As to murder, I have never heard tell of a crime of the kind being committed there, nor, indeed, did I hear of one occurring since the foundation of the colony. Nevertheless, the first consideration entails the maintenance of a very considerable force; and with equal foresight and steadiness the Government has taken precautions against the efforts of these bandits. A second class of society, more formidable still (also much more respectable, but having most to complain about, and the most interesting class for us), is composed of legions of the unfortunate Irish, whom the desire of freeing their country from the British yoke caused to arm in concert with us against the English Government. Overwhelmed by force, they were treated with pitiless rigour. Nearly all those who took up arms in our favour were mercilessly transported, and mixed with thieves and assassins. The first families of Ireland count their friends and relations upon these coasts of New Holland. Persecuted by that most implacable of all kinds of hatred, the hatred born of national animosity and differing convictions, they are cruelly treated, and all the more so because they are feared. Abandoned to themselves, it is felt, they can do nothing, and the Government gains several interesting advantages from their residence in this country. First, a population as numerous as it is valiant is fixed upon these shores. Secondly, nearly all being condemned to a servitude more or less long, they provide many strong arms for the laborious work of clearing. Thirdly, the mixing of so many brave men with criminals seems to obliterate the character of the settlement and to provide, by the retention of a crowd of honest men, some sort of a defence against the opprobrium cast upon it. Fourthly, the Government has relieved itself in Europe of a number of enraged and daring enemies. At the same time, one must admit, this policy has its defects. The Irish, ruled by a sceptre of iron, are quiet today. But if ever the Government of our country, alarmed by the rapidly increasing strength of this colony, should formulate the project of taking or destroying it, at the mere mention of the French name every Irish arm would be raised. We had a very striking example when we first arrived at Port Jackson. Upon the appearance of the French flag in the harbour the alarm in the country was general. We were again at war with England. They regarded our second ship,*[15] *which had been separated from us and compelled to seek shelter at Port Jackson, as a French ship of war. At the name the Irish commenced to flock together. Everywhere they raised their bowed foreheads, bent under an iron rule; and, if their mistake had not been so rapidly dispelled, a general rising would have taken place amongst them. One or two were put to death on that occasion, and several were deported to Norfolk Island. In any case, that formidable portion of the population will always compel the English to maintain many troops upon this continent, until, at all events, time and inter-marriage shall have cicatrized [healed] the recent wounds of the poor Irish and softened their resentment.*

The Government, however, appears to feel that considerably larger forces are required than are now available. At the time of our departure the regiment forming the garrison at Port Jackson did not number more than 800. But some were being continually removed to India, and to replace them 5,000 men were expected. The news of the war must have led to the changing of these dispositions, because the troops, which were to

[15] *Le Naturaliste.*

have been transported on warships, were drawn from Europe, and probably the English Government will have been careful not to despatch so considerable a force to New Holland in the critical situation in which it now finds itself. Moreover, General, do not believe that so many troops are indispensable to the security of the coasts of New Holland, but rather consider the advantages that the English nation is likely to draw from its establishments in that part of the world. The climate of India, inimical to newcomers from Europe, is still more so to these British regiments, drawn from the frosty counties of the north of England and from the icy realms of Scotland. A considerable loss of men results from their almost immediate transportation to the burning plains of India. Forced to look after a population which has little affinity with its immense possessions in both hemispheres, England has always set an example of great sacrifices for all that can tend to the conservation of the health of its people. The new colony of Port Jackson will serve in the future as a depôt for troops destined for India. Actually the whole of the territory occupied up to the present is extremely salubrious. Not a single malady endemic to the country has yet been experienced. The whole population enjoys the best of health. The children especially are handsome and vigorous, though the temperature at certain times is very high. We ourselves experienced towards the close of our visit very hot weather, though we were there in the months of Fructidor, Vendémiaire and Brumaire[16] *nearly corresponding to our European spring. The temperature of New Holland, rather more than a mean between those of England and India, ought to be valuable in preparing for the latter country that large body of soldiers which the Government despatches every year to Bengal, the Coromandel coast, Malabar, etc., etc. Consequently the loss of men will be much less, and you will easily realise the advantage that will accrue to a power like England, when it contemplates the invasion, with a mediocre population, of archipelagoes, islands, and even continents.*

NOTE:—This portion of New Holland appears to owe its salubriousness:

(1) To a situation resembling that of the Cape of Good Hope (Port Jackson is in about latitude 34°);

---

[16] From Fructidor to Brumaire would be from 22 September to 20 December.

(2) To the nature of the soil, which is very dry, especially round Sydney;
(3) To the nature of the vegetation, which is not vigorous enough to maintain a noxious stagnation in the lower strata of the atmosphere;
(4) To the great, or rather enormous, quantity of aromatic plants which constitute the principal part of the vegetation, including even the largest species;
(5) To the vicinity of the Blue Mountains, the elevation of which contributes largely to maintain a certain salutary freshness in the atmosphere;
(6) To the remarkable constancy of the light fresh breezes which blow from the south-east towards the middle of the day.
I have not yet finished the account of the important advantages that England draws from this colony. If time were not so pressing and if I had at my disposal the abundant material consigned to our Government, I could write more. I venture to sum up those considerations to which I have referred, in a form which will be useful for determining your opinion upon this important and rising colony.
(1) By means of it England founds an empire which will extend over the continent of New Holland, Van Diemen's Land, all the islands of Bass Strait, New Zealand, and the numerous archipelagoes of the Pacific Ocean.
(2) She thereby becomes the mistress of a large number of superb ports, several of which can be compared with advantage to the most fortunately situated harbours in other parts of the world.
(3) She thereby excludes her rivals, and, so to speak, blocks all the nations of Europe from entry to the Pacific.
(4) Having become the neighbour of Peru and Chile, she casts towards those countries hopes increasingly assured and greedy.
(5) Her privateers and her fleets in time of war will be able to devastate the coasts of South America; and, if in the last war she attempted no such enterprise, the reason appears to be that her astute policy made her fear to do too much to open the eyes of Spain, and even of all Europe.
(6) In time of peace, by means of an active contraband trade, she prepares redoubtable enemies for the Spaniards; she furnishes arms and ammunition of all kinds to that horde of untamed people who have not yet been subjugated to the European yoke.

(7) By the same means she enables the products of her manufacturers to inundate South America, which is shabbily and above all expensively supplied by Spain.

(8) If amongst the numerous archipelagoes that are visited constantly some formidable military position is found, England will occupy it and, becoming a nearer neighbour to the rich Spanish possessions, will menace them more closely, more certainly, and above all more impatiently. Mr. Flinders, in an expedition of discovery which is calculated to last five years, and who doubtless at the present moment is traversing the region under discussion, appears to have that object particularly in view.[17]

(9) The extraordinarily lucrative whale fishery of New Zealand is exclusively[18] *assured to them. No European nation can henceforth, according to the general opinion, compete with them for that object.*

(10) The fishery, no less lucrative, of the enormous seals which cover the shores of several of the islands of Bass Strait; and from which is drawn an oil infinitely superior to whale oil, guarantees them yet another source of greatness and of wealth. Note: the seals in question, distinguished by the English under the name of sea elephants, are sometimes 25 or 30 feet long. They attain the bulk of a large cask: and the enormous mass of the animal seems, so to say, to be composed of solid, or rather coagulated, oil. The quantity extracted from one seal is prodigious. I have collected many particulars on this subject.

(11) A third fishery, even more lucrative and important, is that of the skins of various varieties of seal which inhabit most of the islands of Bass Strait, all the Furneaux Islands, all the islands off the eastern coast of Van Diemen's Land, and all those on the south-west coast of New Holland, and which probably will be found upon the archipelagoes of the eastern portion of this vast continent. The skins of these various species of seal are much desired in China. The sale of a shipload of these goods in that country is as rapid as it is lucrative. The

---

[17] 'M. Flinders, dans une expedition de découverte qui doit durer cinq ans, et qui sans doute parcourt en ce moment le théatre qui nous occupe, paroit avoir plus particulièrement cette objet en vue.' The passage is peculiarly interesting. At the time when Péron was writing, early in December, 1803, Flinders was, as a matter of fact, sailing towards Ile-de-France in the *Cumberland.*

[18] Underlined in original.

ships engaged in the business are laden on their return to Europe with that precious merchandise of China which gold alone can extract from the clutch of its rapacious possessors. Accordingly, one of the most important objects of the mission of Lord Macartney[19] *to China, that of developing in that country a demand for some of the economic and manufacturing products of England, so as to relieve that country of the necessity of sending out such a mass of specie—that interesting object which all the ostentatious display of the commercial wealth of Europe had not been able to attain, and all the astute diplomacy of Lord Macartney had failed to achieve—the English have recently accomplished. Masters of the trade in these kinds of skin, they are about to become masters of the China trade. The coin accumulated in the coffers of the Government or of private people will no longer be sunk in the provinces of China. That advantage is incontestably one of the greatest that they have derived from their establishment at Port Jackson.*

(12) This augmentation of distant possessions is likely to occasion a fresh development in the British Navy. The practice of voyaging round the world should exalt the enthusiasm of their sailors, whilst it increases their number and efficiency. I may add here that to attain the last-mentioned end the English Government compels each ship which sails for these regions, and above all for New Zealand, to carry a certain number of young men below nineteen years of age, who return from these voyages only after having obtained a very valuable endowment of experience.

(13) The temperature and salubriousness of the country will enable it to look after a very large number of soldiers who used to be incapacitated every year by the burning heat of Asia.

(14) The abundance of the flocks, and the superiority of their wool, will furnish an immense quantity of excellent material to the national manufactures, already superior to those of the rest of Europe.

(15) The cultivation of hemp and vines gives cause to the English to hope that before very long they will be freed from

[19] Lord Macartney's embassy to China, 1792–94, was, says the *Cambridge Modern History* (II, p. 718), 'productive only of a somewhat better acquaintance between the two Powers and an increased knowledge on the part of British sailors of the navigation of Chinese waters'.

the large tribute which they now pay for the first-named to all the Powers of the north of Europe, and for the second to Portugal, France and Spain.

(16) I will not discuss with you some substances indigenous to the country which are already in use, whether in medicine, or in the arts—of eucalyptus gum, for example, which is at once astringent and tonic to a very high degree, and is likely soon to become one of our most energetic drugs. Nor will I say much about the resin furnished by the tree which the English misname gourmier,[20] *a resin which by reason of its hardness may become of very great value in the arts. It will be sufficient to say, General, that I possess a native axe obtained from the Aboriginals of King George's Sound. It is nothing better than a chip of very hard granite fastened to the end of a piece of wood, which serves as a handle, by means of the resin to which I have referred. I have shown it to several persons. It will rapidly split a wooden plank and one can strike with all one's force, without in the least degree injuring the resin. Though the edge of the stone has several times been chipped, the resin always remained intact. I will say little of the fine and abundant timber furnished by what is called the casuarina tree, and by what the English improperly call the pear. This pear is what the botanists term* Xylomelum, *and by reason of its extremely beautiful and deep grain, and the fine polish which it is susceptible of receiving, it appears to be superior to some of the best known woods. I will not refer at length to the famous flax of New Zealand, which may become the subject of a large trade when its preparation is made easier; nor to cotton, which is being naturalised; nor to coffee, of which I myself have seen the first plantations, etc., etc. All these commodities are secondary in importance in comparison with others to which I have referred; yet, considered together, they will add greatly to the importance of this new colony. Similarly, I will pass over the diverse products which are sure to be furnished by the prolific archipelagoes, and of which several are likely to become of great value and to fetch high prices for use in the arts and in medicine. For example, the cargo of the last vessel that arrived in Port Jackson from the Navigator Islands, during our stay, consisted partly of cordage of different degrees of thickness, made from a plant peculiar to*

[20] Péron's word.

those islands, the nature of which is such that, we were assured, it is almost indestructible by water and the humidity of the atmosphere; whilst its toughness makes it superior to ordinary cordage.

(17) The English hope for much from mineral discoveries. Those parts of the country lying nearest to the sea, which are of a sandstone or slaty formation, appear to contain only deposits of excellent coal; but the entire range of the Blue Mountains has not yet been explored for minerals. The colony had not up to the time of our visit a mineralogist in its service, but the Governor hoped soon to obtain the services of one, to commence making investigations; and the nature of the country, combined with its extent, affords ground for strong hope in that regard.

(18) There are, finally, other advantages, apparently less interesting, but which do not fail to exert an influence upon the character and prestige of a nation. I refer to the conspicuous glory which geographical discoveries necessarily following upon such an establishment as this bring upon a nation's name; to all that which accrues to a people from the discovery and collection of so many new and valuable things; to the distinguished services which new countries call forth and which confer so much distinction upon those who watch over their birth.

Time does not permit me to pursue the enquiry. I wish only to add here one fresh proof of the importance which England attaches to this new colony. When we left Port Jackson, the authorities were awaiting the arrival of five or six large vessels laden with the goods of English persons formerly domiciled at the Cape of Good Hope, whom the surrender of that possession to the Dutch had compelled to leave.[21] *That very great accession of population ought sufficiently to indicate to you how great are the projects of the British Ministry in that region.*

Before concluding I should have liked to point out the impossibility, for France, of retarding the rapid progress of the establishment at Port Jackson, or of entering into competition with its settlers in the trade in seal-skins, the whale fishery, etc. But it would take rather too long to discuss that matter. I think I ought to confine myself to telling you that my opinion, and that of all those among us who have more particularly occupied themselves with enquiring into the organization of

[21] The Cape was surrendered to Holland in 1803, but British rule was restored there in 1806.

that colony, is that it should be destroyed as soon as possible.[22] *To-day we could destroy it easily; we shall not be able to do so in 25 years' time.*

I have the honour to be, with respectful devotion,
Your very humble servant,
PÉRON.

P.S.—M. Freycinet, the young officer, has especially concerned himself with examining all the points upon the coast of the environs of Port Jackson which are favourable to the landing of troops. He has collected particular information concerning the entrance to the port; and, if ever the Government should think of putting into execution the project of destroying this freshly set trap of a great Power [see editor's note on p. 185],[23] *that distinguished officer would be of valuable assistance in such an operation.*

[22] 'Mon sentiment et celui de tous ceux déntre nous qui se sont plus particulièrement occupés de l'organisation de cette colonie seroit de la détruire le plus tot possible.'

[23] 'Le projet de détruire ce piège naissant d'une grande puissance.'

APPENDIX C
NAMES GIVEN BY FLINDERS TO IMPORTANT AUSTRALIAN COASTAL FEATURES

Among the Flinders' Papers is a list of names given by Flinders to points on the Australian coast, with his reasons for doing so. The list is incomplete, but has served as the basis of the following catalogue, for help in the enlargement of which I am greatly indebted to Mr Walter Jeffery:

TOM THUMB VOYAGE, WITH BASS

Hat Hill, named by Flinders from Cook's suggestion that it 'looked like the crown of a hat'.
Red Point.
Martin's Isles, after the boy who accompanied them.
Providential Cove (from the Aboriginal name, Watta-Mowlee).

VOYAGE OF THE *FRANCIS*

Green Cape.
Cape Barren Island.
Clarke Island, *Hamilton's Rocks*, after members of the crew of the *Sydney Cove.*
Kent's Group, after the captain of the *Supply*.
Armstrong's Channel, after the master of the *Supply*.
Preservation Island.

VOYAGE OF THE *NORFOLK*

Chappell Islands, after Miss Ann Chappell.
Settlement Island, *Babel Islands* (from the noises made by the sea-birds), and other names in the Furneaux Group.
Double Sandy Point.
Low Head.
Table Cape.
Circular Head.
Hunter Islands, after Governor Hunter.

Three-Hummock Island.
Barren Island.
Cape Grim.
Trefoil Island.
Albatross Island.
Mount Heemskerk and *Mount Zeehan*, after Tasman's ships.
Point Hibbs, after the Master of the *Norfolk.*
Rocky Point.
Mount de Witt.
Point St Vincent, after the First Lord of the Admiralty.
Norfolk Bay and Mount.
Cape Pillar.
After the voyage was over, Hunter, apparently at Flinders' suggestion, named *Cape Portland*, *Bass Strait*, *Port Dalrymple* and *Waterhouse Island.*

VOYAGE OF THE *NORFOLK* TO QUEENSLAND

Shoal Bay.
Sugarloaf Point.
Pumice-stone River.
Point Skirmish.
Moreton Island.
Curlew Inlet.

VOYAGE OF THE *INVESTIGATOR* (Western Australia)

Cape Leeuwin, 'the most projecting part of Leeuwin's Land'.
Mount Manypeak.
Haul-off Rock.
Cape Knob.
Mount Barren.
Lucky Bay, discovered when the ship was in an awkward position.
Goose Island.
Twin Peaks Islands.
Cape Pasley, after Admiral Pasley.
Point Malcolm, after Capt. Pulteney Malcolm.
Point Culver.
Point Dover.

VOYAGE OF THE *INVESTIGATOR* (South Australia)

Nuyts' Reefs and Cape.
Fowler's Bay and Point, after the first lieutenant of the *Investigator.*

Point Sinclair, after a midshipman on the *Investigator.*
Point Bell, after the surgeon of the *Investigator.*
Purdie's Islands, after the assistant-surgeon of the *Investigator.*
St Francis Islands, adapted from the name given by Nuyts.
Lound's Island, *Lacy's Island*, *Evans' Island*, *Franklin's Island* (in Nuyts' Archipelago), after midshipmen on the *Investigator.*
Petrel Bay.
Denial Bay, 'as well in allusion to St. Peter as to the deceptive hope we had found of penetrating by it some distance into the interior country'.
Smoky Bay, from the number of smoke columns rising from the shore.
Point Brown, after the botanist of the *Investigator.*
Streaky Bay, 'much seaweed floating about'.
Cape Bauer, after the botanical draftsman of the *Investigator.*
Point Westall, after the painter.
Olive Island, after the ship's clerk.
Cape Radstock, after Admiral Lord Radstock.
Waldegrave Isles.
Topgallant Isles.
Anxious Bay, 'from the night we passed in it'.
Investigator Group.
Pearson's Island, after Flinders' brother-in-law.
Ward's Island, after his mother's maiden name.
Flinders' Island, after Lieut. S. W. Flinders.
Cape (now *Point*) *Drummond,* after Captain Adam Drummond, R.N.
Point Sir Isaac, *Coffin's Bay*, after Vice-Admiral Sir Isaac Coffin.
Mount Greenly, *Greenly Isles*, after the lady to whom Sir Isaac Coffin was engaged.
Point Whidbey, *Whidbey's Islands*, after 'My worthy friend the Master-attendant at Sheerness'.
Avoid Bay and *Point*, 'from its being exposed to the dangerous southern winds'.
Liguanea Island, after an estate in Jamaica.
Cape Wiles, after the botanist on the *Providence.*
Williams' Isle.
Sleaford Bay, from Sleaford in Lincolnshire.
Thistle Island, after the master of the *Investigator.*
Neptune Isles, 'for they seemed inaccessible to men'.
Thorny Passage, from the dangerous rocks.
Cape Catastrophe, where the accident occurred.
Taylor's Island, after a midshipman drowned in the accident.
Wedge Island, 'from its shape'.

Gambier Isles, after Admiral Lord Gambier.
Memory Cove, in memory of the accident.
Cape Donington, after Flinders' birthplace.
Port Lincoln, after the chief town in Flinders' native county.
Boston Island, Bay and Point, *Bicker Island*, *Surfleet Point*, *Stamford Hill*, *Spalding Cove*, *Grantham Island*, *Kirton Point*, *Point Bolingbroke*, *Louth Bay and Isle*, *Sleaford Mere*, *Lusby Isle*, *Langton Isle*, *Kirkby Isle*, *Winceby Isle*, *Sibsey Isle*, *Tumby Isle*, *Stickney Isle*, *Hareby Isle.* All Lincolnshire names, after places familiar to Flinders.
Dalby Isle, after the Rev. M. Tyler's parish.
Marum Isle, after the residence of Mr Stephenson, Sir Joseph Banks' agent.
Spilsby Island, after the town where the Franklins lived.
Partney Isles, after the place where Miss Chappell lived, and where Flinders was married.
Revesby Isle, after Revesby Abbey, Banks' Lincolnshire seat.
Northside Hill.
Elbow Hill, from its shape.
Barn Hill, from the form of its top.
Mount Young, after Admiral Young.
Point Lowly.
Mount Brown, after the botanist.
Mount Arden, Flinders' great-grandmother's name.
Point Riley, after an Admiralty official.
Point Pearce, after an Admiralty official.
Corny Point, 'a remarkable point'.
Hardwicke Bay, after Lord Hardwicke.
Spencer's Gulf and Cape, after Earl Spencer.
Althorp Isles, after Lord Spencer's eldest son.
Kangaroo Island and Head.
Point Marsden, after the Second Secretary to the Admiralty.
Nepean Bay, after Sir Evan Nepean, Secretary to the Admiralty.
Mount Lofty, from its height.
St Vincent's Gulf, after Admiral Lord St Vincent.
Cape Jervis, Lord St Vincent's family name.
Troubridge Hill, after Admiral Troubridge.
Investigator Strait.
Yorke's Peninsula, after the Hon. C. P. Yorke.
Prospect Hill.
Pelican Lagoon.
Backstairs Passage.
Antechamber Bay.

Cape Willoughby.
Pages Islets.
Encounter Bay.

VOYAGE OF THE *INVESTIGATOR* (Victoria)

Point Franklin.
Indented Head (Port Phillip).
Station Peak (Port Phillip).

VOYAGE OF THE *INVESTIGATOR* (Queensland)

Tacking Point.
Mount Larcom, after Captain Larcom, R.N.
Gatcombe Head.
Port Curtis, after Admiral Sir Roger Curtis.
Facing Island, the eastern boundary of Port Curtis, facing the sea.
Port Bowen, after Captain James Bowen, R.N., Naval Commandant at Madeira when the *Investigator* put in there.
Cape Clinton, after Colonel Clinton of the 85th Regiment, Commandant at Madeira.
Entrance Island.
Westwater Head.
Eastwater Hill.
Mount Westall, after William Westall the artist.
Townshend Island, Cook had so named the Cape which is its prominent feature.
Leicester Island.
Aken's Island, after the master of the *Investigator.*
Strongtide Passage.
Double Mount.
Mount Funnel, from its form.
Upper Head.
Percy Isles, after the Northumberland family.
Eastern Fields, coral banks near Torres Strait.
Pandora's Entrance, after the *Pandora.*
Half-way Island, convenient anchorage for ships going through Torres Strait.
Good Island, after Peter Good, the botanist.

VOYAGE OF THE *INVESTIGATOR* (in the Gulf of Carpentaria)

Duyfken Point, after the first vessel which entered the Gulf of Carpentaria.

Pera Head, after the second vessel that sailed along this coast in 1623.
Sweers Island, after a member of the Batavia Council in Tasman's time.
Inspection Hill.
Lord William Bentinck's Island (now Bentinck Island), after the Governor of Madras.
Allen's Island, after the 'Miner'—i.e., geologist—of the *Investigator.*
Horseshoe Island.
Investigator Road.
Pisonia Isle, from the soft white wood of the *Pisonia* tree found upon it.
Bountiful Island.
Wellesley Island, *Mornington Isle*, after the Marquess Wellesley, Governor-General of India, whose earlier title was Lord Mornington.

VOYAGE OF THE *INVESTIGATOR* (Northern Territory)

Vanderlin Island, the Dutch 'Cape Vanderlin'.
Sir Edward Pellew Group, *Cape Pellew*, after Admiral Pellew.
Craggy Isles.
West Island.
North Island.
Centre Island.
Observation Island.
Cabbage-Tree Cove.
Maria Island, the Dutch 'Cape Maria'.
Bickerton Island, after Admiral Sir Richard Bickerton.
Cape Barrow, after Sir John Barrow.
Connexion Island.
North Point Island.
Chasm Island, 'the upper parts are intersected by many deep chasms'.
North-West Bay.
Winchelsea Island, after the Earl of Winchelsea.
Finch's Island, after the Winchelsea family name.
Pandanus Hill, from the clump of trees upon it.
Burney Island, after Captain James Burney, R.N.
Nicol Island, after 'His Majesty's bookseller'.
Woodah Island, 'it having some resemblance to the whaddie, or woodah, a wooden sword used by the natives of Port Jackson'.
Bustard Isles, they 'harboured several bustards'.
Mount Grindall, *Point Grindall*, after Vice-Admiral Grindall.
Morgan's Isle, after a seaman who died there.
Bluemud Bay, 'in most parts of the bay is a blue mud of so fine a quality that I judge it might be useful in the manufacture of earthenware'.

Point Blane, after Sir Gilbert Blane of the Naval Medical Board.
Cape Shield, after Commissioner Shield.
Cape Grey, after General Grey, Commandant at Cape Town.
Point Middle.
Mount Alexander.
Point Alexander.
Round Hill Island.
Caledon Bay, after the Governor of the Cape of Good Hope.
Cape Arnhem, extremity of Arnhem's Land.
Mount Saunder's.
Mount Dundas, *Melville Isles*, after Dundas, Viscount Melville, a colleague of the younger Pitt.
Mount Bonner.
Drimmie Head.
Cape Wilberforce, after W. Wilberforce, M.P., the slave-emancipator, who was a friend of Flinders.
Melville Bay, after Viscount Melville.
Harbour Rock.
Point Dundas.
Bromby Islands, after the Rev. F. Bromby, of Hull, a cousin of Mrs Flinders.
Malay Road.
Pombasso's Island, after the chief of the Malay praus.
Cotton's Island, after Captain Cotton of the East India Co.'s Directorate.
English Company Islands, after the East India Co.
Wigram Island.
Truant Island, 'from its lying away from the rest'.
Inglis Island.
Bosanquet Island.
Astell Island.
Mallison Island.
Point Arrowsmith, after the map-publisher.
Cape Newbald, *Newbald Island*, after Henrietta Newbald, *née* Flinders, who introduced him to Pasley.
Arnhem Bay.
Wessell Islands, name found on a Dutch chart.
Point Dale.
Wreck Reef.

MAPS FROM ORIGINAL EDITION

***Note:** These maps were placed throughout the first edition. In this reissue, we have collected them in the pages following. The note below is from the original edition.*

The maps have been copied from Flinders' atlas, with the omission of a few details, which, on the small scale necessarily adopted, would have caused confusion: it has been thought better to make what is given quite legible to the unassisted eye. All names on the maps are as Flinders spelt them, but in the body of the book modern spellings have been adopted. In the case of the *Duyfhen* the usual spelling, which is also that of Flinders, is retained; but the late J. Backhouse Walker has shown reason to believe that the real name of the vessel was *Duyfken*.

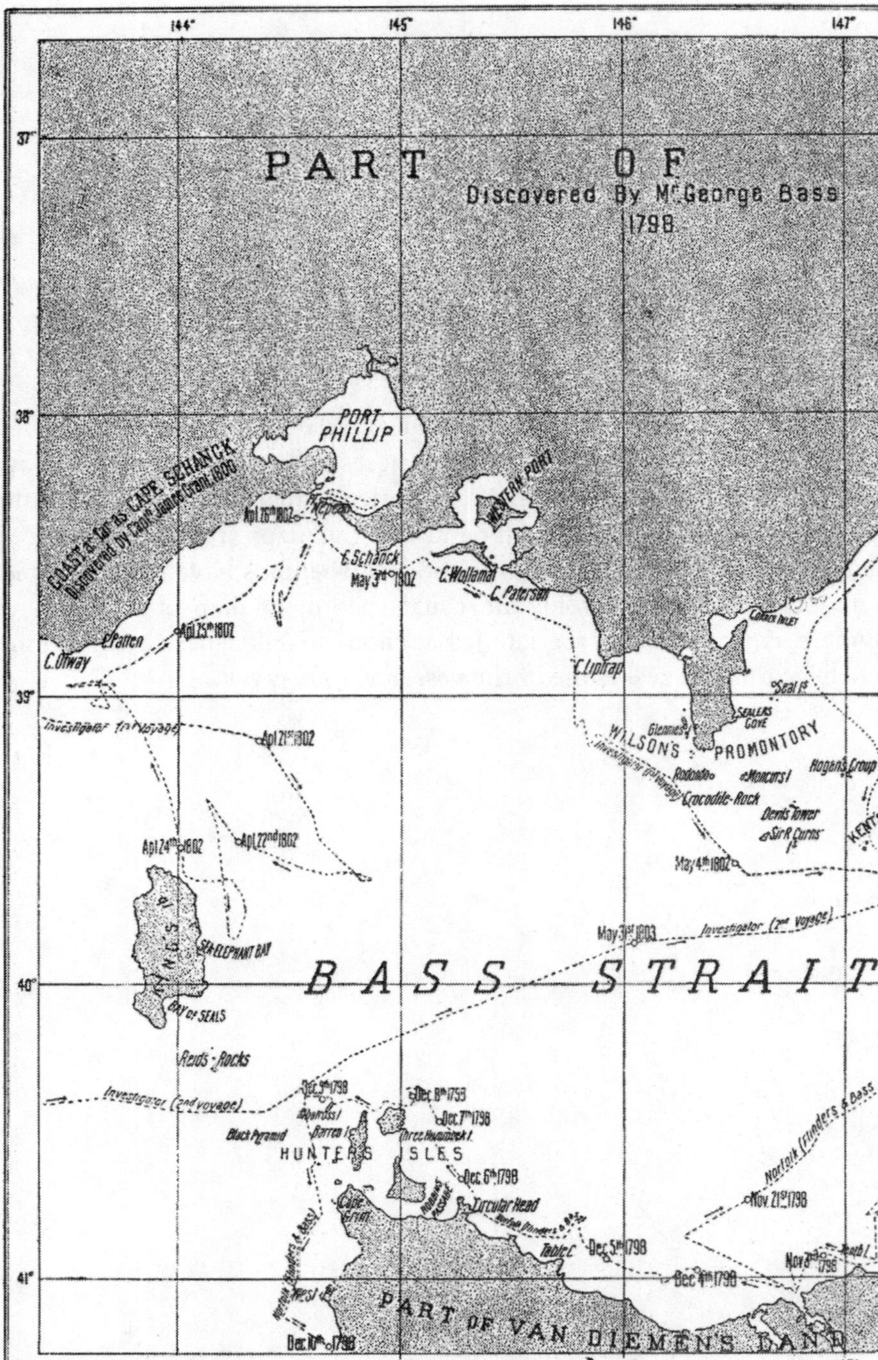

Flinders' voyages in Bass Strait in the *Francis*, *Norfolk* and *Investigator.*

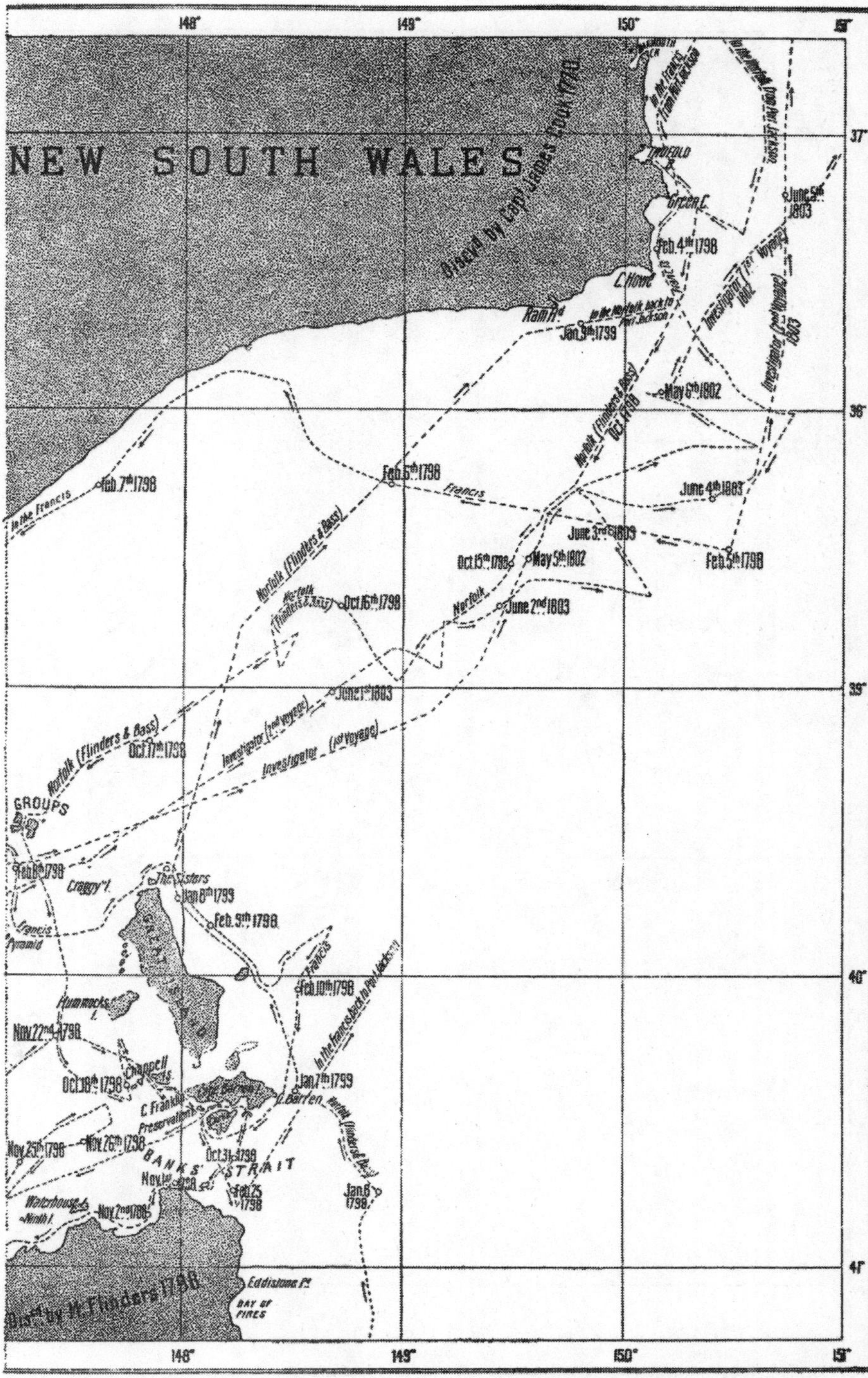

NEW SOUTH WALES
Discov.d by Capt. James Cook 1770
148°
149°
150°
151°
37°
38°
39°
40°
41°
Green C.
C. Howe
Feb. 4th 1798
Jan. 3rd 1799
June 5th 1803
May 6th 1802
Feb. 6th 1798
Feb. 7th 1798
In the Francis
Francis
June 4th 1803
June 3rd 1803
Feb. 5th 1798
Oct. 15th 1798
May 5th 1802
June 2nd 1803
Oct. 16th 1798
Norfolk (Flinders & Bass)
Norfolk
June 1st 1803
Investigator (2nd Voyage)
Investigator (1st Voyage)
Oct. 17th 1798
GROUPS
Feb. 8th 1798
Craggy I.
The Sisters
Jan 8th 1799
Feb. 9th 1798
Pyramid
Feb. 10th 1798
Hummocks I.
Nov. 22nd 1798
Chappell
Oct. 18th 1798
Jan 7th 1799
C. Barren
C. Franklin
Preservation
Nov. 25th 1798
Nov. 26th 1798
BANKS' STRAIT
Oct. 31st 1798
Feb. 25 1798
Jan. 8 1798
Waterhouse
Ninth I.
Nov. 2nd 1798
Eddistone Pt.
BAY OF FIRES
Disc.d by M. Flinders 1798

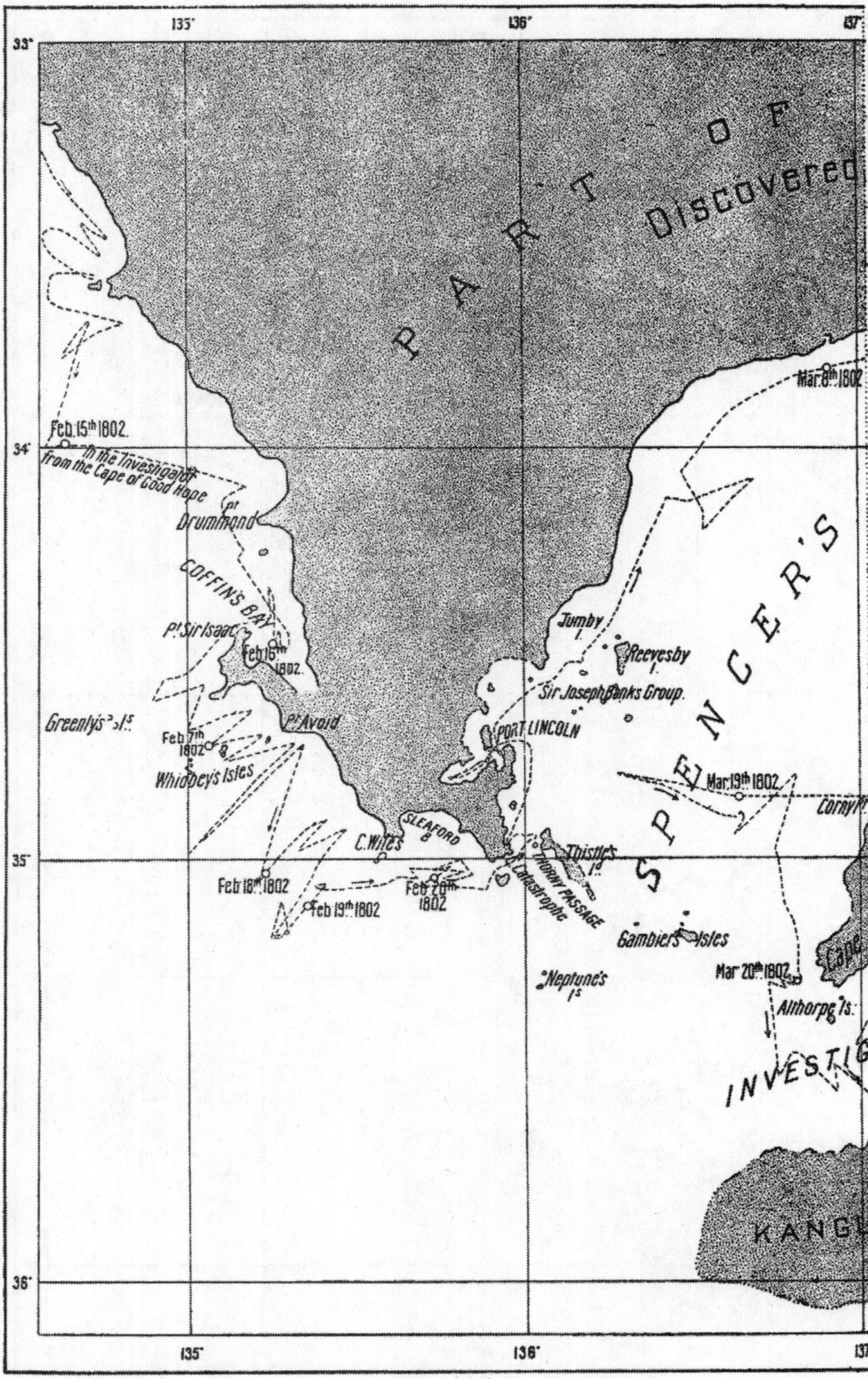

Flinders' chart of Spencer's Gulf, St Vincent's Gulf and Encounter Bay.

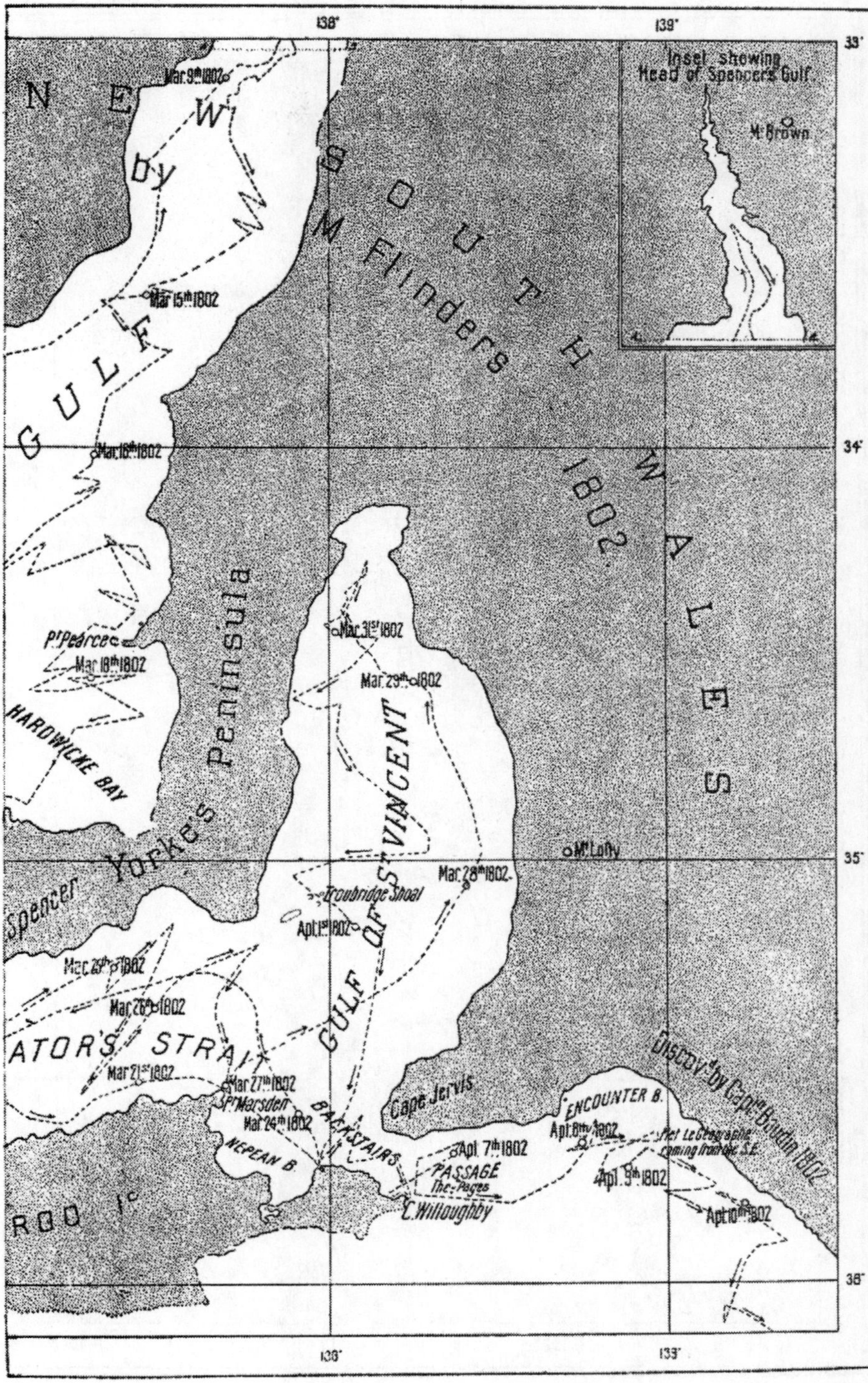
138°
139°
35°
34°
35°
36°
Inset showing Head of Spencers Gulf
Mt Brown
NEW SOUTH WALES
by M. Flinders 1802
Mar. 9th 1802
Mar 15th 1802
GULF
Mar 16th 1802
Pt Pearce
Mar 18th 1802
HARDWICKE BAY
Yorke's Peninsula
Spencer
Mar. 31st 1802
Mar. 29th 1802
GULF OF ST VINCENT
Mt Lofty
Mar 28th 1802
Troubridge Shoal
Apl. 1st 1802
Mar. 25th 1802
Mar 26th 1802
ATOR'S STRAIT
Mar 21st 1802
Mar 27th 1802
Pt Marsden
Mar 24th 1802
BACKSTAIRS
NEPEAN B.
Cape Jervis
ENCOUNTER B.
Apl. 8th 1802
Apl. 7th 1802
PASSAGE
The Pages
C. Willoughby
Apl. 9th 1802
Apl 10th 1802
ROO Ic
Discovd by Captn Baudin 1802
138°
139°

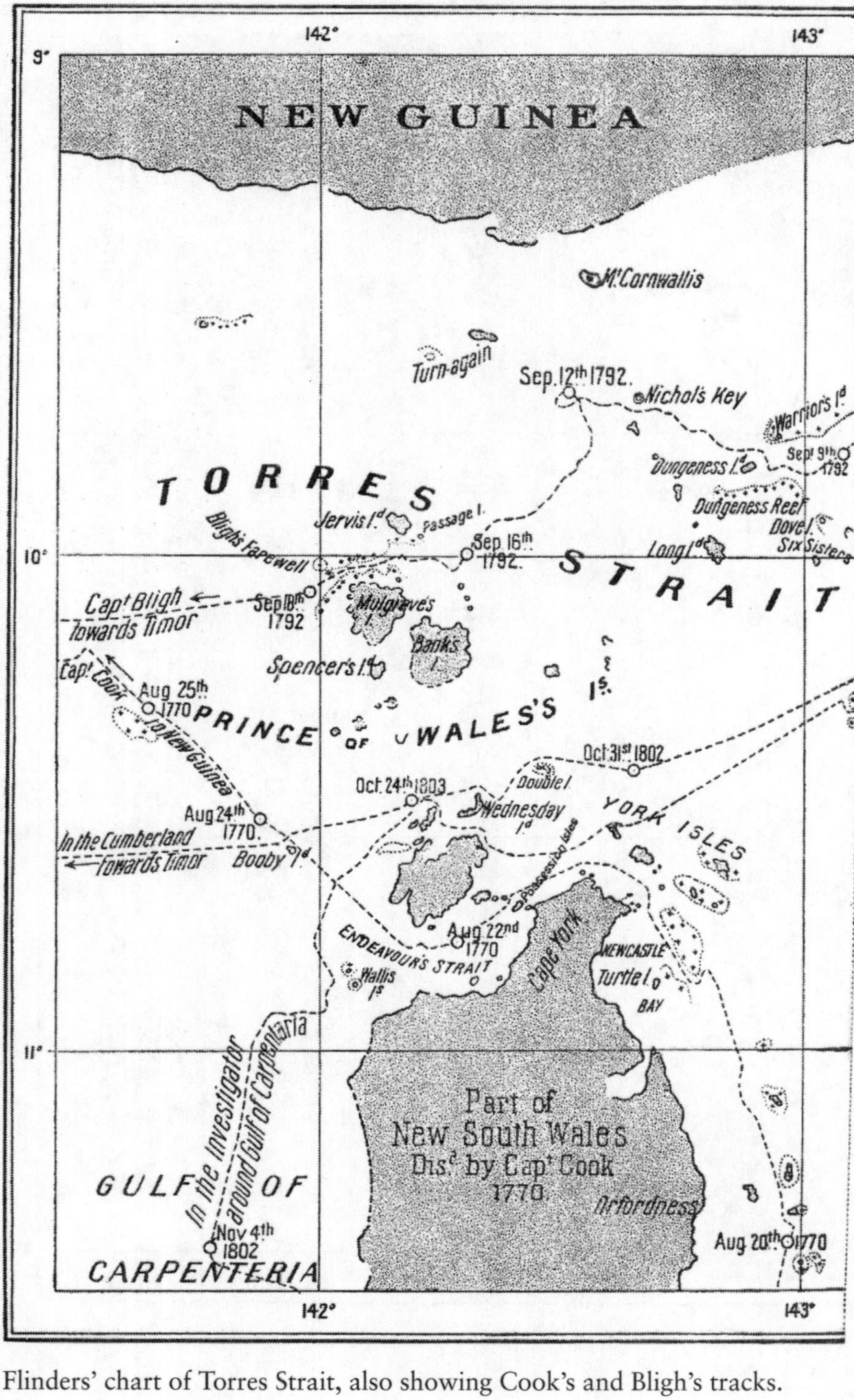

Flinders' chart of Torres Strait, also showing Cook's and Bligh's tracks.

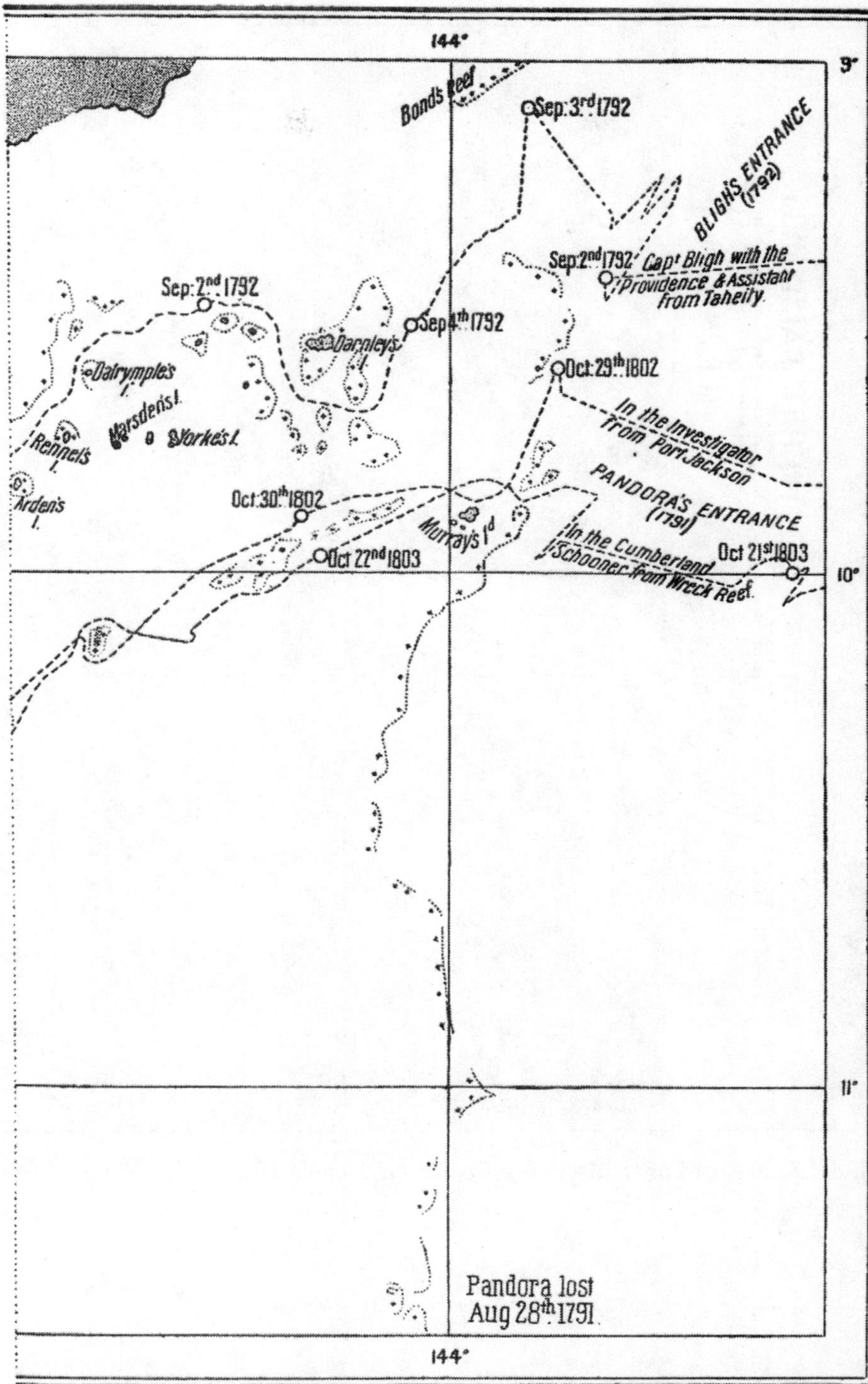
144°
9°
Bonds Reef
Sep: 3rd 1792
BLIGH'S ENTRANCE (1792)
Sep: 2nd 1792
Capt Bligh with the Providence & Assistant from Taheity
Sep: 2nd 1792
Sep 4th 1792
Darnley's I.
Dalrymple's I.
Marsden's I.
Yorke's I.
Rennel's I.
Arden's I.
Oct: 29th 1802
In the Investigator from Port Jackson
PANDORA'S ENTRANCE (1791)
Oct: 30th 1802
Murray's Id
Oct 22nd 1803
In the Cumberland Schooner from Wreck Reef.
Oct 21st 1803
10°
11°
Pandora lost
Aug 28th 1791
144°

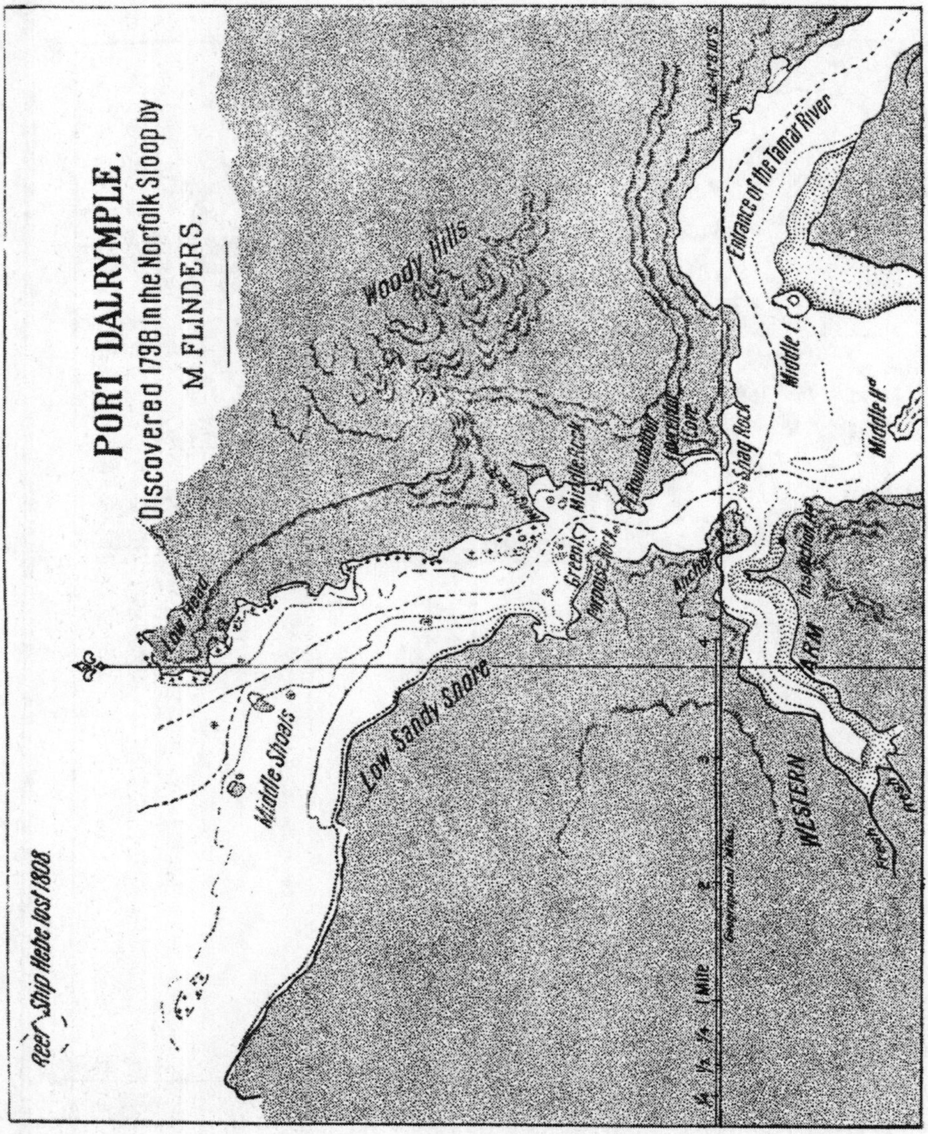

Flinders' chart of Port Dalrymple, Tasmania, discovered in the *Norfolk*, 1798.

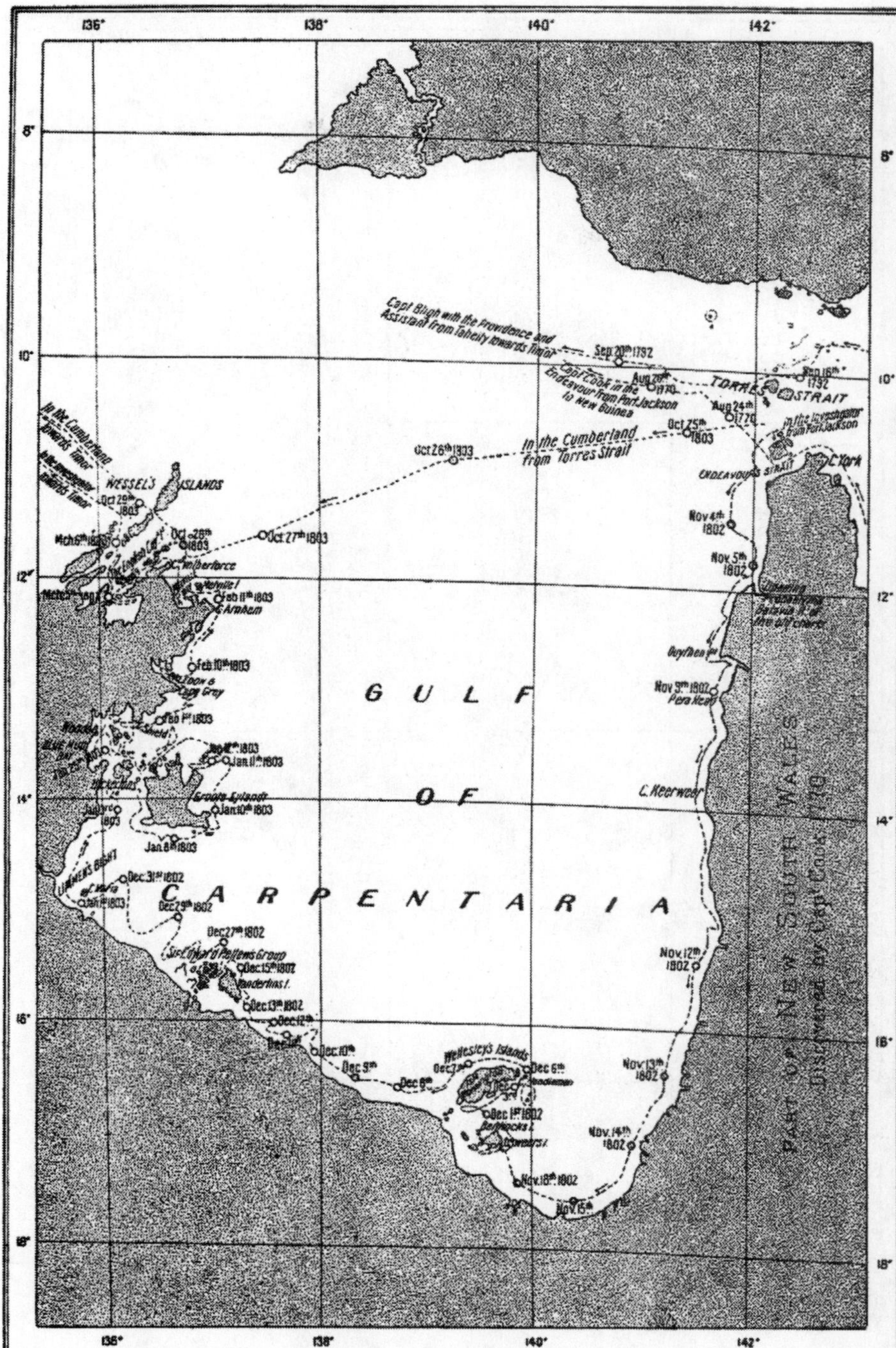

Flinders' chart of the Gulf of Carpentaria.

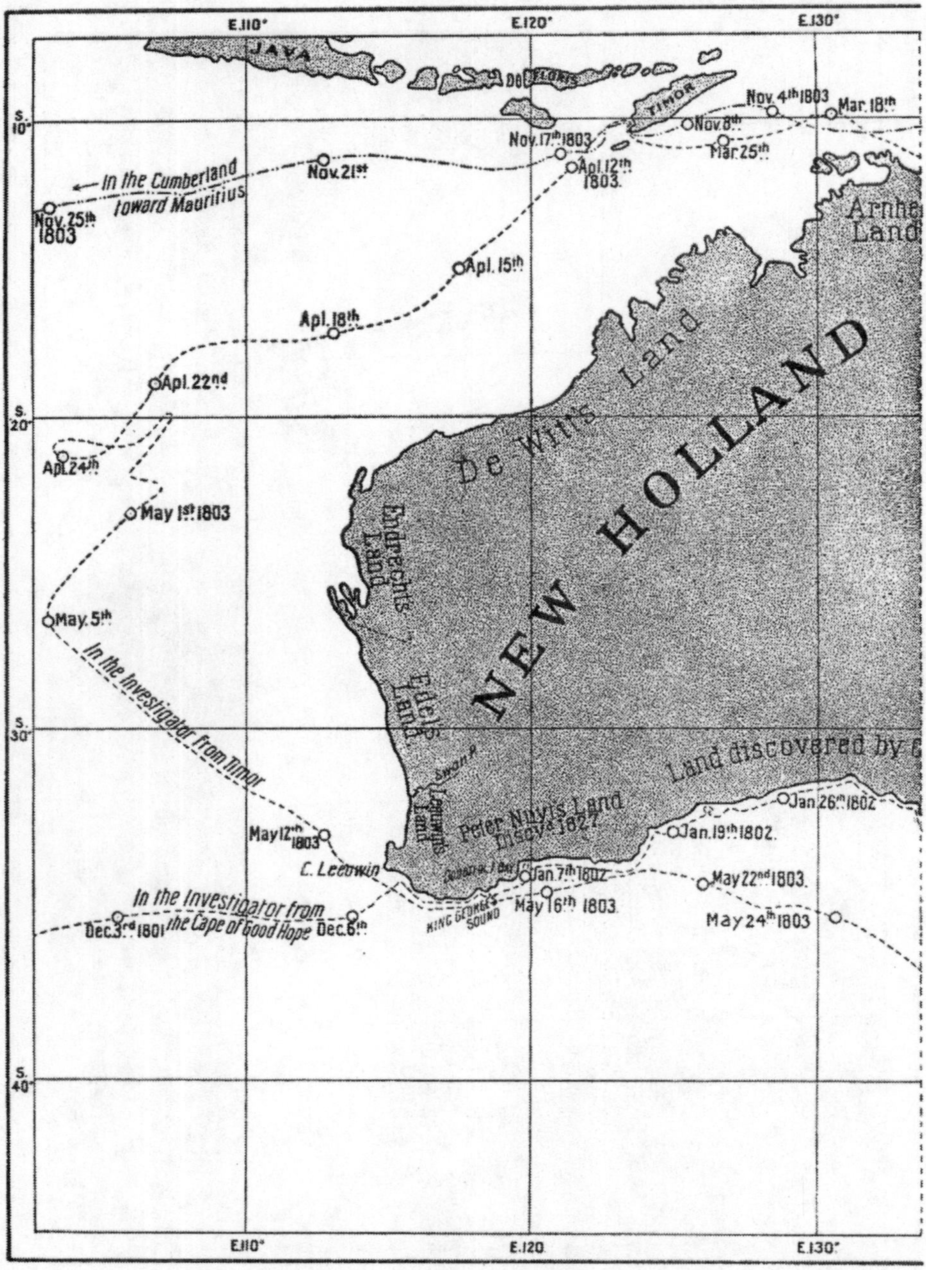

Flinders' map of Australia, showing his principal voyages.

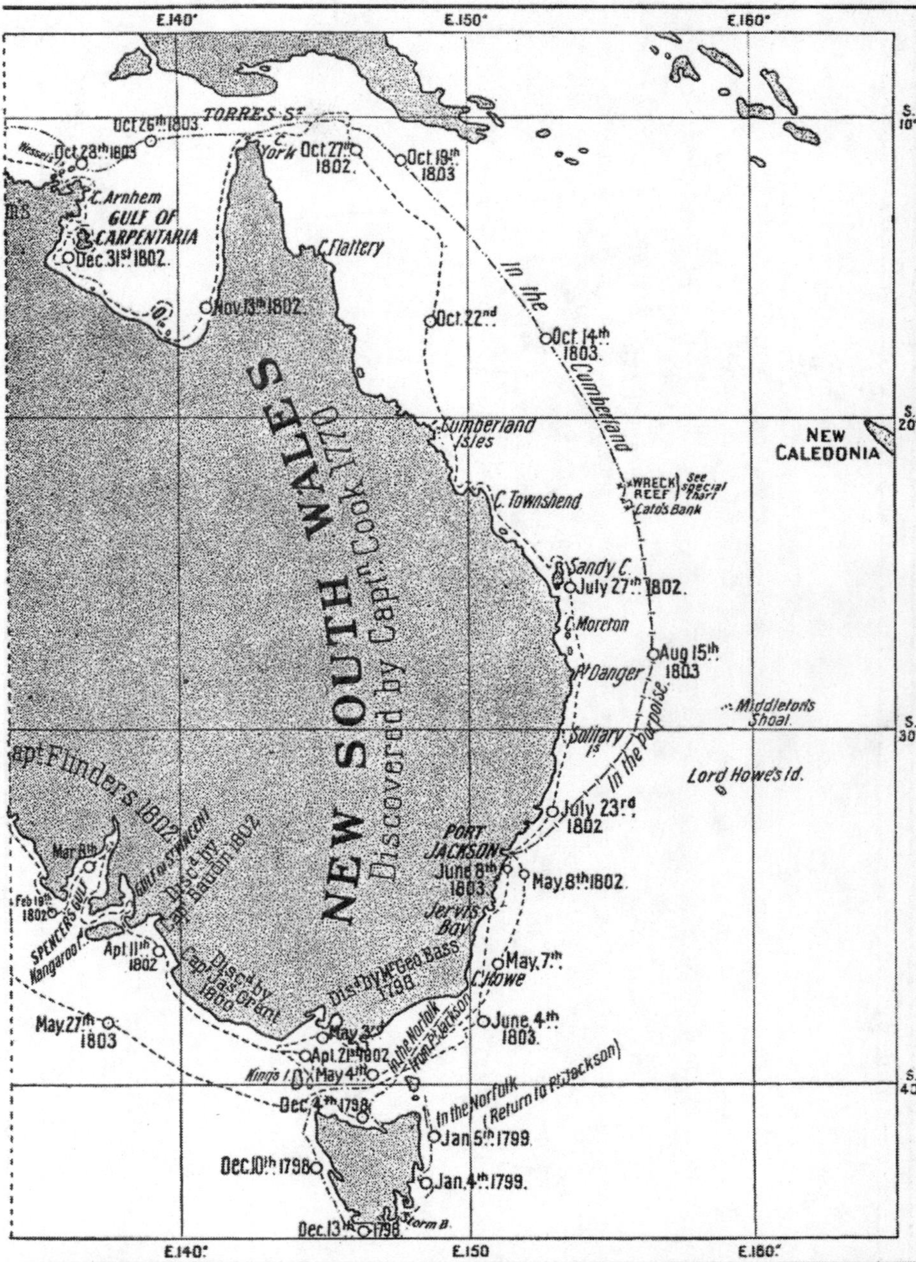
E.140°
E.150°
E.160°
TORRES ST.
Oct.26th 1803.
Oct.28th 1803
C. York
Oct.27th 1802.
Oct.19th 1803
C. Arnhem
GULF OF CARPENTARIA
Dec.31st 1802.
C. Flattery
Nov.13th 1802.
In the
Oct.22nd
Oct.14th 1803.
Cumberland
NEW SOUTH WALES
Discovered by Captn. Cook 1770
Cumberland Isles
NEW CALEDONIA
WRECK REEF
See special chart
Cato's Bank
C. Townshend
Sandy C.
July 27th 1802.
C. Moreton
Aug 15th 1803
Pt. Danger
Middleton's Shoal.
Solitary Is.
In the Porpoise.
Lord Howe's Id.
Capt. Flinders 1802
July 23rd 1802
PORT JACKSON
June 8th 1803.
May.8th 1802.
Mar.8th
Gulf of St. Vincent
Disc.d by Capt. Baudin 1802
Feb.19th 1802
SPENCER'S GULF
Jervis Bay
Kangaroo I.
Apl.11th 1802
Disc.d by Capt. Jas. Grant 1800
May.7th
Dis.d by Mr. Geo. Bass 1798
C. Howe
May.27th 1803
June.4th 1803.
May.3rd
Apl.21st 1802
In the Norfolk from Pt. Jackson
King's I.
May.4th
In the Norfolk (Return to Pt. Jackson)
Dec.4th 1798
Jan.5th 1799.
Dec.10th 1798
Jan.4th 1799.
Storm B.
Dec.13th 1798
E.140°
E.150
E.160°
S. 10°
S. 20°
S. 30°
S. 40°

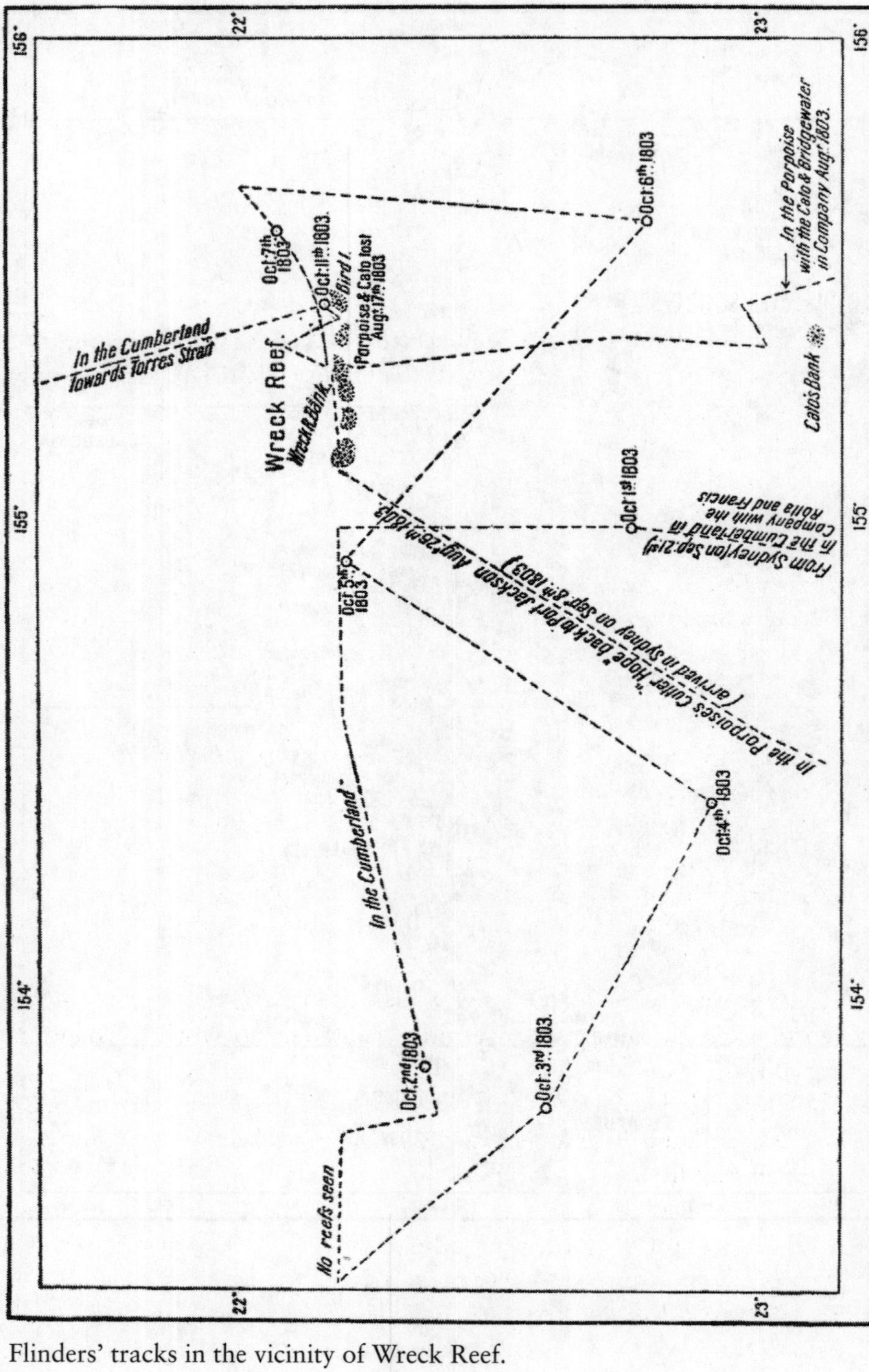

Flinders' tracks in the vicinity of Wreck Reef.

BIBLIOGRAPHY

MANUSCRIPT SOURCES

1 The Flinders Papers, in the Melbourne Public Library, consisting of a letter-book of Flinders (31 Aug. 1807, to 31 May 1814); ms. narrative of the voyage of the *Francis*; miscellaneous notes and memoranda by friends and relatives, a short ms. memoir, and a large quantity of transcripts of journals, family letters, etc. This material is not at present numbered, and allusions to it in the text of the book are therefore made by the general reference, 'Flinders Papers.'

2 Decaen Papers, in the Municipal Library of Caen, Normandy. General Decaen's manuscripts fill 149 volumes. The documents relating to Flinders, including a translation of portions of the *Cumberland*'s log, are principally in volumes 10, 84, 92, and 105. Péron's important report upon the British colony at Port Jackson is also in this collection, which includes many original letters of Flinders.

3 Archives Nationales, Paris, Marine BB4, 996–9, contains a quantity of manuscripts relative to Baudin's expeditions, including reports and letters by him, and many miscellaneous papers.

4 The Bibliothéque Nationale, Paris, nouveaux acquisitions, France, contains many documents relative to Baudin's expedition, including the diary of the commander.

5 The Archives du Muséum d'Histoire Naturelle de Paris contain reports and documents concerning the scientific work of Baudin's expedition.

6 The Depôt de la Marine, service hydrographique, Paris, cartons 6, 22, and 23, contains many reports upon the Australian coast made to Captain Baudin by his officers.

7 The Library of the Royal Colonial Institute, London, contains Westall's original drawings executed on the *Investigator* voyage. Photographed copies are in the Mitchell Library, Sydney.

8 The Mitchell Library, Sydney, contains Smith's ms. journal of the *Investigator* voyage, and many Flinders and Franklin papers, as cited in the text.

PRINTED DOCUMENTS

Most of the Flinders material contained in the Record Office, London, and the British Museum, is printed in Vol. III, IV, V, VI and VII of the *Historical Records of New South Wales*, edited by F. M. Bladen (Sydney, 1893–1901). Copies of other letters and documents, mainly from the same source, are in course of publication by the Commonwealth Government, under the direction of the Commonwealth Library Committee, edited by Dr. F. Watson.

WORKS BY FLINDERS

FLINDERS, MATTHEW, *A Voyage to Terra Australis*, 2 vols., London, 1814. The principal authority for the voyages of the navigator.

FLINDERS, M., *Observations on the Coasts of Van Diemen's Land*, etc., London, 1801.

FLINDERS, M., Papers on the Marine Barometer and on Variations of the Mariner's Compass, printed in the *Philosophical Transactions* of the Royal Society, London, 1806–07.

FLINDERS, MATTHEW, *Reise nach dem Austral-Lande, in der Absicht die Entdeckung desselben zu vollenden unter nommen in den Jaksen, 1801, 1802 and 1803.* Aus dem Englischen, von F. Götze. Weimar, 1816. A German translation of the *Voyage to Terra Australis.* An accompanying map is of great interest, as it essays [endeavours] for the first time to indicate by colours the portions of the Australian coast discovered by the English, the Dutch and the French. The map errs with regard to Kangaroo Island, in attributing the discovery of the north to the French and the south to the English. The reverse was the case.

MATTHEW FLINDERS, *Ontdekkings-reis naar het Groote Zuidland anders Nieuw Holland; bezigtiging van het zelve in 1801, 1802 en 1803; noodlottige schipbreak, en gevangenschap van 6½ jaar by de Franschen op Mauritius.* Uit het Engelsch. 4 vols., Haarlem, 1815–16. A Dutch translation of the *Voyage to Terra Australis.*

OTHER PRINTED BOOKS

BARROW, SIR JOHN, articles in *Quarterly Review*, 1810 and 1817, strongly condemning the work of Péron and Freycinet (see below), and championing the cause of Flinders. Barrow had access to material in possession of the Admiralty, sent to England from Mauritius by Flinders.

BECKE, L., and JEFFERY, W., *Naval Pioneers of Australia*, London, 1899. Very useful.

DALRYMPLE, ALEXANDER, *Collection of Voyages and Discoveries in the South Pacific Ocean*, 2 vols., London, 1770.

EDINBURGH REVIEW, 1807, reviews with commendation Flinders' 'Observations upon the Marine Barometer'.

GRANT, *Narrative of a Voyage of Discovery*, London, 1803.

LABILLIÈRE, F. P., *Early History of the Colony of Victoria*, 2 vols., London, 1878–79. Prints extracts from Flinders' ms. journals relating to Port Phillip.

LAUGHTON, SIR J. K., article on Flinders in *Dictionary of National Biography.*

MAIDEN, J. H., *Sir Joseph Banks, the Father of Australia*, Sydney, 1909.

FOWLER, T. W., 'The Work of Captain Matthew Flinders in Port Phillip,' Victorian Geographical Journal, 1912. Good topographical account.

MALTE-BRUN, *Annales des Voyages*, 1810 and 1814. Interesting references to Flinders; biographical sketch in Vol. XXIII, 268.

NAVAL CHRONICLE, Vol. XXXII (1814), contains a biography of Flinders, with portrait.

PATERSON, G., *History of New South Wales*, Newcastle-on-Tyne, 1811. Contains account of the early discoveries of Bass and Flinders.

PÉRON and FREYCINET, *Voyage de découvertes aux Terres Australes*, Paris, 1807–17. Second edition, with additions by Freycinet, 1824. Very important, but the historical statements have to be checked by reference to Baudin's ms. diary and letters (see reference to mss. above).

SCORESBY, W., *Journal of a Voyage to Australia for Magnetic Research*, 2 vols., London, 1859. The introduction by A. Smith deals with Flinders' discoveries regarding variations of the compass.

SCOTT, ERNEST, *Terre Napoléon*, London, 1910. Deals generally with French explorations in Australia and particularly with the work of Baudin and Flinders. See also the bibliography to that book.

SCOTT, ERNEST, 'English and French Navigators on the Victorian Coast', with maps, etc., in the *Victorian Historical Magazine*, 1912.

SCOTT, ERNEST, 'Baudin's Voyage of Exploration to Australia', in *English Historical Review*, April 1913.

SMITH, E., *Life of Sir Joseph Banks*, London, 1911.

South Australian Geographical Society's *Proceedings*, 1912. Prints from Baudin's letter to Minister of Marine in his account of the meeting with Flinders in Encounter Bay, and Decaen's statement of his reasons for detaining Flinders.

PICARD, ERNEST (editor), *Memoires et Journaux du Général Decaen*, 2 vols., Paris, 1911.

PITOT, ALBERT, *Esquisses historiques de l'Ile de France*, 1715–1810, Port Louis, Mauritius, 1899.

PRENTOUT, HENRI, *L'Ile de France sous Decaen*, Paris, 1901. Very important.

Victorian *Geographical Journal*, Vol. XXVIII (1910–11) prints a biographical sketch of Flinders from a ms. found in a copy of *A Voyage to Terra Australis* in Donington vicarage in 1903. It is printed with an Introduction (by G. Gordon McCrae) wherein it is stated to be 'hitherto unpublished'. But it is simply the *Naval Chronicle* sketch, with a few paragraphs added, and it is from the same pen as the ms. sketch mentioned above.

WALCKENAER, C. A., biography of Flinders in the *Biographie Universelle*, Vol. XIV; excellent.

WALKER, J. BACKHOUSE, *Early Tasmania*, Hobart, 1902. Gives an admirable account of Flinders' explorations in Tasmania.

INDEX

Where the reference is to a footnote, the letter *n* follows the number of the page.

Aborigines, references to, 64–5, 97, 101–2, 113, 114–16, 126, 148, 149–50, 156–7, 174, 191, 196
Admiralty's treatment of Flinders, 263, 287
Aken, John, 191, 201, 207
  Sails in *Cumberland*, 217
  At Ile-de-France, 220, 232, 233
  Departure of, 256
Albatross Island, 101
Allen, John, miner, joins *Investigator*, 129
Althorp Isles, 151
Amiens, treaty of, 143, 227
Arnhem Bay, 197
Arthur's Seat, Port Phillip, 172
Australasia, name of, 304
Australia, discovery of, 1
  Name of, 1*n*, 304 *et seq.*
  Geography of, before Flinders, 47 *et seq.*
  Theories concerning, 52 *et seq.*, 152
  French expedition to, 142 *et seq.*
  South Coast discovery, 147 *et seq.*
  Influence of Flinders on discovery, 171
  Circumnavigation of, 190 *et seq.*
'Australian', Flinders' use of word, 157
Babel Isles, 100
Backstairs Passage, 155
Banks, Cape, 168
Banks' Group, 151
Banks, Sir Joseph, promotes breadfruit expedition, 17, 20
  His friendship for Flinders, 102, 117–18
  His interest in Australian development, 102–3, 118
  Dedication of Flinders' *Observations* to, 123
  His letters concerning Mrs Flinders' proposed voyage on *Investigator*, 133 *et seq.*
  Disapproves of Flinders' conduct towards Decaen, 237, 266
  His dislike of word 'Australia', 308
Barmouth Creek, 75
Barois, Colonel, 249
Barometer, marine, Flinders' paper on use of, 262, 299–300
Barrow, Sir John, his article on Flinders' case, 261–2
Bass, Elizabeth, her marriage to George Bass, 105
  Letters from her husband, 106
Bass, George, family of, 4
  Medical training of, 60
  Sails in *Reliance*, 60
  Character of, 60–1
  Friendship with Flinders, 61
  Discovery of Bass Strait, 70 *et seq.*, 86 *et seq.*
  Exploration of Blue Mountains, 70 *et seq.*
  Discovery of coal, 72
  Plans discovery voyage, 72 *et seq.*

Bass, George, *cont'd.*
Whaleboat crew, 74
Discovery of Twofold Bay, 75
Discovery of Wilson's Promontory, 78
Adventure with escaped convicts, 79–81
Discovery of Western Port, 82
French admiration for, 87
Report on Derwent, 100
Fate of, 104 *et seq.*
Indifference to fame, 104
Marriage of, 105
Purchase of *Venus*, 105
Voyage to Tahiti, 105
New Zealand fishing project, 106
South American projects, 106 *et seq.*
Reports concerning his end, 111
Letters to his mother, 111
Flinders' last letter to, 202–3
See also Flinders
Bass Strait, discovery of, 70 *et seq.*, 86 *et seq.*
Governor Hunter on, 72–3, 95–6, 100
Naming of, 100
Importance of discovery, 102
Flinders' chart of, 346–7
Baudin des Ardennes, Lieut Charles, wounded, and visited by Flinders, 294–5
Baudin, Captain Nicolas, his expedition to Australia, 142 *et seq.*
Instructions to, 143–4
His career, 144
Reaches Ile-de-France, 145
Sails for Southern Tasmania, 146
At Waterhouse Island, 146
In Encounter Bay, 160 *et seq.*, 311 *et seq.*
At Kangaroo Island, 166
At Port Jackson, 176 *et seq.*
Rumours of intended French settlement, 179
Baudin, Captain Nicolas, *cont'd.*
Letter to Governor King, 180–1
Report on Port Jackson, 183
His account of the Encounter Bay meeting, 311 *et seq.*
Bauer, Cape, 150
Bauer, Ferdinand, botanical draftsman, joins *Investigator*, 128–9, 201, 205, 234*n*
Baye du Cap, 220
Beautemps-Beaupré, 148
Bell, Point, 150
Bellerophon, HMS, 12, 14, 20–1
Flinders appointed to, 31
Battle off Brest, 31 *et seq.*
Bennelong Point, 177*n*
Bergeret, Captain, 250
Blaxland, Gregory, his exploration of Blue Mountains, 71–2
Bligh, Captain William, voyage under Captain Cook, 15
Command of the *Bounty*, 17
Mutiny of the *Bounty*, 18
Character of, 20
Second breadfruit expedition, 20, 21
Expedition reaches Tahiti, 23
Voyage from Pacific to West Indies, 24
Introduces Flinders to Duke of Clarence, 282–3
Asks for dedication of Flinders' book, 283
Blue Mountains, exploration of, 70 *et seq.*
Blue Mud Bay, 196
Bolger, Commandant, 221
Bongaree, Aboriginal, accompanies Flinders on Queensland voyage, 113
On *Investigator*, 191
Boston, Point, 151
Botany Bay, 318
Bougainville, 264
Boullanger, hydrographer on *Le Géographe*, 313*n*

Bounty, HMS, voyage to Tahiti, 17
  Mutiny of, 18
Bowling Green, Cape, 193
Breadfruit, 16 *et seq.*
Bridgewater, 202, 206, 207–9
  Behaviour at Wreck Reef, 208–9
  Wreck of, 209
Bridgewater, Cape, 168
Brisbane River, 113
Brouwer, Henrick, his new route to Java, 50
Brown, Point, 150
Brown, Robert, botanist, 162, 201, 205, 234*n*, 312*n*, 314*n*
  Joins *Investigator*, 128
  His *Prodromus*, 128, 205*n*
Burney, Captain, and name Australia, 308
Cape of Good Hope, Flinders at, 23, 141
  Importance of to Australia, 57–8
  Voyage of *Reliance* to from Sydney, 67
Carpentaria, Gulf of, 195
Catastrophe, Cape, 151
Cato, 206
  Wreck of, 207, 208
Cattle Point, 177
Chappell, Ann, *see* Flinders, Mrs Ann
Chappell Isles, 118
Chappell, Mount, 118
Clarence River, 113
Clarke's Island, 94
Coal, discovery of in New South Wales, 72
Coalcliff, 72
Coffin's Bay, 151
Compass, variations of, Flinders' experiments, 300
Convicts, 74
  Escaped, 79 *et seq.*, 93
  Isaac Nichols, 113
  Irish, Péron on, 185, 186
  On *Investigator*, 191, 198
Cook, Captain James, his voyage, 51
  His belief in a strait between New Holland and Van Diemen's Land, 54
  Pension to his widow, 288
Coral reefs, Flinders on, 194–5
Crossley, J., 129
Cumberland, schooner, voyage to Ile-de-France, 215 *et seq.*
  At Kupang, 218
  Arrival at Ile-de-France, 220
  Enters Port Louis, 231
  End of, 287
Dalrymple, Alexander, naval hydrographer, 98
  His use of word 'Australia', 305–6
Dalrymple, Port, 98, 283
Dampier, William, 16–17
Dance, Commodore Nathaniel, 218
D'Arifat, Madame, 257 *et seq.*
Darwin, on coral reefs, 194
Decaen, General Charles, 180*n*, 182, 183, 186, 188, 221
  Career of, 222 *et seq.*
  Napoleon's opinion of, 225
  Sent to India, 227
  Arrival at Pondicherry, 228
  Sails for Ile-de-France, 229
  Arrival at Port Louis, 229
  Character of, 229–30
  Examination of Flinders, 231
  Interrogates Flinders, 233
  Invites Flinders to dinner, 236
  Flinders' refusal, 236–7
  Accuses Flinders of impertinence, 238
  His intentions, 239
  Report to French Government, 242
  Motives for detaining Flinders, 242 *et seq.*
  Anger against Flinders, 244
  Despatch arrives in France, 249
  Flinders' opinion of, 252
  Receives order for Flinders' release, 264–5

Decaen, General Charles, *cont'd.*
Refuses to liberate Flinders, 267–8
His reasons, 268
Release of Flinders, 274
Decrès, French Minister of Marine, 249, 265
D'Entrecasteaux, 52, 55, 124, 142, 147
Derwent, estuary of the, 100, 283, 321*n*
Dirk Hartog Island, 50
Donington, birthplace of Flinders, 2, 6–7
Flinders' monument at, 7
Free school, 9
The Flinders' house, 11
Donington, Cape, 151
Dunienville, Major, 220, 221
Dutch navigators, discoveries in Australia, 49 *et seq.*
East India Company, its interest in Australia, 125, 129–30
Interest in *Investigator* voyage, 129
Elder, John, Flinders' servant, 201, 283
Sails in *Cumberland*, 217
At Ile-de-France, 243, 258, 263
Encounter Bay, 146
Flinders and Baudin in, 160 *et seq.*, 311 *et seq.*
Everard, Cape, 77, 93
Fitzroy, Sir Charles, 310
Fleurieu, Comte de, prepares instructions for French discovery voyages, 124, 143, 147, 253, 264
Flinders, John, naval career, 11
Flinders, Matthew, surgeon, father of the navigator, 2, 6
Marriage into Franklin family, 122
Death of, 199
Flinders, Matthew, genealogy, 5
School days, 9
Study of *Robinson Crusoe*, 9–10
Anecdotes of childhood, 11
Desire to go to sea, 11
Advice of uncle, 12–13
Study of navigation, 13
Introduction to Admiral Pasley, 14
Flinders, Matthew, *cont'd.*
Anecdote of visit to Pasley, 14
On the *Scipio*, 14
On the *Bellerophon*, 14
On the *Dictator*, 14
Midshipman on *Providence*, 21
Description of Teneriffe, 22
Description of Dutch at the Cape, 23
In Torres Strait, 24–5
Return to Europe, 29
Aide-de-camp on *Bellerophon*, 31
First experience of war, 32
Anecdote of battle, 33
His journal of the engagement, 35 *et seq.*
Estimate of French seamen, 44
Appointed to *Reliance*, 57
Careful record of observations, 59–60
Arrival at Port Jackson, 60
Friendship with Bass, 61
Exploration of George's River, 62
Voyages in *Tom Thumb*, 62 *et seq.*
Adventure with Aboriginals, 64–5
Voyage on *Francis*, 88 *et seq.*
Discovery of Kent Group, 90
Biological notes, 90
On the sooty petrel, 91
Description of wombat, 94
Voyage to Norfolk Island, 95
Exploration projects, 95–6
Voyage of *Norfolk*, 96
Character as an author, 97
Discovery of Bass Strait, 98
Circumnavigation of Tasmania, 95 *et seq.*
Description of Tasmanian mountains, 99
Banks' friendship for, 102, 117–18
On Queensland coast, 112 *et seq.*
Adventures with Queensland Aboriginals, 114–15
Return to England, 117
Marriage of, 118, 121*n*
His *Observations*, 118, 123

Flinders, Matthew, *cont'd.*
Naming of Mount Chappell, 118
Letters to his wife, 120, 139, 198, 200, 252, 296
Suggests new discovery voyage, 123–4
Instructions for voyage, 130 *et seq.*
Passport from French Government, 131
Correspondence concerning Mrs Flinders' proposed voyage in *Investigator*, 132 *et seq.*
Reports sandbank at the Roar, 137
Management of crew, 140–1
On Australian coast, 148
Method of research, 148–9
Coastal names given by, 150 *et seq.*
On the character of John Thistle, 152–3
Exploration of Spencer's Gulf, 154
Discovery of Kangaroo Island, 155
Discovery of St Vincent's Gulf, 155
In Encounter Bay, 160 *et seq.*, 311 *et seq.*
In Port Phillip, 167 *et seq.*
At King Island, 169
Description of Port Phillip entrance, 169
Influence on Australian discovery, 171
Departure from Port Phillip, 174
Arrival at Port Jackson, 174
On François Pèron, 188
Circumnavigation of Australia, 190 *et seq.*
On coral reefs, 194–5
Forced to return to Port Jackson, 195, 198
Death of father, 199
Last letter to Bass, 202–3
Sails in *Porpoise*, 205
Observations on Sydney, 206
Wrecked on *Porpoise*, 206
Sails for Port Jackson in *Hope*, 211
Arrives at Port Jackson, 215

Flinders, Matthew, *cont'd.*
Arrival at Wreck Reef, 216
Arrival at Kupang, 218
Decides to sail for Ile-de-France, 219 *et seq.*
Sights Ile-de-France, 220
Appears before Decaen, 231
Seizure of his papers, 232
Detained, 232
Interrogated by Decaen, 233
Invited to dinner by Decaen, 236
His refusal, 236–7
Accused of impertinence, 238
Carries despatches for Governor King, 239–40
Letters to Decaen, 243 *et seq.*
Obtains books and papers, 245
Prolongation of captivity, 250 *et seq.*
Occupations in Garden Prison, 251
Opinion of Decaen, 252
Solicits examination by French officers, 253
Refuses to surrender his sword, 254
Removal to Wilhelm's Plains, 257
Life at Wilhelm's Plains, 258 *et seq.*
Works on his *Voyage*, 261
Paper on marine barometer, 262
Treatment by Admiralty, 263
Release ordered, 264–5
Decaen refuses release, 267–8
Knowledge of weakness of Ile-de-France, 269
Allegations as to taking soundings, 269
Possibilities of escape, 271
Released, 274
Arrival in England, 275
Receipt for books, papers, etc., 277
Interest in French prisoners of war, 282
Honoured in London, 282
Evidence before House of Commons Committee, 283
Works at his *Voyage* and charts, 283
Illness of, 284

Flinders, Matthew, *cont'd.*
Death of, 285
Place of burial, 286
Characteristics, 290 *et seq.*
Visit to wounded French officer, 294
Advice to young officers, 295–6
As a navigator, 299 *et seq.*
Naming of Australia, 304 *et seq.*
Flinders, Mrs Ann, marriage to Matthew Flinders, 118
Flinders' letters to, 120, 139, 198, 200, 252, 296
Proposed voyage in *Investigator*, 132 *et seq.*
On Admiralty's treatment of Flinders, 263
Meets Flinders on his return, 275
Pension voted by Australian colonies, 288
Flinders, S. W., joins *Investigator*, 128
On Wreck Reef, 216–17
Flinders' bar, invention of, 300
Flinders' Entrance, 193*n*
Flinders' family, 2
Connection with Tennysons, 4
Flinders' Island, 93
Foigny, Gabriel de, his *La Terre Australe connue*, 305
Forfait, French Marine Minister, instructions to Baudin, 199*n*
Fowler, Robert, joins *Investigator*, 128, 150, 197, 201
On *Rolla*, 217, 218*n*
Fowler's Bay, 150
Francis, schooner, voyage of, 88 *et seq.*, 95, 205
Sails with *Cumberland*, 215 *et seq.*
Franklin, Sir John, connection with Flinders' family, 5
On the *Polyphemus*, 122
Influenced by Flinders, 122
Joins *Investigator*, 128
At wreck of *Porpoise*, 212
On *Rolla*, 217
On Flinders' return to England, 275
Franklin's Isles, 150
French Island, 82
French Revolution, 30
Freycinet, Lieut Louis de, at Sydney, 181
On military situation at Port Jackson, 185, 186, 187
His hydrographical work, 278
Charge of plagiarism against, 278–9
Publication of his charts, 279 *et seq.*
Furneaux, commander of *Adventure*, 54, 78
Furneaux Land, 78
Gambier Isles, 154
Gambier Mount, 168
Gambier Prison, *see* Maison Despeaux
Géographe, Le, 136, 145–6, 161 *et seq.*, 176 *et seq.*, 181–2, 220, 230, 311 *et seq.*
George's River, exploration of, 62
Glasshouse Bay, 113
Glasshouse Mountains, 113
Good, Peter, gardener, joins *Investigator*, 129
Grant, Captain, in command of *Lady Nelson*, 167
Governor King on, 168
Sails for Australia, 168
Harrington, brig, and the American contraband trade, 109 *et seq.*
Hartog, Dirk, his metal plate, 50
Hawkesbury River, the, 187, 204, 319
Heemskerk, Mount, 100
Hervey Bay, 113
Hicks, Point, 77, 93
Hindmarsh, Sir John, his naval career, 12
Hohenlinden, battle of, 225
Hope, cutter, 211–12, 215, 277
Howe, Lord, battle off Brest, 31–2
Hunter, Captain John, appointed Governor of New South Wales, 56
Interest in Australian colonisation, 57

Hunter, Captain John, *cont'd.*
Discourteous treatment of by Portuguese Viceroy, 59
Encourages Bass and Flinders, 61–2
On Bass Strait, 72 *et seq.*
Ile-de-France, 218
Flinders at, 220 *et seq.*
Interior of, 258
Military situation of, 268–9
Regulations concerning visiting ships, 270
Blockade of, 273
Captured by British, 275
Investigator, 117 *et seq.*
Reasons for expedition, 124–5
Formerly the *Xenophon*, 125
Refitting of, 125–6
Leakiness, 125–6
Selection of crew, 127
Sailing delayed, 136
Sailing of, 137, 138
On South Coast, 147 *et seq.*
In Encounter Bay, 160 *et seq.*, 311 *et seq.*
In Port Phillip, 167 *et seq.*
Arrival at Port Jackson, 174
Circumnavigation of Australia, 190 *et seq.*
Decrepit condition of, 195, 197, 198
Taken to England, 204
End of, 204
Investigator Strait, 155, 280
Jervis Bay, 75
Julia Percy Island, 168
Jussieu, French botanist, recommends Baudin to command discovery voyage, 144, 183, 189
Kangaroo Island, discovery of, 155, 313
Wildlife on, 157
Baudin at, 166, 198, 280
Kent, Lieut William, 68, 90, 112, 134, 288
Kent's Group, 90
Keppel Bay, 192
King, Governor, P. G., and Bass's South American project, 109 *et seq.*
His hospitality to French expedition, 177
Receives news of *Porpoise* wreck, 215
Entrusts despatches to Flinders, 239–40
Protest against Flinders' imprisonment, 262
King George's Sound, 147
King Island, 163
Discovery of, 169
French at, 179
Kupang, 197
Lacépède, 183
Lacy, midshipman, 172, 282
Lady Nelson, 53, 86, 167 *et seq.*, 191, 205
La Pérouse, 52, 55, 143, 159, 173, 177, 192, 260, 302
Launceston, 98
Lawson, Lieut, his share in crossing Blue Mountains, 71–2
Leeuwin, Cape, 141, 147
Linois, Rear-Admiral, 218, 228–9
Little Bay, 75
Liverpool, Lord, 308
Lofty, Mount, 155
Louis XVI, his interest in discovery voyages, 124
Louth Bay, 151
Louth Isle, 151
Lucky Bay, 151
Macquarie, Fort, 177*n*
Macquarie, Governor, his use of word Australia, 310
Maison Despeaux (Garden Prison), 248
Malaspina, Admiral, 316
Malte-Brun, 264
Championship of Flinders, 278–9, 299
Maria Island, 196
Marsden, Rev Samuel, 317

Martin's Isles, 65
Mauritius, *see* Ile-de-France
Melville Bay, 196
Memory Cove, 153
Monistrol, Colonel, 231, 233, 237, 243, 245, 248, 267, 276–7
Moreau, General, 224 *et seq.*
Moreton Bay, 113, 115
Mornington, 172
Mornington Island, 196
Murray, Lieut John, discovers Port Phillip, 170
  Accompanies Flinders, 191
Mutton-birds, 91 *et seq.*
Napoleon, authorises French discovery voyage, 124–5, 142, 182
  His opinion of General Decaen, 225
  Sends Decaen to India, 227
  Hears of the Flinders case, 250
  Orders release of Flinders, 265
  His comment on oaths of allegiance, 275
Naturaliste, Le, 82, 136, 145–6, 161 *et seq.*, 177 *et seq.*, 181, 220, 242, 313*n*–4,
Navy, the British, promotion in, 11–12
  Entrance to, 13
Nelson, 12, 151
Nelson, Cape, 151, 168
Nepean, Evan, Secretary of the Admiralty, 126, 170
Nepean Peninsula, 169*n*, 170, 173
Nichols, Isaac, case of, 112–13
Norfolk, sloop, 96
  Flinders' description of, 99
  Importance of voyage, 102–3
  Voyage to Queensland coast, 113 *et seq.*
Northumberland, Cape, 168
Nuyts, Pieter, 50, 147
Observations on the Coast of Van Diemen's Land, publication of, 123
Otto, L. G., 124–5
Otway, Cape, 168, 169
Palmer, Captain of *Bridgewater*, 209
Pandora's Entrance, 193
Papuans, fight with in Torres Strait, 25 *et seq.*
  bartering with, 193–4
Park, Mungo, and the *Investigator*, 128
Parramatta, 318
Partney Isle, 151
Pasley, Admiral Sir Thomas, Flinders' introduction to, 14
  His interest in Flinders' career, 21–2
  Command of *Bellerophon*, 31
  Wounded in battle off Brest, 33
  Character of, 45–6
Pasley, Cape, naming of, 46
Paterson, Lieut-Col, 179, 184, 317
Peel, Sir Robert, 308
Pellew, Rear-Admiral, his interest in Flinders' case, 262
Pellew Group, 196
Pelsart, Francis, on the Australian Coast, 50–1
Percy Isles, 192
Péron, François, at Sydney, 181
  His report on British settlement, 182, 315 *et seq.*
  Plays the spy on British designs, 184
  Flinders on, 188
  Scientific work of, 189
  Effect of his report on Decaen, 243
  Malte-Brun on, 279
  Death of, 279
Petrie, Professor W. M. Flinders, grandson of Matthew Flinders, 5, 289*n*
Phillip Island, 82
Pinkerton, *Modern Geography*, 52
Pitot, Thomas, 257, 258, 294
Pitt, Mount, 93
Plagiarism, allegation against the French, 236, 278 *et seq.*
  Freycinet on, 281

Pondicherry, 228
Porpoise, Flinders sails in, 205
Wreck of, 206, 247, 277
Port Bowen, 192
Port Curtis, 192
Port Hacking, 67, 75
Port Jackson, *see* Sydney
Port Lincoln, 151
Discovery and survey of, 153
Port Louis, 220, 221, 231 *et seq.*
Port Phillip, 83, 161
Flinders in, 167 *et seq.*
Discovery of, 170
Attempted settlement of, 174
Portland Bay, 168
Portlock, Lieut N., Commander of *Assistant*, 20
Portsea, 173
Preservation Island, 91
Providence, HMS, 21 *et seq.*, 193
Providential Cove, *see* Watta-molla
Quarterly Review, article on Flinders' case, 261–2, 278
Queensland coasts, Flinders' voyages on, 112–16, 191–6
Quiros, voyage of, 51, 304
Red Point, 64
Reliance, HMS, 56, 58, 62*n*, 63, 67 *et seq.*, 72, 95, 100, 113, 117, 171
Revesby Isle, 151
Robbins, Acting-Lieut, 179
Robinson Crusoe, influence of on Flinders, 9–10
Rowley, Commodore, 273
St Alouarn, 147
St Vincent's Gulf, 150–1
Discovery of, 155, 280
Schanck, Cape, 169
Schanck, Captain John, designs *Lady Nelson*, 167
Seal-fisheries, 321
Shaw and Smith, their use of the word Australia, 306
Shinglar, Rev John, schoolmaster of Flinders, 9
Ships not elsewhere indexed—
Adventure, 54, 78
Advice, brig, 135
Agincourt, 288
Albion, 36, 37
Alert, 14
Aquilon, 36
Assistant, 21 *et seq.*
Audacious, 32, 35, 38, 40*n*, 41
Barwell, 95
Batavia, 50
Bedford, 275
Bélier, brig, 228
Belle Poule, La, 228
Berceau, Le, 253
Blenheim, 267
Blonde, La, 36
Brunswick, 44
Buffalo, 134, 153*n*, 205
Caesar, 33, 38*n*, 39, 40, 42
Cape Chatham, 147
Captivity, see also *Bellerophon*, 14
Casuarina, 179, 180
Cerberus, 117
Circe, frigate, 31
Cygnet, 13
Defence, 35, 43
Dictator, 14
Duyfhen, yacht, 51
Eendragt, 50
Eliza, sloop, 90
Elligood, 157
Endeavour, 54, 77
Eole, 33, 34
Espérance, 147
Ganges, 35
Glatton, 213
Glory, 36
Greyhound, frigate, 265, 267
Harbinger, brig, 169
Harriet, cartel, 274–5
Heemskerk, 100
Heir Apparent, 282
Hercules, 191
Hunter, 232
Java, 267

Ships not elsewhere indexed, *cont'd.*
Latona, 31, 34, 35, 36, 43
Leviathan, 32, 38, 38*n*, 39, 43
Lowestoft, frigate, 12
Marengo, French frigate, 228–9
Marlborough, 32, 38, 39, 43
Matilda, whaler, 23
Minerva, frigate, 242
Nautilus, 96
Niger, 37
Olympia, 275
Orient, L', 12
Orion, 40
Otter, 275
Pandora, 193
Phaeton, 41
Phoenix, 36, 37
Piémontaise, La, privateer, 261
Polyphemus, 122
Pompey, 282
Queen, 38*n*, 41, 43, 44
Queen Charlotte, 32, 38*n*, 39, 40, 43, 56
Recherche, 147
Resolution, 14, 54
Resource, 212*n*
Révolutionnaire, 32, 38*n*, 40*n*, 45
Rolla, 215 *et seq.*
Royal Sovereign, 39
Russell, 32, 35, 38, 39, 42, 45
Scipio, 13–14
Seahorse, 132
Sémillante, La, 294
Serpente, Le, see *Le Géographe*
Sirius, 56, 93
Southampton, 36
Supply, tender, 56 *et seq.*, 67, 68, 90
Terpsichore, 294
Terrible, 32
Theseus, 132
Thetis, 262
Thunderer, 32, 38, 39, 45
Trajan, 33
Tremendous, 42
Vengeur, 44
Vésuve, Le, see *Le Naturaliste*
Vianen, 50
Warren Hastings, 261
Warrior, 282
Xenophon, see *Investigator*
Zealand, 127
Zeehan, 100
Shoalhaven, 75
Sibsey Isle, 151
Sleaford Bay, 151
Smith, Samuel, journal of, 140*n*, 141, 149–50, 165–6, 174, 207, 208, 211–12, 216
Spanish-American colonies, 107
Contraband trade with, 110 *et seq.*
Alleged British designs on, 184, 323–4, 332
Spencer, Earl, First Lord of the Admiralty, supports Flinders' exploration project, 124
Grants passport to French discovery voyage, 125
Visited by Flinders, 282
Spencer's Gulf, 150–1, 152
Exploration of, 154, 280
Spilsby Isle, 151
Stamford Hill, 151, 154
Station Peak, 173, 173*n*
Stickney Isle, 151
Streaky Bay, 151
Surfleet Point, 151
Swan Harbour, 173
Swans, black, 100–1
Sydney, growth of, 70
Arrival of *Investigator* at, 174
Baudin's expedition at, 176 *et seq.*
Péron's report on, 182, 315–37
Military forces at, 185
Flinders' observations on, 206
Sydney Cove, wreck of, 80, 88 *et seq.*
Tahiti, 15 *et seq.*
Bass's voyages to, 105
Tamar, discovery of, 98
Tasman, voyage of, 51, 100
Tasmania, circumnavigation of, 95 *et seq.*
Taylor's Isle, 150, 153

Teneriffe, Flinders' description of, 22
Tennysons, connection with Flinders' family, 4
Termination Island, 147
Terra Australis, 49, 126
Thistle, John, drowning of, 152–3
  Character, 152–3
Thistle Island, 150
Tides, theory of, Flinders' writings on, 302
Tom Thumb, measurements of, 62*n*
  Second boat of same name, 63, 75
Torres, voyage of, 51
Torres Strait, 193
Trafalgar, battle of, 188, 268
Transportation system, Péron on, 184
Twofold Bay, discovery of, 75
  Adventure with Aboriginal in, 97
Vancouver, voyage of, 51
  His discoveries on Australian coast, 147
Van Diemen, Cape, 196
Venus, brig, Bass's purchase of, 105
  Voyages to Tahiti, 105–6
  Voyages to South America, 108–9
  Seizure of, 110
Venus Bay, 106
Vlaming, his metal plate, 50
Waterhouse, Captain Henry, 57, 68 *et seq.*, 146, 203*n*
Waterhouse, Elizabeth, *see* Bass, Elizabeth
Waterhouse Island, 146
Wattamolla (Watta-Mowlee), 66, 75
Wellesley, the Marquess, Governor-General of India, 196*n*, 228
  His interest in Flinders' case, 262
Wellesley Isles, 196
Wentworth, W. C., his share in crossing Blue Mountains, 71–2
Westall, Point, 150
Westall, William, artist, joins *Investigator*, 128, 201
Westernport, discovery of, 82
  Le Naturaliste in, 146
Whaleboat, Bass's measurements of, 74
Wilhelm's Plains, Flinders' residence at, 257 *et seq.*
William IV inspects Flinders' charts, 282–3
  On proposed pension to Mrs Flinders, 288
Williams, mate of *Bridgewater*, 209
Williamson, acting commissary, 72
Wilson's Promontory, 78, 84, 161, 168
Winceby Isle, 151
Wombat, Flinders' description of, 94
Woolgrowing, 326–7
Wreck Reef, 205 *et seq.*
Yorke's Peninsula, 151, 156
You-yang Range, 172
Zeehan, Mount, 100

PICTURE CREDITS

Page 1 of picture section
Top left: Miniature portrait of Matthew Flinders, watercolour on ivory, artist unknown. Image Library, State Library of New South Wales, ML ref: Min 52.
Top right: Matthew Flinders' hat. Image Library, State Library of New South Wales, Mitchell Library Relics LR24.
Bottom: *Trim's shortcut, glass all smashed to flinders*, George Gordon McCrae, pen and ink, National Library of Australia R8203.
Page 2
Top: *View of Port Jackson taken from the South Head*, engraving, John Pye (engraver), William Westall (artist), in *Views of Australian Scenery*, National Library of Australia S2275.
Bottom: *Seal Island in King George's Sound, Western Australia*, William Westall, watercolour, National Library of Australia R10660.
Page 3
Top: *View on the north side of Kangaroo Island*, engraving, William Woolnoth (engraver), William Westall (artist), in *Views of Australian Scenery*, Rex Nan Kivell Collection NK1730/6, National Library of Australia U2150.
Bottom: *Murray Isles c. 1802*, William Westall, watercolour, National Library of Australia R4347.
Pages 4–5
Main picture: Flinders' map of Terra Australis. Reproduced with permission from the Tooley Collection, National Library of Australia.
Inset: Marine chronometer. © Powerhouse Museum, Sydney, 2001, photo by Marinco Kojdanovski. Courtesy of Powerhouse Museum Collection H3940.
Page 6
Top: *View in Sir Edward Pellew's group, Gulph [sic] Carpentaria*, engraving, John Pye (engraver), William Westall (artist), in *Views of Australian Scenery*, National Library of Australia S2284.
Bottom: *View of Wreck Reef bank taken at low water, Terra Australis c. 1803*, William Westall, pencil and wash, Rex Nan Kivell Collection NK9938, National Library of Australia T1992.
Page 7
Top left: Bongaree (or Bungaree). Image Library, State Library of New South Wales, hand-coloured lithograph by Augustus Earle, 1826. ML ref: P2/4.
Top right: George Bass. Image Library, State Library of New South Wales, ML Portrait File P1/B (FM1/4624).
Bottom left: Captain Nicolas Baudin. *N. Baudin, Capitaine de Vaisseau, c. 1880*, Francois Bonneville, engraving, Rex Nan Kivell Collection NK1998, National Library of Australia U6257.
Bottom right: General Charles Mathieu Isidore Decaen. Reproduced from original edition of Scott's *The Life of Matthew Flinders*.
Page 8
Page from Matthew Flinders' journal of the *Investigator*, vol 1, 3 September 1801, p. 88. ML Flinders Project digital ref: A055.